HISTORY OF THE UNIVERSITY OF EDINBURGH

HISTORY OF THE UNIVERSITY OF EDINBURGH

1883-1933

EDITED ON BEHALF OF THE
HISTORY COMMITTEE BY

A. LOGAN TURNER
M.D., LL.D., F.R.C.S. Edin.

EDINBURGH
PUBLISHED FOR THE UNIVERSITY BY
OLIVER AND BOYD, TWEEDDALE COURT
LONDON: 33 PATERNOSTER ROW
1933

PRINTED IN GREAT BRITAIN BY
OLIVER AND BOYD LTD., EDINBURGH

PREFACE

THIS volume owes its inception to the Executive Committee of the University of Edinburgh Graduates' Association. At a meeting of the Committee held on 24th January 1930, the suggestion was made that the approaching 350th anniversary of the foundation of the "Town's College" presented a suitable occasion for the publication of the History of the University, subsequent to the period covered by Principal Sir Alexander Grant in *The Story of the University during its first Three Hundred Years*, and published, in 1884, in connection with the Tercentenary celebration. A sub-committee of the Executive was appointed, consisting of Professors W. P. Paterson, R. K. Hannay and William Wilson, and Sir Ludovic J. Grant, with Dr A. Logan Turner as convener. Subsequently, the name of Principal Sir Thomas Holland was added, to act as chairman, and the committee thus constituted became the History Committee. The proposal received the cordial approval of the University Court.

As the Principal in his introductory chapter has indicated the scope of the volume and has briefly sketched the main events in the history of the University during the half-century under review, it is unnecessary to make any further reference to its contents.

While there are obvious advantages associated with the preparation of a historical volume by one author, the History Committee formed the opinion that, in view of the great developments not only in University administration but also in the expansion of the Faculties during this period, it would be more satisfactory to place the compilation of the book in the hands of those best qualified from personal knowledge to undertake it. This course was accordingly adopted and a number of writers were invited to participate in the work of preparation.

Information, undoubtedly useful for purposes of reference,

but which could not be suitably introduced into the text, has been tabulated in the form of Appendices. The Committee is desirous of recording its indebtedness to, and appreciation of, the services of those responsible for their compilation: in particular to Mr James Clarkson Corson, M.A., assistant librarian, for the time and labour expended upon the difficult task of preparing the Biographies of the Professors, Readers and Lecturers, 347 in number, and in the construction of the Index; to Mr Thomas F. Harley, secretary to the General Council of the University, for the lists of Office-bearers; to Mr George D. Stewart, University accountant, for the preparation of the table of Donors and their Benefactions; and to Miss Helen Cormack and Miss E. L. Stewart for their assistance in compiling, from the University Register, the figures showing the Geographical Distribution of the Graduates.

The portraits of the Right Hon. John Inglis, Chancellor of the University, of Principal Sir Alexander Grant and of Professors John Stuart Blackie and Samuel Henry Butcher are reproduced from drawings and etchings executed by William Hole, R.S.A., and selected from the interesting series of portraits which illustrate the volume, *Quasi Cursores*, printed by T. & A. Constable, Edinburgh, in 1884, in connection with the Tercentenary Celebration of the University.

Finally, the Committee desires to thank the publishers for valuable advice and for the care which they have bestowed upon the production of the volume and the illustrations.

THE EDITOR.

EDINBURGH, *July* 1933.

CONTENTS

CONTENTS

CONTENTS

CONTENTS

LIST OF ILLUSTRATIONS

INTRODUCTION

According to the plan originally approved by the Editorial Committee, the Principal was allotted the task of explaining in a Foreword the aim and scope of this work, which was designed to record the progress made in each Faculty and main division of activity during the past fifty years. The Editor, however, has extended this task by demanding a brief review, in chronological order, of the main events that are more fully discussed in the later chapters.

The chapters which follow are, for the most part, devoted to a discussion of the administrative measures which have accompanied and facilitated our development; but most graduates are interested in more than one Faculty and there have been accessory incidents of importance, especially of a personal nature, that fall outside the particular provinces that have been allotted to my colleagues.

Although this volume is intended to continue the story told in Sir Alexander Grant's History,* the majority of the contributors have found it necessary to look back beyond the boundary and to dovetail their stories into pre-1884 events, in order to show how the organic unity of the University has been maintained. The chapter, indeed, that immediately follows this introduction goes further; as Professor Hannay has been able recently to unravel records which were not accessible when Sir Alexander Grant wrote, and he has contributed a new and specially valuable analysis of the circumstances which led to the origin and affected the early infancy of the Old College, in which Master Robert Rollock commenced teaching the first class of students in 1583.

What began as a purely local institution afterwards attracted students from distant lands; and Edinburgh is still, so far as its matriculates show, the most cosmopolitan among British

* *The Story of the University of Edinburgh during its first Three Hundred Years*, London, 1884.

universities. There are now over 19,000 graduates scattered throughout the world—over 16,000 in Europe, 1034 in Asia, 1003 in Africa, 573 in Australasia, and 590 in the Americas. The present distribution of graduates is an approximate but not an exact expression of their origin, as many of those who came as undergraduates from British, and especially from Scottish, homes have since made new homes beyond the seas: the sun never sets on the General Council of the University.

THEN AND NOW

When the Tercentenary Festival was held in April 1884, the New Buildings for the Faculty of Medicine were approaching completion; but there was no McEwan Hall, the Degree ceremonials being held in the Synod Hall, Castle Terrace; there was no University Union, no such thing as a recognised Students' Representative Council, and no athletic grounds at Craiglockhart; there was no Faculty of Music or of Science. Although women students of extra-academical training were granted certificates in Arts, they were not admitted to the ordinary University classes or to graduation. Evidently it was a very different institution fifty years ago. Conditions were, however, just ripening for a definite move forward.

The Right Honourable John Inglis who, as Lord Advocate, successfully piloted the Universities (Scotland) Bill through Parliament in 1858 and was Chairman of the Commission that promoted the consequent ordinances, was then Chancellor of the University; he was still the leading spirit, working in co-operation with Sir Alexander Grant to meet the obvious need for expansion in staff, in extended variety of teaching, in buildings and equipment, and in providing facilities for the students' social and athletic activities.

In 1884 there were 39 professors, 3 lecturers and 26 assistants—a total of 68 teachers for 3374 students. To-day for 4327 students there are 59 professors, 9 readers, 148 lecturers and 99 assistants—a total of 315 teachers, without counting the Clinical Teaching Staff. This change in the ratio of staff to students is partly due to the increased specialisation in all branches of culture, but mainly to improvements, which were long overdue, in meeting the requirements of students. Expenditure has increased accordingly from an ordinary annual budget of about £70,000 to more than £286,000. Without counting interest on the capital expenditure during this period, the annual outlay on a student by the University has thus been more than trebled; and the cost incurred by those who pay for the accessories of student life has probably increased in a similar ratio.

What we now call the Old College must have been packed like a bee-hive prior to fifty years ago. The transfer, soon after, of the large body of medical students was followed by some twenty years of readjustment within the old building; and further serious migrations from the hive did not occur until 1906, when the movement began again with the transfer of Engineering and Natural Philosophy to the High School Yards.

1884-1889

The beginning of the fourth century of our history was noticeably a time of rapid change, more serious than was imagined at the time. Sir Alexander Grant, already burdened with the control of normal administrative work under difficult conditions, had the task of preparing the history of the University and the planning of the new Medical School, as well as the organisation of the Tercentenary celebrations; and obviously this excessive overwork was a contributory cause of his early death a few months afterwards. But he had laid the foundations and prepared the way for expansion; his successor was thus enabled to carry on under more favourable conditions.

For the students the first five years of the new half-century formed the most important quinquennium in the whole history of their organisations: it was indeed their Reform period; for, within the first three years, the Students' Representative Council, the University Union and *The Student*—the Edinburgh University Magazine—were founded in quick succession, three different but complementary outlets of one general desire for the self-expression of feelings that were lying dormant, till they were awakened and developed by Robert Fitzroy Bell, David Orme Masson and Robert Cochrane Buist.*

Fitzroy Bell was undoubtedly the pioneer: he gathered together the representatives of clubs and societies, first with the intention of organising the students' share in the Tercentenary celebrations, and then to form a Council as a permanent representative body. The ceremonies planned for the 350th birthday of the University in October will thus coincide with the jubilee of the Students' Representative Council. Student populations rapidly change their configuration, and so, within a few years, doubts arose about the relative functions of the first two leaders, possibly because Masson was elected the first Senior President. A formula, however, found by *The Student* in 1888, seemed to express the general feeling:—"If it be true that Bell could not have started the Council without Masson, it is also true that Masson could not have started the Union without Bell."

The Student, however, was Buist's own venture: he was founder, proprietor and editor from November 1887 until he left the University. The length of a student's academic life is short, and those who undertake the work of initiating a new movement get little or no personal benefit for themselves; these three pioneers therefore—Bell, Masson, Buist—deserve to be remembered by the students among their great ones, as men—

> "Who knew the seasons when to take
> Occasion by the hand, and make
> The bounds of freedom wider yet."

The Students' Representative Council was the first of its kind in the country, but it was quickly copied in the other

* Another manifestation of the spirit of reform in student life occurred within this period, although it was extra-academical and independent; for it was in 1887 that Patrick Geddes, then Assistant to the Professor of Botany, started "University Hall," and so laid the foundation of hostel life. Beginning with ten rooms and seven students, University Hall has since grown to three houses with over ninety student residents, who treasure the right of electing new residents and of managing the internal affairs of the houses.

Scottish Universities, and later by universities in the South. Within a few years it proved to be of the greatest service to the administrative authorities as well as to the various specialised clubs and societies. Before the end of the quinquennium it was given formal recognition by the Universities (Scotland) Act, 1889, followed by Regulations approved by Ordinance in 1895.

The first Council was elected on the 17th January 1884 with Orme Masson,* Fitzroy Bell,† and J. F. Sturrock‡ as the three Presidents; and, among its first activities, was the institution of a successful campaign for the collection of money to build a suitable home for its headquarters—a University Union.

The way in which the staff and friends of the University were enrolled to share in this work showed the remarkable efficiency as well as the popularity of the new Council. One of the most successful of these efforts was a Fancy Fair which was held in the Waverley Market in November 1886, when an amusing *Journal*, published daily, was edited by W. K. Dickson, then a law student and member of the Students' Representative Council, but since known to a wider public by his historical works and as the head of the National Library of Scotland.

The Student first appeared as a free-lance—"a casual," as Buist called it—on 8th November 1887; it was an eight-page quarto, issued fortnightly, sold for a penny, and a good pennyworth too—portraits of professors with critical sketches of their work, verses, reports of athletic events, articles and reviews, and, in addition, one unusual feature to which may be traced the beginning of the Scottish Students' Song Book—a fortnightly series of songs with music, first appearing on the 22nd November 1887.

When Buist left the University in 1888, the Students'

* Now Sir David Orme Masson, K.B.E., F.R.S., Emeritus Professor of Chemistry, Melbourne. M.A., Edin., 1877.

† Afterwards Secretary of the Scottish Universities Commission. Died 23rd Oct. 1908. M.A., Edin., 1879.

‡ Afterwards Medical Officer of Health, Dundee. Died 13th Feb. 1916. M.B., Edin., 1885.

Representative Council adopted *The Student* as its official journal; and, in the first number of the new series, published on 10th May 1888, an article reviews the founder's manifold activities with the prediction that "the medical student we knew will by and by reappear as a hygienist, the coach and lecturer as an educationist, the ex-editor as a publicist, and the Representative Councilman as a citizen." Dr Buist's subsequent medical and public work in his native town of Dundee has abundantly verified these forecasts.

Becoming the official organ of the Students' Representative Council, *The Student* adopted a more pontifical tone, and some of its later victims probably resent the fact that it still claims the right of apostolic succession. In 1889 it severely criticised the "unfortunate style" of "a young writer" named J. M. Barrie who, however, had committed the error of contributing to the *British Weekly*, a contemporary with which *The Student* had then a bitter feud. The spirit of the critical historian and that of the prophet are not always united in the same person! Possibly the founder of *The Student* little thought that his notes of the proceedings of clubs and societies in his own time would become of special interest to us fifty years later. He has left, however, a model for his modern descendants to copy with suitable modification; for they, too, are now writing a chronicle that will be read at the 400th anniversary, when some of the students of to-day will be occupying positions of leadership here, in other parts of Great Britain and in countries beyond the seas.

Before *The Student* entered its third year of life, the Editorial Committee had realised its value and its responsibilities in this respect. At the opening of the new session in 1889, the Commitee reviewed the purpose and scope of the magazine and pointed out that "its object is faithfully to record the passing events of University life and . . . . to form a bond of union between present and absent sons of our Alma Mater." From this germ the modern Graduates' Association and the *University of Edinburgh Journal* have grown.

When Sir William Muir was appointed Principal, in

1885, the chief problem before the University was preparation for fresh legislation, partly necessary to repair the shortcomings found by experience in the Act of 1858, and partly to meet the subsequent developments in university education generally.

In matters internal it was obviously desirable meanwhile to mark time, and some new lectureships in the Faculty of Medicine remain as the only outward signs of expansion, during that period, among the regular teaching staff. But Adam Gifford, Senator of the College of Justice, died in 1887 and bequeathed £100,000 to found short courses of lectures in the four Universities of Scotland on questions ranging round the general term "Natural Theology." At Edinburgh this series was opened, in 1888, by J. Hutchinson Stirling who had commenced life as a medical practitioner; but, soon after, he turned to philosophy and quickly established a lasting reputation by his scholarly analysis of Hegelian dialectics, which introduced a series of works of equally high standard.

1890-1899

The year 1890 opened a new chapter in the history of the Scottish Universities, for, on 1st January, the Universities (Scotland) Act, 1889, came into force. The venerable John Inglis was still Chancellor of the University, but his unsurpassed record of work on behalf of Scottish university education was just over; he died in the following year at the age of eighty-one. He had been largely responsible for placing the 1858 Act on the Statute Book, had acted subsequently as chief of the Executive Commissioners in prescribing new ordinances, and as chairman of the Royal Commission which was appointed in 1876, with Huxley and Froude among its members. The General Council showed remarkable foresight in choosing as Inglis's successor Arthur James Balfour, then only forty-three years of age, but already leader of the House of Commons, although the youngest member of Lord Salisbury's Cabinet.

A number of changes was introduced by ordinances made

by the Scottish Universities Commission created by the new Act; the Court, in recognition of its extended powers of administration, was increased in number from eight to fourteen members by additions to the representatives of the General Council and the Senatus, each nominating four instead of one member; provision was made also for adding, if necessary, representatives of affiliated colleges, not exceeding four in number. Power was given to the Court, subject to sanction by the Universities Committee of the Privy Council, to alter or revoke ordinances and to institute new ordinances after the expiration of the powers of the Scottish Universities Commission. The Students' Representative Council was formally recognised by statute. Women students were to be admitted to graduation and to the regular classes of instruction on terms of equality with the men. The professors were no longer to draw fees from the students, but by special Ordinance were appointed with regular salaries. The Scottish Universities Committee of the Privy Council was constituted, and in the list of various "Lords" with *ex officio* rights to membership, occurs the only statutory use of the term "Lord Rector." Possibly this was a slip due to the use of the courteous and correct address of "Lord and Rector," for the five preceding Rectors. The incorrectly shortened term Lord Rector was in fact in common use before 1889, and appears, for example, in the first number of *The Student* in November 1887.

A few products of the new Universities Commission appeared in 1891; for example, the constitution of the University Library Committee, limited to twenty-one members, and a Museums' Committee, limited to nine members.

In the year 1892, however, a larger and more far-reaching group of Ordinances was issued. It included one which prescribed the procedure for electing Assessors to represent the General Council on the Court, with regulations for the election of a Chancellor.

In the same year a new title was prescribed for the first qualifying degrees in Medicine, which have since been known as Bachelor of Medicine (M.B.) and Bachelor of Surgery

(Ch.B.), with the higher degrees recognising specialisation in the form of M.D. and Ch.M. The course of study, especially to meet the desire for clinical training, was extended at the same time from four to five years, and this was followed by an immediate drop in the numbers of new entrants from 2044 to 1369, which has remained till recently the effective capacity of the Medical School.

The most far-reaching reform of major importance introduced at this time was contained in the well-known Arts Ordinance No. 11 of 1892, which also prescribed a Preliminary Examination for all students before admission to the curriculum; instituted the Summer Session in addition to the Winter Session as a qualifying period of teaching; and increased the range of subjects qualifying for a first graduation, giving, at the same time, a certain degree of freedom in the graduand's choice of his seven subjects.*

In order to control the preliminary examinations for admission to the four Scottish Universities a special Joint Board of Examiners was set up.

To organise the studies required for the degrees of B.Sc. and D.Sc., which were authorised by the Commissioners in 1892, a Faculty of Science, with Professor James Geikie as its first Dean, was established in the following year; it comprised the departments which had till then been administered by a Committee of the Arts Faculty. It consisted at first of eleven members, but these have since been trebled with the institution of the new Chairs and with the establishment, at about the same time, of additional independent lecturers for the control of special departments that were then beyond the natural range of any existing Chair. Independent lectureships were also added about the same time to the Faculty of Arts; for example, those in German and French, which were both established in the session 1894-95.

In 1893 the Faculty of Music was instituted by a special Ordinance which was drafted under the influence of Professor Niecks who had succeeded Sir Herbert Oakeley, two years

* Further changes in all these respects were made by the University Court's Arts Ordinance of 1908.

before, as Reid Professor of Music. Two degrees—Mus.B. and Mus.D.—were authorised, preparation for which required a residential qualification, a regulation previously unknown, but which was afterwards copied by other universities for degrees in Music. The first Mus.B. was granted in 1898 to Matthew Shirlaw.

A new Professorship of History was created by Ordinance in 1893, provision being made for the existing Chair to be changed to Constitutional Law and Constitutional History on the retirement of Professor John Kirkpatrick.

Regulations for two degrees in Law were also prescribed by the Commissioners in 1893, a junior degree of B.L. requiring a course of study extending over two academical years,* and the LL.B. requiring a course of three years in the Law School in addition to the Arts degree.

1890-1899

For a number of years the subject of Public Health had been taught in association with the Chair of Forensic Medicine and very limited laboratory accommodation had been provided in that department for its practical study. Stimulated by Louis Pasteur's great contribution to science, and in memory of his visit to Edinburgh at the time of the Tercentenary celebrations, Alexander Low Bruce, a partner in the firm of William Younger & Co., resolved to found a Chair of Public Health in the University. Supplementary donations from his widow and family, from his firm and from John Usher of Norton supplied the necessary endowment; and, in 1898, the Bruce & John Usher Chair of Public Health was instituted.

Laboratory accommodation for scientific study and research, on a larger scale than that already in existence, was essential for a progressive science and in the interests of the health of the community. Consequently, through the munificence of Sir John Usher, Bt., there was handed over to the University, in 1903, the Usher Institute of Public

* Extended in 1911 to three years.

Health. Erected in the Warrender district of the City, the building represented the first step in a process of decentralisation of the departments of science, a movement which has been extended in more recent years.

Among the Presidents of the Students' Representative Council during this decade the following names will be familiar to modern students: Robert Munro, 1891-92, now Lord Alness, the Lord Justice Clerk; David (now Sir David) Milne Watson, 1892-93; James Young Simpson, 1895-96, now Professor of Natural Science in the New College; and John Dixon Comrie, 1898-99, the author of the chapter on the Faculty of Medicine.

1900-1909

Andrew Carnegie's munificent donation, in 1901, of ten million dollars to the Universities of Scotland was perhaps the most important event of this decade. A large portion of the income of the fund has been devoted to the financial assistance of students who, otherwise, would not have been able to enter a Scottish university. In addition, part of the income has been spent upon the construction of buildings and other extensions requiring capital outlay; and a larger share has been applied to assist the work of research and publication, including research scholarships and fellowships. After spending £3$\frac{1}{3}$ millions of the income the Trustees find themselves now in possession of a capital that is £1$\frac{1}{3}$ millions larger than the original sum. Possibly no other similar fund can show a record more satisfactory financially and with results so great and so definite to the public good.

With its help, long over-due extensions were undertaken at Edinburgh. One of the first was the provision of better laboratory accommodation for Engineering and Natural Philosophy; and these two departments were moved in 1906 to the High School Yards, where the buildings previously occupied by the old Infirmary and the High School were modified for the purpose.

The Students' Representative Council celebrated its coming-of-age in January 1905, when nineteen of the past-Presidents attended the celebration dinner. A memorial volume, *Twenty-one Years of Corporate Life*, was prepared by J. I. Macpherson * who was Senior President in the session 1901-2 ; it recorded a graphic description of the changes which had occurred in student life from 1884.

In 1903 Sir William Muir, who had been in office as Principal since 1885, decided to retire, having given, with rare distinction, sixty-six years of his life to the public service. As his successor the Curators were fortunate in finding, and they showed their wisdom in selecting, Sir William Turner, who had, during his thirty-six years' tenure of the Chair of Anatomy, extended the fame of the Edinburgh Medical School and had earned for himself a position of great distinction among comparative anatomists. His appointment occurred at a time when public opinion in this country was specially stirred by the rapid development of technical industries in Germany and America, and when demands were being made for a marked extension of the facilities for higher education. He had already had a share in moulding the Carnegie Trust and had saved it from the danger of incurring onerous financial obligations as a qualification for accepting its benefits. He had shown, too, a special *flair* for finance as Convener of the Finance Committee of the Court. These and other administrative qualities were recognised by the Curators and, in the subsequent thirteen years, were abundantly verified.

Anatomy, however, was not allowed to suffer by the promotion of Sir William Turner ; for he secured the return from Dublin of one of the most brilliant of his old students—Daniel John Cunningham—as his successor.

Among the Presidents of the Students' Representative Council in this period mention has been made already of Sir Ian Macpherson who was Senior President in 1901-2. D. Oswald Dykes, now Professor of Constitutional Law, was one of the Presidents in 1900-1 and the later lists include William Browne Brander, 1902-3, now Secretary of the Universities Bureau of the British Empire.

* Now the Right Hon. Sir Ian Macpherson, Bt.

INTRODUCTION

1910-1919

In 1911 an addition to the Faculty of Science was made by the institution of a Lectureship in Genetics and Heredity—an outgrowth of the brilliant research work carried on by Professor Cossar Ewart, who still occupied the Chair of Natural History to which he had succeeded in 1882. Arthur D. Darbishire, who was appointed to the new lectureship, died four years later, and it was then held in abeyance until after the War.

Although, during this decade, four years of war interfered with the normal life of the University and many academic questions were necessarily held in suspense, nevertheless the University continued unobtrusively to enlarge her sphere of usefulness. Thus the period was remarkable in the number of additions made to the professoriate. No fewer than ten new Chairs were founded between 1913 and 1919—six in the Faculty of Medicine, three in Arts and one in Science.

In 1913 the Chair of Bacteriology came into the patronage of the University Court, its endowment being then made possible through the accumulation of the necessary funds derived from the estate of the late Robert Irvine of Granton. In the same year the Chair of Clinical Medicine was instituted, the Court applying for this purpose a portion of the legacy bequeathed by James Moncrieff Arnott of Chapel, Fife, and his daughter. In 1917, through the generosity of the Trustees of the Royal Victoria Hospital Tuberculosis Trust, the Chair of Tuberculosis was created; and, at the same time, by arrangement with the Corporation of the City, who were then administering the Tuberculosis Scheme under the Insurance Act, every facility for teaching and research was provided in the Dispensary, the Hospital and the Farm Colony.

The remaining three Chairs in the Faculty of Medicine were founded in 1919: that of Chemistry in Relation to Medicine, promoted by an Ordinance of the University Court in 1918; the Christison Chair of Therapeutics, instituted by agreement with the Managers of the Royal Infirmary, when the wards previously under the charge of the Professor of Materia Medica became vacant; and the Chair of Psychiatry, in greater part endowed by the Managers of the Royal Edinburgh Hospital for Mental and Nervous Disorders.

In the Faculty of Arts two Modern European Languages had been represented since 1894 as Lectureships, but, in 1918, French and, in 1919, German were raised to professorial status, the French class in particular having attracted a large number of students. In 1919, in connection with the new department of Commerce, the Chair of Accounting and Business Method was instituted, endowed by subscriptions from members of the Edinburgh and Leith Chambers of Commerce, from the Merchant Company of Edinburgh and other bodies.

Finally, in 1919, the subject of Forestry, instruction in which had been given for thirty years by means of a Lectureship, was similarly treated. The new Chair was established in the Faculty of Science, endowed in part by a capital grant from the Development Commissioners.

Early in 1914 the transfer of three departments to new quarters relieved to some degree the congestion in the Old College. Mathematics went to a new home in Chambers Street, whilst Agriculture and Forestry were transferred to a new building in George Square.

After an interruption of over four years development was resumed in 1918. The separation of the two administrative offices of the Court and Senatus was abolished, and the secretarial organisation consolidated.

The appointment of Lecturers, regularised by Ordinance in 1892—some for independent subjects and some under the older professorships—necessitated a change in the constitution of the Faculties. An Ordinance which was passed in 1919, followed by amendments in later years, recognised their position on the teaching staff by creating a Grade of Readers (in Medicine, Senior Lecturers). These officers were made eligible for seats on their Faculties and on the Senatus, and eligibility to Faculties was also extended to Lecturers.

In the same year the School of Theology extended the area of its activities beyond its accustomed function of vocational training for the ministry: a post-graduate school of study was organised and soon attracted graduates from abroad, more especially from Canada and the United States, a large proportion of them working for the degree of Ph.D.

1920-1929

In consequence of the growing demand for more space for science laboratories, the Court acquired 115 acres of open land at Liberton; and, on the 6th July 1920, the King laid the foundation stone of a new building designed to accommodate the department of Chemistry. Thus was inaugurated the policy of forming a new colony of science departments separated by two miles from the Administrative Offices, Library and University Union, a policy which necessarily opened up a wholly new and difficult problem — that of ensuring the maintenance of unified social relations between science students and those of the other Faculties. This new accommodation for Chemistry was followed by separate buildings in the same area for Zoology, Geology, Animal Genetics and Engineering.

In 1922 the third Universities (Scotland) Act was passed, abolishing the old system of life tenure for the Principal and Professors, giving power to each of the Scottish Universities to limit these tenures by ordinance, with provisions for the replacement of the old pension scheme by a contributory superannuation allowance. At Edinburgh the limits of tenure laid down by Ordinance in 1924 were, for the Principal, the age of seventy-five, and for Professors that of seventy, except in the case of those whose retirement was otherwise regulated.

Within this decade regulations were sanctioned for the B.Sc. and D.Sc. degrees in Pure Science (1921), in Mining and Metallurgy (1921), in Agriculture (1922), in Technical Chemistry (1922), in Forestry (1924), and in Engineering (1924). In the same decade four new Chairs were established; the James A. Hood Professorship of Mining (1923); Organisation of Industry and Commerce (1924); the Abercromby

Chair of Archæology (1925); and the Buchanan Chair of Animal Genetics (1928).

At the end of the last session of this decade Sir Alfred Ewing decided to apply to himself the new rule by which future holders of the office of Principal are limited in service to the session in which they attain the age of seventy-five years. Although his thirteen years' term of office was interfered with by war work at the Admiralty, he shared the responsibility of creating eleven new Chairs—French, German, Archæology, Accounting, Organisation of Industry and Commerce, Mining, Forestry, Animal Genetics, Tuberculosis, Therapeutics and Psychiatry. The southern colony for scientific departments was inaugurated and further funds were obtained for extensions there, for the reorganisation of some of the medical buildings, for the institution of hostel accommodation for men in George Square, and for various developments in other departments of University activity. It was a period of active expansion, especially marked by the laying of foundation stones on which we have yet to build. His energy overflowed the boundaries of the University into affairs of civic life and, at the close of his term of office, his fellow-citizens marked their appreciation of his work by conferring on him the Freedom of the City.

1930 to Date

In 1930 authority was obtained by Ordinance to charge an additional half-guinea to the annual matriculation fee, the money so obtained being devoted to the physical welfare of the students. All students are now entitled to free medical examination and are given advice regarding suitable exercises. Colonel Ronald Bruce Campbell, the Director of Physical Education, co-ordinates the activities of the various athletic clubs, and has organised a number of new classes for those who have previously had little or no chance of physical training. Under the class-rooms in Minto House a gymnasium, recently equipped, is now available for the free use of the students. This scheme of extending facilities for physical training was designed especially for the benefit of the average student, not for the athlete who finds his opportunities in the established clubs. Experience of the first three sessions proves its value and promises real success.

Until 1930 the women students had no athletic grounds of their own. With the help largely of grants made by the Carnegie Trustees and the University Grants Committee a pavilion was built at Peffermill on a plot of land, covering 15 acres, which was fenced and prepared for hockey and lacrosse pitches. This ground was opened on 18th March 1931, by Mr John Buchan.

Two new buildings in the southern science colony were opened by the Prime Minister, the Right Hon. J. Ramsay MacDonald, F.R.S., on 28th January 1932—the Engineering laboratories built by a bequest of the late Mr James Sanderson of Galashiels, and the Geological laboratories by a donation from Sir Alexander Grant, Bt. of Logie.

Following the Union, in October 1929, of the Church of Scotland and the United Free Church, an Act was passed, in 1932, authorising the addition of the professorial staff of the United Free Church College to the Faculty of Divinity, which will now include eight instead of four Professors. By agreement with the Church made this year, appointments to the office of Dean, as well as new appointments made to fill Chairs, will require the nomination of a standing Joint Board of twelve members, six appointed by the Church and six by the University. The seat of the whole Faculty will henceforth be the New College on the Mound.

With the help of a generous grant made by the Carnegie Trustees for the quinquennium 1930-35, considerable improvements have been made in the Old College; the quarters vacated by the transfer of Natural History to The King's Buildings have been utilised to extend the reading-room accommodation and storage capacity for the growing library. The rooms vacated by the transfer of Geography to High School Yards have been used partly for the growing needs of Psychology and partly fitted to provide retiring rooms for women students. But the schemes for improving the Old College internally and in the Quadrangle are still far from complete and require more money than is at present in sight.

Three new Chairs were established in 1931 : Geography and Psychology in the Faculty of Arts and the Edward Clark Chair of Child Life and Health in the Faculty of Medicine.

It has not been possible in this opening chapter to do more than refer briefly to a selection of outstanding incidents ; changes in the professoriate, references to generous benefactions and other matters of importance will be found in appropriate subsequent sections. But it is impossible to pass over silently the most recent change in the Chair of Physiology, which forms an outstanding incident in the history of the Medical School. Sir Edward Sharpey-Schafer came, in 1899, with a world-wide reputation, already established as a leading investigator of the endocrine organs and as a recognised authority on histology, having been elected a Fellow of the Royal Society as far back as 1878. After coming to Edinburgh he continued to extend the boundaries of his special subject by his own unremitting work, supplemented by his pupils' researches. In 1912 he was elected President of the British Association, and his distinguished work has been otherwise recognised by the honorary degrees of several universities, as well as by the honorary membership of numerous scientific societies at home and abroad. Sir Edward's retirement closes a chapter in the history of the Medical School made famous by his personality and brilliant work.

"*In Education there is no finality — we cannot stand still in such matters. Every step which we take in the improvement of University Education gives us a new platform from which to start, in order to make other and better arrangements.*"

Sir William Turner.

I

THE FOUNDATION OF THE COLLEGE OF EDINBURGH *

THE project of a College in Edinburgh for higher education was due, in the first instance, to Robert Reid, Bishop of Orkney, and took shape more than two years before the Reformation. As abbot of Kinloss, Reid became in 1532 a Senator in the new College of Justice: as Bishop of Orkney and commendator of Kinloss, he succeeded Alexander Myln in the presidency sixteen years later, and died in 1558. He bequeathed 8000 merks for an institution leading through a literary course towards the study of the Civil and the Canon Law. There were six testamentary executors, of whom Walter Reid, a nephew promoted to the abbacy of Kinloss, and John Reid of Aikinheid, a younger relative, were the two primarily interested. To carry out the proposed foundation, a special charge was laid upon three friends and colleagues of the Session.

At the existing Universities, the Faculties of Law had never taken strong root; and ambitious men preferred to go abroad. If there was provision for theoretical instruction at St Andrews, Glasgow and Aberdeen, any practical experience was limited to the ecclesiastical and local courts. Edinburgh was not only the seat of the diocesan Official of St Andrews deputed for Lothian, transacting a more extensive business than his senior colleague in the primatial city: it had become the centre of the royal government, and the normal meeting-

* This sketch is based upon the results of recent research. Evidence is now available to elucidate that crucial passage of our history which was not known when Principal Sir Alexander Grant wrote *The Story of the University*, and which, if it had been known, would have modified some of his conclusions regarding the rather obscure course of these events. The figures in the text refer to the authorities quoted in Appendix I (see p. 362).

place of Parliament, of the Privy Council, and of the Session in civil causes. The legal element in the population was growing rapidly. Young men of the burgh, as well as from the country, aspired to practise as lawyers, often without any proper academic training. Reid no doubt considered that facilities for instruction would be salutary for the profession, and an advantage to individuals whose means and opportunities were limited.

During the turmoil of the religious revolution, which began almost immediately after his death, the Bishop's will was not produced for confirmation; and there was a gap of some four years between the disestablishment of the Roman episcopal authority and the appointment, under the Court of Session, of the new Commissaries who took over testamentary jurisdiction from the old spiritual tribunals. Meantime educational schemes different in origin and character were under discussion.

In May 1560 the First Book of Discipline, a report "touching the reformation of religion," was hastily drafted. One recommendation was that "in every notable town," especially at the diocesan centres of the new ecclesiastical Superintendents, a "college" or advanced grammar school should be provided, capable of giving at least the instruction usual during the first year of a university curriculum. In the fifteenth century, the movement at Paris to secure increased moral supervision by means of college residence affected academic institutions at St Andrews. The compilers of the Book of Discipline proposed to develop the collegiate system at Glasgow and Aberdeen; and their town colleges were designed not only to afford facilities for the poor, but also to prolong home influence, so that "the youtheid and tender children sall be nurischit and brocht up in virtue in presence of thair freindis."[1]

Another section, dealing with finance, was to have an important bearing upon educational plans in Edinburgh. The poor and the schools, as well as the ministers, were to be a charge upon the reformed Kirk. In the landward parishes, the teinds must be supplemented by such local endowments as became obsolete with the cessation of the mass: in the burghs, where there were no predial tithes, the obsolete endowments would be the main source of income, supplemented by contributions from the merchants and craftsmen.

The Town Council of Edinburgh had been discussing these recommendations even before the Parliament of 1560 renounced the Papacy;[2] and in the spring of 1561 there were schemes afoot, based upon the rash assumption that superstitious mortifications were to be readily available.[3] This expectation was soon disappointed. That the Kirk should fall heir to the whole ecclesiastical property, with the exception of the monastic estates, proved to be a devout imagination rendered still more visionary by the return of the widowed Mary from France and the diplomacy of Lord James Stewart and Maitland of Lethington, who declined to override her religious prejudices by the forcible methods that Knox would have employed, and thought rather, as Maitland put it, to "allure" her into alliance with England.

In 1562 the Town Council had an eye upon the Kirk o' Field as easily adaptable for the college or school which the Book of Discipline suggested.[4] St Mary's in the Fields, like the foundation dedicated to the Holy Trinity by the Queen of James II, was a collegiate church with provost and prebendaries and an attached hospital for the sick and destitute. The eleemosynary work of such institutions had suffered in latter years from lack of supervision; and St Mary's was particularly unfortunate, since its hospital was never rebuilt after the destructive English invasion of 1544. The kirk itself was in a ruinous condition, so that the ground and masonry, with the sinecure emoluments of provost and prebendaries, might well be turned to account for education.

Master William Penicuik, however, who had been admitted to the provostry before the Reformation, took good care to anticipate the designs of the Council by obtaining an express confirmation of his right from Mary, after her return from France.[5] There was great uncertainty as to the fate of such ecclesiastical property; and Penicuik, afraid of missing his market, proposed a sale to the burgh of ground, buildings and endowments, his desire to accelerate the transaction being proportionate to a very natural doubt as to his title to alienate. While the Town hesitated to close with him, he proceeded to demolish the masonry of the kirk, and invited purchasers of the material.[6]

Along with its scholastic plans, the Town Council had schemes also for an hospital to meet the clamant needs of the deserving poor.[7] Mary granted a site at the Blackfriars for the hospital, on condition that building should be begun within a year and completed in seemly fashion in a given time.[8] A start was made, though the work was afterwards discontinued; and Penicuik's activities in demolition at Kirk o' Field had the effect upon which he counted. In 1564 it was decided that the burgh must transact with him, either for the fabric of the neighbouring hospital "or for ane universite there."[9] But this ambitious educational design—if "ane universite" implied more than a college—had in any case to be dropped.

One reason may have been disappointment over Bishop Reid's legacy. The new Commissary Courts were empowered to call in testaments for confirmation under penalties for defaulting executors. Among the Commissaries was Master Clement Litil, a strong supporter of the academic enterprise, and intimately acquainted with the affairs of the Reids, as a curator appointed by the Session for young Aikinheid in 1561, when Walter of Kinloss was in France.[10] A summons to the Bishop's executors in 1564 was probably due to him. Kinloss and Aikinheid, appearing for the rest, were given a term to produce the will duly confirmed.[11] What happened thereafter is not clear; but it is certain that the money was not obtained, and that twelve years later Kinloss was held answerable by the Privy Council for the whole of this special bequest.[12]

It was undoubtedly the attitude of the government to the claims of the Kirk upon ecclesiastical property that most effectually arrested progress. Maitland and Lord James, convinced that financial demands on the scale outlined in the Book of Discipline, if brought into debate before Parliament, would split the reforming party, avoided the issue. To appease Knox and his followers, some provision must be made for the Kirk: vested interests, by no means exclusively Romanist, had to be recognised: the Crown, long accustomed to exploit the resources of the old Church by methods more or less indirect, was now compelled to appropriate a portion of its revenue. One third was to be deducted from the incomes of all beneficed men: out of this tax the royal treasury would be relieved, and the ministers have assigned allowances. Mary's religious scruples would not be seriously offended, though she was in fact committed to a measure of confiscation: the more extreme reformers, on the other hand, could be kept under government control through command of the purse. For a time, as Knox says, the ministers lived "upon the benevolence of men." So niggardly and ill-paid was their dole that the Comptroller, personally "ane earnest professor of Christ," was consigned in his official capacity to "the mekle devill."[13] As to the ministers in the burghs, any obligation upon the Crown to support them was questioned, in view of the comparatively small income obtained by deduction of thirds from burgh benefices.[14] Edinburgh appealed in 1563 to "the faithful" for voluntary aid on behalf of the poor and the ministry; and when the faithful were unresponsive, and the magistrates approached the Queen, her answer was a command to impose taxation.[15] This was the situation at the end of 1564.

Moray and Maitland did not succeed in shepherding Mary; and the Kirk, taking fresh alarm at the announcement of the Darnley marriage, insisted upon vigorous suppression of the mass, adequate provision for the ministry, restoration of hospital revenues to their intended use, application of the friars' property and the endowments for masses to the maintenance of the poor and the schools.[16] When Moray rebelled, the Edinburgh Council lent 10,000 merks to the King and Queen for military expenses, under a degree of compulsion which did not preclude a desirable bargain.[17] The superiority of Leith was obtained;[18] and there seems to have been at least an expectation of the miscellaneous lands and annuals which the Book of Discipline had marked for burgh use, and out of which it was hoped to provide John Knox with a permanent stipend.[19]

This year 1565 was a hard one for the reformed ministers, who were all, according to Moray, "frustrated of their livings."[20] As Mary's troubles accumulated and her calls upon the ill-administered fund of thirds increased, she was compelled at length to placate the Kirk by undertaking to confer upon ministers the small benefices in her patronage so as to eke out a specific assignation made to them for stipend.[21] Though it was still maintained that the burghs ought to find money by taxation for their ecclesiastical purposes, the Crown, for its own peace and safety, consented to relieve them by granting the obsolete endowments so long sought.[22] In the spring of 1567, after the murder of Darnley, no fewer than ten burghs had gifts in a common form, described as *fundatio regia ministerii et hospitalitatis.* Subject to the life interest of persons instituted before the Reformation, Edinburgh received the lands, buildings, and revenues pertaining to chaplainries, altarages and prebends in whatsoever church, chapel, or college within the liberty: the ground and rents of the friars: all mortifications within the burgh or burdens upon its common good for mass endowments anywhere in Scotland.[23] This royal gift, diplomatic rather than benevolent, of which burghs continued to avail themselves during the next few years, was of great educational importance: in particular, it was destined to give the University of Glasgow fresh life and, later, to bring the College of Edinburgh into being.

Meanwhile, in 1566, William Penicuik had been made Master of Wardrobe to the infant Prince James.[24] He resigned the provostry of Kirk o' Field, which was given on 9th December to Robert Balfour, with power to dispone upon the prebends and the kirk masonry.[25] There is reason to believe that Balfour's brother, the sinister Sir James, was concerned; and the writ of gift is remarkable for the inclusion of a precept of sasine, adroitly calculated to secularise the benefice, if possible, and safeguard it against transference to the town under the impending royal benefaction.

With the accession of James VI in 1567, with the final establishment of the reformed faith and Moray as regent, the

Kirk expected an endowment adequate to the maintenance of the ministry, the poor, and the schools. All that Moray could effect was to procure for it the collection of thirds on condition that a portion was paid to the public exchequer. There was, indeed, some effort to bestow vacant benefices upon qualified ministers; but no compulsion was applied to lay patrons, while the action of the Crown since 1560, in frequent disregard of its own promises and ordinances, had created a fresh crop of rights which Parliament was forced to admit. When Moray died, the Assembly was intent upon the needs of the landward parishes. The regent seems to have provided Knox, as minister of Edinburgh, with a grant out of the thirds;[26] but that was a personal favour, and did not affect the financial position of the town sufficiently to warrant a resumption of the college enterprise.

In 1572, the year in which Knox died and Morton became regent, a phase of the controversy opened which turned the attention of the Kirk seriously to the problem of education. Morton, among other imputations of cupidity, was charged with stinting the reformed ministry for the benefit of his revenues, so that able men had little inducement or prospect in entering the Church. He replied by complaining about the dearth of competent persons: when they presented themselves, stipends should be found for them. Whatever their differences on ecclesiastical polity, both sections of the Protestant party were agreed on the grave lack of qualified men. In 1567 there were 257 ministers of the sacraments: by 1574 there were only 289, undertaking with the cheap assistance of 715 readers the cure of about a thousand parish kirks.[27]

The burgh of Glasgow, looking for "champions of the faith" and regarding schools as the "seminaries of the Kirk and the whole commonwealth," was authorised by Parliament to devote Mary's *fundatio ministerii et hospitalitatis* towards revival of the almost defunct University,[28] which was thus enabled, in 1574, to engage the learning of Andrew Melville. Visiting St Andrews in that year, Morton himself alluded to the "necessity and scarcity of ministers."[29] Edinburgh was not in a position to act. It had suffered heavily during the civil strife and the siege of Mary's partisans in the Castle: it was maintaining three ministers and a reader only by resort to special taxation:[30] money had to be borrowed to build a lodging for them in the kirkyard of St Giles—an opportunity, by the way, for Robert Balfour to dispose of timber extracted from the Kirk o' Field steeple.[31] Master James Lawson, Knox's successor, formerly an academic teacher at St Andrews and Aberdeen, was among the men sent by the Assembly in 1576 to report upon the state of affairs at St Andrews;[32] and it was no accident that another effort was made, this time before the Privy Council, with Morton in the chair and the King's Advocate pursuing, to lay hands upon Bishop Reid's elusive legacy.[33] The money would be welcome, because it might be used in part for secondary education, and the place which accommodated the High School was now so ruinous that a resort to building had become unavoidable.[34] Kinloss, though ordered to produce the 8000 merks, succeeded somehow in postponing the evil day. The Town could not find the £1800 for ministerial stipend and the cost of a school without special taxation for the one or the other; and it was not until the summer of 1579 that the new High School on the site of the kirk of the Blackfriars was in occupation.[35]

By this time the University of Glasgow had acquired additional resources for the training of "useful members to serve the Kirk of God and the commonwealth," and obtained a *nova erectio* from the Crown, embodying the ideas of Andrew Melville. In 1579 the Assembly, anxious to keep students away from Paris and other Romanist places, invited action by the government for a thorough reform at St Andrews.[36] By the *nova erectio* which resulted, the College of St Mary, or New College, as good Protestants preferred to say, begun by the two Betouns and equipped by Archbishop Hamilton with an eye to the theological deficiencies of churchmen, was appropriated entirely to studies in Divinity. Nor was the Law forgotten. In 1574 Morton had laid stress upon the need for theoretical instruction; and it was now again recommended that some academic qualification should be required from all pleaders in the courts—an interesting justification of Bishop Reid's design.[37]

These developments were not lost upon Edinburgh. No sooner was the High School finished than the town approached Master Robert Pont, minister at St Cuthbert's and a Lord of Session, who held the provostry of Trinity Collegiate Kirk.[38] Moray had granted the lands and buildings of that foundation, though not the benefice revenues, for the main purpose of hospital extension;[39] and it might be easier to establish an academic institution on that ground than at Kirk o' Field, where there were many legal complications. In April 1579, a meeting of town councillors with Master Clement Litil and Master Alexander Sym, official procurators of the Kirk,[40] was convened in the lodging of the ministers beside St Giles's.[41] Nothing was settled; but negotiations were resumed in the following winter for what was now designated "a college of Theology."[42] While these plans were being discussed, Robert Balfour was involved in the downfall of the Hamiltons, and his provostry was forfeited:[43] in addition, the house built by Châtelherault upon the old hospital tenement, feued to him in 1554,[44] fell to the Crown. John Gib, the King's valet, who never overlooked such opportunities, contrived to secure a gift of the provostry, with ample powers of disposition.[45] Unable to make anything of the Trinity College scheme, the Town Council had now to revert, a little late in the day, to Kirk o' Field, and was haggling with the domestic, when the financial straits of his royal master became an important factor in the situation.[46]

The personal government of James VI began in 1578. If Morton had sought to assimilate the Scottish ecclesiastical order to that of England, had "mislyked the General Assemblies," and was not on good terms with the ministers and burgesses of Edinburgh, his policy was at least soundly Protestant. When he fell, instead of a Presbyterian establishment according to the Second Book of Discipline, which the Assembly had matured and completed, the Kirk was faced with the danger of a Romanist reaction under the influence of Esmé Stuart, first cousin of Darnley and representative, through his father's adoption, of the distinguished French family of Aubigny akin to the house of Lennox. Elizabeth was sufficiently alarmed to intervene. Hints of forcible action by England were a god-send in the state of the Scottish treasury. The government produced the King's Confession, denouncing all things papistical, a document which, though discreetly vague on the polity of the Kirk, was taken for a satisfying condemnation of prelacy. On the strength of this manifesto, and the attitude of the old enemy, Edinburgh was invited to lend £20,000, but declined on the ground of troubles and losses since the beginning of the reign. When a Convention of Estates proceeded to impose upon the country a general taxation of £40,000, the burgh was persuaded to advance 10,000 merks on security for repayment by Whitsunday in 1581.[48]

The occasion was seized to point out that Kirk o' Field, by the forfeiture of Balfour, seemed to have fallen under Mary's *fundatio*. The King was prepared in the circumstances to admit that it "justly pertained" to the Town; and his face was saved when Gib resigned any right, for a consideration.[49] James also declared, *verbo principis*, that Balfour should have no title to restitution if his sentence of forfeiture was afterwards reduced.[50] So far, so good. But Whitsunday passed without any signs of the covenanted repayment: a serious matter, because the merchants who had subscribed in 1565 for the loan to Mary and Darnley had not yet seen their money, and were restive.[51] Besides the financial difficulty, there was trouble over the Hamilton lodging, which the Town had expected to have at its disposal for college use. Captain James Stewart, the accuser of Morton, was raised in 1581 to the vacant earldom of Arran, and in his capacity as tutor to Châtelherault's demented son and heir he instituted proceedings before the Session.[52] Nevertheless the Town Council resolved to take advantage of the royal indebtedness, on the well-founded suspicion that James would stand in still further need. Parliament was to meet in the autumn. Two bills were drafted, one empowering action by the burgh against Kinloss for the Reid bequest, the other no doubt embodying the terms of the charter which James ultimately granted.[53]

These petitions, owing to pressure of business, were not heard by the Lords of the Articles, but were remitted with many others to a Commission, of which Patrick Adamson, Archbishop of St Andrews, was a member.[54] At the present juncture the relations of the King and the prelatical party with Lawson and the Edinburgh ministers were becoming strained. When the see of Glasgow fell vacant, the Crown roused violent controversy by a discreditable appointment made without regard to the views and claims of the Kirk. Both Lawson and the Provost of Edinburgh served upon a committee of Assembly distinctly hostile to the government;[55] and the Archbishop of St Andrews was not likely to encourage a scheme advanced by his bitter political enemies to the prejudice of his own seat of learning. The success of the burgh deputation which attended at Stirling in April 1582, when ecclesiastical feeling ran high, must have been due very largely to the King's debt, even if his personal interest in the educational design had been awakened. Looking back, in 1617, James could forget the mercenary aspects of the transaction, and attributed the beginning of the College entirely to his own enlightened initiative. "After the founding of it had been stopped for sundry years in my minority," Craufurd makes him say, "so soon as I came to any knowledge I zealously held hand to it."[56]

The three lawyers charged under Bishop Reid's will were all dead. The Privy Council empowered Edinburgh to sue Kinloss, and placed it under obligation to spend the sum upon a College within a year after recovery.[57] Of the 8000 merks, half was to come from a bond on Strathnaver, long since hopelessly inextricable owing to the vicissitudes of that territory: even the remaining 4000 could not be wrung from the improvident or unfortunate Commendator. The King, who from all accounts was probably himself also interested in Walter Reid's solvency, advised a compromise for 2500 merks, of which 700 actually came to hand in July of next year, the residue not until late in 1587.[58]

Three days afterwards, on 14th April 1582, a signature[59] was passed for the charter under which the College took shape.

James confirmed his mother's *fundatio regia* for the ministry and hospitals, and by a *novodamus* extended the scope of the gift so as to include educational purposes, leaving the allocation of revenue to the discretion of the Town Council. He ratified John Gib's renunciation of any right in Kirk o' Field, which had been made to the burgh in name of the ministers and the poor; but he did not include it expressly under the enlarged destination, or tie down the grantees to place the College there. The ecclesiastical sites available were stated to be more than sufficient for hospital needs; and the Town Council might erect or repair buildings to accommodate studies in Arts, Theology, Medicine, the Laws, or any other liberal branch of knowledge, without breach of the mortification: might appoint or remove teachers, with the advice of the ministers, and enjoy the sole right of admitting to the profession of these subjects.

The charter was not the foundation of a College, but a *libertas collegium erigendi.*[60] In the circumstances no other line of procedure was possible. A corporate body was certain to develop. At the outset, however, the enterprise was only one more item in a general policy prosecuted by the Town under the new order outlined in the First Book of Discipline, and could have no endowment independently of the common fund at the disposal of the Council. The legal advisers of the burgh, too, were thinking of more than the immediate question of a College. They knew the lamentable condition of the royal finances, and feared that the revocation of alienations passed in the Parliament of 1581 might be followed by further acts of reduction. From exceptions subsequently introduced in its special favour, it is plain that Edinburgh must have been nervous about the permanent integrity of Mary's gift, and took the opportunity to procure a *novodamus* in order to strengthen its hold upon the lands and revenue.[61]

This was the charter which determined the relations of the community to its College until tutelage became impossible. Sir Alexander Grant in *The Story of the University* was undoubtedly right in maintaining that a document has been lost; but it was not a detailed academic foundation, as he was inclined to suppose.[62] The extant gift, as we have seen, did

From an etching by] [*William Hole, R.S.A.*

SIR ALEXANDER GRANT, BT., D.C.L., LL.D.

Principal and Vice-Chancellor
1868-1884

not confine the College to Kirk o' Field, or include that property within the larger scope of the mortification. The lost document, which probably disappeared during subsequent legal controversy with Hamilton, and is now known only through one or two references, seems to have been an annexation of Kirk o' Field, remedying an obvious defect of the *novodamus,* and at the same time definitely locating the College there. As in Mary's grant in 1562-3 of an hospital on the site of the Blackfriars, the proviso was inserted that operations should begin within a year and be continued. It looks as if the Town's petition, upon which the royal signature for a charter was based, intended to leave some freedom, possibly to revive the Trinity College design, for the question of title to the Hamilton house was always a difficulty. That building was now occupied by a number of families as tenants of the burgh;[63] but the interloping Earl of Arran desired to have it for his own convenience.[64] Whether the King disapproved any adaptation to academic ends of the place founded by his devout ancestress, Mary of Gueldres, for the benefit of the destitute, while the royal favourite agreed to relinquish the pursuit of his claim upon Châtelherault's lodging if it was definitely appropriated to the College, there is no express testimony to show.

During the remainder of 1582 Edinburgh was distracted by the bitter quarrel over prelacy and the see of Glasgow, by the Raid of Ruthven which removed Esmé Stuart and Arran from power about the throne, and by domestic controversy between merchants and craftsmen regarding representation on the Town Council. Owing to inevitable delays and financial obstacles, it was found eventually that the tenants in the Duke's lodging could not be ousted till Whitsunday 1583;[65] and not until that date approached were active operations undertaken so as to open the College in the following autumn.[66]

Beginning in 1583, at first single-handed, Master Robert Rollock had by 1587 conducted a batch of students, as was the practice, through a complete course. Means were limited. Balfour reappeared; and in his remission the exception promised *verbo principis* was not included.[67] Lord Hamilton, upon his restoration, was naturally somewhat difficult about his house, especially as the burgh had been trying to reduce the feu in his absence.[68] Additional sources of income, however, were secured from the fruits of the archdeaconry of Lothian and the provostry of Trinity College; and the royal signature for the former of these annexations held that upon this small beginning "thair is guid expectatioun that be the favour of God and his hienes clemencie thair sall ane mair happie succes follow."[69] The College was gradually equipped to provide the normal type of instruction in Arts received at the Universities. Degrees were conferred as a matter of ordinary routine, just as at St Andrews the licence *ubique terrarum* continued to be granted, though the papal authority which gave the licence its meaning had been disowned.[70] The next step at Edinburgh, consistently with the development, was to be the establishment of a Faculty of Theology, which Rollock was now free to initiate.[71]

It was at this stage that the Town obtained all that was recoverable of the Reid bequest: yet no steps were taken towards any endowment of the Law. Undoubtedly there was a suggestion that regard should be had to the intention of the Bishop's will; and if it did not come from the King himself, it seems to have had his support. In 1564 the Lords of Session, very inadequately remunerated from the prelatical contributions obtained by James V in 1532, had a grant from Mary of £1600 out of the "quot silver" or legacy duty, and in 1566 a gift of the whole surplus accruing after the Commissary Court judges of Edinburgh were paid.[72] Like the Town itself, the Senators were nervous about the permanence of a favour procured when the Queen was in difficulties, and were prepared to hand over £1000 of the surplus to endow "a teacher and professour of the lawis" in the College, provided that the burgh put down an equal sum and that the King ratified his mother's gift. The advocates and other members of the College of Justice, it was assumed, would be ready to contribute a third £1000 of capital.[73]

The matter was in train before James sailed for Denmark to be married; and during his absence, on 20th February 1589-90, the triple contract was finally approved by the Town.[74] It is not clear whether Adrian Damman, a Fleming from the neighbourhood of Ghent, had come to Scotland during the lifetime of George Buchanan, or whether he appeared first about the time of the royal wedding;[75] but he was in favour with the Chancellor Thirlestane, and with the influential Senator Master John Lindsay, was recognised as an eminent scholar by Melville and Pont, and tactfully dedicated to the magistrates of Edinburgh verses describing the ceremonial entry of Queen Anne.[76] The original suggestion was for a "professour of the lawis"; but the wording of the contract referred to "ane publict professour in the lawis or humanitie," according as it should seem expedient for the benefit of the youth.[77]

The Advocates were dissatisfied, and declined to implement their part of the bargain. A curious document, discovered by W. C. Dickinson, formulates some of their objections.[78] They make no specific reference to Damman, but wish to know who will occupy the chair and to have evidence of his learning. The project is likely to fail, "and than peradventure sum courteour gett our silver to spend." Facilities at St Andrews and Aberdeen, they contend, have not elicited much response: one lecturer in Edinburgh on so wide a subject is ludicrous: serious students will resort to properly equipped schools: there are now seventy Advocates, where the nine admitted in 1532 would be sufficient, and most of them are unemployed: "thair is as mekle law in Edinburgh as thar is silver to pay for it." Nothing is said about any interest the Advocates had in the instruction of their servitors, though admission to the bar was very frequently obtained through a form of apprenticeship, and the College of Justice had been tending to develop functions of an almost academic character.

The office of "professour in the lawis or humanitie" was either created or used for Adrian Damman, who held it from 1590 till the spring of 1594, when he became Resident for the United Provinces at the Scottish Court.[79] Having obtained in 1591 the royal confirmation of gifts bestowed since 1542 upon the College of Justice,[80] the Senators were now free to lend a helping hand to an Advocate, and appointed Master

Adam Newton, without consulting the Town Council. The latter indignantly ordered repayment to the Lords of their £1000, and refused to remunerate the intruder.[81]

It was hardly safe for the Senators to break the undertaking upon which their confirmation rested ; and both the Advocates and the Writers to the Signet were induced to furnish their joint contribution of £1000 on receiving the assurance that no instruction in the Law was to be given. On 21st September 1597, a fresh deed provided for a Regent of "humanitie in authouris Greek and Latene," with six bursars, of whom each contracting party should nominate two. The new teacher had a "private" and subsidiary task. He was to take boys prior to their first *annus academicus*, without prejudice to the proper grammatical functions of the High School, or to the right of an ordinary Regent to receive a student competent to proceed at once with his qualifying course.[82]

Such was the end of Robert Reid's plan to endow academic study of the Law in Edinburgh. The growth of the College in the direction of a *studium generale* was effectually arrested ; and it was destined to remain for many years an institution confined in scope to the Faculties of Arts and Divinity.

II

ADMINISTRATION

FIFTY YEARS OF EVER-WIDENING SCIENCE

"There is nothing more moving than that endless procession of students who pass under our eyes and go forth from our walls, generation after generation, bearing their new-lit torches—go forth into the darkness of the future, some of them destined to emerge in the full blaze of fame and success, but thousands of others who can never win their way to that light, but of whom now and again we catch some unexpected glimpse, which reveals them at their task, with torches still undimmed, it may be in some lonely parish of their own land, or it may be at some distant outpost of the Empire."

Professor S. H. BUTCHER's *Farewell,*
20th January 1904.

IN 1789, according to a writer in *The Scots Magazine*, "the most celebrated University at present in Europe" was "the worst accommodated"; and Lord Cockburn in his *Memorials* recalls how "in November we got a half holiday to see the foundation-stone of the new College laid, which was done with great civic and masonic pomp. Forty years more did not see the edifice completed. Only those who knew the adjoining grounds at this time can understand how completely its position has been since destroyed. With the exception of a few paltry and easily removable houses on the west and north, the ground all round it was entirely open. Nicolson Street was partly, and College Street entirely, unbuilt; and the College was so perfectly free on its east or front side, that I saw the ceremonies both of laying the foundation-stone and of President Dundas's funeral in 1787 from a window in the west wing of the Royal Infirmary. The spaces now occupied by the various buildings pressing on the College were then covered with grass fields or gardens. How often did we stand to admire the blue and yellow beds of crocuses rising through the clean earth, in the first days of spring, in the garden of old Dr Monro (the second), whose house stood in a small field entering from

Nicolson Street, within less than a hundred yards south of the College." In his letter to the Lord Provost on the "Best ways of spoiling the beauty of Edinburgh," written sixty years later, in October 1849, Cockburn records that "when the College was begun, it was in a large piece of nearly open ground; laid out chiefly in gardens. There were no houses on its eastern or southern sides; nothing on its west side except rubbish, that could easily have been bought; and nothing on its north side that did much harm. It might have stood, though rimmed by street, with much turfed and shrubberied space beyond this rim, with little noise; and the possibility of being seen. It is now jostled by houses all round; without a foot of soil except what it stands on. To be sure, the spare ground could not have been kept clear without a price; and, considering how long and ominously the College itself remained unfinished for want of funds, nobody perhaps is blameable for its present state. But it is an example, and a striking one, of danger that might have been avoided, and of the imprudence of letting such things take their own course, and trusting to accidental deliverances. What has happened should either have been foreseen and prevented; or the College ought not to have been placed where it is, and probably would not. As it is, it is nearly lost, externally, as an ornament to the town."

Lord Cockburn's criticism and censure have been completely justified by the course of events. The Thirty Years' War of litigation between Town and Gown, concerning the respective rights of the parties to make regulations for degrees, began in 1825 and ended in a judicial victory in the House of Lords for the Town Council, to whose generally wise and disinterested administration of the affairs of the College Principal Sir Alexander Grant has paid a generous and a warm tribute in *The Story of the University.* That victory, however, was to be followed by legislation. The Universities (Scotland) Act, 1858, the *Magna Charta* of the University, transferred the authority and control, exercised by the Town Council for over two centuries and a half, to the Senatus Academicus who, in addition to superintending and regulating the teaching and the discipline of the University, were to administer its property and revenues, their decisions being subject to the review of a newly-established University Court of eight members.

It may be that this rift in the relations between Town and Gown, at a critical period of the history of the University, caused the lack of foresight which Cockburn deplores, and of which the results are so apparent to-day.

At the commencement of the period under review, the academical year, 1883-84, a Buildings Extension Scheme had been launched with a representative Acting Committee under the convenership of Principal Sir Alexander Grant. Sites in Park Place and Teviot Row had already been purchased at a cost of about £33,000; and on that ground in the immediate vicinity of the new Royal Infirmary "complete Class-Rooms, Theatres, Laboratories, and Museums with the latest scientific improvements for the Medical Faculty of the University," were in the course of erection. It was also proposed "to erect a University Hall for the conferring of degrees, the holding of Examinations, and for all public Academical Ceremonials."

Before the fifty years covered by this History had run their course, the *New* College, crowned by Sir Rowand Anderson with a dome—in place of that designed by Robert Adam—and a figure of Youth bearing the torch of Knowledge had been renamed the *Old;* the Medical Faculty had been transferred to the University New Buildings in Teviot Row; an Academic Hall had been erected there by the generosity of William McEwan; the historic High School (at which Cockburn was educated) and the Royal Infirmary (to which he refers) had been procured to accommodate the Faculty of Science; Minto House—once a School of Medicine, and a name immortalised by John Brown in *Rab and His Friends*—and other buildings in Chambers Street, had been purchased to meet the growing needs of the Faculty of Arts; Sir John Usher had provided an Institute of Public Health in Warrender Park Road; the Departments of Agriculture, Forestry and Entomology had been housed in George Square; and in 1919 an area of 115 acres had been purchased on the south side of the City, and within its present boundaries, for the erection of scientific laboratories. This stretch of land is not uninteresting historically as the West Mains of the ancient Barony of Nether Liberton adjacent to the lands of Over or Upper Liberton which belonged, in the sixteenth century, to Clement Litil, an advocate in Edinburgh who, in 1580, left his books to "Edinburgh and the Kirk of God," a bequest which was to lay the foundation of the University Library.

The laboratories on the Liberton site are known collectively as "The King's Buildings"—permission to use his name having been graciously given by His Majesty King George the Fifth on the occasion of the Laying of the Foundation-Stone of the Department of Chemistry on 6th July 1920. They now include that department—except the department of Chemistry in Relation to Medicine, which is separately housed in the University New Buildings in Teviot Row—and the departments of Natural History, Animal Genetics, Engineering and Geology.

Town and Gown have long forgotten the litigations of the first half of the nineteenth century; and well might the Lord Provost of the day, Sir Thomas Whitson, in his Inaugural Address to the Fourth Congress of the Universities of the Empire, held in Edinburgh in July 1931, reflecting on the scattered character of the University Buildings and conjuring up the future, make an appeal for academic planning which would be the visible embodiment of a great ideal, the outward sign that, in one form or another, the University had some connection with the other educational institutions of the city, and that it was "in fact the head and forefront of Edinburgh's most important industry—Education."

THE ROYAL COMMISSIONS OF 1826 AND 1876
THE UNIVERSITIES (SCOTLAND) ACTS OF 1858 AND 1889
THE EXECUTIVE COMMISSIONS OF 1858 AND 1889

Fifty years of ever-widening Science have caused the University to expand far beyond the physical bounds of the College which was commenced in 1789. It was not, however, to prove to be beyond the power of the administrative machinery which had been created during the nineteenth century to deal with the multitude of problems of every kind which were to arise. That century saw no fewer than four Commissions on the Universities of Scotland; and, in the case of the University of Edinburgh, it witnessed the complete transference of control, in the first place from the Town Council to the Senatus and, in the second place, from the Senatus to the University Court.

The devoted labours of many men, bearing names illustrious in the history of Scotland and in its legal annals, who served on the Royal Commissions of 1826 and 1876, bore fruit in the legislation embodied in the Universities (Scotland) Acts of 1858 and 1889. But to one man pride of place is due: the Right Honourable John Inglis of Glencorse—"ille clarissimus"—Lord Justice General and President of the Court of Session and Chancellor of the University, who played a supremely important part in moulding the academic destinies of the Scottish nation. In April 1858 it had fallen to him, as Her Majesty's Advocate, to bring before the House of Commons a Bill "to make provision for the better government and discipline of the Universities of Scotland." The Scottish Universities, he pointed out, had lost sight of their proper objects; and their educational establishments had descended below the requirements of the age. The Bill was founded to a great extent upon the Report of the Royal Commission of 1826 on which, *inter alios,* Sir Walter Scott had been nominated to act as a member. This Report had been presented to Parliament in 1830, but it had lain dormant for over a quarter of a century. The Lord Advocate now proposed to confer for the first time upon the graduates of the University a certain share in the administration of its affairs by the foundation of a University Council; to institute for each University a University Board, or a University Court, consisting of a Rector, the Principal, and a certain number of Assessors (in Edinburgh six); and to appoint an Executive Commission to carry out these and other details of the Bill. The Bill became law as the Universities (Scotland) Act, 1858. The election of the Rector of the University was entrusted to the students, and that of the Chancellor to the graduates or General Council, William Ewart Gladstone being elected to the former office, and Lord Brougham to the latter. The Executive Commission continued in office for more than four years; and Sir Alexander Grant records that during that time the Commissioners held one hundred and twenty-six meetings, at every one of which Inglis presided. "He was, in fact, the soul of the Commission, and the excellent ordinances which resulted from the labours of the Commissioners may be regarded as especially the product of his judgment, and of his untiring attention to the mass of details with which the Commission had to deal."

The Commission left the University in the possession of constitutional autonomy, with its studies and degrees regulated by ordinances, and, should any change in the ordinances appear desirable, with the power, under due check, of revising them. But there was one matter in which the autonomous University seemed powerless to act, and which could only be regulated by an external authority, and that was the general reform of the Arts Faculty. Consequently, in 1876, the Government appointed a Royal Commission with Inglis as its Chairman, once more to enquire into and report upon the institutions of the Universities of Scotland. On this Commission the growing claims of Science and History for an adequate recognition were represented by the selection of Thomas Henry Huxley and James Anthony Froude as two of the Commissioners. The Commissioners presented, in February 1878, a Report which concluded with a summary of sixty-one recommendations. Although many of these recommendations have remained inoperative, and others have been modified by subsequent legislation, this Report is, and will remain, a mine of wisdom for the guidance of academic administrators.

Froude appended a Memorandum of Suggestions for a Law and History School, in which he laid down the following as "a Method of a School of History": "A general chart of universal history should first be laid down. Then a chart on a larger scale of the history of the country to which the student

From an etching by] [*William Hole, R.S.A.*

THE RIGHT HONOURABLE JOHN INGLIS OF GLENCORSE, D.C.L., LL.D.

Chancellor of the University
1868-1891

belongs. His own country is nearest to him; he knows the localities of it; he is what he is, because he inherits his character from his forefathers, and their actions and fortunes will touch him more nearly than those of others. Lastly, the Professors should choose particular epochs on which they should specially lecture and specially examine. In Scotch Universities those epochs should be chosen from the history of Scotland. No nation in Europe can look with a more just pride on their past than the Scots, and no young Scotsman ought to grow up ignorant of what that past has been."

The attitude of Huxley is reflected in the following passage in a letter written by him in 1892: "My own ideal is for the present day at any rate hopelessly impracticable. The University or Universities should be teaching bodies devoted to Art (literary and other), history, philosophy, and science where any one who wanted to learn all that is known about these matters should find people who could teach him and put him in the way of learning for himself. It will be a place for men to get knowledge and not for boys and adolescents to get degrees. That is what the world will want one day or other as a supplement to all manner of high schools and technical institutions in which young people get decently educated and learn to earn their bread—such are our present universities."

The venerable Chancellor of the University whose patience, foresight and sagacity had, in the words of Sir William Turner, placed him in "the highest rank amongst the benefactors of education in Scotland," was to live to see much that the Commission of 1876 had recommended translated into law in the Universities (Scotland) Act, 1889. *Quasi Cursores vitai lampada tradunt,* he was now to hand on his torch to another eminent Senator of the College of Justice, Lord Kinnear, the Chairman of the Commission of 1889 of which one was the Professor of Greek, Samuel Henry Butcher. "For myself," Professor Butcher said, "it taught me much. I got to know the University through and through, and became almost as much interested in every department of it as I was in my own. Incidentally, I had the opportunity of mastering some curious intricacies and requirements of the law which needed all the wisdom of the House of Lords to disentangle. Many of these details have now slipped from me; but what I shall never forget is that through that Commission I was brought into close intimacy with Lord Kinnear—with whom it was a pride and privilege to act—with Lord Kyllachy, Sir Arthur Mitchell, Sir Patrick Heron Watson, Mr Donald Crawford, Sir John Stirling-Maxwell, and, not least, with Lord Kelvin."

The Act, which had been placed on the Statute Book on the motion of the Lord Advocate, the Right Honourable J. P. B. Robertson, afterwards Lord Robertson of Forteviot, a Rector of the University, came into force on 1st January 1890. It is to be read and construed, so far as is consistent with its tenor, with the Universities (Scotland) Act, 1858.

In these two Statutes, with certain modifications introduced by the Universities (Scotland) Act, 1922, there are to be found the provisions enacted for the administration by the University of Edinburgh of its own affairs. It is a remarkable fact that, although the State has not hesitated to enforce its rights by Royal Commissions followed by legislation, the University so reformed has been left with larger powers and greater autonomy.

THE CONSTITUTION OF THE UNIVERSITY

i. *The University Court*

The University Court, as constituted by the Act of 1858, consisted of eight members, of whom five were a quorum: (1) A Rector elected by the matriculated students; (2) The Principal; (3) An Assessor nominated by the Chancellor; (4) The Lord Provost of Edinburgh; (5) An Assessor nominated by the Lord Provost, Magistrates and Town Council of Edinburgh; (6) An Assessor nominated by the Rector; (7) An Assessor elected by the General Council of the University; and (8) An Assessor elected by the Senatus Academicus. The Act of 1889 increased the number of members to fourteen, and the quorum to seven, adding three Assessors elected by the General Council and three by the Senatus, as it had long been felt that the representation of these two important bodies was inadequate.

The Rector and his Assessor continue in office for three years; and when the Chancellor, or the Rector, ceases to hold office, his Assessor continues to be a member of the Court until an Assessor is nominated by the new Chancellor or Rector. The other Assessors hold office for four years; and all Assessors are eligible for re-election. It is specially enacted that no principal or professor of any Scottish University shall be elected Rector or be nominated or elected Assessor to any other person or body than the Senatus Academicus. The Rector, and in his absence, the Principal, presides at meetings of the Court; normally, it is the latter; and, in the absence of both, a chairman is elected by the meeting. The person presiding at any meeting has a deliberative vote and also a casting vote.

As has been pointed out by Sir Charles Grant Robertson,* the Universities of Scotland are closely associated with the life of all classes in the civic community which have acquired both an interest and a share in their government and working. Nothing corresponding to the University Court in Scotland—*i.e.* the mixture of academic and civic persons in government—was, or could be, developed at Oxford or Cambridge. Whereas the Senatus had, since 1858, administered the property and revenue of the University, subject to the review of the Court, they were now by the Act of 1889 confined in the main to regulating and superintending the teaching and discipline. The Court became the chief governing body and received a very considerable extension of its powers, which are defined in Sections 6 and 21 of the Act. It is a body corporate, with perpetual succession and a Common Seal; and it can now, in addition to administering and managing the revenue and property of the University, review decisions of the Senatus on appeal; elect Professors to Chairs which are in the patronage of the University, and appoint Examiners and Lecturers; grant recognition to the teaching of any college or individual teacher for the purpose of graduation; define

* *The British Universities,* p. 16.

the nature and limits of a Professor's duties under his Commission; take proceedings for the purposes of discipline against any person employed in teaching or examining; appoint a certain proportion — one-third—of the Standing Committees charged with the immediate superintendence of the libraries or museums; and appoint Committees of its own members, with powers to report on any business that may be entrusted to them, or to carry out special instructions. The Court is also empowered to elect the representative of the University on the General Medical Council, and to found new Professorships with the approval of the Universities Committee of the Privy Council.

Of paramount importance is the power conferred by Section 21 of the Act of 1889 to alter or revoke any of the ordinances affecting the University, and to make new ordinances. The Commissioners under the Act of 1889, Section 14 (14), had been entrusted with power, which they did not exercise, to establish a General University Court of the four Scottish Universities, "with a view of taking in review the general interests of the Universities, especially in regard to degrees and examinations, and with the duty of reporting to Her Majesty on new ordinances, or changes in existing ordinances, affecting all or any of the Universities, and with power to report to the Secretary for Scotland on matters connected with the Universities upon which they may deem it to be of importance to represent their views, or upon subjects which may be specially referred to them by the Secretary for Scotland." This proposal was strenuously opposed by Sir William Turner. In an address on Medical Education delivered at Birmingham on 1st October 1890, he said: "I claim for the Universities in Scotland that the power of making, altering and revoking ordinances and regulations connected with the discharge of their degree-conferring functions should be vested in the authorities of each University, after communication with the sister Universities and reference to the Universities Committee of the Privy Council, and that they should not be subjected to a prolonged and complicated procedure such as has been imposed by the Act of 1889.

Educational freedom has been conferred on the younger Universities south of the Border, and it is difficult to understand why we in Scotland, with an educational history of which we have no cause to be ashamed, should be bound in swaddling clothes and impeded in our progress."*

Turner's view prevailed. The Court of each of the four Scottish Universities can make its own ordinances, subject to a duty of communicating their terms to the Senatus and General Council of its own University and to the Courts of the other Universities, and subject also to the Parliamentary control provided for in Section 21, to which no exception can be taken as new ordinances may involve financial expenditure and grants of money are made by the State.

ii. *The Scottish Universities Committee of the Privy Council*

The Universities Committee of the Privy Council, to which reference has been made, plays an important part in this connection. It is constituted by Section 9 of the Act of 1889, and consists of the Lord President of the Privy Council and the Secretary of State for Scotland, and also the Lord Justice General, the Lord Justice Clerk, the Lord Advocate, and the Chancellor and the Rector (designated in this section of the Act "the Lord Rector") of each of the Universities if they are members of the Privy Council, and at least one member of the Council's Judicial Committee.

The Commissioners under the Act of 1889 had utilised freely the Report of the Royal Commission of 1876 in framing ordinances. In particular, they had instituted a Faculty of Science and a Faculty of Music, and had regulated, in addition to the finances of the University, the retirement of Principals and Professors. The University Court, in virtue of the powers conferred upon it by Section 21 of the Act, powers which came into force after the expiration of the Commission, has made about sixty ordinances, most of which regulate specific matters within a Faculty; and, in conjunction with

* *Sir William Turner: A Chapter in Medical History*, by A. Logan Turner, M.D., 1919.

the other University Courts, it has regulated, by General Ordinances, admission to the Scottish Universities for purposes of graduation, has established a Scottish Universities Entrance Board, and has fixed the fees for matriculation and graduation. The matter of pensions to Principals and Professors has been regulated by another General Ordinance, which is subject now to the provisions of the Act of 1922. The University Court has also by ordinance instituted new degrees, a Doctorate of Philosophy and Bachelorships of Education and Commerce; it has founded over twenty new Chairs, it has instituted and regulated the offices of Reader and Senior Lecturer, and has admitted members of the teaching staff, in addition to Professors, to the Senatus Academicus and to the Faculties.

In contradistinction to the Royal and Executive Commissions and the legislation of the nineteenth century, the twentieth century may be regarded as the era of self-government by ordinance.

iii. *The Senatus Academicus*

The Principal and the Professors of the College of King James the Sixth, commonly called the Senatus Academicus of the University of Edinburgh, to adopt the title used in the legal proceedings already referred to, under the regime of the Town Council had been left to draw up their own schemes for studies and degrees; and they had built up from the foundation the whole system of medical graduation, the activities of the Town Council being limited to the appointment of Principals and Professors, the regulation of finances, and the care of the buildings. The Town Council claimed, however, to be entitled to intervene in the matter of regulations for degrees, and they were successful in the legal issue which followed.

The Universities (Scotland) Act, 1858, by Section 5 defined the powers of the Senatus in the following terms: "The Senatus Academicus of each of the Universities shall consist of the Principal . . . and whole Professors in each University, and shall possess and exercise the powers heretofore belonging to a Senatus Academicus in so far as the same are not modified or altered by or in pursuance of the provisions of this Act, and shall superintend and regulate the teaching and discipline of the University, and administer its property and revenues, subject to the control and review of the University Court . . . one-third of the Senatus shall be a quorum, and the Principal . . . shall be the ordinary President of the Senatus Academicus with a deliberative and casting vote. . . ."

Section 7 of the Universities (Scotland) Act, 1889, modified these provisions as follows: "The Senatus Academicus shall continue to possess and exercise the powers hitherto possessed by it so far as they are not modified or altered by the Universities (Scotland) Act, 1858, or by this Act, and shall have power (1) to regulate and superintend the teaching and discipline of the University; (2) to appoint two-thirds of the members of any Standing . . . Committee charged . . . with the immediate superintendence of any libraries or museums or the contents thereof. . . ."

To the Principal and Professors there have now been added by an Ordinance of the University Court, No. 39, approved by an Order in Council on 11th October 1923, Readers in the Faculties of Arts, Science and Law, and Senior Lecturers in the Faculty of Medicine to a number not exceeding one-fourth of the number who are members otherwise.

The Principal is the President of the Senatus, with a deliberative and also a casting vote; and, in his absence, the senior Professor present acts as Chairman.

Among their privileges the Senatus have the right to elect two of the Managers of the Royal Infirmary of Edinburgh, two of the Governors of George Heriot's Trust, and a Representative on the Board of Trustees of the National Library of Scotland.

Degrees in the Faculties of Divinity, Law, Medicine, Arts, Science and Music, and also the Honorary Degrees in Divinity, in Laws and in Music are conferred, on the recommendation of the Senatus, by the Chancellor, the Vice-Chancellor, the Principal, or the senior Professor present.

Every additional Chair adds to the number of the Senatus and, consequently, from mere numerical strength, to the difficulty of a satisfactory transaction of business. To Sir William Turner it was obvious that the Senatus might at some time become too large an administrative body, and that it might be necessary to appoint an executive from its members. The Principal, he thought, and the Deans of the various Faculties might be members *ex officiis* and, in addition to these, one or two representatives from each Faculty would complete the Executive Committee. Turner's fear has been realised. While the Court is invested with supreme power, the Senatus continue to wield great influence; but, in practice, this influence has in effect to be exercised by two committees—subject to review—the Committee on Educational Policy, constituted on the lines foreseen by Turner, and the Principal and Deans Committee of seven members. The experience of the Senatus is the most eloquent argument against increasing the number of members of the Court. Executive bodies, if they are to be effective, should be small numerically, so long as they are representative.

iv. *The Secretariat*

A survey of the Minutes of the Senatus Academicus and of the University Court, since the institution of the latter body, reveals the outstanding fact that in their mutual relations harmony has been the prevailing rule after certain preliminary adjustments and interpretations had been made with regard to their respective spheres of action. Financial control and educational arrangements are, of course, interdependent, and the body with the power of the purse must inevitably control educational policy at the end of the day. But in actual practice there has been the most active co-operation and the friendliest intercourse between the two bodies.

Until 1918 the Court and Senatus were separately organised, each with an administrative office and an Executive Officer. A multitude of communications passed from the Secretary of the Senatus to the Secretary of the Court, and from the Secretary of the Court to the Secretary of the Senatus. During the greater part of the period under review two outstanding personalities held these offices, Professor Malcolm

Campbell Taylor and Professor Sir Ludovic Grant. Professor Taylor was a member of the reconstituted Court which assumed office in 1890, and, shortly after that date, he succeeded John Christison, Writer to the Signet, the third son of the great Sir Robert, as its Secretary. He held office until 1916, and for a period of over twenty years his services were of the utmost value alike to the University, to the body whose deliberations he guided, and to two successive Principals, Sir William Muir and Sir William Turner. Sir Ludovic Grant, who in 1897 succeeded Professor John Kirkpatrick (a historiographer of the University in English and in French) as Secretary of the Senatus, had touched academic interests at every point. Born in the academic purple, he held with high distinction the offices of Regius Professor of Public Law and Dean of the Faculty of Law. As Dean, it was his duty to act as the Promotor of the Honorary Graduands in Law, a duty he discharged with

> "the touch of the Magician's finger,
> His Golden Keys."

Moses, when he strove with Amalek, was not more fortunately placed than the Principal of the University with two lieutenants such as these to sustain him.

In 1916 Professor Taylor retired and was succeeded by Professor Sir Richard Lodge—*clarum et venerabile nomen*—as Interim Secretary of the Court. At his instance a Joint Committee of the Court and Senatus was appointed to consider the question of the union of the two secretarial offices and, after considerable discussion, it was resolved to institute the office of Secretary to the University, and to place in the hands of a whole-time official the duties previously discharged by the Secretary of the Court and the Secretary of the Senatus, and also the general secretarial business of the University. This step might well have proved disastrous, alike to harmony and to efficiency, but for the self-sacrifice of Sir Ludovic Grant, who agreed to undertake and to discharge the duties of the office for a year. Professor William Wilson, for a period of five years, was given the opportunity to work out in detail the broad lines of principle which his distinguished predecessor had laid down, and was associated, in close collaboration, with a chief, Sir Alfred Ewing, who inspired at once affection, admiration and esteem. The Secretaryship of the University in the hands of William Arnot Fleming, who assumed office in November 1924, has justified the hopes of the founders of the office. In 1922 the offices of Deputy-Secretary and Assistant Secretary were instituted. They are filled respectively by Alexander Falconer Giles and Thomas F. Harley. But the officials with whom the students come into closest contact during their University careers are those of the Matriculation Office, and by the *alumni* of the University now scattered throughout the world the names of Thomas Gilbert and James Dowie will be gratefully remembered.

The Secretary's Office is the Clearing House for all the administrative business of the University, and the Secretary is in direct touch with the Court, the Senatus and the other Officials; he communicates with the Factor and the Accountant and he has, in practice, as members of his staff the Secretary and Registrar of the General Council of the University, an arrangement with advantages which are obvious from the point of view of efficiency.

v. *The Curators of Patronage*

In September 1583 the Town Council made their first academic appointment in favour of Master Robert Rollock of St Andrews, and from the outset they assumed the right, without control, to appoint and remove regents or teachers. Rollock's appointment was for one year and further, so long as he "uses himself faithfully according to the rules and injunctions which shall be given to him by the Provost, Bailies and Council."

The problem of patronage, which was peculiar to the University of Edinburgh as a municipal foundation, was solved in 1858 by the creation of the Curators of Patronage, in so far as the patronage previously exercised by the Town Council was concerned, and no alteration was made in 1889. The Town Council in 1858 was deprived of its ancient right which was transferred to seven Curators, four nominated by the Town Council and three by the University Court. The

Curators have now the patronage of all the Chairs previously in the gift of the Town Council, and a share in the patronage of certain others. Most important of all, they elect the Principal of the University.

The exercise of patronage by the Town Council had at no time been open to serious criticism. Inglis, in his Inaugural Address as Chancellor, dealing with the question of the exercise of patronage, referred to the qualities of honesty and firmness which were required, and the capacity for making a discriminating choice: "It will be found that the men who possess these gifts, and who know best how indispensable is their use in the administration of such a trust are, generally speaking, the most apt to shrink from undertaking its duties. It is no easy task, at least for most men, to disregard the claims of kindred, the appeals of friendship, the pressure of influence; to cast aside political and politico-religious prejudices and sympathies; to wade, it may be, through a morass of faithless and verbose testimonials in the almost vain hope of gathering a few modest blossoms of truth; to extract all other available and trustworthy materials for forming a sound judgment, and then to address oneself to the task of selection, but such are the qualities and such the amount of honest labour indispensable in the right administration of University patronage."

The Commissioners under the Act of 1889 had been empowered to prepare a scheme by which a detailed and reasoned report on the qualifications of candidates for Chairs might be submitted to the patrons, including the Crown, so as to assist them in the discharge of their patronage; but this power they did not exercise.

Patronage in the University of Edinburgh, apart from certain special cases, is now exercised normally either by the Crown, by the Curators, or by the University Court. Sir William Turner suggested one source of patronage which would be representative of all three. Any alteration in the present system, however, would require legislation; and vested rights were successfully defended before a Departmental Committee presided over by Lord Elgin in 1909.

vi. *The General Council of the University*

The General Council of the University was constituted by Section 6 of the Universities (Scotland) Act, 1858, "to take into consideration all questions affecting the well-being and prosperity of the University, and to make representations from time to time on such questions to the University Court, who shall consider the same, and return to the Council their deliverance thereon." All proposed improvements in the arrangements of the University "shall be submitted to the University Council for their consideration." The Council now consists of the Chancellor, the members of the University Court, the Professors, the graduates of the University and, since the passing of the Act of 1922, the Lecturers of one year's standing, who, however, have not the right to vote as Parliamentary electors unless they are otherwise qualified. Section 8 of the Act of 1889 contains provisions as to meetings and a quorum; but otherwise it leaves the provisions of the Act of 1858 unaffected.

The Council elects the Chancellor of the University and four of the Assessors on the Court. The regulations as to their election are contained in Ordinances of the Commissioners of 1889. At Council meetings the Chancellor presides and, in his absence, the Rector, the Principal, the Chancellor's Assessor, or the Rector's Assessor, in that order. The Register contains the names of over 19,000 members. Thousands of the members reside at a distance, many of them abroad, with little or no connection with the University, and without practical knowledge of University matters.

> "Far and sure our bands have gone—
> Hy-Brazil or Babylon,
> Islands of the Southern Run
> And Cities of Cathaia!"

It would therefore obviously be inexpedient to give the Council powers; but, since its institution, it has wielded a great and growing influence in University affairs, and it has never been more beneficially active than it is to-day under the Conveners of its two Standing Committees on Business and Finance.

William A. Coutts, now the Chief Clerk in the Matriculation Office, acts as the Registrar, and Thomas F. Harley as the Secretary of the Council. Both are members of the staff of the Secretary to the University.

The General Councils of the four Scottish Universities now together return three Members of Parliament by a statutory alteration of the arrangement contained in the Representation of the People (Scotland) Act, 1868, whereby one member was returned by the General Councils of the Universities of St Andrews and Edinburgh, and one member by the General Councils of the Universities of Glasgow and Aberdeen.

It will be noted that the Council has no executive authority. It can only make representations. The Royal Commission of 1876 was against placing increased power in the hands of the Council, as a small section, residing in or near Edinburgh, might thus exercise control.

vii. *The Chancellor and the Vice-Chancellor*

In Edinburgh the office of Chancellor of the University was created by Section 2 of the Act of 1858 : "in time coming there shall be a Chancellor of the University of Edinburgh." Degrees are conferred by the Chancellor. He is to hold office for life and to have power to appoint a Vice-Chancellor "who may in the absence of the Chancellor discharge his office in so far as regards conferring degrees, but in no other respect." Normally, but not necessarily, the Chancellor nominates the Principal of the University as Vice-Chancellor. As has been stated, the Chancellor is elected by the General Council of the University, of which body he is the President, and although he has no seat on the Court, he nominates an Assessor. Under the Act of 1858 changes in the internal arrangements of the University, proposed by the University Court, were to receive his sanction; but, this arrangement having proved cumbrous in practice, it was not re-enacted in 1889.

The Vice-Chancellor acts as Returning Officer at Parliamentary Elections and, if there be no Vice-Chancellor at the time, the University Court appoints a Returning Officer.

The office of Chancellor has proved to be of very real value to the University, and grateful record is made of the long and distinguished services of Chancellor Inglis and the Earl of Balfour.

viii. *The Rector*

In contradistinction to the office of Chancellor, that of Rector could not be said to be a creation of the legislature. In 1620 it was given to Andrew Ramsay, the Lord Provost, who treated the post apparently as a merely nominal one. The office shortly afterwards went into abeyance, but was revived by the Town Council in 1640 by an Act of Council, entitled "Laws for the conduct of, and Act creating a Rector for the College." This Act bestowed the office on the Reverend Alexander Henderson and gave lengthy instructions as to his duties. He was to preside at ceremonials; there was to be carried before him "ane maisse"; he was to be "the eye of the Council of the town for universal inspection and as the mouth of the college for giving information to the Council"; he was to supervise the Principal and Professors and adjudicate on all complaints and debates, labouring to compose them "joyslie and without scandle." In 1665 the Council decided that "the Provost of Edinburgh present and to come be always Rector and Governor of the College of this Burgh in all time coming."

The office of Rector created by the Acts of 1858 and 1889 was wholly divorced from past history. In Section 11 of the former Act, and in Section 5 (4) of the latter, the name "Rector" alone is used; but in Section 9 of the Act of 1889 the officer is referred to as "Lord Rector." The Rector in the pre-Reformation Universities was *dominus*. The Rector of statutory title in Scottish Universities is elected by the matriculated students of the University, and holds office for three years. He may, before he appoints his Assessor on the Court, confer with the Students' Representative Council.

Photo by] [*Russell, London*

THE RIGHT HON. THE EARL OF BALFOUR, K.G., O.M.

Chancellor of the University
1891-1930

ix. *The Students' Representative Council*

The Regulations for the Students' Representative Council are to be found in a General Ordinance of the Commissioners of 1889, No. 60, the Act of that year having given statutory authority for its formation. The Council is entitled to petition the Senatus with regard to any matter affecting the teaching and discipline of the University, and the University Court with regard to any other matter affecting the students.

"The students, in common with the Professors and other teachers, are deeply interested in the advancement of education, and in maintaining the position of the University in the front rank both as regards the quality of the teaching and the character, conduct and reputation of the students." *

The Act of 1858 had authorised the students to elect a Rector to preside at the meetings of the University Court; he in his turn was to nominate an Assessor on the Court, but, at each triennial period, as soon as the Rector was elected, the students became dormant in regard to the official life of the University.

x. *The Universities (Scotland) Act,* 1922

Whereas Robert Rollock was appointed for a year, the custom grew up of appointing Principals and Professors *ad vitam aut culpam.* The Act of 1922 empowered the Court to make ordinances for the superannuation and pensioning of Principals and Professors. It provided also for the admission of Lecturers and Readers to the Senatus Academicus and to membership of the General Council.

At the University of Edinburgh a Professor appointed after the date of the Act must, by the provisions of an ordinance, unless his retirement is regulated otherwise, as in the case of Professors holding Clinical posts in Hospitals, retire at the end of the academical year in which he shall have attained the age of seventy years; and the Principal at the end of the academical year in which he shall have attained

* *Twenty-one Years of Corporate Life at Edinburgh University,* 1905, preface by Sir William Turner.

the age of seventy-five years. *Eheu fugaces anni!* A Professor formerly held his Chair for life, not merely for the "allotted span," and in place of a non-contributory pension he must now, if appointed after the effective date of the Act, become a contributory towards a superannuation allowance.

THE TEACHING STAFF

So far as the present constitution of the University is concerned, one may say that it existed, in embryo, from the passing of the Act of 1858; subsequent legislation did no more than develop, in the light of the experience which had been gained and to meet altered conditions, institutions which had proved themselves suitable for the times. But a glance at the *University Calendar* of fifty years ago shows at once that the University was then a very different institution from what it is to-day. The most marked changes concern the number and the personnel of the teaching staff, the admission of women to graduation, the administration of the finances, and the attitude of the University to the social life of the students.

To-day there are 59 Professors, 9 Readers, 4 Senior Lecturers, 144 Lecturers and 99 Assistants, a staff of 315 altogether, and, in addition, over 60 members of the Clinical Teaching Staff. In the academical year 1883-84, there were 4 Professors in the Faculty of Divinity, 5 in the Faculty of Law, 12 in the Faculty of Medicine, and 18 in the Faculty of Arts, a total of 39—but known to the profane as "The Forty Thieves," because the students paid the class fees to the Professors personally. There was no Faculty of Science and no Faculty of Music. There were only 3 Lecturers, of whom 2 were in the Faculty of Medicine and 1 in the Faculty of Arts; only 26 Assistants, of whom 8 were in the Faculty of Arts, 3 in the Faculty of Law, and 15 in the Faculty of Medicine.

The total number of matriculated students in 1883-84 was 3374, of whom 108 were in the Faculty of Divinity, 505 in the Faculty of Law, 1763 in the Faculty of Medicine, and

998 in the Faculty of Arts; and although it would be incorrect to say that there were no women students, women were not admitted to graduation in any of the Faculties and they were taught extra-academically. For the last academical year for which the returns are complete, 1931-32, the total number of matriculated students was 4327, of whom 3121 were men and 1206 were women, distributed among the Faculties as follows:—

	Divinity.	Law.	Medicine.	Arts.	Science.	Music.
Men . . .	140	241	1157	971	595	17
Women . .	2	33	155	904	85	27

During the same year, 1931-32, the students coming from homes outside the British Isles numbered 649; of this total, 551 were whole-time students, of whom 369 came from the British Empire and 182 from Foreign Countries; of the remainder, 98 were part-time students and of these 67 were from the Empire and 31 from Foreign Countries.

The numerical growth of the teaching staff is obviously out of all proportion to the increase in the number of students. It is indeed startling; and it has brought with it problems not easy of solution. In the nineteenth century many subjects, new and old, were not taught within the University; and there were special branches of subjects which were not usually, or fully, dealt with in the professorial lectures. The professorial system, with its security of tenure, had attracted to the University many men of eminence as teachers. But to found a new Chair, the occupant of which would hold office for life, involved the provision of an adequate endowment; to create a lectureship was an altogether different and an easier matter depending on annual revenue.

Sir William Turner foresaw the danger which might arise from the institution of a number of appointments filled by comparatively young men, whose object was to gain experience in teaching and to acquire a more thorough knowledge of the subject. There was a risk that some might fail in due course to obtain promotion and thus, with advancing years, tend to become disappointed with their want of success in life, a condition which would not conduce to the value of the

Lectureships in the scheme of University instruction. Now, however, with the great variety of academic instruction and the multiplicity of subjects, the number of Lecturers far exceeds the number of Professors; they are in fact roughly in the proportion of three to one. They include many men of eminence and many excellent teachers, loyally devoted to the institution which they serve. Failure to attain to the academic eminence of a Chair can no longer be regarded as in any degree a sign of want of success. There are many men and women well qualified, and there are few Chairs. The Professors and the Lecturers are now in the fullest sense of the word *Colleagues* as University Teachers; and gradually the latter branch of the teaching staff has acquired a status and a security of tenure. They are fully represented on the Boards of Studies and, in a certain proportion, on the Faculties and in the Senate; and it is possible for them to obtain direct representation on the University Court.

In 1919 the University Court adopted the Federated Superannuation System for Universities on a contributory basis, for the teaching staff, except Professors, and for those engaged in administration and in the Library. Since the Act of 1922, however, the non-contributory scheme of pensions for Professors, formerly the rule, no longer applies in the case of appointments made to Chairs after that date; and now the professorial and non-professorial members of the teaching staff are on the same footing in respect of provision for resignation or retirement. Under this system the member insured contributes five per cent. of his salary and the University Court ten per cent., in addition to the salary, in order to pay the premium on a policy of insurance selected by the member of the staff from a great variety of options.

THE ADMISSION OF WOMEN TO GRADUATION

On 5th November 1872, the Principal of the University delivered an Address on "Happiness and Utility as promoted by the Higher Education of Women." The subject was much in the air, and Lord Neaves contributed to the discussion in verse:—

"Ye fusty old fogies, Professors by name,
A deed you've been doing of sorrow and shame;
Though placed in your Chairs to spread knowledge abroad,
Against half of mankind you would shut up the road;
College honours and lore from the fair you withdraw
By enforcing against them a strict Salic Law;
Is it fear; Is it envy; or what can it be?
And why should a woman not get a degree?"

There is no doubt as to the views of Principal Sir Alexander Grant on this subject. In *The Story of the University* he writes: "'The Association for the higher Education of Women' now styles itself 'The Association for the University Education of Women,' and in fact it has always been the object of some leading spirits in the Association to obtain the admission of women to the classes within the University walls, and the opening of degrees to women on the same terms as those on which they are open to men. So long as the University is overflowing with male students and every class-room is overcrowded, it is, of course, impossible to think of admitting a number of ladies in addition. But, waiving this, the whole policy which aims at such a thing seems mistaken:—

'For woman is not undeveloped man,
But diverse.'

And therefore, though undoubtedly women should have facilities for obtaining a University education, it should probably be one cast on different lines from the present University system for men. What the Woman's University of the future will be, time and experience have yet to determine."

The facilities which existed fifty years ago for women to obtain a University education are to be found on page 14 of the Appendix to the *University Calendar* for the academical year 1883-84. The University granted Certificates in Arts to women. Candidates were required to study in at least three of the classes of the "Edinburgh Association for the University Education of Women," recognised by the Senatus, and to have passed the Local Examinations of the University of Edinburgh, or of one of the other Scottish Universities, or of the Universities of Oxford or Cambridge. They might then present themselves at the Edinburgh University Examinations for the Certificate in Arts and, after passing in not less than three subjects, they were entitled to receive a Certificate in Arts. The Certificates were of two grades, Pass and Honours. The classes sanctioned and approved by the University were, *in the Department of Languages and Literature*: English Literature, Latin, Greek, and Biblical Criticism; *in the Department of Philosophy*: Psychology and Logic, Moral Philosophy, Political Economy, Theory of Education and Fine Art; and *in the Department of Mathematics and Physical Science*: Mathematics, Experimental Physics, Chemistry, Geology, Botany, Zoology, and Physiology.

So matters remained until the passing of the Act of 1889, Section 14 (6) of which empowered the Commissioners "to enable each University to admit women to graduation in one or more Faculties, and to provide for their instruction." The Commissioners, we may assume, embarked on this part of their task *con amore*, for one of the earliest ordinances which they made contains the regulations for the graduation of women and for their instruction in the Universities. All the barriers have now disappeared and, in every Faculty, women are admitted to the class-rooms and to the examination halls on terms of complete equality with men. It was not, however, until Parliament extended the franchise to women that women graduates were permitted to vote as members of the General Council of the University for a Parliamentary candidate. The point was tested in a law-suit which ended, in 1909, in the House of Lords in a decision against the claim of the women graduates to exercise the University franchise as of right and independently of sex, as it was a principle of the unwritten constitutional law of the country that men only were entitled to vote.*

There may still be questionings as to whether or not "the happiness and utility of women" have been adequately promoted by the higher education provided in the curricula of to-day. Has the problem of the Woman's University been solved?

* Nairn and Others *v.* the University Courts of St Andrews and Edinburgh. 1909 S.C. (H.L.) 10.

Without attempting to answer this question, it is realised that problems there are in plenty to confront the woman undergraduate in the course of her University career. To assist her she has the tact, the sympathy and the understanding of a General Adviser of Women Students, an office now held by Miss Marjorie Rackstraw.

FINANCE

A third great change is in the domain of finance. The financial problem is always with the University. When in 1893 an attempt was made by the Treasury to come to an arrangement by which an annual sum of £40,000 was to be paid to the four Universities of Scotland to cover all their claims, past, present and future, Sir George Harrison, the Lord Provost of Edinburgh, pointed out to the Financial Secretary of the Treasury that the proposal to dispose for the future of the claims of the Universities to public moneys would require to be coupled with the condition that the people of Scotland would also have to be freed from all future increase of taxation. There the matter rested. In fifty years the annual Government Grant to the University of Edinburgh alone has increased to substantially more than twice the amount which the Treasury had proposed, in 1883, finally to pay to all four Universities.

A student undertaking research on "The Emoluments of Scots Professors" might fall into a grievous error. The salaries of the Professors of the seven basic Arts subjects, half a century ago, were as follows:—

Subject	£	s.	d.
Humanity	£247	10	0
Mathematics	258	6	8
Greek	247	4	4
Logic and Metaphysics	322	4	4
Moral Philosophy	322	4	4
Natural Philosophy	282	4	4
Rhetoric and English Literature	280	0	0

But these annual salaries were exclusive of class fees. It was the Golden Age of the Scots Professor, and he sat personally at the receipt of custom.

The Chancellor of the University, Sir James Barrie, was a student in the days of "The Forty Thieves," and he has given us, in *An Edinburgh Eleven*, a graphic picture of the system as he knew it: "Having immediately before taken lodgings in a crow's nest, my first sight of Masson was specially impressive. It was the opening of the Session, when fees were paid, and a whisper ran round the Quadrangle that Masson had set off home with three hundred one-pound notes stuffed into his trouser pockets. There was a solemn swell of awe-struck students to the gates and some of us could not help following him. He took his pockets coolly. When he stopped it was at a second-hand bookstall, where he rummaged for a long time. Eventually he pounced upon a dusty, draggled little volume, and went off proudly with it beneath his arm. He seemed to look suspiciously at strangers now, but it was not the money but the book he was keeping guard over. His pockets, however, were unmistakably bulging out. I resolved to go in for literature."

The Commissioners of 1889 were to make a radical change and to substitute a fixed normal salary. Schedule 1 of their Finance Ordinance of 5th June 1893 contains a schedule of the normal salaries of the Professors. Taking again for purposes of comparison the same seven subjects, we find the salaries fixed as follows:—

Humanity	£1100
Greek	1100
Mathematics	1100
Natural Philosophy	1100
Logic and Metaphysics	900
Moral Philosophy	900
Rhetoric and English Literature	900

In the event, however, of the Fee Fund, when added to the sums payable out of the Salaries Account, not being sufficient in any year to make good the normal salaries of the Professors, the claims of the Professors upon the Fee Fund were in that year to suffer a deduction proportionate to their normal salaries.

These sums remain the stipends fixed by Ordinance, but the University Court has, in the exercise of its powers,

SIR JAMES MATTHEW BARRIE, Bt., O.M., LL.D., M.A.

Chancellor of the University

1930

augmented them in view of the change in the purchasing power of money and to meet other altered conditions.

It has been argued that with security of tenure and a normal salary all incentive to exertion on the part of a Professor would disappear. But, had the system not been changed, it would have been impossible to make provision, especially in the Arts curriculum, for the inclusion of optional subjects, as the more advanced or the less popular the subject, the smaller normally would be the class. No system could possibly be worse than one where Professors might bid against one another for students. There was little or no such competition so long as the Arts curriculum was rigidly confined to the seven subjects, for every Professor drew practically the same amount in class fees.

It is impossible to compare the University Accounts of fifty years ago with the Accounts to-day. George D. Stewart, the University Accountant, an office which was instituted in 1922 and which has proved to be of great value, has drawn up the following comparison between the year 1893-94, when the Commissioners' Ordinance had come into operation, and the year 1930-31 :—

INCOME.	1893-94.	1930-31.
Class Fees of Students	£26,559	£79,388
Matriculation, Examination and other Fees	11,212	30,744
Endowment Income	7,742	51,856
Annual Government Grants	25,920	105,800
Other Income—all sources	...	19,552
	£71,433	£287,340

EXPENDITURE.	1893-94.	1930-31.
Salaries of Professors, Lecturers and Assistants	£45,947	£162,292
Maintenance of Laboratories, Libraries and Class Expenses	5,278	36,921
Upkeep of Buildings, including rates, attendance, heating, lighting and general repairs, but excluding extraordinary items	6,002	29,222
Examination Expenditure	2,688	6,865
Other Expenditure, ordinary and extraordinary	6,540	48,785
	£66,455	£284,085

The regulations as to the Finances of the University are now contained in an Ordinance of the University Court (No. 27), which was approved by an Order in Council on 14th January 1919. It superseded the Commissioners' Ordinance, simplified the Accounts of the University and, in particular, discontinued the keeping of the separate Fee Fund and Salaries Account.

A succession of Principals and Vice-Chancellors—sturdy beggars in the interests of the University—Sir Alexander Grant, Sir William Muir, Sir William Turner and Sir Alfred Ewing—have each in turn added to its capital and its revenue, its efficiency and its prestige. The labours of the first were brought to a brilliant conclusion with the celebration by the University of the Tercentenary of its Foundation, and the virtual completion of the Buildings Extension Scheme, to which reference has been made. The reign of the second saw the completion of that scheme with the erection of the McEwan Hall. For years before he assumed office as Principal, in 1903, Sir William Turner had acted as Convener of the Finance Committee of the University Court and, with prudent sagacity, had managed the finances of the University in the years before the war. The purchase, in his period of office, of the site and buildings at High School Yards, where the Royal High School and the Royal Infirmary of Edinburgh had been situated, for what would now be regarded as a nominal sum, was a triumph of administrative skill, the value of which has perhaps not yet been fully realised. In the words of Lord Justice Clerk Macdonald (Lord Kingsburgh): "His life work was great and strenuous. His memory will always be revered by all who knew him. He sought no praise. He was no *poseur*. He had no enemies and had the regard of hosts of friends. His best epitaph is—'He did his duty.'" In 1919 the acquisition of a new site, unencumbered with buildings, had become a matter of the utmost urgency, and Sir Alfred Ewing's name will be associated with "The King's Buildings," a permanent memorial to his characteristic foresight. In 1929, on his retirement, he was succeeded by Principal and Vice-Chancellor Sir Thomas Holland.

Address to the
King's Most Excellent Majesty

May it please Your Majesty to receive from the UNIVERSITY OF EDINBURGH the homage of a profoundly loyal and grateful welcome. Your Majesty comes to us not only as King but as Emperor, for the members of this University are drawn from all places of Your Dominions. We tender Your Majesty a welcome that is Scottish indeed in its warmth and Metropolitan in its pride, but is none the less Imperial in its scope. This gracious visit to a University which may in a unique sense claim to be a servant of the Empire will gladden hearts in India, in Canada, in Australia, in New Zealand, in Africa, in the Islands of the Seas, who look to Edinburgh as their own Alma Mater, or the Alma Mater of their sons.

When Your Majesty last visited Edinburgh we were privileged to make You a loyal Address, and even as it was being spoken the Navy of Your late enemy was brought to an inglorious anchorage in the Forth. With kingly magnanimity Your Majesty had chosen to be absent from the scene of their humiliation. Then Your people had but just laid down their arms, and this University, like others, was only beginning to recover after the empty years of war. But coming now You find us full, to overflowing, of young life which has lost nothing of its eagerness though it is enriched with a strange experience, which is resolute to redeem the time, to build where others have broken. Never before have our class-rooms been so crowded: never has the value of University training been more plainly recognised, especially in all that relates to the development and application of Science. We believe that the demand for higher education will not only continue but will grow, and that the Universities are destined to play a still larger part in the national life. It is to meet the responsibilities of the present and the future that the bold step has been taken of acquiring a great new site on which buildings may be erected that will adequately serve modern needs. We have entered on this scheme in the faith that the friends of the University will not suffer her activities to languish for lack of necessary support. With Your Majesty's permission, and in memory of Your visit, we propose to call these 'The King's Buildings' of the University. The first of them, in the midst of which this Memorial Stone is placed, is a Laboratory for the study of Chemistry—a science no less potent in peace than in war.

With particular pleasure the University greets Her Majesty Queen Mary, who has graciously consented to allow us to enrol Her among our Honorary Graduates. It is our happy fortune to offer Her Majesty this tribute on the anniversary of a day which has already brought Her, as we believe, much happiness, and has brought lasting good to the Royal House, to the Nation, and to the world. And though He is far away, our eyes turn with affectionate admiration to Your Royal Son The Prince of Wales, whose upbringing was the subject of so much wise parental solicitude, who now passes lightly from triumph to triumph, linking up the Empire by the magic of his personality, by his genius for the kindly thought, the happy and witty word. May God prosper such a messenger of goodwill.

Again, and from the bottom of our hearts, we thank Your Majesties for this evidence of interest in the work of the University, and sympathy with its aims.

J. A. Ewing,
Principal and Vice-Chancellor.

THE UNIVERSITY OF EDINBURGH,
6th July 1920.

PRESENTED TO HIS MAJESTY ON THE OCCASION OF THE LAYING OF THE FOUNDATION STONE OF "THE KING'S BUILDINGS"

Any record of financial administration during the last half century would be incomplete without a reference to Sir Henry Cook who, succeeding his father and succeeded by his son, and combining all the best qualities of the highest type of Scottish legal practitioner, managed the investments of the University as its Factor.

The Carnegie Trust for the Universities of Scotland

The twentieth century opened with a new era of hope for the Scottish Universities. Andrew Carnegie, a Scottish millionaire and philanthropist, was born and brought up in Dunfermline. At an early age he went to America where he achieved remarkable commercial success, the details of which are related in his *Autobiography*, published in 1920. He was the creator of many endowments to promote the cause of international peace and other interests which he had at heart; and in 1901 he proposed to create a trust with an original capital of £2,000,000 to relieve Scottish parents of the necessity of paying their children's fees at the Universities of Scotland. At a conference at Dover House, at which Sir William Turner was present, it was pointed out to the donor that a natural question to consider would be the effect of such a change, a change which would involve legislation on the finances in the University system. The scheme would not add to the revenue of the University unless the number of students underwent a proportionate increase. It would mean no more than that fees paid by parents would be paid by the Trust. If there was a large increase of students—and the number of students was practically determined by the standard of the Entrance Examination—the Universities would then be called upon to make payments on capital account for larger class-rooms and, in the scientific departments, for larger laboratories, more apparatus and other teaching appliances; and additional teachers would be needed. The scheme, in short, would call for an increase in the capital of the Universities to provide for all these improvements in educational methods. Carnegie's essentially practical mind at once responded to these considerations. The Trust, as eventually created, provided that one-half of the net annual income should be devoted to the improvement and expansion of the Universities in the Faculties of Science and Medicine, and the extension of opportunities for scientific study and research, and of facilities for acquiring a knowledge of History, Economics, English Literature and Modern Languages, and such other subjects cognate to a technical or commercial education as could be brought within the University curriculum. The other half of the Trust's revenue was to be devoted on a permissive basis—and now after a means test—to the payment of the whole or part of the ordinary class fees exigible by the Universities from students of Scottish birth or extraction, of sixteen years or upwards, or scholars who had given two years' attendance after the age of fourteen at schools in Scotland under the inspection of the Scottish Education Department.

The Carnegie Trust is thus a very valuable source of capital endowment, which enables the University to keep abreast of modern progress by the erection of buildings, equipment of laboratories, and by the provision of scholarships for the purpose of encouraging scientific and literary research. The Trustees are in the closest touch with the four Universities and make capital grants, payable under a quinquennial scheme, for the purposes mentioned.

The following distributions have been made to the University by the Trust from its inception in 1902 to the end of the current quinquennium on 30th September 1935 :—

Buildings and Permanent Equipment	£227,850
Endowment of Chairs and Lectureships	115,440
Endowment of Pension Scheme for Lecturers and Assistants	20,000
Hostels and Playing Fields	29,700
Library Catalogue	5,000
Library Maintenance	45,750
In supplement of Income (War period)	8,650
	£452,390

ADMINISTRATION

The University Grants Committee of H.M. Treasury.

In July 1919 the Chancellor of the Exchequer appointed a University Grants Committee of His Majesty's Treasury as a Standing Committee "to enquire into the financial needs of University Education in the United Kingdom, and to advise the Government as to the application of any grants that may be made by Parliament towards meeting them."

In order to survey the position of University Education throughout the country, it was necessary to arrange, in consultation with the various institutions concerned, for the preparation of statistics on a uniform basis. The Scottish Universities had for many years made returns of the numbers of students and of financial statistics; and the creation of the Committee furnished a suitable opportunity for the introduction of a uniform system for presenting the chief facts and figures relating to all the Universities and University Colleges in receipt of Treasury grants. The first Chairman of the Committee was Sir William S. McCormick who had been the first Secretary of the Carnegie Trust for the Universities of Scotland. No man was more familiar with academic administration and with the problems which at that time confronted the Universities, thronged as they were with a multitude of students, many of whom had rendered distinguished service to their country at a time of crisis. In Edinburgh the number of matriculated students had increased from 3282 in the academical year 1913-14 to 4643 in the academical year 1919-20. Sir William and his Committee, composed of men of eminence not only in the academic world but in the world of affairs, kept in close and sympathetic touch with the Universities, and administered in a liberal spirit the sums which were voted by Parliament for their aid. Periodical visitations of the Universities are made when the Committee meets, in friendly consultation, with the Governing bodies and representatives of the teaching staff and of the students. The Committee has already rendered invaluable service to the Universities; and its annual reports present a conspectus of the academic life of the country. The criticism has, however, been made that the Scottish Universities are now for the first time linked with the old English Universities and the newer institutions in London and the provinces as claimants for a share in the general grant for University purposes, although their history, traditions and circumstances are wholly different.*

Benefactors

THE McEWAN HALL

"Riches are for spending, and spending for honour and good actions." Fortunate indeed has the University been in her Benefactors.

Every undergraduate who hopes eventually to receive the academic accolade passes day-in day-out the McEwan Hall on whose walls this simple inscription is cut in stone:—

HANC AULAM ACADEMICAM
GULIELMUS McEWAN
UNIVERSITATI EDINBURGENSI
LIBENS ANIMO DONAVIT
MDCCCXCIV

On 4th November 1896, the University Court adopted the following minute:—"The University Court have heard with much satisfaction that the Trustees expect the McEwan Hall to be completed early in 1897. They regard the presentation of the Hall as forming an epoch in the life of the University, which will for the first time in its history be provided with adequate accommodation for the conferring of degrees and for other University functions and ceremonies. The Court wish to put on record their profound sense of the magnificence of the gift, and of Mr McEwan's unsparing liberality in providing funds for an Academic Hall. In both the dignity of its architecture and the beauty and completeness

* *The Case for a New Universities Commission* by Professor James Mackintosh —*Aberdeen University Review,* July 1929.

Photo by] [*Valentine*

THE UNIVERSITY UNION AND THE McEWAN HALL

of its internal arrangements, the Hall is an edifice of which both the University and the City may well be proud."

In the course of his Rectorial Address to the students on 6th December 1895, on *The Duty of Educated Intellect to the State*, the Lord Advocate, the Right Honourable J. P. B. Robertson, said: "This is, I suppose, the last great function of our University which will take place in a hired room. Hitherto our *Alma Mater*, on those occasions on which she assembles her children around her, has flitted about the City from one public hall to another, homeless and vagrant. The signal generosity of an individual is about to remove that reproach, and although it has not been given to me as your Rector to enter the promised land, I have had glimpses of it. Within that stately pile, the eyes of generations of University men in the future, when they scan the highest splendours of the lofty dome, will rest on these words — graven there as the first and last lesson to be learned — "Wisdom is the principal thing, therefore get wisdom, and with all thy getting get understanding." *

The University makes grateful record † of the benefactions she has received since 1884, and of one of her sons she would make special mention—Daniel Mackintosh Forbes, East India merchant, who bequeathed to her his fortune. Others there are who are nameless "who might say to their *Alma Mater*, 'Silver and gold have I none, but such as I have give I thee,' and who have given her the quiet memorials of a student's life, the example of patient and unobtrusive work, pursued often under difficulties, inspired by duty and lit up with courageous hope, a college life of strenuous simplicity and hardness, of high ideals and unworldly aims. Men such as these have stamped their mark, the authentic impress of

* A complete account of the University Buildings Extension Scheme which culminated in the McEwan Hall will be found in the McEwan Hall number of *The Student*, published by the Students' Representative Council in 1897. It was written by George Somerville, the Clerk to the Buildings Extension Trustees (incorporated by an Act of Parliament in 1886). He rendered invaluable services to the University in connection with this and other Schemes over a long period of years.

† Appendix, p. 422.

their character, on our University and on all the Universities of Scotland. The bequest they have left is of priceless value. How often has one wished to follow into later life those whom one has watched in the opening of their career."*

THE ATTITUDE OF THE UNIVERSITY TO THE SOCIAL LIFE OF THE STUDENTS

The Physical Welfare Fund

In a fourth aspect, there has been a complete transformation in fifty years—the attitude of the University towards the social life of the students. While no doubt the Principal and the Professors individually watched over the welfare of the students and showed them much hospitality, there was no attempt on the part of the University, as such, to assist in organising their social life. The students, in societies and clubs, did a great deal for themselves. The Associated Societies—the Dialectic, the Scots Law, the Diagnostic, the Philomathic and the Celtic — were all in existence and flourishing long before the period of this History opens. But nothing had been done to meet the famous plea of Thomas Carlyle. On the 20th September 1931, the British Broadcasting Corporation caused to be relayed from London the Rectorial Address which he delivered to the students—his constituents—on 2nd April 1866: "In the midst of your zeal and ardour—for such, I foresee, will rise high enough, in spite of all the counsels to moderate it that I can give you —remember the care of health. I have no doubt you have among you young souls ardently bent to consider life cheap, for the purpose of getting forward in what they are aiming at of high; but you are to consider throughout much more than is done at present, and what it would have been a very great thing for me if I had been able to consider, that health is a thing to be attended to continually, that you are to regard that as the highest of all temporal things for you. There is no kind of achievement you could make in the world that is equal to the possession of perfect health."

* Professor Butcher's *Farewell,* 20th January 1904.

Tempora mutantur! In Lord Constable a Rector's Assessor was found, a fitting successor to the illustrious Senators of the College of Justice who had rendered signal service to the University, who appreciated to the full this defect in the academic system; and, thanks to his efforts, by a small increase in the amount of the Matriculation Fee, a Physical Welfare Fund was instituted in 1930, and Colonel Ronald Campbell was appointed Director of Physical Education. The sphere of his duties is to co-operate in fostering the forms of physical recreation which are already provided, and to assist in taking further steps for the physical welfare of the students.

In 1884 the University Union for men was founded. It was watched over, with a loving care, by James Walker, its Treasurer, who, as Rector's Assessor and Convener of the Finance Committee of the University Court, served his *Alma Mater* faithfully and well. In him the students of the University never had a better friend. In the course of the present century a Union for women was founded; and, from humble beginnings, it has grown to its present dimensions in George Square.

Playing fields for men and for women have been provided and equipped—before the war mainly as the result of the efforts of the students themselves, and, since then, with the growing recognition of the importance of the development of academic life as a whole and not merely as a mental exercise, partly from grants made by the Treasury and the Carnegie Trust.

Halls of Residence for women students have been provided. For the men University Hall was formed in 1887 by Professor Sir Patrick Geddes. It comprises three houses—Ramsay Lodge, Blackie House and St Giles's House—primarily intended for the use of students in any of the Faculties, who themselves manage the purely internal affairs of each house, without control, direct or indirect, by the authorities of the University. One Hall of Residence for men is under the direct control of the University, with a Resident Warden appointed by, and responsible to, the University Court—Cowan House in George Square, founded and endowed by Thomas Cowan, Shipowner, Leith.

In the University Settlement at High School Yards, and at Prestonfield, the students can participate in social work, study social problems, and consider and advance plans calculated to further the welfare of the community.

In the choice of a future career they have a guide, a philosopher and a friend in Thomas A. Joynt, the Appointments' Secretary.

In a host of University Societies and Clubs, Associated and Non-Associated, it is possible for the undergraduates *desipere in loco;* and, in the Officers' Training Corps, the martial spirit can "sound the clarion" and "fill the fife."

Finally, they have before them the inspiration of the sacrifice of those, many of whom would have been their leaders to-day, whose names are commemorated in bronze on the walls of the Old Quadrangle, and who "turned without fear or question from these Gates of Learning to those of the Grave in order that free men might still continue to learn freedom." *

THE UNIVERSITY OF EDINBURGH GRADUATES' ASSOCIATION

With the inauguration of the University of Edinburgh Graduates' Association in the summer of 1924—originally designated the Alumnus Association—a definite attempt was made to create, on a voluntary basis, a corporate spirit among the graduates and a link between them and the

* In 1921 the University Court caused to be compiled a Record of War Service relating to those who served in the Forces of the Crown. The Record, which was edited by Major John E. Mackenzie, comprises first, the "Roll of the Fallen" on which are the names of 944 members of the University, with a brief account of their military careers and with photographs, when these could be obtained; and, secondly, a Record of War Service, giving details—necessarily in a very concise form—of service in the Navy, Army and Air Force on the part of about 7000 members of the University. Then follows a list of Orders, Decorations and Mentions in Despatches, which includes, with many other honours, five awards of the Victoria Cross.

On the outbreak of hostilities about 600 students and young graduates who had been members of the Officers' Training Corps, which in this University includes Artillery, Infantry, Engineering and Medical Units, at once received Commissions in the Army, and the Corps continued to be an active training centre for Cadets during the whole of the War.

University. The movement owed its initiation to the enthusiasm and energy of Professor Sir Harold Stiles who became the first Acting-President of the Association.

Its objects, as set out in its constitution, were to maintain the association of former students with the University and with one another, and to foster their permanent interest in her welfare; and, further, to promote the formation of associations or clubs of Edinburgh graduates, at home and overseas, in centres where such did not already exist, and to assist established associations or clubs in any way possible. Under the constitution, membership is not limited to graduates of the University, but is open to students of the final year of study and to all former students; to any member or former member of the teaching and administrative staffs whether graduates or not; and to honorary graduates of the University.

Through the pages of the *University of Edinburgh Journal*, published twice annually under the auspices of the Association, a medium of contact between *Alma Mater* and her sons and daughters has been established, so that those living at the periphery may be kept in touch with the centre and those at the centre with the periphery.

III

THE FACULTY OF DIVINITY

THE FACULTY RECORDS

Of the four quarto volumes containing the Minutes of the Faculty written and, after approval, signed by successive Deans, a touching and characteristic series of records for one who is himself an alumnus of the Faculty to hold in custody and to peruse, the first opens with the words, "Edinburgh College 20 Nov. 1837. Present, Drs Chalmers, Welsh, and Brunton—Dean." At that date the Faculty consisted of three Professors, having to wait till 1847 for the creation of the Chair of Biblical Criticism and Biblical Antiquities. In 1843 the Dean, Alexander Brunton, had to make the melancholy entry: "There was no quorum of the Faculty." Thomas Chalmers and David Welsh had left the Church. The Principal, the Rev. John Lee, was, during this session, doing the duty of both. In 1844 he was received by the Senatus as Professor of Theology; and James Robertson as Professor of Church History. When the final entry in the first volume was made on 7th November 1884, the Tercentenary Celebration had taken place, and Archibald Hamilton Charteris, on account of failing health, resigned the office of Dean in favour of Malcolm C. Taylor. The other three manuscript volumes accordingly cover the period, and supply most of the material of the present survey of the history of the Faculty.

THE PERSONNEL OF THE FACULTY

In 1884 the Faculty formed a notable group of teachers and personalities, two of whom had reached the highest eminence as representatives respectively of churchmanship and of theological learning.

Archibald Hamilton Charteris, who had succeeded John Caird in the Park Church, Glasgow, and made his mark both as a preacher and as a pastor before succeeding Robert Lee, in 1868, as the second Regius Professor of Biblical Criticism, was the senior member of the Faculty and had been Dean since 1875, except for a year of illness during which Professor Flint held office. To him the Church of Scotland owes more than to any other leader for the inspiration and development of its social work and, in particular, of women's work in its service. He retained his Chair till 1898, honoured not only by the Church and the University but by the Sovereign, who appointed him one of her chaplains.

The Professor of Divinity, called, in 1876, from the Chair of Moral Philosophy in St Andrews, was Robert Flint, whose writings on Theism, Anti-theistic Theories, Socialism, the History of the Philosophy of History, and Agnosticism, exercised world-wide influence, and whose massive learning had gained for him the honorary membership of learned societies on the Continent. His impressive lecturing is still gratefully remembered by many students whose faith he confirmed, and in whom he implanted an austere and exacting ideal of scholarship and judgment.

In Malcolm Campbell Taylor, Professor of Ecclesiastical History, previously Minister of the parish of Crathie and continued as one of the royal chaplains, the Faculty possessed for fifteen years a dignified and accomplished Dean, whose devotion to its interests, and capacity for affairs, led to his appointment as Secretary to the University Court. Though his burden of administration left him small leisure for research and authorship, the high regard entertained for him by his colleagues in all Faculties was shared by his students who appreciated the lucid and graceful style and the devout and cultured standpoint of his lectures.

Youngest of the four, David Laird Adams had followed David Liston in 1880 and, himself a pupil of the Faculty, was endearing himself to his colleagues and, by his zealous development of the Hebrew classes into a Semitic Department, was amply vindicating his appointment. Obtaining an assistant, he was able to begin courses in Syriac and Arabic, and did much to raise the standard of Semitic scholarship in the University. His untimely death, in 1892, was followed exactly two years later by that of his successor, John Dobie—a victim of the tragic railway accident at Newtonmore—whose delightful personality and precocious gift for languages gave promise of an exceptionally useful career.

In 1894 the Curators called Archibald Robert Stirling Kennedy from Aberdeen University to the vacant Chair of Hebrew and Semitic Languages, and formed that link with the triumvirate of 1884, which happily remains unbroken to-day. Professor Kennedy has placed our School of Semitic Studies on the highest level, assiduous as a teacher and devoted to his pupils, a keen advocate of reforms in theological instruction, the friendliest of colleagues, an authority and an author on his subject, not only a teacher but a maker of teachers, since not a few Chairs in his subject have been occupied by his pupils.

Not till 1898 did the series of resignations begin which withdrew into well-earned retirement the three honoured figures who, at the time of the Tercentenary, were conspicuous ornaments of the Faculty. In that year Professor Charteris, after thirty years of service, gave place to John Patrick, Minister of Greenside Parish Church, Edinburgh, an educationist and scholar who brought to his new duties a well-stored and meticulously accurate mind, great powers of work, gifts of lucid and learned exposition, and an unerring judgment in affairs not less than in learning. Till his resignation, in 1915, when one of his earliest pupils, William Alexander Curtis, was chosen by the Crown to be his successor after holding the Chair of Systematic Theology at Aberdeen for twelve years, Professor Patrick rendered service of great value to the Faculty, not only as an efficient instructor in Biblical Criticism, whose mastery of his subject invested his teaching with authority, but as a vigilant and able Dean. He will long be remembered for his standard works on Origen's Reply to Celsus and on Clement of Alexandria, books which are models of theological exposition. He died on 17th January, 1933.

FACULTY OF DIVINITY

In 1903 Professor Flint bade farewell to his Chair and class-room, hoping—alas! in vain—to devote to a Gifford Lectureship and to other enterprises the late evening of his uniquely laborious life. From the Chair of Systematic Theology at Aberdeen, as by acclamation, the Curators called William Paterson Paterson, first of the series of Pitt Club Scholars in the Faculty, to the vacant Professorship at Edinburgh. Gifted as a scholar in languages, in philosophy and in theology, Professor Paterson was already a public figure, known as a keen educationist and economist, an advocate of social reform, a fascinating speaker in the General Assembly, on public platforms and in the pulpit and, not least, a striking personality. During his Edinburgh professoriate he has played a leading part in Scottish life, commanding equal powers of extempore thought and speech and of premeditated utterance, welcome as perhaps no other orator on public occasions in the service of patriotic, philanthropic, social, academic and religious causes, while firmly establishing his reputation as an inspiring teacher and as a brilliant writer. The centre of attraction in his Faculty, and its Dean from the time of Professor Patrick's resignation in 1912 until a serious illness compelled him, in December 1928, to transfer the office to younger hands, he has continued to hold a unique position in the counsels and esteem of the whole University.

In 1908 Professor Malcolm Taylor, after the long period of thirty-two years of tenure, handed over the Chair of Ecclesiastical History to James Mackinnon who, as Lecturer on History at the University of St Andrews, had proved his capacity for research and constructive writing in that wider field, and who, in the fruitful years of his instruction both to Arts and to Divinity students at Edinburgh, has amply realised the high expectations based upon his earlier activity. An assiduous explorer of the proper sources for the periods on which he lectured, he set an example of thorough historical method and, in an imposing series of solid volumes, he has given to a wider public the ripe results of his scholarly devotion. His massive biography of Luther has taken high rank among the world's authoritative treatises on the Reformer, combining sobriety of judgment with illuminative appreciation; and his work on the Life of Jesus Christ is a monument of reverent critical reconstruction of the Gospel sources. It may justly be asserted that in the discharge of the duties of his Chair James Mackinnon invested his subject with a degree of scientific precision and a systematic documentation never attained by his predecessors, and reached a leading position among its exponents not only in Scotland but throughout the Protestant world. In 1931 he was succeeded by one of his own pupils, John Henderson Seaforth Burleigh, a former holder of the Aitken Travelling Scholarship in Theology.

To have been admitted to a place in the succession to, or in the fellowship of, such men is indeed no mean privilege and imposes no ordinary obligation. The future of the Faculty will indeed be secure if it is staffed by members who share their spirit and cherish their ideals.

THE FACULTY IN RELATION TO THE CHURCH OF SCOTLAND

During the period under review only ministers of the Church of Scotland were eligible to hold theological Chairs in the Scottish Universities. Changes pending in this respect will be noticed later. From the time of the founding of the University the students in training for the Ministry of the National Church have formed the great majority of the membership of the classes; and it was natural that their teachers, though members of the University Senatus and, as such, under academic authority and protection, should themselves be ministers holding a recognised office in the Church as doctors of the accredited theology, and therefore under ecclesiastical jurisdiction. The endowments of their Chairs, adequate or inadequate, had an ecclesiastical origin, and most of the bursary endowments under their administration were restricted to students in preparation for the service of the Church of Scotland. The decrees of the General Assembly and the regulations of the Church's Committee on the

Education of the Ministry shaped the contents and directed the course of the ordinary curriculum, due performance of which on the part of the regular student the Faculty had to certify to the proper Church authority. Only as regards the courses for the degree of Bachelor of Divinity, was the Faculty free to frame its plans, and even these had to bear a sufficiently close relation to the ecclesiastical requirements. But year after year, the student enrolments have included pupils drawn from other Churches at home and abroad, and valuable links have thus been formed with other ministries and other teaching centres. As one looks back across half a century, it may be doubted whether the Church of Scotland was ever more consistently, or more loyally, served by any Faculty than by this. Not a few of the staff have acted leading parts in the Church's organisations and courts, and been for many years conveners of its greater committees. Professors Charteris, Kennedy, Paterson, Patrick and W. A. Curtis may be named in this connection as having maintained responsible touch with the Church's organised activities. Professors Charteris and Paterson also occupied with distinction the Moderatorial Chair of the General Assembly. On that side, among others, of its functions the Faculty has abundantly exemplified the vital relation which the University has sustained to the Scottish Church, and asserted the spiritual element in the University's character. As distinguished from the Faculty of Arts, through which its students have all passed on their way to Divinity, it shares with Law and Medicine and, in a lesser degree, with Science and Music, the burden of specifically professional instruction, and is under a similar obligation to co-ordinate its work with the professional life for which it trains. It may be added that it has also had to its credit the education of a very large proportion of the occupants of theological Chairs in Scotland and throughout the Presbyterian world—at least seventeen since 1884—and of its own members. Although Professor Flint was mainly trained at Glasgow and Professors Taylor and Kennedy at the same School of Theology, all the others were native products of Edinburgh. Some part of the credit for this record may justly be assigned to the unique equipment of the Faculty in post-graduate travelling scholarships, which have enabled outstanding Bachelors of Divinity to continue their special studies for two or three years abroad before taking up the work of the Ministry. In this respect the Faculty still holds a leading position among Protestant schools.

THE FACULTY IN RELATION TO THE UNIVERSITY

If the repute and standing of the Faculty within the University at the time of the Tercentenary was on the highest level, its high reputation has been maintained in the interval. In the Senatus Academicus its monthly reports may have formed but a slender item on the agenda as a rule, since much of the business recorded in its minutes fell within its own competence and called for no review. An occasional dissent from its earlier conclusions may be discovered, but no single appeal. But its members were active in the general service of University affairs and took their place, as occasion arose, in debates on policy and procedure. Represented by their Dean on the Principal and Deans' Committee, then, as now, entrusted with an omnibus responsibility and initiative, they were in touch with every department of academic responsibility. The office of Principal of the University had ceased to be held by Ministers of the Church in 1860 when John Lee passed away and ecclesiastical tests had been removed. Among the four assessors whom the Senatus is empowered to elect to the University Court the Faculty has had but a precarious opportunity to be directly represented: Professor Malcolm Taylor, however, held office with acceptance as Secretary to the Court from 1892 over a period of years, and Professor Curtis had the honour of being elected to its membership in 1930, at a time when prospective changes in the Faculty of Divinity were under serious consideration.

In a great variety of ways the administrative duties of the Faculty have increased since 1884. Bursary and scholarship endowments have largely grown in number, calling for the

From the painting by] [*Fiddes Watt, R.S.A.*

THE VERY REV. WILLIAM PATERSON PATERSON, D.D., LL.D.

Professor of Divinity
1903

formulation of schemes for their administration, and for their revision and adjustment. The Gunning Lectureship and Prizes, provision of assistance in teaching, revision of ordinances and regulations for B.D. examinations, the extension of the teaching session and the duplication of classes, the widening of the range of Semitic instruction and the inclusion of Hebrew and Ecclesiastical History within the Faculty of Arts, the formation of a Post-graduate School and Board of Theological Studies, including the staff of New College and representatives of the Episcopal and Congregational Colleges and the lecturer on Arabic, are examples of new interests which have arisen on its horizon. Prior to 1895 the Faculty as a whole had the duty of nominating for the Honorary Doctorate in Divinity but, since that date, three of its members share that charge with other members of the Senatus in a special standing committee. Among other committees its members serve on the Gifford Lectureship Committee, on the Library Committee, and on the Educational Policy Committee. On the University Services' Committee the Dean and his colleagues, with other members, arrange for six official services, each year, in the Cathedral of St Giles.

Although the Faculty, still under the ecclesiastical test, was thereby ineligible to receive the augmentation of its professorial stipends from Parliamentary grants to the University, the inclusion of two of its Chairs within the Faculty of Arts (Oriental Languages in 1888, followed by Ecclesiastical History) and generous action by the University Court in view of the serious war-time diminution of the endowments of the other Chairs, resulted in the placing of all four Chairs upon the minimum basis of remuneration, as at the other Scottish Universities. The humaner standards which have emerged during the fifty years have brought about a general provision whereby, in cases of illness, the acting substitute is paid by the Court instead of by the disabled teacher.

DEVELOPMENT AND CHANGE IN THE FACULTY

The Curriculum of Study

Three winter sessions remained, during the greater part of the period under consideration, as the normal course of study in Divinity, but the session was lengthened in the later 'nineties by two terms, each of ten weeks; and whereas in the subjects of Divinity, Ecclesiastical History, and Biblical Criticism it was customary for the Professors to deliver one lecture daily to all students of the years concerned, the division of the two former classes into Senior and Junior was introduced by Professors Paterson and Mackinnon on their arrival—an obvious improvement, which followed the example offered already in the teaching of Hebrew. Time-table considerations postponed the same change in Biblical Criticism until the new conditions under which a serious increase in the number of students deficient in Greek began to assert itself; and readjustments in view of the reunion of the Church of Scotland and the United Free Church, and the requirements of the most recent revision of the B.D. regulations led, in 1930, to its adoption.

Since that date regular students have had a comprehensive scheme of classes prescribed for them in each separate year of study; the entire staffs, both of the Faculty and of New College, being associated in providing not only Junior and Senior instruction in each of the old subjects, together with courses in Pastoral Theology, Christian Sociology, Religious Education, Elocution, etc., but also advanced instruction, over a third year, for specialist candidates for the B.D. Degree in their selected subjects. It was at first necessary for the students of the two united Churches to enrol and matriculate separately, and to compete for the separate series of bursaries and scholarships and special prizes at their disposal, as well as to pay separate fees; but steps were taken to secure the earliest possible merging of the two systems through legislative sanction and provision for a reunited Faculty. Whereas the preceding half-century had witnessed the disruption of the Faculty, it was the happy fortune of its successor to close with its restoration, and to usher in a period of renewed vigour with an enlarged staff, two short summer terms added, a more comprehensive curriculum, a more than double enrolment of students, and a worthier equipment both in the service of the Church and in the service of the University. In the last decade the traditional system of class prizes has passed away, except for certain special endowed rewards for the first and second places in each class. The students pass from the Old College to New College, there to assemble daily for common prayer at 11, and for dinner at 1.15. It was a picturesque detail in the necessary changes, incidental to the combined curriculum, which involved the use of the Old College accommodation from 9 to 11 A.M. daily, and of the New College class-rooms from 11 A.M. to 1 P.M., that the New College Professors of Church History and of Old Testament found themselves transferred to the University, and the University Professors of Divinity and of Biblical Criticism, the ex-Dean and Dean respectively, to New College, even before legal reunion could be achieved!

Bursaries and Scholarships

If the curriculum has moved with the times, the provision of bursaries and scholarships has not lagged behind. Fresh endowments have come to the Faculty's assistance to an extent and in a variety unparalleled in Scotland. Among the Bursaries, restricted to Edinburgh and mainly open, are the Archibald or McGuffie (£35 for 3 years), 1914; the Brown (three of £18 for 1 year), 1900; the Hunter (two of £65 for 2 years), 1884; the Lockerby (£38 for 3 years), 1892; the Simson (twelve of £25 for 3 years, tenable in Arts by prospective students of Divinity and in the gift of the Presbytery of Edinburgh), 1889; the Cobb (£76 for 3 years), 1889. Others are open to all the four Scottish Faculties of Divinity. Among the Scholarships, the Blackie (in memory of Professor John Stuart Blackie—£190 for 1 year, for travel in Greece and, as now arranged, in Palestine also), the Richard Brown (£100 for 1 year, in turn with the other Faculties in the University), 1930; the Jeffrey (two of £130 for 2 years), 1887; the Keith (two of £100 for 2 years), 1924; along with the Crombie Scholarship (£50 for 1 year), the Maclean Scholarship (£200 for 1 or more years), 1919; and the Union Seminary Fellowship (three of £250 for 1 year), a group of three open to the four Divinity Halls. The Barty Memorial Prize of £50 in Hebrew and Hellenistic Greek is open to entrants into the four Halls. The Gunning Victoria Jubilee Prizes (originally five in Natural Science and five in Theology of values ranging from £50 to £10 and open to candidates who had completed their courses in Arts and Divinity), 1889, have recently been reconstituted on the basis of five awards of similar value in the aggregate theological subjects only. The Gunning Victoria Jubilee Lectureship (1889) continues to be available as an encouragement to scholarly ministers, expert in some department of scientific, philosophic, linguistic, antiquarian, or sociological research. Taken in conjunction with the endowments of an earlier date, several of which were of considerable value, these constitute a remarkable total not easy to match in the world of theological learning.

It has, however, further to be recorded that whereas, in 1888, the Faculty turned an unresponsive ear to the Universities Commission on Endowments of that date, stating that there were none in its custody "which it is desirable that the Commission should deal with," in 1928 the Faculty willingly associated itself with other faculties in the University in taking advantage of the Educational Endowments (Scotland) Act which set up a new Commission, and in presenting an elaborate and far-reaching scheme, prepared by Professor Curtis, for the revision and reorganisation of its bursaries and scholarships.

The need for change was not small, and several of the alterations were considerable, though the main purpose and spirit of the foundations were scrupulously conserved. The risks taken were serious, since the Commissioners, though without power to compel a reference, had full powers, when consulted, to determine the result, but it deserves to be acknowledged that the representations of the Faculty were most courteously heard and weighed, and in almost every detail were finally granted. The changes in the Blackie and Gunning awards have been mentioned above. The combination, however, of minor bursaries when desirable, and the conditional opening of preferential bursaries have been authorised, while the two Jeffrey Scholarships have been turned into four annual travel-prizes in each of the four main subjects, to enable the ablest students, during their regular curriculum, to spend a full summer in study abroad; the travel scholarships, already a special feature of the Edinburgh equipment, now termed Fellowships, are augmented by the combination of three of the smaller scholarships to form a new Fellowship and complete a three-year sequence of practically equal awards. It may be of interest to state that, in addition to sharing in the scholarships open to all four universities, Edinburgh students and graduands in Divinity are now eligible for the following competitive Fellowships providing for advanced study and travel:—the Aitken (£290 a year for 2 or 3 years), the Blackie (£190 for 1 year), the Richard Brown (100 for 1 year every sixth year), the Bruce of Grangehill and Falkland (£150 a year when vacancies occur in any of the three Arts Scholarships), the Glover, Kidd and Maxton (combined to yield £200 for one or more years), the Pitt Club (£252 for 3 years), and with them the Jeffrey Prizes (four of £65 each year). The Faculty believes that it is of peculiar advantage alike to the individual students and to the Church, as well as to the University and to Learning, that in this way so many of its alumni are enabled to widen their knowledge not only of theological teaching and science but of Christendom and of the world. The Richard Brown Scholarship, allotted for the first award in 1930 to the Faculty's patronage, was awarded, in furtherance of international student exchange, to a German scholar for a year of study at Edinburgh. And, it may be added, from time to time the Faculty's students are awarded grants abroad, not only at New York but also at Elberfeld, Zürich, Prague, Buda-Pest, and Montpellier, to enable them to continue their education as guests of Continental Faculties or Seminaries, a very gracious and friendly return of hospitality which, in spite of recent economic troubles, has been established.

A special feature of the decisions of the Educational Endowments Commission as from session 1932-33 was the establishment, at the request of the Faculty, of two comprehensive funds, (i) the Divinity Fellowship Fund by the administrative amalgamation of the various fellowship endowments; (ii) the Divinity Bursary Fund by the similar amalgamation of bursary endowments. In connection with the former it is provided :—

(1) "If at the end of any financial year the whole of the free income of the Divinity Fellowship Fund has not been appropriated . . . it shall be in the power of the Court to apply the unappropriated balance of such income towards such of the following purposes as the Senatus may direct, that is to say (*a*) Towards the cost of extending, in special circumstances, for one year the period of tenure of the holder of any of the fellowships named: (*b*) Towards the cost of making additional payments to the holder of any of the said fellowships whose total income is, in the opinion of the Senatus, insufficient to maintain him: (*c*) Towards the cost of awarding from time to time an occasional fellowship in Divinity, subject to the general conditions of this Scheme and to such special conditions as the Senatus may prescribe.

(2) "Any residue not applied to the foregoing purposes shall be added to and form part of the capital of the Divinity Fellowship Fund.

(3) "If at any time owing to additions to the capital of the Divinity Fellowship Fund, or from any other cause, the income of the fund shall increase to such an extent as in the opinion of the Court to permit of the establishment of an additional fellowship in Divinity, it shall be in the power of the Senatus to establish such additional fellowship which shall be awarded subject to the general conditions of this Scheme and to such special conditions as the Senatus may prescribe by regulations. . . . The Court shall pay such additional fellowship from the Divinity Fellowship Fund."

In connection with the latter it is provided :—

"The Court shall . . . pay each year from the free annual income of the respective funds the bursaries described." And thereafter :—

(1) "If at the end of any financial year the whole of the free income of the Divinity Bursary Fund has not been appropriated for the purposes . . . of this Scheme it shall be in the power of the Court to apply the unappropriated balance of such income to such of the following purposes as the Senatus may direct, that is to say :—

"Towards the cost of making additional payments to the holders of bursaries who have been accepted as candidates for restricted bursaries. . . .

"Towards the cost of making special grants to students in necessitous circumstances who are attending the Faculty :

"Towards the cost of awarding from time to time an occasional bursary tenable in the Faculty (either by a first-year student or by a student in a later year) :

"Towards the cost of awarding prizes in the Faculty.

(2) "Any residue not applied to the foregoing purposes shall be added to and form part of the capital of the fund to which it belongs.

(3) "If at any time the income of the Divinity Bursary Fund shall increase to such an extent as in the opinion of the Court to permit of the establishment of an additional bursary payable from such fund, it shall be in the power of the Senatus to establish such additional bursary . . . it shall be in the power of the Senatus to establish additional prizes in Divinity."

Thanks to the considerable help of the Commissioners the Faculty is now able to employ its funds to much better purpose for the encouragement of scholarly industry and talent, not only among men but also among women. A new flexibility has been given to its endowments. Anomalous or obsolete conditions of tenure have been removed, and administration simplified. And while preferences have been respected, they no longer stand in the way of a useful employment of the normal income to which they have been attached. Instead of an irregular and awkward sequence of awards which made no provision for years in which an exceptionally numerous group of gifted candidates are forthcoming, the Faculty has now such a control of the unexpended residues as to be in a position to cope with such occasions. Not seldom in the past it would have been only too thankful to have been given such authority. It may well count itself fortunate, in view of the great increase of students brought by ecclesiastical reunion, to have received at this time powers so urgently required.

Degree of Bachelor of Divinity

While the degree of B.D. as awarded at Edinburgh had maintained its character as an essentially Honours Diploma, presupposing an Arts Degree and a three-years' curriculum of theological instruction, it had come to be held, at Edinburgh and elsewhere, that the time was ripe for changes in its character. Conferences with the Faculties of Divinity in the other Scottish Universities were initiated, and it was agreed that a new Ordinance should be promoted which would terminate the existing discrepancies among the four Universities, and establish a practically homogeneous system. It was felt that the degree should be based upon a more intensive or specialised study of one of the recognised departments and, accordingly, a fresh ordinance was promoted, which became operative in 1924, and was followed by a series of administrative regulations in 1925. It was provided that the degree should be taken in two stages, the second of which consisted of the full examination in five or six papers on the special subject selected by the candidate, Old Testament, New Testament, Ecclesiastical History, or Systematic Theology, while the first part included, on a lower scale of reading and proficiency, the other three subjects. "Distinction" was to be awarded to candidates who obtained a sufficiently high percentage of marks in their special subject. The result of the change thus effected has been satisfactory. It has encouraged advanced study in the several departments, and it has led to the provision of advanced teaching in each of them, largely in the form of "seminar" and tutorial instruction during the third year of the course. On the other hand, it is open to the objection that it entails a severe concentration on the student's part upon the work of all four departments during the two earlier sessions. It may be that further changes will be required in the near future, *e.g.* the introduction of options to replace the comprehensive system, or the readjustment of the teaching syllabus. But it may be claimed that the Scottish B.D. Degree compares favourably in scope and standard with any other in the theological world.

The Post-Graduate School of Studies in Theology and the Degree of Doctor of Philosophy in Theology

No development during the period under review is more interesting or important than the formation, in 1919-20, of the Post-graduate School of Theological Instruction at Edinburgh. Its original aim was simply to provide advanced tuition for ministers desirous of continuing their special studies. But at the close of the war the wish was expressed in Canada and elsewhere that instruction and guidance in research with a view to the degree of Ph.D. might be furnished in the British Universities, so that advanced students might obtain in them the facilities which previously they had secured in Germany. The Faculty, while in full sympathy with the movement which has instituted the Ph.D. Degree throughout our University system, was not without misgivings about the future status of a doctorate of considerably lower standing than the D.Litt. and D.Sc. But when the decision was made in favour of the institution of the new degree, the Faculty recognised the peculiar responsibility of Edinburgh as a theological centre. Approach was made to the sister theological Colleges in the City with the happiest results. With the express authorisation of the General Assembly of the United Free Church the New College staff promised hearty cooperation. The Principals of Coates Hall (Episcopal Church in Scotland) and of the Congregational College responded in like manner. Accordingly the Faculty was able, with the willing assistance of Professors in the Faculty of Arts—Sanskrit, Fine Art, Arabic, Philosophy, and Psychology—to form a well-equipped Board of Studies in Theology, with a three-term schedule of classes, and ample resources for teaching and supervising research students over a very wide field. So instituted, without advertisement beyond the pages of the *University Calendar*, the School has steadily grown in numbers and in extension, drawing its students from many Christian denominations, and from every part of the United States as well as from the Dominions overseas and from Great Britain and Northern Ireland. The response, both of candidates for the new degree and of senior students and ministers who engage in advanced study simply for its own sake, has been such as to justify the experiment, and to attest the appeal which Edinburgh still makes as a theological centre. By itself the Faculty would have been powerless to meet the need which had arisen. It acknowledges on behalf of the University a debt of gratitude to the external colleagues whose generous and slenderly remunerated collaboration has made this enterprise a success.

As illustrating the progress of the new School, it may be recorded that the first year's enrolment consisted of five Scottish and five American members. In 1920-21 the enrolment rose to 31, of whom nine were from Scotland, five from Canada, twelve from the United States, two from New Zealand, and three from Japan. The ecclesiastical quotas were Presbyterian 25, Congregational 3, American Episcopal 2, and Scottish Episcopal 1. The average enrolment for a number of years continued to be about 30 till 1927-28 when 40, of whom three were women, matriculated. Australia, Cape Colony and China also contributed to the list, and further denominations were represented. Leaving out of account the numerous students who entered without contemplating the Ph.D. Degree, the admissions to December 1931 totalled 263, of whom 81 graduated, three of these after re-submission of their theses, and six were rejected. Of the total, 53 were already

Sir WILLIAM MUIR, K.C.S.I.

Principal and Vice-Chancellor
1885-1902

graduates of Edinburgh, 208 of other universities (23 Scottish, 8 English and Welsh, 2 Irish, 66 Colonial, 2 European, 107 American), while only two were admitted without degrees but with adequate certification in the shape of diplomas held to be sufficient; 28 worked in the Old Testament and Semitic Department, 46 in New Testament, 78 in Ecclesiastical History, and 109 in Systematic and Philosophical Theology.

Candidates for the degree are admitted only after production of certificates of distinction from approved universities and colleges, and from their teachers in the subjects which they specially profess, followed by favourable reports from their instructors in the School as to their fitness to engage in the research which they propose. They are assigned to one or more supervisors, generally to two and, unless they are already graduates of Edinburgh, are required to devote the four terms of their minimum period of study at the University to work upon their special subject of investigation. In addition to annual matriculation they pay an inclusive fee of eight guineas for instruction and guidance. The high standard of the degree is maintained not only by the tests indicated but by the selection of eminent scholars as the external examiners of the theses submitted. Judged by the rough and ready test furnished by proportional statistics of the passes and failures, the standard in theology has proved to be at least as exacting as that of any other Faculty. The University, therefore, may justly regard this School, established and maintained hitherto without any material charge upon its funds, as one of the most efficient and popular of all post-graduate enterprises, as unrivalled in the theological sphere, and as a powerful instrument for the promotion of closer academic and ecclesiastical relations throughout the Empire and the English-speaking world. Among the candidates already admitted not a few have been young scholars of the highest promise whose work, published or unpublished, has constituted a notable advancement of knowledge. With such material at its disposal the School has an honourable future awaiting it.

The Admission of Women to Graduation

As early as 1897 the Faculty addressed itself to the question of the admission of women to its classes, on the motion, as might have been expected, of Professor Charteris who had done so much on behalf of their employment in the service of the Church. On that occasion it contented itself with a cautious and measured pronouncement. So far as class instruction was concerned there was no real difficulty. But so long as admission to the Ministry was barred to them, women could not be expected to appear in numbers. That barrier still stands, under a threat it is true, and it has been strengthened by the legal restriction of bursaries and scholarships in theology to men in preparation for the Ministry of the Church of Scotland. But without prejudging the general question, the Faculty has secured from the Educational Endowments Commission equality of both sexes as candidates for bursaries. The way is thus cleared within the University for action by the Church should it resolve to sanction the ministry of women in any form requiring a theological education. Many of the bursaries, however, can only be awarded to candidates who are regular students proceeding to the Ministry of the Church, and it must depend upon the Church's own action whether these are eventually to be thrown open irrespective of sex. Meanwhile two women have passed for the B.D. Degree, one a Scottish graduate now serving with distinction in the Chinese mission field, the other a Japanese graduate of unusual capacity now returned to her own country for theological service. The Ph.D. Degree has been similarly gained by a woman student from America, and advantage is taken, by a considerable number of women, of the post-graduate facilities in theology.

Degree of Doctor of Divinity

Till 1895 nominations for the Honorary Degree of Doctor of Divinity were made by, or submitted for consideration to, the Faculty and passed on to the Principal and Deans' Committee, and thence to the Senatus. In that year a special

Committee of Selection was set up under Ordinance, consisting of a majority of the members of the Faculty, together with three Professors selected from other Faculties, the Principal being Convener. The maximum number of five presentations per annum was established, an advance upon the previous practice; but care was taken to preserve the tradition which selected nominees from all branches of the Church that permitted their Ministry to receive the degree. Not only has Edinburgh an exceptionally extensive body of theological alumni in all parts of the world, prominent in religious learning or in ecclesiastical leadership, but it has given thought to the recognition of theological eminence beyond the pale of Presbyterianism. More than once it has bestowed its highest degree in Divinity upon laymen, Professor Sir William M. Ramsay, the Hon. Lord Sands and Joseph H. Oldham having received the honour. In order to facilitate the recognition of scholars and leaders in the wider world, the number five was recently increased to six at the request of the Dean, and Continental as well as Dominions representatives are now regularly selected for laureation.

University Services in the Cathedral of St Giles

Alone among the Scottish Universities, Edinburgh as a secular foundation has lacked a Chapel of its own for academic worship. At St Andrews, Glasgow and Aberdeen the University meets for Divine Service every Sunday during term. At Edinburgh the University is represented once a month in its official stalls in St Giles's, and once a year holds its post-graduation Commemoration Service in that Church. Opinion is still divided in the University as to the desirability of erecting a University Chapel for separate worship. The time-honoured association with a shrine so historic and so national as the Cathedral is not lightly to be broken, despite the fact that the building lays an obvious restraint upon the freedom and intimacy of the preacher's appeal, and is not available for frequent academic use. There would be great advantage in many ways if the University possessed a Chapel of more limited capacity for religious assemblies than either the Cathedral of St Giles or the Graduation Hall, both of which present acoustic difficulties to most speakers. But the circumstances at Edinburgh differ largely from those at the other Scottish centres, and when, among other schemes, it was proposed that, as at Glasgow, the University War Memorial should take the form of a University Chapel, it was decided to adhere to the Church of St Giles. A substantial donation from some benefactor might at any time reopen this by no means easy question.

Early in the half-century now ending the Faculty instituted a brief series of University Services in the McEwan Hall, among the preachers being Dean Farrar and John R. Mott. Much later the Students' Representative Council arranged afternoon services for students for a few years in Greyfriars' and in St Giles's, which were conducted by members of the Faculty. Finally, on a petition from the students to the Senatus that the University should officially participate in these, Professor Curtis moved that the whole matter be remitted to the Faculty for consideration and report. The result was that a scheme was devised and accepted by the Senatus and the Students' Representative Council, which placed the services upon a new basis in charge of a University Services' Committee containing, in addition to the Faculty, the Principal, the Minister of St Giles's, Professors from other Faculties, and Student Representatives, the Dean presiding. Under this scheme, with the cordial consent of the Minister and Session of St Giles's Cathedral, two evening services are held each term in the Cathedral, attended officially by members of the various governing bodies in the University, and open, by reservation of a large area in the building, to students. The special preachers are selected by the Committee. The experiment has not been unsuccessful during the past three years, and it is hoped that the new arrangement will continue to fulfil the sacred purpose which its promoters among the staff and the students had at heart.

FACULTY OF DIVINITY

Scottish Church Reunion—Enlargement of the Faculty

The section dealing with changes in the Curriculum of Study has indicated some of the consequences which have already followed the achievement of union between the Church of Scotland and the United Free Church of Scotland. But no account of the story of the Faculty during the past fifty years can end without describing in some detail the significance of that long-delayed but happy event in relation to the position and prospects of Theology within the University. At the moment of going to Press,* the process of reunion on its academic side is still incomplete and, even when this volume issues from the Press, the final stages may still have to be traversed. But with certain reservations the general outline of the settlement to which the Church of Scotland, the Universities and Parliament are willing parties is clear enough to be recorded. Only in matters of local agreement between the Church and the four separate Universities is there room for a measure of uncertainty, since it has been recognised that the circumstances in each centre present distinctive features and demand variety of treatment.

By the Union of 2nd October 1929, the two great sections of the Scottish Churches ended their long separation, and the overwhelming majority of the Scottish people found themselves included again in one ecclesiastical household. The years of war had protracted the union negotiations, but quickened the longing for their success. The goodwill of Government and the consent of Parliament, irrespective of party, had prepared the way on the civil side by sanctioning the memorable Articles Declaring the Constitution of the Church of Scotland, formulated to serve as a charter of spiritual autonomy and a basis for reunion. There resulted a Church at once National, by right of history and by extension throughout the land, and spiritually Free, recognised as such by the supreme authority in the realm. In a world sated by strife a settlement of old controversies by consent was secured, without disestablishment and without disendow-

* April 1933.

ment, but by means of readjustment and by the annulling of such elements in ancient statutes as savoured of a coercive or exclusive spirit in connection with the national recognition of religion as embodied in a Church. In the interests of Christian unity and of the Scottish people, the traditions and principles of both Churches had been combined, and that with the cordial help of the State and the Law whose earlier actions had helped to precipitate past separations.

But the Reunion left one gap unfilled. The National Church now possessed three Theological Colleges of its own on the United Free Church side, Colleges of the highest standing at Edinburgh, Glasgow and Aberdeen, maintained by its own resources; and on the Church of Scotland side, it retained its ancient inheritance in the Faculties of Divinity within the four National Universities, whose distinctive endowments—Chairs, Bursaries and Scholarships—had been destined to its service and devoted to the training of its Ministry. No question of the Church's title to retain its heritage had arisen. But the principles on which the union was based called for a readjustment of the Church's relations with the Universities, as well as with the State. It was clear that the right of the Church's authorised theology to a place in the Universities could be justified by its national status, its history, and its long prescription from the foundation of those institutions, and equally by its supply of the main body of the students under training, and by the explicit destination of the endowments. It was also recognised that in the Scottish Universities the Theological Faculties had the same title to be Presbyterian as their sisters in other lands had to be Anglican, Lutheran, Presbyterian, Roman Catholic or Orthodox. But agreement had been reached in the Plan of Union that while enlarged Faculties of Divinity were to be secured by the inclusion of the Church College Chairs, the statutory test restricting the University Chairs in effect to Church of Scotland ministers should, with consent of the Crown and other appointing authorities, be abolished. Hence these Chairs would be open to scholars of other denominations, and appointments to them made by *a method which would secure their continued practical serviceableness for the training of the Church's ministry.* The Church Colleges were to remain and to be maintained within the Universities as the Church's property and as, in association with the University Professorships, seats of the Faculties; and certain of their Chairs were to be re-erected as new Chairs within the full fellowship of the University Faculty and Senatus, maintained, staffed, and controlled by the Church's direct, or delegated, authority.

To enable the Scottish Universities to give effect to this scheme, a Bill was presented to Parliament, the Universities (Scotland) Bill, 1932. Behind it lay a remarkable consensus of University and Church opinion. The University Courts, headed by the four Principals, guided by the Faculties, and supported by the Senatus and Councils, had shaped it through conferences, and through negotiation with the Church's Committee on the Training of the Ministry, a special Committee set up for the purpose. The National Government, at the instance of the Secretary of State for Scotland, granted it facilities and support, and, with one or two minor agreed amendments, it speedily passed through Parliament and duly received the Royal Assent in the same year. The way was thus open for the formulation of the basic Agreements between the Church and the separate Universities, resting upon the enabling authority of the Act, by which the details of the local adjustments and arrangements for the enlargement of the Divinity Faculties by the incorporation of the Church Chairs in their new form to an agreed number would be determined. Ordinances setting up the new Chairs in terms of the Agreements will then be promoted, and the Union completed.

The situation, gratifying as it appears to all who have the interests of theological instruction at heart, is not without an element of shadow. The financial resources of the Church are grievously straightened by the economic disturbance through which the world is passing. Its desire to contribute generously to the formation of a strong Faculty in each centre is tempered by the necessities of the stern times. It has to supply two new Chairs to the St Andrews

Faculty, and it is under a moral obligation to respond to the hope of the Universities that the salaries of the Church Chairs to be established will not fall below the University minimum. But it is expected that, at Edinburgh, at least four of the New College Chairs will be re-erected within the University—Old Testament, New Testament, Church History, and Christian Dogmatics—on a permanent basis. The Chair of Science and Religion will be recognised as a Lectureship for the present, and part-time lectureships in Pastoral Theology, Sacred Elocution, and Christian Sociology, will be continued, as the Church's contribution to the widened scope of the Faculty's equipment. Unfortunately, this would mean the loss of one of the New College Chairs, Pastoral Theology and Christian Apologetics, but it is hoped that the loss may in the future be made good. With the tasks at present laid upon the Faculty, in association with its colleagues in the Post-graduate School, not only in the regular training of candidates for the Ministry during their three-years' curriculum, and of candidates for the B.D. Degree, but also in the teaching and direction of research for the Ph.D. Degree, there is ample need for the resources of New College, if the opportunities and responsibilities of Edinburgh are to be worthily met.

Provision is made in the scheme of Reunion for the continuance of the office of Principal or Administrative Head of New College at the Church's discretion. Consideration is also being given to the problem of its adjustment or combination with the corresponding office of Dean of Faculty, in order that there may be no conflict of authorities, or overlapping of duties, and that the unity of the enlarged Faculty may be secured. The Faculty's strenuous plea for a homogeneous composition of its future membership, whereby all its Professors might hold the same position both in the Church and in the University, was not realised in form, since the new Chairs, though within the University, will be under test, and the old will be test-free. Nevertheless the composition of the Joint Board of Nomination—six representatives of the General Assembly and six, including the Principal, of the University

Court—was devised in order to secure a working solidarity in the teaching staff, Church and University requirements being equally satisfied in the interests both of vocational training and of theological science.

An element of practical compromise has of necessity entered into the reorganisation thus planned. But it is believed that no vital interest on either side has been sacrificed, and that mutual goodwill and good sense are all that is required to secure a happy working of the scheme. Upon that spirit both Church and University may surely count in their future relations, realising the advantage which accrues to both from an alliance through which the Church secures for its teachers and students a continuation and a deepening of their old association with the national schools of cultural and professional training, and the University obtains, without cost, a doubling of the strength of its Divinity Faculty and an enhancement of the spiritual element in its general teaching and fellowship, and of its touch with the religious centre of the national life. The Church will as formerly control the curriculum of training for its ministry and retain the ownership and administration of its College and its endowments. It will select the occupants of the four new Chairs and have an equal share in selecting those of the four old Chairs. It will be a happy issue of the union now achieved if in the future activities of the enlarged Faculty a combination of the Seminary and the University spirit can be established; the Faculty fostering its own distinctive esprit-de-corps as a College loyal to the Church and to its missionary ideals at home and abroad, without forfeiting or betraying its other birthright as an integral and essential member of the academic body to which, not less than to the Church, the passion and search for the Truth and for its publication have been entrusted. In the past dissensions and divisions of the Scottish Church, the University has had no part, either provocative or partisan. The healing of the old schism should be the easier accordingly, and the prospect of a swift oblivion for past differences the nearer. At Edinburgh it has meant much for the promotion of that end that the theological personnel of the Faculty and of New College have for a generation been on terms of such fraternal intimacy as to facilitate, at every stage, the steps towards that merging of their work which is now legally as competent as it has, in recent years, been practically effective. Within the existing Senate of New College, as reconstituted after the ecclesiastical union, the two staffs are already one, with a co-ordinated teaching schedule, and with much of their business to transact in common. Neither in doctrine nor in religious standpoint, neither in zeal for the service of the Church nor in devotion to Scottish University ideals, would it be easy to distinguish them from one another. The way is clear for a reunion within the University also, as natural and as unobtrusive as it will be complete. Looking back upon the momentous changes of this time, the future historian may well be moved to reflect that the separation of 1843, which arrested the natural development of the Faculty and invested it with something of a sectarian and invidiously privileged character, has in the end led to a singular enrichment of its resources and an impressive vindication of its fitness to bear the name and sustain the trust which devolves upon the representative of a National Church within a National University.

A RETROSPECT

The sketch now completed has been sufficient to show that, small though the Faculty has been in numbers, its activity and growth have kept pace with the general progress of the metropolitan university as a whole. Its share of public responsibility, equipment for its work, literary output, and the stewardship of its growing endowments; the extension of its teaching and examining duties, its touch with the ever-changing needs of the religious world, its place in the University and relation to the Church, these have been solidly maintained. Its members may not seldom envy the academic leisure which was enjoyed by their predecessors in a less burdened age. But they can also look back upon substantial and enduring gains which they have been privileged to see attained, and they can look forward to a future larger and happier than earlier eyes were permitted to see.

IV

THE FACULTY OF LAW

GENERAL SURVEY OF THE LAST FIFTY YEARS

THE academic anniversary which the University is celebrating this year synchronises very nearly with a notable legal anniversary which is of special interest to the Faculty of Law. The College of Justice was founded four hundred years ago, just half a century before the reputed institution of the University. The systematic founding of Law Chairs and the laboured birth of a Faculty of Law were unaccountably delayed until the first quarter of the eighteenth century. From its first institution the Faculty has naturally been in close and constant association with the law courts and the legal societies, its main function being to train recruits for their service.

The Tercentenary of the University found the Faculty in a flourishing state; its students numbered about five hundred, its staff consisted of five Professors and a sixth shared with the Faculty of Medicine, its work was proceeding with marked efficiency and commendable economy. The last fifty years have seen a slight shrinkage in numbers; but in other respects there has been continuous progress in adapting the old and tried traditions of legal education to modern conditions. Among the outstanding events that fall to be recorded are: the expansion of the curriculum by the recognition of new subjects; the institution of Lectureships, no addition to the Professoriate having been found practicable; the increasing popularity of the two Law Degrees which has practically transformed the Faculty from a non-graduating to a graduating basis; and the admission of women to the privileges of attendance and graduation. The immediate source of these and other novelties is to be found in the Universities (Scotland)

Act, 1889, and the executive action that followed in the shape of new ordinances and regulations designed to give effect to its provisions. Account must also be taken of changes in the entrance regulations of the various professional bodies. But the mainspring of progress has been the informed opinion of the legal profession as a whole, which is well qualified to voice an intelligent criticism of educational arrangements and, if united, is practically master of the situation. The Chairman of the 1889 Commission, Lord Kinnear, and two of its members, Lord Kyllachy and Sheriff Crawford, were themselves lawyers of great ability and long experience. The Commissioners invited advice from every competent quarter, and their decisions for the most part simply gave effect to the consentient views expressed by the three Scottish Faculties of Law, and various recommendations made by the best authorities.

THE NUMBER OF STUDENTS

The number of Law students has fluctuated very widely in the period under review. The official record shows a decline from about five hundred at the beginning of the period to about three hundred at the close; but the figures of 1884 and 1932 are not really comparable owing to administrative changes. At the former date all who attended a Law class for whatever purpose were enrolled in the Faculty of Law; whereas now a considerable proportion are entered under the Faculty of Arts, on the ground that they are still in the early part of a combined M.A.-LL.B. course, or are studying for the Degree in Commerce which for the present is included within the Faculty of Arts. The full number receiving instruction in Law at the present time may be estimated at about four hundred. One reason for the decline in numbers is the completion of the Law Faculties at Glasgow and Aberdeen and the establishment of certain Law courses at Dundee; these new facilities keep some students at home who would formerly have been obliged to come to Edinburgh. Perhaps a more potent cause is the clerical revolution which has been in progress for some time in all business offices. A lawyer's chambers used to be staffed by male clerks and apprentices who, in general, attended the Law classes with a view to qualifying for the profession. These have now been replaced to a large extent by female clerks and typists, few of whom aim at a University training in Law.

ADMISSION OF WOMEN

On the whole, however, women have taken as full advantage of their new privileges as could be expected in a profession where the public do not seem to welcome the female practitioner. The attendance of women in the Law classes has now reached an average of about forty, most of whom aim at secretarial appointments, or employment in Government offices (*e.g.* the Inland Revenue and Estate Duty Departments), where a Law degree improves the prospects of promotion. In general they have proved diligent and hard-working students; a fair proportion of them have shown decided talent and aptitude for the subject, and have carried off more than their share of class honours, scholarships and other rewards of merit.

GRADUATION IN LAW

When the Commissioners under the 1889 Act came to deal with graduation in Law, they found two degrees already established, but sparingly sought after: (1) the Bachelorship of Laws (LL.B.) which was instituted in 1864 by their predecessors under the Act of 1858, and was practically an Honours Degree, open only to graduates in Arts, and requiring attendance on each of six departments in the course of three academical years; and (2) the Bachelorship of Law (B.L.), a degree on a lower standard dating from 1874, open to non-graduates possessed of certain qualifications, and including four legal subjects to be studied during two academical years. Neither degree had proved attractive to the great majority of Law students; they preferred to qualify by means of the examinations conducted by the various professional bodies, or under the Law Agents Act. The Commissioners, after some hesitation, decided to retain both degrees and to confirm generally the existing regulations and the list of prescribed subjects. But they resolved to make the conditions, particularly for the LL.B. Degree, more elastic by introducing certain optional subjects to suit the case of persons who intended to practise in England or abroad, or who, without any intention of following the Law, desired to enter one of the allied professions or to secure some public or administrative position. It has long been a common practice for the future accountant, banker, or actuary to take one or two Law classes; and the occupational value of such training is now recognised in many other fields (*e.g.* the Civil Service, municipal administration, the higher posts in business, and journalism). Students with some such outlook supply a growing contingent to the Law classes.

Ordinance 39, 1893

With the object of opening up the LL.B. Degree to a wider circle, the Commissioners sanctioned the following changes in the prescribed curriculum: English Law as an alternative for Scots Law; Political Economy or Mercantile Law as alternatives for Conveyancing; and the admission of a group of courses, each consisting of forty lectures—International Private Law, Political Economy, Administrative Law and Forensic Medicine—out of which two subjects had to be chosen. The only other important change was made by a Court Ordinance in 1911, by which a course in Evidence and Procedure was added to the above group, and the Senatus and the Court were empowered to include any other subject from the Department of History and Law or the Faculty of Law.

Ordinance 40, 1893

The Commissioners also revised the regulations for the Degree of B.L., stiffening the preliminary qualification, and offering certain options for Forensic Medicine. This did nothing to remove the prevailing apathy. Consequently, the four University Courts, after prolonged negotiations and almost interminable delays, agreed in 1911 upon the terms of the amending Ordinance which is still in force. It imposed the Arts Preliminary Examination or its equivalent (with Latin as a compulsory subject) as the qualification for entrance to the course. It lengthened the curriculum to three years; it added to the four compulsory subjects a fifth, which might be one full course of eighty lectures or two half-courses of forty lectures; it allowed options for Conveyancing and Forensic Medicine, but not for Scots Law; and it provided that the standard of examination should be the same as for the higher degree.

INCREASE IN NUMBER OF STUDENTS GRADUATING

There has been a decided change within recent years in the attitude of Law students towards graduation, whether it be connected with the above-mentioned reforms in the regulations or not. Fully 75 per cent. of those enrolling for the first time in the last year or two are aiming at a degree. Some no doubt fall out by the way; but at Edinburgh, as also at Glasgow and Aberdeen, the general result is that far more are now qualifying for practice by graduation than by any of the other available avenues. The legal practitioners of the future have evidently come to regard the University hall-mark, with its implication of a liberal training, as something worth striving for; and this is all to the good of the profession whose prestige is thereby enhanced, and of the public who are very directly concerned in the efficiency and honourable standing of their legal advisers.

RECOGNITION OF CERTAIN LAW CLASSES IN THE ARTS CURRICULUM

Another notable innovation due to the Commissioners was the inclusion of three Law classes—Civil Law, Public Law, and Constitutional Law and History—among the subjects recognised for graduation in Arts. The partial transference of these subjects into the province of Arts was a just and proper recognition of their educational value and of their title to rank with the old and recognised instruments of intellectual discipline and mental cultivation. It had the incidental advantage of making possible the double Degree in Arts and Law after a five years' course of study; for an M.A. pass on the proper standard in the above subjects was allowed to count as a pass for the Degree of LL.B. also, which meant the saving of a whole year in the joint curriculum. This provided a strong inducement to take the cultural as well as the vocational course.

NEW LECTURESHIPS

To bring the new options into operation, it was necessary to provide teaching in the several subjects. This has been gradually effected as funds permitted by the institution of the following Lectureships: Evidence and Procedure (1884); International Private Law (1894); Administrative Law (1904); Mercantile Law (1908); English Law (1912).

Mercantile Law is frequently the largest class in the Faculty, for besides being an option for Law Degrees, it is a prescribed subject for the Degree in Commerce, and the Society of Accountants imposes attendance on its entrants: this is one of the subjects for which it is hoped that an endowment will soon be forthcoming to raise it to the status of a Chair, as has been done in Glasgow. Procedure and Evidence, which is practically compulsory for all entrants to the legal profession, is also largely attended. The other Lectureships, being optional subjects, have smaller numbers in attendance. English Law serves the purposes of those who intend to practise in England or abroad; of candidates offering it for Civil Service examinations and appointments; and of Scottish pleaders and advisers who find that they cannot afford to be entirely ignorant of English Law and practice. It is sometimes taken as an extra or post-graduate subject by the best of our students who intend to practise in Scotland. Lectureships in Agricultural Law and Industrial Law have also been instituted in connection with the Degrees in Agriculture and in Commerce. They really belong to the

Faculties of Science and Arts respectively and do not qualify for graduation in Law. Still more recently an experiment has been tried with what may be called Departmental Lecturers, such as are common in the larger Faculties. Two of these have been appointed, one in Public Law and the other in Scots Law, under the supervision and control of the respective Professors.

These additions to the teaching staff have filled many gaps in the educational scheme. The Faculty now offers as complete and thorough a training in the elements of legal science as any Law School in the country. Something has also been done in the way of making the material of study more accessible by providing the nucleus of a law-library for the use of students. There no doubt remain anomalies to be corrected and deficiencies to be supplied—it could hardly be otherwise after the lapse of forty eventful years since the constitution and working arrangements of the Scottish Universities were last overhauled; but the consideration of what reforms are desirable and practicable is outside the scope of this sketch. The experience of the Faculty, however, goes some way to prove that it is almost impossible with the existing machinery to effect a settlement of any of the major problems that confront the University. The difficulties and delays experienced in obtaining some simple amendments on the General Ordinance regulating the Degree of B.L. have been referred to above. Since that date the Faculty, with the aid of representatives of the legal bodies, has made a serious attempt to work out a scheme for the better co-ordination of certain courses of study and for the prevention of overlapping; but in the end the project had to be abandoned owing to practical difficulties, the chief of which was the rigidity of the General Ordinances and the hopelessness of securing the degree of unanimity among the Universities which is necessary for the alteration of a General Ordinance. It would seem that no comprehensive reform is likely to be carried through until another Royal Commission is appointed "for the better administration and endowment" of the Scottish Universities, with full powers of enquiry and executive action.

THE FINANCE OF THE FACULTY

The financial administration has been so careful that this Faculty approaches more nearly to a balanced budget than any other; the deficit to be met out of the General University Fund is surprisingly small. The stipends of the Chairs are almost covered by the income from their endowments and from class fees; a substantial part of the Lecturers' salaries is contributed by the fees of their students; and the expenditure on Assistants, equipment, etc., is negligible, so that every additional student is a clear gain to the University chest. Credit is due to the Commissioners for the sound judgment and careful discrimination with which they apportioned the exiguous funds at their disposal. In dealing with the Law Chairs they fixed normal salaries on the lowest scale (£600) or slightly above it, in respect that the holders were at liberty to engage in practice; and they applied the same principle to all Chairs which were on a similar "part-time" footing. Unfortunately, the same parity of treatment has not been sufficiently kept in view in the post-war readjustment of salaries to meet the increased cost of living. The unsatisfactory result is that, while University salaries in general have been substantially augmented, three important Chairs in the Law Faculty are at present in receipt of smaller stipends (if allowance be made for the change in the value of money) than were considered fair and reasonable forty years ago. That is an anomaly which ought to be redressed before it prejudicially affects the future prospects of the Faculty.

PROFESSORS OF PUBLIC LAW

The appointment of James Lorimer to the Chair of Public Law in 1862 was, in the words of Professor Flint, "a most fortunate event for the University and for the credit of Scottish juridical science, for he stands alone in his century so far as the Philosophy of Law in Scotland is concerned." One instance of Lorimer's prescience and the constructive power of his thought may be cited. In his introductory lecture to his class in November 1870, when the Franco-

Prussian War was engrossing the world's attention, he discussed "The International Significance of Recent Events," and, in seventeen points, outlined a scheme for a League of Nations and a Permanent Court of International Justice on much the same lines as were actually adopted fifty years later at the Peace Conference of Paris. His ingenious speculations on the nature and warrant of all law, whether natural, municipal, or international, were an unfailing stimulus to his students: they took final shape in the two treatises on which his fame will securely rest. As one of the founders of the Institute of International Law, he enjoyed the friendship and esteem of many of its distinguished members all over Europe; and honours beyond count were showered upon him by universities and learned societies. His memory is fittingly perpetuated by the Lorimer Travelling Scholarship, founded for the encouragement of the study of the "Law of Nature and Nations" in a foreign Law School.

Lorimer was succeeded in 1890 by the eldest son of Principal Sir Alexander Grant, who was marked out for the academic life by heredity no less than by personal aptitude. Sir Ludovic James Grant held the Chair from 1890 until his retirement in 1922. To him the University owes a deep debt of gratitude for his administrative capacity and intellectual gifts which were placed ungrudgingly at her disposal. As Secretary of the Senatus, he guided the deliberations of that body for over a quarter of a century, and as Dean of the Faculty of Law from 1894 until 1910, he presented the candidates for the Honorary Degree of Doctor of Laws with a grace and dignity peculiarly his own. Destined to see much of the fabric of his subject shattered by the war, he set himself in 1918 to rebuild the structure anew. But his *Alma Mater* just then made new and urgent demands on his time and energy; to the burden of his Professorship was added the onerous office of Secretary to the University, then created for the first time. The administrative chaos threatened by post-war conditions was thus happily averted; but the task imposed an excessive strain on Sir Ludovic's health and, in

1922, he was reluctantly released from his duties. Many students, in many lands, recall with a profound sense of gratitude the considerate courtesy, the inspiration, and the intellectual stimulus which they received from one who was *factus ad unguem.*

The Commissioners under the Act of 1858 ordained the Professor of Public Law to deliver forty lectures in International Law during the Winter Session. But Lorimer, with the consent of the Senatus, "abandoned the easy lines which the Commissioners had traced," and accepted voluntarily the burden of a full winter course, divided between (1) what is variously known as Natural Law, or the Philosophy of Law or General Jurisprudence; and (2) the Public Law of Nations, or Public International Law. In this he was followed by Grant; but the latter, on his retirement, in view of the rapid development of international organisations, such as the League of Nations and the International Court of Justice, recommended that Jurisprudence should be assigned to a separate Lecturer, and that International Law be developed into a full course of eighty lectures. The University Court, on the recommendation of the Senatus, having adopted this suggestion, the present occupant of the Chair, William Wilson, confines himself to the latter subject, while Jurisprudence is taught by a Lecturer under his supervision.

PROFESSORS OF CIVIL LAW

It is only the closing years of James Muirhead's Professorship which fall within this period. He had already acquired a high reputation for learning and literary skill among civilians at home and abroad, and his remarkable power of presenting a large and complex system in vivid and arresting outline was at its zenith. His gifts as a teacher still live in the recollection of his few surviving pupils—the easy mastery of the material, the lucid exposition of thorny problems, and the rare faculty of holding the attention of a whole class by investing the topic in hand with human interest and permanent significance. His sympathies mainly lay with the Historical School, and he

Sir LUDOVIC JAMES GRANT, Bt.

Professor of Public Law, 1890-1922
Dean of the Faculty of Law, 1894-1910. Secretary of Senatus, 1897-1918

did a real service to legal education by introducing its ideas and methods into his teaching. Sixty years ago it was comparatively new doctrine to regard the law of a country as a living organism growing with the people's growth and changing with the changing conditions of their intellectual, moral and social life; and it was a new departure to insist on the importance, even for practical purposes, of a proper understanding of the history of legal institutions. His pioneer work in this direction has been carried on by his successors, and the historical introduction has developed into a substantive course —the only kind of instruction in the history of law which the present curriculum has to offer.

On the death of Muirhead in 1889 he was succeeded by Henry Goudy, an advocate who had made his mark at the Bar as an authority on the law of bankruptcy. Possessed of a natural bent for the scholar's life, he hailed the opportunity of concentrating upon the scientific side of the law, and devoted himself so assiduously to his academic work that little time was left for outside interests. He found his reward in the cordial appreciation of his students, and in rapid preferment to a post of still wider influence and larger opportunities. In 1893 he was offered and accepted the Regius Professorship of Civil Law at the University of Oxford, a Chair which had ceased to be a sinecure and had taken a place of cardinal importance in the Oxford School of Jurisprudence. For many years Goudy played a leading part in the organisation and teaching of this flourishing Law School, and so it came about that the training and experience of a Scottish lawyer appreciably helped forward the movement for establishing legal education in England on a broad scientific basis.

Since 1894 the Chair has been occupied by James Mackintosh. Considerable changes in the methods and materials of instruction have been rendered necessary by the Ordinances of the University Commissioners and by subsequent regulations, under which Civil Law became a compulsory subject for both legal degrees and an optional subject for graduation in Arts. In particular, graduating students are required at their entry to the class to produce evidence of a sufficient knowledge of Latin to enable them to understand simple Latin law-texts, as the teaching and the examinations must be conducted with reference to the original sources; and the historical part of the course has been considerably extended. The facilities now offered to intending lawyers to give attendance in Civil Law during the preliminary period which they can afford to devote to general education, before the pressure of "bread and butter" studies and of practical work in legal chambers has begun to make itself felt, have helped to popularise the full M.A.-LL.B. course. The inclusion of the subject in the Arts curriculum has also attracted some students who have no such professional goal in view, especially classical students to whom the study naturally makes a strong appeal.

PROFESSORS OF CONSTITUTIONAL LAW AND CONSTITUTIONAL HISTORY

The long history of this Chair, which was founded in 1719, is marked by important developments which occurred within this period and were due to the wise initiative of the University Commissioners and the new regulations for graduation in Arts adopted by the University in 1909. Up to that time it had been known as the Chair of History; but, with the demand for more specialised teaching in the different aspects of History and for a greater subdivision of the subject, a new Chair was founded in 1894, designated the Chair of History, but almost entirely concerned with British History. In consequence of this the old Chair of History had its scope limited and its province defined as "Constitutional Law and Constitutional History"; it was meant to fill an important place in both the Faculties to which it was attached, and its emoluments were substantially increased. At the time of these changes its incumbent was John Kirkpatrick, who rendered valuable administrative services as Secretary of the Senatus. In the later part of his long term of office from 1881 to 1909, his teaching was confined to the special aspect of British History assigned to his Chair. But he introduced a new factor into the class-work by imparting some elementary knowledge of the leading foreign constitutions, and thus made a beginning in the comparative study of Constitutional Law which has more recently become a marked feature of the work of the class. In Kirkpatrick's time the class was composed, as it still is, of students of Law and Arts in varying proportions, and attendance on it, while compulsory for an LL.B. Degree, counted for graduation both in Arts and Law.

In 1909 Kirkpatrick was succeeded by John Hepburn Millar who had for some years held the Lectureship in International Private Law. His induction synchronised with the first effective application of new regulations for the Arts Degree which greatly affected the work of the Chair. British History—the new Chair—became "History" for ordinary Arts Degree purposes, and the course in Constitutional Law and History could normally be taken only by a student for the Degree of LL.B., and by those Arts students who, having previously taken British History, desired to offer Constitutional Law and History as a "cognate" subject to be passed on a higher standard. The result of these changes was to restrict the numbers in attendance. In Kirkpatrick's later years the class had been growing in popularity; but that tendency was now checked, while British History received large accessions of numbers. At the same time, and partly in consequence, the standard of study in Constitutional Law and History was appreciably raised. It remained, however—and still remains—a difficult problem for the Professor to adapt his teaching to a class which contains Arts graduates who are pursuing this subject for graduation in Law, and also the younger and less mature students who are still in the early years of the Arts curriculum.

Even more important for the incumbent of the Chair was the new place assigned to its subject in the scheme of study for the Degree of M.A. with Honours in History. Constitutional Law and History was given, and still retains, a more prominent place in the examination than is usual in other History Schools. It is a compulsory subject. The period from 1688 was assigned to the Professor, while the earlier periods were in the hands of an independent Lecturer. Millar found in this work for his Honours class not only the most exacting part of his duties, but also the chief attraction of his Chair. He made an intensive study of the State Papers and memoirs of the seventeenth and eighteenth centuries, and brought to their exposition a fine literary taste and an incisive style. Letters indeed had always competed with Law for the foremost place in his affections, and the brilliant work he did as literary historian and critic would make the reputation of a Professor of Literature; but that is another story, which cannot be pursued here. He was handicapped in his later years by a serious and ultimately fatal illness.

In 1925 he resigned and was succeeded by David Oswald Dykes, the present occupant of the Chair.

PROFESSORS OF SCOTS LAW

On the retirement of George Moir, in 1865, Norman Macpherson was appointed to succeed him in the Chair of Scots Law. He came of a stock associated with scholarship; for sixty years his father held the Chair of Greek at the University of Aberdeen, and his maternal grandfather was Principal of King's College. He passed advocate in 1851. For nine years before his appointment to the Chair he was editor of the reports of Court of Session cases, and for some years he also edited the *Journal of Jurisprudence*. Among his professional brethren he had a high reputation as an accomplished and learned lawyer, and those who were privileged to hear his lectures unite in bearing testimony to their high order of excellence. But his labours were not confined to the work of his Chair. In 1868 he acted as Secretary of the Commission whose report was the foundation of the important Act of 1868 dealing with procedure in the Court of Session; and nine years later he presided over the Commission appointed to inquire into the salmon fisheries in the Solway. From 1880 to 1890 he was Sheriff of Dumfries and Galloway.

In 1888 he retired and was succeeded by Sir John Rankine (1888-1922), the tenth in the line of distinguished men who have occupied the Chair. He was the son of the Rev. John Rankine, of Sorn, and was educated at Edinburgh and Heidelberg, where under von Vangerow, "my revered teacher," he laid the foundation of the learning exhibited in the works with which his name will always be associated in the legal profession. In 1879 his erudite treatise on the Law of Landownership in Scotland appeared, and eight years later it was followed by his work on the Law of Leases. His literary work is notable not only for a scholarly knowledge of the law, but for conspicuous powers of orderly arrangement and felicitous expression. Throughout his occupancy of the Professorship he maintained a living interest in the scientific study of the law, as was evidenced by the publication, on the eve of his retirement, of his work on Personal Bar. It can never have been easy to treat of so large a subject as Scots Law within the compass of a course of three terms; and the complexities of modern legislation and commerce combined to make his task even more exacting than that which had fallen to his predecessors. It was perhaps not difficult to discover from his lectures that, as with the older school of Scots lawyers, commercial law possessed less attraction in his eyes than those topics which are associated with the law of heritable property; but no student could fail to admire the skill with which, in the comparatively brief time at his disposal, he contrived to present so complete an outline of all the main principles. For many Scots lawyers their legal studies will always be associated with the courtly and kindly figure of the man under whose guidance those studies began; and his retirement meant for them the severing of a link with the days of their apprenticeship to the Law. Sir John held the Chair for a period equalled only by his illustrious predecessor, Baron Hume. He retired in 1922 and died within a few months of the relinquishment of his duties.

He was succeeded in the Chair by Robert Candlish Henderson, the present occupant.

PROFESSORS OF CONVEYANCING

James Stuart Fraser Tytler of Woodhouselee came of a family already distinguished in the Law. He was appointed to the Chair when Conveyancing practice was still in the Parliamentary melting-pot, and before the feudal system had been reduced to the shadow which we now know. As a lawyer he was well versed in feudal lore, and his work during his long tenure of the Chair was efficiently and carefully done. Naturally, like other practitioners of his generation, he had a greater affection for the forms of the past than for the statutory innovations of his day; but his lectures covered the new ground as well as the old in a clear and comprehensive review which put the progressive changes in the Law in their proper perspective. He was the first Chairman of the Board of Examiners set up under the Law Agents (Scotland) Act, 1873, and was largely responsible for the inauguration of that important departure and for its success.

Fraser Tytler was succeeded by John Philp Wood, who is still remembered with affection and respect by former members of his class. Beginning practice towards the end of the transition period in conveyancing, he was naturally less influenced by the older feudal system than his predecessors had been. His lectures broke new ground, widened the horizon of the class, treated the subject in a more practical manner than any of his predecessors had attempted to do. Not only was he a lawyer in large practice and of great experience who communicated to his class the fruits of that experience, but he was deeply interested in the welfare of his students. He always held up to them the necessity for a high moral standard in the conduct of their profession. Members of his class gained more than a knowledge of conveyancing; they came into contact with a teacher who impressed them with his character and ideals. During his tenure of the Chair he published several legal text-books and, after his retirement, prepared his lectures for publication. These works are still held in high esteem by the profession. Failing health, brought on by overwork, obliged Wood to retire after only eight years' tenure of the Chair, and he was succeeded in 1900 by Professor Mounsey.

John Little Mounsey, who had a distinguished career as a student of Law, narrowly missed appointment as successor to Fraser Tytler. He brought to the Chair experience gained in an extensive conveyancing practice, and his lectures were characterised by their logical arrangement and lucidity. He had a wide knowledge of the history and theory of conveyancing; and to this was added the faculty of separating principles from details and of expounding the fundamentals and illustrating their application in such a way as to fix them indelibly in the minds of his students. Methodical and conscientious to a degree, he was unsparing of himself, and his health gave way under the combined strain of an exacting professional life and the duties he owed to the University. He retired in 1922 and died on 26th June 1933.

The present Professor, Ernest Maclagan Wedderburn, has developed the facilities for teaching by extending the course into the summer session and by introducing a system of practical instruction in the framing of writs and deeds, for which purpose the class is divided into groups and works under individual supervision.

V

THE FACULTY OF MEDICINE

In the Faculty of Medicine the fifty years following the Tercentenary celebration have seen considerable expansion as well as change. The alterations in the curriculum introduced after the Universities (Scotland) Act, 1889, affected Medicine very specially through the lengthening of the course of study from four years to five. These changes began to take effect about 1895. The added year was utilised mainly for practical classes in the scientific subjects and to a certain extent for further clinical study. Incidentally too a change was effected in the designation of the degrees qualifying the student for the practice of his profession. In 1705—the year in which the first degree in Medicine was conferred by the University—the single qualification of Doctor of Medicine (M.D.) was granted. The Doctorate remained as the only qualification until, in 1860, an Ordinance of the Commissioners appointed under the Universities (Scotland) Act, 1858, divided the Medical degrees into two classes, the primary qualifying degrees, Bachelor of Medicine (M.B.) and Master in Surgery (C.M.) and the higher degree of Doctor of Medicine. Under the Universities (Scotland) Act, 1889, a further change took place, the two qualifying degrees being entitled Bachelor of Medicine and Bachelor of Surgery (Ch.B.) with two higher qualifications, Doctor of Medicine and Master of Surgery (Ch.M.) At this period Edinburgh, of the four Scottish Universities, had the best chance for medical development, because the new medical buildings, first occupied at the Tercentenary, and the new Royal Infirmary, opened five years previously, afforded increased space and naturally stimulated study and research.

The development that has taken place in the last fifty years is indicated by the fact that the staff of 12 Professors and 2 Lecturers (Mental Diseases and Diseases of the Eye) of 1883 has increased to 19 Professors and 48 Lecturers, with a corresponding augmentation in the number of Assistants. During this period the subject of Chemistry has been transferred to the Faculty of Science, but its place in the Medical Faculty has been taken by the Chair of Chemistry in Relation to Medicine. Other new Chairs have been founded—most of them in subjects previously represented by Lectureships—in Public Health (Bruce-John Usher Chair, 1898), Clinical Medicine (Moncrieff-Arnott Chair, 1913), Bacteriology (Robert Irvine Chair, 1913), Tuberculosis (1917), Therapeutics (Christison Chair, 1919), Psychiatry (1919), Child Life and Health (Edward Clark Chair, 1931). The students matriculating year by year in Medicine give another index of the Faculty's development during the period. The figures for the last years of successive decades are:—1859-60, 554; 1869-70, 560; 1879-80, 1459; 1889-90, immediately before the extension of the course took effect, 2044; 1899-1900, 1369; 1909-10, 1440; 1919-20, the peak of the post-war influx, 1968; and 1929-30, 1318.

With the added facilities and equipment in the University and with the augmented funds provided from various sources, a change in the type of teaching and in the functions of the teaching staff insensibly took place. Before 1890, instruction in Medicine was largely or even mainly conveyed by lectures, and few practical classes, except in Anatomy, were compulsory. Students usually elected to attend some at least of the courses given by extra-academical lecturers who were generally men of great practical experience and distinction in their profession. With the steady improvement in text-books, the necessity for the formal lecture diminished; and as medical knowledge at the same time became wider and its methods more precise, the need for practical instruction increased. Accordingly, the staff of the University Medical departments tended to increase in numbers (including a growing proportion of younger men), and to devote a greater amount of time to individual teaching. Another result that naturally followed was an output of research work much greater in quantity than before, although less revolutionary in effect than that which had been carried out, for example, by Charles Bell, by Simpson, or by Lister. The extra-academical teachers gradually diminished in numbers; and the Professors came to be appointed more frequently from outside Edinburgh. On 10th and 11th June 1926, the Bicentenary of the Faculty of Medicine was celebrated.

ANATOMY

The Chair of Anatomy, though not the earliest founded in the Faculty of Medicine, was the first in connection with which active teaching was carried on. The demonstrators in this subject, serving under the Incorporation of Surgeons, a body with a history of over two centuries, were recognised as "Professors" by the Town Council in 1705. In 1720, Alexander Monro (*primus*) was appointed Professor of Anatomy for life. The subject then included, in a six months' course of lectures, what it was necessary to know of anatomy, physiology, surgery, and several other branches of medical science. Monro was succeeded in 1754 by his son, and in 1798 by his grandson, and he in turn by John Goodsir in 1846. Goodsir's successor in the Anatomy department, Sir William Turner, occupied the Chair for the long period from 1867 to 1903, when he became Principal of the University. During his Professorship 10,500 students passed through the class. The Anatomy department in the New Buildings in Teviot Row was opened in 1880; and in the winter of 1885, 638 students were attending Practical Anatomy in the dissecting-rooms.

The Anatomy department, during and since Sir William Turner's time, has been the training ground of men who have become professors of the subject in other places. Arranged in chronological order, so far as possible, these have been as follows:—Professors of Anatomy at Owens College, Manchester, Morrison Watson and A. H. Young; at Otago University, New Zealand, John Halliday Scott; at Trinity College, Dublin, D. J. Cunningham, afterwards professor at Edinburgh; at Queen's College (after 1909, University), Belfast, Johnson Symington; at the University of Tokio, Japan, F. Dyce

Fraser; at the University of Oxford, Arthur Thomson; at the University of Sydney, J. T. Wilson, who afterwards became professor at the University of Cambridge; at King's College, London, Arthur Robinson, who afterwards became professor at Birmingham and later succeeded Cunningham at Edinburgh; at the University of Liverpool, A. M. Paterson; at the University of Durham, Robert Howden; at Lahore College, India, and afterwards at University College, Dundee, J. C. Lamont; at the University of Toronto, Alexander Primrose; at the University of St Andrews, James Musgrove and afterwards David Waterston; at the University of Bristol, Edward Fawcett; at the University of Glasgow, T. H. Bryce; at University College, Cardiff, David Hepburn; at Melbourne University, R. J. A. Berry; at the University of Leeds, J. K. Jamieson; at Middlesex Hospital, London, Thomas Yeates; at McGill University, Montreal, Auckland C. Geddes; at Guy's Hospital Medical School, T. B. Johnston; at the University of Birmingham, J. C. Brash (now in the Anatomy Chair at Edinburgh); at the University of Winnipeg, Manitoba, Alexander Gibson, J. C. B. Grant (later at Toronto), and R. G. Inkster; at Dalhousie University, N.S., John Cameron and afterwards Donald Maitland; at Bangkok, Siam, and later at the University of Sydney, C. W. Stump; at the University of Cape Town, R. B. Thomson and afterwards M. R. Drennan; at the University of California, I. M. Thompson and afterwards John B. Saunders (Clinical Anatomy); at the Medical School, Cairo, D. E. Derry.

The Edinburgh anatomical department during this period was fertile in research and publication. The doctrine of evolution had received a great impetus by the appearance, in 1859, of Darwin's *Origin of Species*, and it was from the evolutionary point of view that anatomists continued to study their subject well into the twentieth century. One of Turner's early important contributions to Comparative Anatomy was an elaborate study of the surface arrangement of the convolutions of the cerebral cortex, based upon a series of dissections of the brains of apes and man, published in 1866. In this paper he drew attention to a sulcus in the parietal lobe, to which he gave the name of the intraparietal fissure and which was subsequently recognised as the third of the three primary fissures upon the outer surface of the brain. At this time experimental research into the functions of different parts of the cerebral surface was just beginning. David Ferrier, an Edinburgh graduate practising in London, began, in 1873, to publish the results of his basic researches upon this subject. Accordingly it became necessary to ascertain carefully the topography of the cerebral convolutions and delimit their areas before an exact analysis of their function could be made. Turner made an elaborate investigation of the surface convolutions throughout the mammalian series, including the brains of carnivora, whales, seals, apes and man, and his general conclusions, after many years' work, were summed up in his address to the anatomical section of the 10th International Medical Congress at Berlin in 1890. He showed that a smooth surface was the universal type of all brains in an early stage of their development; and the most complex arrangement of the convolutions he found to exist in the elephants, whales, seals, monkeys, and finally in man, although even in some of these orders there was an occasional species in which the surface of the brain was smooth or only feebly convoluted. He came, therefore, to the general conclusion that the convolutions did not exhibit a progressive and continuous development from the lower animals through the apes to man, and that the homologies of the cortical areas must be looked for rather in similarity of microscopic structure and in function than in any morphological arrangement.

A special development of the Anatomical Chair was the subject of Anthropology, a department of research which was first recognised by the British Association for the Advancement of Science, at its meeting in 1884. Turner's eminence in this subject was recognised by his election as president of the section in 1889 and in 1897. His studies were directed especially to the physical side of anthropology, and the skulls and other bones collected by the *Challenger* Expedition were entrusted to him, in 1876, for descriptive purposes.

A line of work of national importance, dealing with the

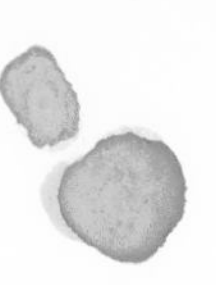

From the painting by] [*Sir James Guthrie, P.R.S.A.*

SIR WILLIAM TURNER, K.C.B.

Principal and Vice-Chancellor
1903-1916

craniology of the peoples of Scotland, was carried out by Turner between 1903 and 1915. Nearly 180 crania had been collected from various parts of the country and, after careful measurements and the weighing of other evidence collected in different parts of Scotland, such as the consideration of specimens of hair, evidence of the colour of the eyes, etc., Turner came to the conclusion that the modern race of Scottish people showed a strong brachycephalic strain, evidence of a bronze age ancestry, little affected by the various subsequent invasions of the country.

When Sir William Turner resigned the Chair of Anatomy in 1903, to become Principal of the University, he was succeeded in the former post by Daniel John Cunningham. Cunningham had graduated in Medicine at Edinburgh and had been appointed Senior Demonstrator in Anatomy in 1876. Six years later he was appointed Professor of Anatomy, first in the Royal College of Surgeons in Ireland and, one year later, at Trinity College, Dublin.

During his period at Dublin he had become acting editor of the *Journal of Anatomy and Physiology*, to which he contributed numerous papers; but his best known work, so far as teaching was concerned, was *A Guide to Dissection*, which he subsequently expanded into *A Manual of Practical Anatomy*. This manual, founded upon the methods of dissection followed in the Practical Anatomy department of Edinburgh University, was first issued in 1893, and speedily came to be used in medical schools all over the English-speaking world. At a later date, in 1902, he projected and edited a larger *Text-book of Anatomy*, of which the sections were written by various men trained in the Edinburgh School, and this also, in various editions, became a standard work upon the subject.

Among Cunningham's papers and monographs were included an elaborate report on the anatomy of the marsupialia collected during the voyage of *H.M.S. Challenger* and published while he was acting as demonstrator at Edinburgh; various papers on the nerves of the head and neck; on acromegaly; on the convolutions of the brain and on the lumbar curve in man and apes; and, after his return to Edinburgh, a memoir on the formation of the stomach.

During the six years of his occupation of the Chair of Anatomy at Edinburgh, he took a great interest in the development of post-graduate instruction in this school, and was one of the most active movers in the inauguration of the post-graduate courses established jointly by the University and the School of Medicine of the Royal Colleges, courses which subsequently attained a great success.

On the death of Professor Cunningham in 1909, he was succeeded in the Chair of Anatomy by Arthur Robinson who, after graduating at Edinburgh, had been Professor of Anatomy at King's College and at Birmingham. During his tenure of the Chair, he was engaged in research upon embryology, including enquiries into the causes of ante-natal death; he also did much to increase the material in the museum by casts of prehistoric specimens, simian skeletons, and tracings and casts of comparative craniology. He also undertook the responsibility for the preparation of new editions of Cunningham's *Text-book of Anatomy* and *Manual of Practical Anatomy*, both of which had attained a very wide circulation. On Professor Robinson's retirement in 1931, he was succeeded in the Chair by James Couper Brash.

The management of the dissecting rooms during many years of Turner's professorship was in the hands of David Hepburn; throughout the years of Cunningham and Robinson, E. B. Jamieson—appointed Lecturer in Anatomy in 1906—was in charge. He published for the use of students *A Companion to the Manuals of Practical Anatomy*, first issued in 1913, also *The Basel Anatomical Nomenclature* in 1916 and, in conjunction with Professor Robinson, a monograph on *Surface Anatomy* in 1928.

During Turner's tenure of the Chair, the teaching of Anatomy in the Extra-academical School continued to flourish. P. D. Handyside, who had lectured for many years at Surgeons' Hall, was succeeded in 1881 by Charles W. Cathcart, with Francis Caird as his demonstrator. In 1884 Cathcart, now devoting himself to Surgery, was followed by

J. Macdonald Brown, until he began practice in London, his successor, in 1895, being J. Ryland Whitaker, who held the lectureship till 1931, becoming very popular as a teacher of Anatomy, and attracting students from all parts of the world. The lectureship at Surgeons' Hall is now held by Charles Richard Whittaker. A School of Medicine had been opened at Minto House, Chambers Street, in 1877, with its anatomical department in the hands of J. Cossar Ewart who, on his appointment in 1879 to the Chair of Natural History at Aberdeen, was succeeded by Johnson Symington who, in 1893, became professor at Queen's College, Belfast. In 1895, the Anatomy department in Minto House was handed over to the Women's School of Medicine. At this time the New School was opened in Bristo Street; and here James Musgrove taught Anatomy for two years till he became lecturer — afterwards professor — at St Andrews. Richard J. A. Berry then filled the position at the New School until 1905, when he was appointed to the Chair of Anatomy at Melbourne University. The anatomical department at the New School was then taken over by the University and used, after 1916, for the teaching of women students.

PHYSIOLOGY

The first arrangement for teaching Physiology or, as it was originally called, Institutes of Medicine, or Theory of Medicine, began with the appointment, in 1724, of William Porterfield as Professor of the Institutes of Medicine, and also of the Theory and Practice of Medicine. He does not appear to have lectured and, in 1726, John Rutherford and Andrew St Clair became professors of these subjects. They were succeeded in both, in 1747, by Robert Whytt, but, in 1766, the Institutes of Medicine were separated from Practice of Medicine, William Cullen professing the former, and John Gregory, the latter. In 1773, Alexander Monro Drummond succeeded William Cullen in the Theory of Medicine, the latter passing to Practice of Medicine; but Drummond, who was in Italy, physician to the King, did not come to

Edinburgh and, in 1776, James Gregory was appointed to the Chair. He was followed successively by Andrew Duncan in 1789; Andrew Duncan, junior, in 1819; William Pulteney Alison in 1821; Allen Thomson in 1842; and John Hughes Bennett in 1848. On the retiral of Professor Hughes Bennett in 1874, William Rutherford was elected to the Chair. He had been assistant to Hughes Bennett, and Professor of Physiology at King's College, London, and, while assistant to the professor at Edinburgh, had introduced a practical class of teaching in Physiological Chemistry. Prior to the time of Hughes Bennett and during his tenure of the Chair, the professors of Physiology had also been professors of Clinical Medicine in the Royal Infirmary; and some of the most important work of Hughes Bennett had been done in connection with clinical medicine. Rutherford did not act as a physician in charge of wards, but confined himself entirely to teaching and to research in physiology. In his earlier days he devoted himself to such experimental work as the investigation of the inhibitory fibres of the vagus, the secretion of bile, and to histological research. Latterly, he occupied himself mainly in the preparation and delivery of his lectures. The arrangement of the experiments which he demonstrated to his class took up the greater part of the day, and much time was also spent in the preparation of diagrams with which the lectures were illustrated.

The habit gradually grew up among students of attending the lectures in Physiology both in the second and third year of study; in consequence, there was a very large class, numbering usually between 400 and 500, although there was no compulsion to take two courses of lectures.

The department, in addition to a large lecture theatre, included a room for histology with preparation rooms attached, a large room for physiological chemistry, and a museum of apparatus used for demonstrations and lectures. Some of this apparatus was of considerable historical interest, and most of it had been accumulated in the time of Professor Hughes Bennett. There was a class in Practical Physiology, which consisted mainly of histology with a few special meetings for the study of physiological chemistry, and this class was taught in sections of about thirty at a time by the assistants, four in number.

On the death of Rutherford, he was succeeded, in 1899, by Edward (later Sir Edward) Sharpey-Schafer, under whom very considerable changes were made in the structure of the department, the nature of the teaching, and the amount of research work carried out. A well-equipped laboratory for teaching Experimental Physiology, combined with a demonstration theatre for showing experiments which the students could not well perform themselves, was presented by Mrs Cox, the daughter of Professor Hughes Bennett, as a memorial of her father. The Hughes Bennett laboratory had 36 working places, and the demonstration theatre accommodated between 70 and 80 students in such a way that they could all see the experiments which were being performed. Afterwards, a new lecture theatre to accommodate 250 students was built adjoining the Hughes Bennett laboratory, and the former large lecture theatre was converted into a biochemical laboratory with 150 working places. Provision was at the same time made for accommodating about eight research workers in biochemistry, and in providing space for workshops, stores, photography, etc. Finally, an entirely new histological laboratory was erected on the flat roof of the Forestry building in George Square, so arranged that, although there were 150 working places, every place had a window, together with all the other necessary equipment such as gas, electric light, etc. A physiological library was also established; Professor Rutherford had left all his scientific books and journals to the University for this purpose, and Sir Edward Sharpey-Schafer afterwards presented his journals and physiological books and a rich collection of reprints accumulated for over fifty years. This is acknowledged to be one of the best physiological libraries in Britain.

With the increased provision for practical teaching and research, the staff has grown in proportion, so that, in 1932, it consisted, besides the professor, of 4 lecturers, 2 senior assistants, 4 graduate demonstrators, 2 technical assistants, a secretary who also acted as librarian, and 8 laboratory attendants—22 in all. This indicates the development of the department when it is compared with the staff of 4 assistants and 2 laboratory boys who constituted it towards the close of the nineteenth century.

A large number of persons who obtained part of their training at Edinburgh, or who, for a time, acted as assistants in the Department of Physiology under Professor Rutherford and Sir Edward Sharpey-Schafer afterwards became professors of this or allied subjects in other places. Arranged, so far as possible in chronological order, these were as follows: at the University of Birmingham, John Berry Haycraft and, later, E. W. W. Carlier; at the University College, Cardiff, John Berry Haycraft and, later, Thomas Graham Brown; at Tulane University, New Orleans, Gustav Mann; at Queen's College, Belfast, T. H. Milroy; at the University of St Andrews, P. T. Herring; at Cornell University, New York, Sutherland Simpson; at the University of Glasgow, D. Noël Paton and, later, Andrew Hunter (Physiological Chemistry); at the University of Otago, N.Z., John Malcolm; at Trinity College, Dublin, Harold Pringle; at the University of Cape Town, W. T. A. Jolly; at McGill University, Montreal, John Tait; at the Royal (Dick) Veterinary College, Edinburgh, H. Dryerre; at King's College, London, R. J. S. McDowall; at the University of New York, E. Ponder; at the London School of Economics, Lancelot T. Hogben (Social Biology); at Peking Union Medical College, R. K. S. Lim.

The books published from this department have included *The Text-book of Physiology* by various authors, in two volumes, edited by Sir Edward Sharpey-Schafer; a work on *The Endocrine Organs*, which has gone through two editions; *The Essentials of Histology* in twelve editions; and *Experimental Physiology* in four editions.

Research that has been of the greatest value, in some cases to physiological science, and in others to practical medicine, has been done in the department during the past thirty years. During Schafer's tenure of the chair, investigations were not confined to one particular branch of physiology but explored nearly the whole field of this subject. Along with an enthusiastic group of assistants, he studied in the early years of the century the structure and functions of the cellular elements of the blood, the phenomena of coagulation, the circulation in various organs and the effect of chloroform and of certain animal extracts on the heart and circulation. The work of P. C. Herring and Sutherland Simpson on the circulation and structure of the liver may be mentioned in this connection. The name of Schafer will always be associated with pioneer work on the function of the endocrine glands, especially the thyroid, pituitary and adrenals. As early as 1913, the relationship of the pituitary to the sex glands was demonstrated by work from this laboratory, and some ten years later Norman Dott published a general description of the functions of the pituitary gland, while other workers in the laboratory achieved a satisfactory standardisation of its products. The action of adrenalin on muscle and its influence on the pulmonary circulation formed further important contributions from this department to science and to practical medicine. The physiology of the nervous system was a branch which received special attention throughout this period; and among the subjects upon which light was thrown by the work of this laboratory may be mentioned the conduction of sensory impulses in the spinal cord, the degeneration following injury of the motor cortex, the connections of the cerebellar tracts, and the regeneration of sympathetic nerves. Among Schafer's personal contributions to this subject may be cited his work on the dilator pupillæ, the paths of volitional impulses, the regeneration of the vagus nerve, the action of the nerves of respiration, and especially on the recovery after severance of cutaneous nerves and on the effects of denervation of cutaneous areas.

Of direct practical importance was the enquiry by Sir Edward Sharpey-Schafer into the phenomena attending death by drowning, carried out before 1904, with a comparison of the relative efficiency of different methods of performing artificial respiration, from which Schafer's simple method has become adopted as the standard all over the world.

Sir Edward retired in September 1933 after thirty-four years of service, being succeeded by Ivan de Burgh Daly.

MATERIA MEDICA AND THERAPEUTICS

The Chair of Materia Medica was separated from that of Botany in 1768, when Francis Home was appointed professor of the former subject. He was succeeded thirty years later by his son, James Home, who was followed in 1821 by Andrew Duncan, junior, and in 1832 by Sir Robert Christison.

Christison was succeeded in 1877 by Thomas (afterwards Sir Thomas) Richard Fraser. In the first six years of his professorship the Materia Medica department, being still housed in the Old College, provided only an attic for the practical class which Fraser started on assuming the duties of the Chair. Until the department removed to the New Buildings in 1883, there was no accommodation for laboratory workers. The professor himself carried out important researches, but the facilities in the department afforded little encouragement to other workers to prosecute original investigation. Fraser's graduation thesis had, on the suggestion of Christison, dealt with the Calabar Bean, and he had recorded the important observation that the pupil contracted under the action of this poison. This investigation largely determined the direction of his future work, as, from the Calabar Bean, he was led through various other ordeal poisons and arrow poisons to his well-known work on the action of remedies derived from plants of the strophanthus group, which occupied him during the first twenty years of his professorship. A line of investigation which proved of great importance to medicine was that dealing with the subject of antagonism between different active substances, and in particular with that between physostigmine and atropine. A subject which seemed at the time to be of productive importance was suggested to him by Professor Crum Brown, in the relation which might be found to subsist between the chemical constitution of remedies and their pharmacological action. This played a great part in the introduction of a number of new drugs, although its importance was found ultimately to be not so great as had at first appeared. Between 1860 and 1870 Fraser and Crum Brown carried out a series of investigations on the effect of introducing methyl and ethyl groups into alkaloids. They showed that this procedure resulted in the production of compounds with a specific paralytic or curariform action. This was the first work that suggested a clear relation between chemical constitution and pharmacological action, and the conception was at the time far ahead of contemporary thought. The researches on strophanthus led to the introduction of this important remedy into medicine as a possible substitute for digitalis. The work on antagonism led up to a long series of researches on snake venoms and anti-venin, on the analogy of the use of anti-diphtheritic serum. Fraser's work was mainly carried out by direct observation of the effects of active substances on animals by the use of simple apparatus, and his methods form an important link between the old materia medica of Christison and the more modern ways of dealing with pharmacology by physiological operations.

Sir Thomas Fraser was for many years Dean of the Faculty of Medicine and a member of the University Court; he also represented the University for a time on the General Medical Council. In 1898 he was president of the Plague Commission in India which reported in 1901. Like his predecessors in the Chair, he also acted as a physician in the Royal Infirmary, but towards the end of his term of office the increasing amount of research in pharmacology made it desirable that these two posts should be separated.

Accordingly, on the retirement of Sir Thomas Fraser, in 1918, the University Court decided that the subject of Therapeutics should be taught by a separate professor who, in addition, would take part in clinical or other practical teaching. The Court, therefore, set apart funds to endow a Christison Chair of Therapeutics. The work of the old Chair of Materia Medica was henceforward to be conducted as a laboratory subject. Sir Thomas Fraser was succeeded by Arthur Robertson Cushny in the Chair thus reconstituted.

The latter was an Aberdeen graduate, had been assistant for a year to Schmiedeberg at Strassburg, and afterwards Professor of Pharmacology at the University of Michigan for twelve years and for thirteen years at University College,

London. During this period he had made a great reputation as a teacher and investigator and had written his celebrated *Text-book of Pharmacology and Therapeutics.* Just before coming to Edinburgh, his monograph on "The Secretion of the Urine" had appeared, treating this subject on a physical and chemical basis, and while at Edinburgh he wrote his important monograph on "The Action and Use in Medicine of Digitalis and its Allies." His work on the latter subject was of great value to practical medicine, especially in showing that auricular fibrillation is the condition of the heart in which digitalis exerts pre-eminently its therapeutic effect. Another important monograph published just after his death dealt with the "Biological Relations of Optically Isomeric Substances." He also had interests outside his chair as he acted as a member of the conferences on biological standards, held under the auspices of the League of Nations; and with Professor J. J. Abel, assisted as editor of the *Journal of Pharmacology and Experimental Therapeutics.* At Edinburgh, he established the laboratory of his department as a centre for pharmacological research by numerous workers, and in the teaching of students he greatly simplified his subject for their study by the introduction of the metric in preference to the imperial system, and by reducing the materia medica of a previous generation to a restricted list of substances of proved utility. Research on a large variety of subjects was prosecuted and, in particular, a number of important papers was produced on the subject of renal secretion. On his death in 1926, Professor Cushny was succeeded by Alfred Joseph Clark who had previously held the Chairs of Pharmacology at University College, London, and at the University of Cape Town.

Among those who acted as assistants in this department and afterwards became professors at other universities were the following, viz.: at the University of Aberdeen, Matthew Hay (Forensic Medicine); at the University of Glasgow, Ralph Stockman; at Oxford University, James Andrew Gunn; at Cape Town University, John W. C. Gunn; at Queen's University, Belfast, Edward B. C. Mayrs; at the University of Witwatersrand, Johannesburg, John M. Watt; at Dalhousie

University, Halifax, N.S., O. S. Gibbs; at Osmania Medical College, Hyderabad, S. W. Hardikar (Pharmacology); at the University of Sydney, C. G. Lambie (Medicine). In the extra-academical school during the period under review T. R. Fraser, prior to becoming Professor in the University, had acted as a Lecturer. Other Lecturers in Materia Medica were William Craig, G. A. Gibson, Ralph Stockman (who later became Professor of Materia Medica in Glasgow), A. L. Gillespie, Francis D. Boyd (who subsequently became Professor of Clinical Medicine in the University), and John Orr.

An important event in this department within recent years has been connected with the general reorganisation of the medical buildings in the years 1929-32. Towards this scheme of internal reconstruction Sir William Dunn's Trustees contributed £20,000, and the Rockefeller Foundation £35,000. When the buildings had been originally constructed each department was practically completely shut off from every other lecture room and set of laboratories, an arrangement that was wasteful of space and that almost completely prevented collaboration in research between workers in two departments. The accommodation both for teaching and research was by the reconstruction improved and extended, a Central Medical Library for research workers in the medical sciences was instituted, and the departments which chiefly benefited by the provision of free intercommunication were those of Pharmacology, Chemistry and Bacteriology.

When the Christison Chair of Therapeutics was established in 1919, Jonathan Campbell Meakins was elected its first Professor. He had previously been Lecturer in Medicine and Bacteriology and Director of the Department of Experimental Medicine at McGill University, Montreal, and afterwards Assistant in Medicine at the Johns Hopkins Medical School, Baltimore. During his period at Edinburgh he interested himself especially in research regarding the functions of respiration and circulation. He published a book on *Respiratory Function in Disease* in collaboration with H. Whitridge Davies, who was then Assistant in the Department of Therapeutics and, later, Professor of Physiology at the University of Sydney, and, along with J. S. Haldane and J. C. Priestley he published a monograph dealing with "Respiratory Response to Anoxæmia." The Department of Therapeutics was at the same time engaged in the early production of insulin and the investigation of its action. Research was also carried out here, into the influence of histamine on gastric secretion. While still teaching at Edinburgh, Meakins accompanied Professor Barcroft on an expedition to the Andes with the object of studying the physiological changes in life at high altitudes, and the results of this investigation were published in the *Proceedings of the Royal Society* in 1923. After five years at Edinburgh, Professor Meakins resigned the Chair, in 1924, to become Director of the Department of Medicine at McGill University, Montreal. He was succeeded by David Murray Lyon, who became Director of the Clinical Laboratory.

In December 1923, the Rockefeller Foundation intimated a grant of £35,000 for building and equipping a clinical medicine laboratory. This was erected in the grounds of the Royal Infirmary and was occupied in 1928. The object of this laboratory was from the outset comprehensive—that it should be available for all members of the Clinical Staff of the Infirmary; and that it should serve the dual purpose of research and of routine reporting work upon the patients. Investigations have been carried out on disorders of the heart, on the treatment of pneumonia and upon other subjects.

CHEMISTRY IN RELATION TO MEDICINE *

This Chair was founded in 1919 following the allocation for endowment of a sum amounting to £15,500 from the Carnegie Trust Quinquennial Grant in 1917; and George Barger was appointed to the post.

On the foundation of the new Chair, instruction was at first limited to that of medical students studying for the first professional examination; later a pre-registration course in

* *See* The Faculty of Science, pages 264-272.

summer was begun. In 1926, the chemical teaching for the Diplomas in Public Health and Tropical Medicine was taken over, and a course of general biochemistry (lectures and laboratory work) was instituted for the B.Sc. Degree. This is also attended by medical graduates desiring to specialise. A considerable amount of research work has been organised and carried out both in biochemistry and in organic chemistry. Under the former heading substances of physiological importance, such as thyroxine and methionine, have been investigated, and work has been done on the respiratory pigment hæmocyanin and on the inhibition of esterases by synthetic urethanes, while problems of calcium, purin, and fat metabolism have been investigated. In organic chemistry the structure of natural products, particularly of toxic alkaloids, has engaged much attention. It may be mentioned that the synthetic preparation of thyroxine was initiated in this department and completed by Professors Barger and Harington.

An important feature of this department is the large number of research workers attracted to it from overseas, including three natives of India and twenty-six of nine nationalities other than British; some of these already held the Ph.D. Degree, and some graduated at Edinburgh. Among those who have worked in the department and afterwards become professors elsewhere are,—at University College Hospital Medical School, London, C. R. Harington (Pathological Chemistry); at the Medical School, Madras, A. S. M. Nayar (Biochemistry); and at George Washington University, Washington, D.C., V. du Vigneaud (Biochemistry).

PATHOLOGY AND BACTERIOLOGY

The subject of Pathology was originally taught by the Professor of Anatomy, and later by the Professor of Clinical Surgery, but, in 1831, the Crown decided to establish a Chair of Pathology and nominated John Thomson for the post. He was followed in 1842 by William Henderson, in 1869 by William Rutherford Sanders, and in 1881 by William Smith Greenfield. Before his appointment at Edinburgh, Greenfield had been demonstrator of Pathology at St Thomas's Hospital, and had contributed numerous papers to the Pathological Society of London, on such subjects as "Visceral Syphilis," "Lymphadenoma," "Pyæmia," and "Granular Contracted Kidney." From 1878 he had been Professor of Pathology in the Brown Institute, where he had worked out the bacteriology of woolsorters' disease.

An important innovation introduced by him at Edinburgh was a course of Practical Pathological Histology, which was conducted by his assistant, German Sims Woodhead, who afterwards became Professor of Pathology at Cambridge. Its subject matter formed the basis of Woodhead's well-known manual of *Practical Pathology*. This work was a new departure in text-book literature and, for thirty years, in successive editions, it brought distinction to the Edinburgh School. Woodhead took a leading part in the movement at Edinburgh towards research, which began about 1884, and he was for a short time the first superintendent of the Royal College of Physicians' Laboratory. His success in organising the work of this laboratory led to his transference to London, in 1890, to perform a similar function in the newly started conjoint laboratory of the Royal College of Physicians, London, and the Royal College of Surgeons, England. While still at Edinburgh, he was one of the originators, and the first secretary, of the Pathological Club, an association which still exists, and which has had a considerable influence in the encouragement of research and moulding of medical scientific opinion in Edinburgh. Some ten years later, Woodhead founded *The Journal of Pathology and Bacteriology*, which greatly stimulated research in these developing subjects.

During Greenfield's tenure of the Chair of Pathology he was also one of the Professors of Clinical Medicine, with the charge of wards in the Royal Infirmary; this dual position was somewhat detrimental to teaching and research in both of these subjects as it distracted his interests and impeded his activities in both directions. It had thus been felt for some time that the two subjects ought to be separated and, when Professor Greenfield retired, in 1912, arrangements were made so that his successor was relieved of clinical duties.

Professor Greenfield was succeeded in the Chair of Pathology by James Lorrain Smith. After taking, at Edinburgh, the Degree of M.A. with first-class honours in Philosophy, and that of M.B., C.M., with first-class honours, he had gone to Oxford as assistant to Professor Burdon Sanderson. Here he became closely associated with another Edinburgh graduate, John S. Haldane, collaborating with him in an important series of physiological studies on the respiratory functions and the oxygen capacity of the blood. In 1895, Lorrain Smith was appointed Lecturer in Pathology at Queen's College, Belfast, where he was later appointed Professor, afterwards filling a similar Chair at the Victoria University of Manchester.

On coming to Edinburgh, in 1912, he developed a special method of teaching morbid anatomy which he had already carried out with success at Manchester. This consisted in a study of individual cases of disease rather than in that of individual organs, with the object of making a closer correlation between clinical and pathological facts. The student under this method was supplied with notes of the clinical history, and with the naked-eye and microscopical specimens from the case, which were studied in detail under the tuition of demonstrators; he was then obliged to write on several such cases a full report, describing, discussing and correlating the clinical and pathological data, which was then submitted to the teaching staff for criticism. This system was carried out during the twenty years of his professoriate and became an essential part of the undergraduate study at Edinburgh.

For twelve years Lorrain Smith acted as Dean of the Faculty. During this time he conducted important scientific researches into such subjects as the determination of blood volume; the metabolism of fat in its physiological and pathological conditions; the antiseptic properties of hypochlorous acid; and philosophic studies on the subject of *Growth*. He took a keen interest in comparative pathology which, in recent years, has been increasingly regarded as having an important bearing upon the production of disease in human beings; and he acted as Convener of the Research Committee of the Animal Diseases Research Association of Scotland.

Professor Lorrain Smith, on his death in 1931, was succeeded by Alexander Murray Drennan.

As a result of the change in the scope of the Chair, which has been mentioned as taking place when Professor Lorrain Smith became its occupant, the latter was appointed Consultant (later Honorary) Pathologist to the Royal Infirmary and executive head of this department: a Lectureship in Morbid Anatomy was established by the University, the holder of which became acting Pathologist in the Infirmary. The first occupant of this post was Theodore Shennan, subsequently Professor of Pathology at Aberdeen.

Another important development of Pathology was the establishment, in 1887, by the Royal College of Physicians of Edinburgh, of a laboratory for the prosecution of original research. Sims Woodhead, who was its first superintendent, was followed by Diarmid Noël Paton, who later became Professor of Physiology at the University of Glasgow, and, in 1907, he was succeeded by James Ritchie. In 1903, an arrangement was concluded with the Carnegie Trustees by which they purchased the laboratory, while the Royal College of Physicians continued to manage it, and its work gradually expanded both in research and in reporting. On Professor Ritchie's resignation from the superintendentship in 1920, he was succeeded by Lt.-Col. Anderson McKendrick.

In consequence of the researches carried out during the late 'seventies and early 'eighties of the nineteenth century by Pasteur and Koch on the relationship of bacteria to disease, an offshoot from Pathology developed in the subject of Bacteriology. Its importance was recognised by the University in 1894, when a Lectureship in Pathological Bacteriology was established, and Robert Muir, who had for some years been chief Assistant to the Professor of Pathology, was appointed to the post. Three years later, in conjunction with James Ritchie, he published a *Manual of Bacteriology*, one of the first and one of the most successful manuals in regard to disease-producing bacteria. The book was copiously illustrated with drawings and microphotographs made by Richard Muir, Laboratory Assistant in the Pathological Department of the University, who came to be recognised as one of the most expert technical laboratory workers in the country. This manual went through many editions and became the leading text-book in English on this subject.

In 1898 Robert Muir became Professor of Pathology at the University of St Andrews, and was succeeded in the Lectureship in Bacteriology by David Arthur Welsh, who subsequently became Professor of Pathology at the University of Sydney.

When the Robert Irvine Chair of Bacteriology was founded in 1913, James Ritchie became the first professor of this subject. A certain amount of romance attaches to the institution of this Chair. Robert Irvine, with chemical interests in Edinburgh, was greatly attracted to biological science, and was a friend of Sir John Murray who had been a member of the *Challenger* Expedition. As a result of examining a piece of rock from the small volcanic Christmas Island in the Indian Ocean, Murray and Irvine found that valuable phosphatic deposits had accumulated upon the island. Murray persuaded the British Government to annex the island, and obtained a concession to work its enormous phosphatic deposits, from which he and Irvine made considerable fortunes. As Irvine was greatly interested in the possibilities of the new subject of bacteriology, he bequeathed the remainder of his estate in trust to found a professorship of this subject at Edinburgh, and to equip a department for teaching and research.

Professor Ritchie, on his appointment, immediately reorganised the courses in Bacteriology, and in the same year he edited, along with Professor Pembrey, a text-book on "General Pathology," to which he contributed a number of chapters. In 1908 he became assistant-editor of the *Journal of Pathology* under the chief editorship of Professor Sims Woodhead. He died in 1923 and was succeeded in the Chair of Bacteriology by Thomas Jones Mackie, then Wernher-Beit Professor of Bacteriology at the University of Cape Town. The latter was also appointed Honorary Bacteriologist to the Royal Infirmary.

In 1923 the University Court decided to increase the accommodation of the Bacteriology department, and five research laboratories were ultimately equipped for bacteriological work. Between 1923 and 1929, about 250 undergraduates and 50 graduates were using these laboratories annually, and it became progressively more difficult to conduct practical classes under these conditions. In 1928 the scheme that has been previously mentioned for reconstruction of the University New Buildings became urgent, and it was pointed out that the department of Bacteriology was in special need of improved accommodation, while that of Medicine required space in which research could be conducted.

The space devoted to lecture theatres for Materia Medica, Forensic Medicine, Chemistry, and Medicine was reduced and converted into laboratories. The Bacteriological department was now concentrated on the top floor of the west side of the quadrangle, and the class laboratories were entirely refitted and provided with a proper corridor of access. A laboratory previously in the Chemistry department, which had now moved out to The King's Buildings, was converted into a large research laboratory for Bacteriology.

In the period under review, numerous persons went out from the Edinburgh School to become Professors of Pathology or Bacteriology, most of these having been attached to the department of Pathology in the University. Arranged in chronological order so far as possible, these include :—At the University of Aberdeen, D. T. Hamilton ; at the University of Cambridge, German (later Sir German) Sims Woodhead ; at Queen's College, Belfast, James Lorrain Smith, later transferred to Manchester and finally to Edinburgh ; at the University of Oxford, James Ritchie, later transferred to Edinburgh ; at the University of St Andrews, Robert Muir, who was later transferred to Glasgow ; at the University of Sydney, D. A. Welsh ; at the University of Birmingham, R. F. C. Leith ; at the

University of Sheffield, J. M. Beattie, later transferred to Liverpool (Bacteriology); at the University of Aberdeen, Theodore Shennan; at the University of Durham, Stuart McDonald; at Queen's University, Kingston, Canada, James Miller; at the University of Otago, A. M. Drennan, later transferred to Queen's University, Belfast, and to Edinburgh; at the University of Melbourne, Peter MacCallum; at the University of Cape Town, Benjamin J. Ryrie; at the University of Cape Town, William Campbell (Bacteriology); at the University of Sydney, Hedley D. Wright (Bacteriology); at the University of Manitoba, William Boyd; at the School of Medicine, Cairo, F. E. Reynolds; at the University of Hong-Kong, Chung Yik Wang; at the University of Aberdeen, L. Stanley P. Davidson (Medicine).

FORENSIC MEDICINE

Forensic Medicine, founded as a Chair in 1807, was for a long time not an obligatory class, and its first three Professors used it as a stepping-stone to other professorships. The first Professor of this subject was Andrew Duncan, junior, who was followed, in 1820, by William Pulteney Alison; in 1822, by Sir Robert Christison; and, in 1832, by Thomas Stewart Traill.

Andrew Douglas (later Sir Douglas) Maclagan was appointed in 1862. He formed a link with the remote past, for his father had been a medical adviser throughout the Peninsular War, and Maclagan himself was baptised by the same minister who had christened Robert Burns; he was still lecturing at the age of eighty-five. He was an erudite and cultured man who had engaged in many departments of medicine before succeeding to the Chair. In his early days, he practised surgery, and became a surgeon to the Royal Infirmary; later, abandoning this for medicine, he lectured upon Materia Medica in the Extra-academical School for eighteen years. At this time, Sir Robert Christison was making a special study of toxicology, which also attracted Maclagan's attention and, in 1862, he was appointed, by the Crown, Professor of Forensic Medicine in the University. From then till 1897, when he resigned the Chair, he acted as the principal medico-legal adviser of the Crown authorities in Scotland, and was concerned in many *causes célèbres*. Although no special discoveries are associated with his name, he was a well-known figure in Edinburgh society and greatly sought at medical meetings on account of his wit and his poetic gifts. A collection of his songs was published under the title, *Nugæ Canoræ Medicæ*.

The subject of Medical Police, as it was originally called, or the application of medicine to regulating the general health of the community, was attracting special notice in the 'sixties of the nineteenth century, not long after Maclagan was appointed to the Chair of Forensic Medicine. Sanitary arrangements in the large towns were very bad and in country places were practically non-existent prior to the year 1870. The year 1862, when Maclagan was appointed to the Chair, marked also the first appointment of a Medical Officer of Health for Edinburgh in the person of Henry Duncan (later Sir Henry) Littlejohn. In the same year, William Tennant Gairdner, an extra-academical lecturer in Edinburgh, published one of the most memorable papers on sanitation, under the title "Public Health in relation to Air and Water," and in the following year was appointed the first Medical Officer of Health for the City of Glasgow. These two appointments were the first of the kind in Scotland. The teaching of Public Health, which from this time became of increasing importance, was associated for over thirty years with the Chair of Forensic Medicine.

When Sir Douglas Maclagan resigned the Chair he was succeeded by Sir Henry Littlejohn who, for many years, had been a prominent authority both in Forensic Medicine and in Public Health. His dramatic power made his course one of the most interesting in the curriculum, upon which no student willingly missed attendance. He was businesslike in method, spare and keen in appearance, alert in movement and in mental grasp, and deeply sympathetic or very brusque according to his humour at the time. The way in which he gave evidence before the courts was entirely his own; no advocate could put him in a difficulty, and he always had a reply ready for every question.

His special achievement, however, had been in the sphere of Public Health. In 1865, he had made a report on the sanitary condition of Edinburgh, which established his reputation as a scientific sanitarian and led to a gradual and steady decrease in the death-rate of the city. At the time when he took office as Medical Officer of Health, the death-rate for some of the wards of Edinburgh was over 37 per 1000, and when he retired it had been reduced to some 14 or 15 per 1000. His most striking single achievement was perhaps in persuading the Town Council of Edinburgh to obtain from Parliament an Act compelling the notification of every case of infectious disease. This Act, for Edinburgh, was passed in 1879 in the face of much medical opposition, which held that notification interfered with the relations of confidence between doctor and patient; but the medical profession, like the public, gradually came to regard the matter as one of practical commonsense, and the whole country soon followed this example.

His activities were associated with the disappearance of smallpox and typhus from Edinburgh at an earlier date than from any other large city in Britain. Along with Lord Provost Sir William Chambers, he was active in a great deal of town-planning which removed many of the old tenements where disease had been incubating for three hundred years, and made new roads through some of the worst parts of the town. At a later date, he was also instrumental in the building of the new City Hospital in 1903.

When Sir Henry Littlejohn was appointed Professor, the subject of Public Health had attained so much importance that, as stated elsewhere, it was removed from the duties of this Chair; and the Bruce and John Usher Chair of Public Health was founded, followed a few years later by the John Usher Institute of Public Health. It may be pointed out in passing that although Sir Henry Littlejohn was appointed Professor at the age of seventy-one, his course of lectures was one of the most highly appreciated by students in the University until he retired nine years later.

In 1906, Sir Henry Littlejohn was succeeded by his son, Henry Harvey Littlejohn, who had been a lecturer in the Extra-academical School since 1898, and previously Medical Officer of Health for Sheffield. Like his father, he was an impressive lecturer. His most noteworthy published work was an *Atlas of Forensic Medicine* (1925) profusely illustrated with photographs of the material contained in the museum of his department which had been collected mainly by his father and himself. To the compilation of this book he had devoted much time and thought, in association with his assistant, Douglas J. A. Kerr. For many years he acted as Dean of the Medical Faculty with conspicuous success, and rendered valuable service in furthering the interest of the Edinburgh Medical School and in the establishment of its post-graduate instruction. On his death, in 1927, he was succeeded in the Chair by Sydney Alfred Smith, who became Dean of the Faculty of Medicine after the death of Lorrain Smith.

PUBLIC HEALTH

The foundation of the Chair of Public Health was directly inspired by Louis Pasteur. This great Frenchman and founder of the science of bacteriology, while attending the Tercentenary celebrations of the University in 1884, was the guest of Henry J. Younger and, later, of Alexander Low Bruce, partners in the brewing firm of William Younger & Co. He was delighted to find, on visiting the Abbey and Holyrood breweries, that the practical application of his researches upon yeast and other organisms was being systematically carried out in the brewing industry.

In memory of this visit and as an acknowledgment of Pasteur's great contribution to science, A. L. Bruce determined to found a Chair of Public Health in the University. Supplementary donations from his widow(the daughter of Livingstone the African explorer), as well as from Sir John Usher and from the firm of William Younger & Co., raised the sum available for the endowment of a Chair to £15,000, and, on the resignation, in 1897, of Sir Douglas Maclagan, who had taught the subjects of Forensic Medicine and Public Health together, it was decided that the time had come to separate these two subjects which had no essential connection with one another. In 1898 Charles Hunter Stewart was elected to the newly-instituted Bruce and John Usher Chair of Public Health, the first on this subject in Britain.

The accommodation for the practical and research work connected with the Chair was at this time limited to one or two rooms in the Department of Forensic Medicine, and Sir John Usher, who had contributed to its endowment, was immediately approached to provide a laboratory. He at once agreed to complete the endowment of the Chair of Public Health by providing a building and equipment where the work of this rapidly developing branch of medical science could be carried on. A site was secured by the University in Warrender Park Road and, three years later, the John Usher Institute of Public Health was completed at a cost of over £21,000. This Institute was formally opened in 1902. In it the instruction of medical students and of those proceeding to a degree or a diploma in Public Health was subsequently carried out, and for many years also the reporting work in connection with the Public Health Department of the City. In 1928 the diagnostic work on behalf of the City was transferred to the bacteriological department of the University. Professor Hunter Stewart was succeeded, in 1925, by Colonel Percy Samuel Lelean.

MEDICINE

The subject of Medicine was recognised by the Town Council of Edinburgh in 1685 when Sir Robert Sibbald, James Halket and Archibald Pitcairne were appointed professors in the Town's College. Although Sibbald and Pitcairne gave lectures in connection with the Royal College of Physicians and the Incorporation of Surgeons, there is no definite proof that they lectured as Professors of Medicine in the College. A similar statement applies to William Porterfield who was appointed Professor of Medicine in 1724, but, in 1726, John Rutherford and Andrew St Clair were actively teaching students in a room allotted to them in the Town's College. After them, came a succession of Professors in the subject, Robert Whytt from 1747, John Gregory from 1766, William Cullen from 1773, James Gregory (son of John Gregory) from 1790, James Home from 1821, William Pulteney Alison from 1842, and Thomas Laycock from 1855.

In this department Thomas (later Sir Thomas) Grainger Stewart held the Chair from 1876, in succession to Laycock. Grainger Stewart had previously been a Lecturer in Pathology in the Extra-academical School from 1864. In 1870 he had commenced a course of lectures on the practice of medicine and in this class he had been very successful because, possessed of considerable oratorical gifts, he contrived to present to his students a vivid picture of disease, which was not readily forgotten. The same success attended his lectures in the Chair of Medicine. Prior to his appointment to the Chair, he had devoted considerable attention to research into the diseases affecting the kidneys, and his *Practical Treatise on Bright's Disease*, published in 1868, was a well-known book in its time.

When Sir Thomas Grainger Stewart died in 1900, John Wyllie was appointed to the professorship. He also had lectured with success on Pathology in the Extra-academical School before attendance on this subject was compulsory for students and, in 1879, beginning to lecture on Practice of Medicine, he attained great success as a result of the clearness and simplicity with which he brought the essential facts before his students. He had completed the usual term of office as a Physician to the Royal Infirmary and had retired from this post, in 1897, at the age of fifty-three. Three years later, however, he was brought back to duties as Professor of Medicine and Physician to the Infirmary, and he held the Chair till 1915. Wyllie was more a teacher than a writer or practitioner of medicine, but his *Disorders of Speech*, published in 1894, was a book which enjoyed considerable popularity. He was succeeded, in 1915, by George Lovell Gulland, whose books, *The Blood; a Guide to its Examination,* published in collaboration with Alexander Goodall (1912), and *Pernicious Anæmia,* published in collaboration with L. Stanley P. Davidson (1925), as well as numerous articles in the same department of Medicine, are well known. Professor Gulland was succeeded in 1928 by William Thomas Ritchie.

The class of Medicine which, from its institution until 1922, had been a six-months' lecture course taken in the fourth year of study was, in 1923-24, divided into a junior and senior section. The junior section was taught in the autumn term of the third year as an introduction in the principles of medicine prior to the clinical study of this subject, while the senior section, meeting in the spring term, was taken by students of the fourth year. This division of the class was successful and highly appreciated by the students. A still further innovation was made in 1929-30 when a co-ordinated class, including the subjects of Pathology, Bacteriology, Medicine, Surgery, Materia Medica and Therapeutics, under the direction of the Dean of the Faculty of Medicine, was held by the professors of these various subjects.

In the internal reconstruction of the medical buildings, 1929-32, the space used by the department of Medicine was considerably remodelled. The former lecture theatre was divided horizontally so that the upper floor became a large modern demonstration room, while the lower floor was made into a suite of research laboratories, the Professor of Medicine henceforward sharing the existing Surgery lecture theatre with the Professor of Surgery.

During the latter part of the nineteenth century, the reputation of Edinburgh as a School of Medicine was greatly enhanced by the presence of several distinguished teachers in the Extra-academical School. Byrom (later Sir Byrom) Bramwell had commenced to lecture on Medicine in 1880, after a term of office as Pathologist to the Royal Infirmary. He was an eminently successful teacher of Medicine, and he especially elevated to an art the examination and diagnosis of cases applying for out-patient treatment at the Royal Infirmary. For many years hardly a single student failed to attend these weekly clinics which were held by him first on Saturdays and afterwards on Wednesdays. The substance of his lectures was later published as *Clinical Studies.* He was specially celebrated for investigations into diseases of the nervous system and did much to clear up such intricate subjects as those of intracranial tumour and aphasia. His manuals on *Diseases of the Spinal Cord* and *Diseases of the Heart and Thoracic Aorta* were popular text-books in the last twenty years of the nineteenth century, while his *Intracranial Tumours,* published in 1888, contained many new facts on this subject drawn from his own observations, and is generally regarded as a medical classic. His *Atlas of Clinical Medicine* was a more comprehensive work, of which three volumes appeared during the 'nineties.

George Alexander Gibson, after spending a short time as Assistant Physician to the General Hospital in Birmingham, returned to Edinburgh and became a lecturer in the Extra-academical School in 1886. He was a prolific contributor to medical journals and acted for a time as editor of the *Edinburgh Medical Journal,* a publication which did much to augment the reputation of the Edinburgh Medical School. Many of his researches and publications were concerned with the heart and circulation, and he was an earnest investigator of problems in this department of Medicine at a time when new aspects and phenomena were opening up as a result of new instrumental methods. He was a clear and vivid lecturer who attracted large classes of students.

Alexander Bruce was for a time a lecturer on Medicine while acting as a physician and successful teacher of Clinical Medicine in the Royal Infirmary. He had previously lectured, from 1886, on Pathology in the Extra-academical School and had devoted special attention to the subject of neurology. His works, the *Topographical Atlas of the Spinal Cord* and *Illustrations of the Mid and Hind Brain,* were valuable contributions to the elucidation of the nerve paths, a subject which was receiving great attention towards the end of the nineteenth century. He founded at Edinburgh *The Review of Neurology and Psychiatry,* a periodical which is now published in London. Other lecturers on Medicine in the Extra-academical School at this time were James Ormiston (later Sir James) Affleck, Robert William (later Sir Robert) Philip, J. J. Graham Brown, Alexander James and Robert Alexander Fleming, their successors to-day being W. Alister Alexander and John Dixon Comrie.

CLINICAL MEDICINE

On the retirement, in 1912, from the Chair of Pathology of Professor Greenfield, who had also acted as a Physician to the Royal Infirmary, and in consequence of the fact that the change in scope of this Chair excluded its holder from the charge of wards, there was a vacancy on the staff of the Royal Infirmary. As the University had in the past requested, and the Infirmary had granted, charge of wards in the case of new professors, the Board of Management of the Royal Infirmary, designing to give every facility for the advancement of the Medical School, came to an agreement with the University Court, in 1913, to appoint, by joint selection, a Professor of Clinical Medicine to take charge of the vacant wards. This arrangement had been made possible by the fact that the University, in 1908, had received a bequest sufficient for the endowment of a Chair and not ear-marked for any particular object. This legacy had been bequeathed by James Moncrieff Arnott, a former graduate of Edinburgh University, who had had a distinguished career in London as Surgeon to the Middlesex Hospital, and by his daughter. The new Chair was accordingly named the Moncrieff Arnott Chair of Clinical Medicine, and William Russell, one of the physicians to the Royal Infirmary, was appointed the first occupant, in October 1913.

On his retiral, in 1919, Francis Darby Boyd, also a physician in charge of wards in the Royal Infirmary, succeeded to the post. He had previously carried out a considerable amount of research work in connection with disease of the kidneys, and during the war had served as consulting physician to the Forces in Egypt and Palestine. After the war, he had presided over a commission on pellagra, his report on the occurrence of this disease among Turkish prisoners and others being issued as a Government White Paper. His tenure of the Chair of Clinical Medicine came to an end after three years, with his death in 1922, when he was succeeded by Edwin Bramwell.

SURGERY

The Chair of Surgery was founded in an unusual manner. The Incorporation of Surgeons, from about the middle of the eighteenth century, continued to agitate for the appointment of a professor of this subject, but following upon a specially vigorous agitation, in 1777, the Town Council, on the representations of Alexander Monro, *secundus*, that he had a special right to teach surgery, although he was not a surgeon, gave him a new commission, appointing him Professor of Medicine and "particularly of Anatomy and Surgery." In 1804 the Royal College of Surgeons, as the Incorporation was now called, appointed John Thomson to be Professor of Surgery to the Royal College of Surgeons, a post in which he was succeeded, in 1821, by John William Turner. The Crown, in 1831, appointed the latter, Professor of Surgery in the University, but after a short tenure of office he was succeeded by Sir Charles Bell in 1836, who was followed by James Miller in 1842 and James Spence in 1864.

John Chiene succeeded Professor James Spence in 1882, and held the Chair till his retirement in 1909. He had previously been a successful lecturer on Surgery in the Extra-academical School, and during Lister's second period at Edinburgh he was closely associated with the latter, whose surgical principles in their primitive simplicity he adopted and maintained throughout the tenure of his office.

He early instituted in connection with the Chair a small laboratory for the examination of pathological and bacteriological specimens; this is said to have been the first of its kind in Britain. He wrote little beyond a small *Treatise on Surgical Anatomy*, but he enjoyed a reputation among his students for the care with which he inculcated the broad principles of surgery in his lectures and in his wards.

On Chiene's retirement, he was succeeded by Henry Alexis Thomson, who had also been a successful lecturer, with an incisive and epigrammatic style, in the Extra-academical School. He contributed many valuable papers on Surgery, and especially on Surgical Pathology, to current medical literature, particularly to the *Edinburgh Medical Journal* of which he acted for a time as editor. In 1904 he published, in collaboration with Alexander Miles, *A Manual of Surgery* and *A Manual of Operative Surgery*, which were of great importance as forming an exposition of surgical practice at this period in the Edinburgh School of Medicine. These works passed through numerous editions and established themselves as standard text-books in many other medical schools both at home and abroad.

Thomson was specially interested in surgical pathology, and one of his methods in this department was the introduction of large paraffin sections of whole organs by which he used to demonstrate pathological changes, *e.g.*, the changes that occur in fibromatosis of the stomach. The same interest led to the foundation of a Lectureship in Surgical Pathology, established in 1914. During his period of office, Thomson with the means at his disposal encouraged experimental investigation into surgical problems, and research was carried out in his department by James M. Graham on blood-vessel surgery, and by A. Pirie Watson on bone grafting, although the experimental part of this work was of necessity done in the departments of Pathology and Physiology.

On the death of Professor Alexis Thomson, in 1924, he was succeeded by David Percival Dalbreck Wilkie. It had by this time become evident that the Medical buildings of the University, which had been designed and completed in the days when the formal lecture was the most important part of University education, had now become ill-suited for the practical teaching and research which were becoming more and more prominent as an essential part of a university's function. Although well-equipped laboratories had been installed in other departments, such as those of Physiology and Pathology, the department of Surgery possessed, in addition to its magnificent lecture theatre, only a small museum and the still smaller laboratory for histological work, which had been instituted by Professor Chiene. It seemed, therefore, that the time had come for complete remodelling of the surgical department and of the conditions under which the work was carried on in it.

In December 1923, the Rockefeller Foundation had intimated a grant of £15,000 as an endowment for this Chair to enable the University Court to supplement the stipend so that a whole-time appointment, or one under conditions of restricted practice by the Professor, might be made. They also paid £750 a year, for five years, towards staff salaries in this department. In 1928 this annual payment was capitalised by gifts of £5000 from Thomas Cowan of Leith and £10,000 from the Rockefeller Foundation, to be used as an endowment for the department. Immediately on the appointment of Professor Wilkie, the reconstruction of the Surgery department was commenced and was carried out during 1925-26, at a cost of about £10,000, of which £1000 was given by T. S. Thomson, brother of the late Professor Alexis Thomson, the rest being provided out of the general funds of the University. A grant of £5000 for equipment was made by the Rockefeller Foundation. A sum of approximately £45,000 was thus expended on the reconstitution of the Chair and the reorganisation of the Surgical department.

The old surgical theatre was a lofty auditorium with a gallery, and by flooring it across at the level of the gallery sufficient space was provided above for lecturing purposes, and below for practical rooms in which bandaging, surgical anatomy and operative surgery could be taught. A teaching museum with gallery was also provided, and the room which had formerly served as a museum was fitted out as a students' reading room, in which specimens could be displayed and studied at the student's leisure. The old laboratory on the ground floor of the building was converted into photographic and preparation rooms.

Accommodation for a department of experimental research was obtained by reconstructing a two-storey building in the rear of the teaching department. This had been erected three years earlier as an anatomy department for women students. It was now altered so as to give facilities for routine histological and bacteriological investigation of material from the Infirmary ; to provide an operation department with radiological and recording apparatus where operations on animals could be conducted under conditions at least equal to those found in a modern hospital; and to accommodate research workers, with benches, common room, library, etc. On the ground floor, a large laboratory was laid out for histological and bacteriological work, and a research laboratory, with the most modern fittings, capable of accommodating twelve workers. On the upper floor, private laboratories were designed for the professor and assistants, and the operating theatres, with their necessary adjuncts and X-ray department were also installed on this floor.

In the establishment of this research department, the achievement of two objects was attempted, and the success with which they have been attended will appear from the outline of work accomplished, which is given below. The first of these objects was the encouragement of the younger surgeons at Edinburgh to take some part in work of investigation, and to have a training provided by controlled experiment; this applied especially to the surgical tutors in the Royal Infirmary. The second object was to provide facilities for post-graduate research which might attract workers from abroad to spend six months or a year profitably at Edinburgh. During the past seven years, young surgeons have come from Montreal, Toronto, Halifax, Boston, Philadelphia, San Francisco, India, South Africa and Ireland for the purpose of working in this laboratory, and most of these have remained for nine months or a year, investigating experimentally some problem more or less directly connected with surgery.

The work done in this laboratory has been published by the various workers in about thirty papers dealing with the experimental investigations, and correlated with its clinical aspect in some twenty further communications. The subject of gall-stone formation and its effects was one which received special attention from a number of workers ; thus, the practice of cholecystography was greatly advanced by studies in a long series of cases, and the mechanism of cholesterol deposit was specially dealt with ; the toxic effects of the substances used in radiography of the gall-bladder were investigated ; the bacteriology of cholecystitis, especially in relation to its cause by a specific streptococcus, was studied ; and the clinical aspect of biliary infection, cholecystography, and the surgery of the bile passages were treated in seven papers, forming a practical application of the facts experimentally discovered.

A series of investigations on the nature of the cancer process, and on the properties of the Rous chicken sarcoma, was carried out and several points in regard to surgical diseases of the urinary tract were experimentally determined. A considerable amount of attention was paid to the determination of subjects connected with intestinal obstruction and the surgery of the stomach ; while the clinical results of operative treatment in regard to gastric ulcer, intestinal obstruction, appendicitis, and other abdominal conditions were published in a series of twelve papers. Tannic acid as a method of treatment for burns and scalds was investigated prior to being introduced as a useful remedy. Other subjects on which important research work was done were the pathology of congenital torticollis, and post-operative collapse of the lung ; the effect of anæsthesia upon the blood sugar content, peritoneal lymphatic absorption and vascular changes in splenic anæmia.

CLINICAL SURGERY

The Town Council, in 1803, obtained from the Crown an endowment of £50 per annum for a Chair of Clinical Surgery, and elected James Russell as the first Professor. He was one of the six surgeons to the Royal Infirmary, and permission was granted to all the six to deliver clinical lectures in this Institution, while, in the case of Professor Russell, the Managers subsequently granted him this privilege for life. In 1833, he was succeeded by James Syme, who was followed, in 1869, by Joseph Lister.

Although it would be out of place here to attempt any general account of Lister's life and work, it is necessary, in speaking of the Clinical Surgery department, to say something regarding that part of his work done in connection with the Edinburgh School of Medicine.

Prior to his appointment as Professor of Clinical Surgery his work had had important points of contact with the Edinburgh Medical School. In his early days at University College, he came under the influence of three men—Thomas Graham, Wharton Jones and William Sharpey, all of whom had studied medicine at Edinburgh. On the advice of Professor Sharpey, Lister had come, at the age of twenty-six, to spend a short period in attending the surgical clinic of Professor Syme at Edinburgh. From 1853, however, he remained, first as house surgeon with Syme, and afterwards as an Extra-academical Lecturer on Surgery; and he did not leave Edinburgh until 1860, on his appointment as Professor of Systematic Surgery at Glasgow.

The value of the influence exercised by contact with students upon the mind of a teacher is emphasised by Lister in the letter given in facsimile on pages 316-318, where he says: "It was thanks to its" (Edinburgh University's) "very liberal and wise policy regarding the extra-academical school that I was induced to teach Surgery when a very young man; and this led to my work on Inflammation which was the essential preliminary to that of the Antiseptic Principle." For five years he was a successful lecturer on Surgery outside the University.

During this first Edinburgh period, he was actively assisting Syme in his operations and in teaching the class of Clinical Surgery, as well as in writing weekly summaries of Syme's clinical lectures, and in preparing records of Syme's cases for the press. Some of the important work on physiological subjects, to which he devoted much attention in his earlier days, was also done during this period, such as a paper read before the Royal Society of Edinburgh, in 1856, on "The Minute Structure of Involuntary Muscular Fibre," and his celebrated investigation regarding the nature of inflammation, upon which three papers were read, in 1867, before the Royal Society, London. Experiments upon the coagulation of the blood occupied him in 1856 and, in 1858, he read a paper on "Spontaneous Gangrene" before the Medico-Chirurgical Society of Edinburgh.

After ten years in the professorship at Glasgow, where the earlier experiments on antiseptic surgery and its practice were carried out, Lister, on the retirement of Syme from the Chair of Clinical Surgery, returned to Edinburgh in October 1869, as his successor. In the Royal Infirmary fifty beds were allotted to his charge, situated in that part of the building which had previously been the High School, and which still stands facing the lower end of Infirmary Street. During the earlier part of this second Edinburgh period, two important modifications of the antiseptic treatment were introduced; one of these was the substitution of a gauze dressing for the plaster containing carbolic acid and other antiseptics, with which he had previously covered the operation wounds. This was a muslin gauze impregnated with a mixture of resin, paraffin and carbolic acid, which, however, he subsequently replaced by gauze charged with double cyanide of mercury and zinc. The other important modification which he introduced at this time was the spray; this apparatus was intended to create an antiseptic atmosphere surrounding the wound in all directions. The spray-producer, used at first as a small instrument worked by a hand-bulb, went through rapid development, and the spray was ultimately produced by steam. It was first recommended publicly by Lister at a British Medical Association meeting in 1871, and he continued to employ it until 1887, although it was earlier abandoned by other surgeons. He also introduced, in 1871, the use of boracic acid as an antiseptic.

Speaking in 1875 at the opening of the Surgical Section of the British Medical Association meeting at Edinburgh, Lister was able to say "Six years ago" (*i.e.*, in the course of his introductory lecture as Professor of Clinical Surgery at Edinburgh), "when writing on the very remarkable improvement which had been brought about by 'enforcing strict

LORD LISTER, O.M.

Regius Professor of Clinical Surgery
1869-1877

attention to the antiseptic principle' in the wards of which I had charge in the Glasgow Royal Infirmary, 'converting them from some of the most unhealthy in the kingdom into models of healthiness,' I ventured to express myself thus: 'Considering the circumstances of those wards, it seems hardly too much to expect that the same beneficent change which passed over them will take place in all surgical hospitals, when the principle shall be similarly recognised and acted on by the profession generally.' That prediction, I think I may say, is now in course of fulfilment."

Speaking of Lister's work at Edinburgh, the present incumbent of the Chair of Clinical Surgery, John Fraser, said: "Surgery tolerated the incubus of infection, unable to apply in its own field the discoveries which the sciences were beginning to announce. Cribbed, cabined and confined, there could be no real progress in surgical art so long as men worked under the shadow of an ever-threatening disaster. With the golden key of genius, Lister unlocked the gates which had never hitherto been opened, and the stream thus released is now a torrent of great volume, carrying our art to regions which time alone can reveal."

In 1877, when Lister was in his fiftieth year, Sir William Fergusson, Professor of Clinical Surgery at King's College, London, died, and his Chair was offered to Lister. Although attempts were made to retain him in Edinburgh, as, for example, by a petition signed by about 700 medical students, he severed his connection with the Edinburgh Chair of Clinical Surgery at the end of the winter session 1876-77.

On his retirement, the Chair was filled by the appointment of Thomas Annandale, who had been assistant to Syme, and a successful Extra-academical Lecturer on Surgery. Annandale was a surgeon of great manipulative skill, possessed of a charming personality and sympathetic nature. Upon his death the Chair was filled, in 1908, by the appointment of Francis Mitchell Caird, who had been a highly successful lecturer on Surgery from 1887. Caird had graduated in 1877, and in the next ten years he had paid many visits to Continental schools of surgery. At this period, thanks largely to Lister's work, the performance of abdominal operations had become safer than ever before, and several Continental surgeons, such as Billroth of Vienna and Mikulicz of Breslau, were now performing with great frequency and success numerous operations upon the stomach and intestinal canal. Caird, influenced by the study of their work, was performing gastric and intestinal operations at an earlier date and on a larger scale than any of his colleagues in Edinburgh.

The development of abdominal surgery in Edinburgh at an earlier date than elsewhere in Britain, was mainly due to him, and many surgeons of a later period, who were his pupils, owed much to his precept and training. He was a prolific contributor to current medical literature and in this way exercised a great influence on the practice of surgery outside Edinburgh; especially valuable were several comprehensive papers which he published, giving the results of a long series of cases such, for example, as on the results of operations for perforated gastric ulcer; of excision of the rectum for carcinoma, and of excision of the tongue for cancer. His most generally known work was the *Surgical Handbook*, which he published in collaboration with C. W. Cathcart, and which passed through many editions.

On his retirement in 1919, he was succeeded in the Chair of Clinical Surgery, by Harold Jalland (later Sir Harold) Stiles. When the latter retired in 1925, his successor in the Chair was John Fraser.

Among other Edinburgh surgeons of this period who lectured on surgery and clinical surgery in the Extra-academical School should be mentioned: Joseph Bell, Sir Patrick Heron Watson (who in early life had served in the Crimea), P. H. Maclaren, John Duncan, A. G. Miller, C. W. MacGillivray, C. W. Cathcart, Sir Montagu Cotterill, Alexander Miles, Sir James W. B. Hodsdon, Sir David Wallace (who organised the activities of the Red Cross in the East of Scotland during the war), J. W. Dowden, A. A. Scot-Skirving, George Chiene, W. J. Stuart, J. W. Struthers, and Henry Wade.

FACULTY OF MEDICINE

MIDWIFERY

It is a noteworthy fact that in the year 1726 when John Rutherford and Andrew St Clair began assiduously to teach medicine, the Town Council made, in the person of Joseph Gibson, the first appointment of a Professor of Midwifery in Britain. He was succeeded by Robert Smith in 1739, Thomas Young in 1756, Alexander Hamilton in 1780, James Hamilton in 1800, and Sir James Young Simpson in 1840. It is remarkable that the class of Midwifery did not become compulsory for students until 1833, after great exertion and legal action by James Hamilton, the Professor.

The Maternity Hospital of the present day had its origin in the attic storey of the old Royal Infirmary which, under Professor Thomas Young, early in the eighteenth century, had been devoted by the Managers of this Institution to the treatment of lying-in women. Here practical instruction in obstetrics was given by Young and by Alexander Hamilton who, towards the close of that century, took over Park House, on the site of the present University Union, as a private hospital for this purpose. This continued for some forty years to be the maternity hospital under the latter's son, Professor James Hamilton. After his death, the Institution assumed a more public character as the Royal Maternity Hospital, and through various transfers was situated successively in St John Street, Milton House, Minto House and Chapel House. For two years, 1872-74, the Managers of the Royal Infirmary accommodated it in the Watson's Hospital building before this was used as the new Infirmary. Once again, 1874-79, it moved to St John Street, but in the latter year the present Royal Maternity and Simpson Memorial Hospital was opened in Lauriston for the reception of patients and as a permanent memorial to Sir James Young Simpson. Here it has continued to the present time, but the scheme has now been carried through for its reception, for the third time, under the management of the Royal Infirmary. It can be readily understood that, after more than half a century of service, the building has become out-of-date and insufficient in accommodation. The necessity for more beds is indicated by the fact that while the cases treated in this hospital in 1870 numbered 489, in 1923 they had risen to 1852.

In the Chair of Midwifery in the University, Sir James Young Simpson, on his death in 1870, was succeeded by his nephew, Alexander (later Sir Alexander) Russell Simpson. He was a voluminous contributor to medical journals, a skilful operator and a successful lecturer, dealing in his lectures with the subjects both of Obstetrics and Gynæcology. On his retirement, in 1905, John (later Sir John) Halliday Croom was elected to the Chair of Midwifery. He had for many years delivered in the Extra-academical School a summer course of fifty lectures on Midwifery, but he had not dealt with Gynæcology, and when he was appointed Professor of Midwifery, the University Court elected Alexander Hugh Freeland Barbour as Lecturer in Gynæcology.

When Croom and Barbour retired from their respective posts, in 1922, the two subjects were again conjoined, and Benjamin Philp Watson was appointed Professor of Midwifery and Gynæcology; upon his resignation, in 1926, to take up a similar post at Columbia University, New York, he was succeeded in the Chair by Robert William Johnstone.

Sir James Young Simpson, by his recognised skill in practice, his association with the introduction of anæsthetics, his outstanding position in the literary and social world, and the many advances he made in relation to diseases of women, had raised the Edinburgh School of Obstetrics and Gynæcology to great eminence. This prominent position of the School was maintained by a number of his successors. Sir John Halliday Croom had attained great fame as a lecturer before he was appointed to the Chair. Almost every student of Medicine at Edinburgh attended his summer course of lectures as a preparation for the cases which were requisite before presenting themselves for examination. He took immense pains in the preparation of every lecture that he delivered, and he was celebrated rather for his lecturing than for his publications on the subject of Obstetrics. A. H. Freeland Barbour had attained great success as an Extra-academical Lecturer in Gynæcology before he was appointed to this post in the University; but he had also gained a world-wide reputation by some of his publications, especially by the *Manual of Gynæcology,* written in conjunction with Dr Berry Hart. He had also published a well-known *Atlas of the Anatomy of Labour,* which formed the foundation for much subsequent research in pelvic anatomy and in the pathology of labour.

A teacher of still wider fame was David Berry Hart who, after graduation, had been for a time Assistant to Professor A. R. Simpson and afterwards an Extra-academical Lecturer in Midwifery. In 1880 he published, as a result of research work, *The Structural Anatomy of the Female Pelvic Floor.* This was of the greatest importance in throwing light, where medical ideas had previously been confused, upon the behaviour of the pelvic floor in various physiological conditions, including labour, especially in the explanation of the true nature of prolapsus uteri, or, as he named it, sacro-pubic hernia; in elucidating the mode of action of the Sims's speculum; and in rendering possible the modern method of examination of the bladder by cystoscopy. Hart also introduced the method of investigating various problems of obstetrics by means of large frozen sections. In 1882 he published, along with Barbour, *A Manual of Gynæcology,* which for a generation was the chief text-book on this subject used throughout the English-speaking world. It passed through many editions, was translated into several foreign languages, and raised the fame of the Edinburgh School of Medicine to a high level in the new specialty of Scientific Gynæcology. It has been described as "a model for all time in the precision of its language, in the accuracy of its references, in the appreciation of the work of others, and in the restraint of its opinions." Hart, in addition to being an Extra-academical Lecturer, was Physician to the Royal Maternity Hospital and Gynæcologist to the Royal Infirmary. He was the first operator in Scotland to perform successfully the operation of abdominal section for ruptured tubal pregnancy, although his fame depended more upon his expert scientific investigations than upon his skill as a surgeon. He also published several general works, such as *Some Phases of Evolution and Heredity*, which attracted great attention on its publication, in 1910, and *A Guide to Midwifery*.

Robert Milne Murray, who was for a time Assistant to Halliday Croom, became a successful lecturer on, and practitioner of, Midwifery in the last twenty years of the nineteenth century. His name is specially associated with the mechanical and mathematical investigations which led to a modification of the midwifery forceps by the principle which he introduced of axis-traction. Sir Alexander Simpson also introduced a slightly modified form of forceps on the same principle. Milne Murray was further distinguished for his knowledge of electricity in its practical applications, and he constructed several pieces of electrical apparatus which were much used in medicine.

Another department of obstetric medicine which was initiated at Edinburgh, and which has come to occupy an important position all over the world, is especially associated with the name of John William Ballantyne. This concerns the care of the expectant mother before the birth of the child, and has resulted in the wide development of antenatal clinics. Ballantyne was for some years Assistant to Professor A. R. Simpson, and, in 1889, presented a thesis for the M.D. Degree on "Some Anatomical and Pathological Conditions of the New-born Infant in their Relation to Obstetrics." He devoted a great part of his subsequent attention to this subject, and his volumes on *Diseases of the Fœtus* and *Antenatal Pathology and Hygiene* became standard works. By constantly speaking and writing on this subject, he gradually impressed the medical profession with his views regarding the importance of antenatal pathology and the necessity for antenatal care, and he was the first physician in Great Britain to establish a clinic for antenatal supervision of expectant mothers. Referring to maternity clinics, he wrote: "It must never be forgotten that the chief, almost the only, purpose of these pregnancy clinics in maternity centres is to detect signs of impending danger, and to prevent their maturing. . . . They are as listening-posts for the recognition of the slightest whisper of danger." His advocacy of this subject was recognised when a bed for this purpose was endowed, in 1901, in the Royal Maternity Hospital. The antenatal department was later, in 1915, established in this hospital under his charge.

The Edinburgh School in the early part of the twentieth century exerted a wide influence upon the development of Obstetrics and Gynæcology in other places, both through the publications of its lecturers, which have been mentioned, and also by the teaching of men who were trained in it, and who afterwards took up teaching posts in other schools. Among these may be mentioned Professors William Stephenson at Aberdeen, Clarence Webster at Chicago, W. W. Chipman at Montreal, B. P. Watson at New York and John McGibbon at St Andrews.

CLINICAL TEACHING IN THE ROYAL INFIRMARY

The old Infirmary, part of which had been completed in 1741 and which was associated with the work of Liston, Syme, and other celebrated older surgeons, and more recently with that of Lister, had become unsuitable after more than a century of occupation. Accordingly a new site on the grounds of George Watson's Hospital in Lauriston Place was obtained, and the new Infirmary was opened on 29th October 1879 for the reception of patients. The old buildings in Infirmary Street were sold to the Corporation of the City for a fever hospital. The original "medical house" was demolished, but the surgical part of the old Infirmary continued to be used as the City Hospital for Infectious Diseases until 1903, when the new City Hospital at Colinton Mains was opened. In the same year that the new Royal Infirmary was opened, the Royal Maternity and Simpson Memorial Hospital was erected in Lauriston Place, thus giving wider scope for the treatment of maternity cases and the teaching of obstetrics.

It was fitting and convenient that when the University New Buildings for medical classes were begun in 1878, these should have been erected in immediate juxtaposition to the new Infirmary buildings. It may be mentioned in passing that when the agitation for a new Infirmary, and for increased medical accommodation began about 1869, the number of students in the University had risen to 1500, and that of professors to 33, while there were only 17 class-rooms available for their use. When the University New Buildings, therefore, were in full occupation after the Tercentenary of 1884, great possibilities for the further development of the Medical School of the University were opened up.

The Royal Infirmary in the past fifty years has continued to expand in size and to develop in equipment. In accordance with the widening of medical knowledge, the most noteworthy feature in this, as in other great hospitals, has been the evolution of special departments. The physicians and surgeons connected with these departments have, in general, begun to lecture on their special subjects in the Extra-academical School, and have later, in some cases, been absorbed into the University as lecturers. The earliest of these special departments was that of Ophthalmology, as, at Edinburgh, diseases of the eye had attracted the attention of several surgeons at an early date. This subject had received a great impetus through the invention of the ophthalmoscope by Helmholtz, and the introduction of new operations on the eye by von Graefe, shortly after the year 1850. The Managers of the Royal Infirmary had, in 1855, appointed William Walker, the first ophthalmic surgeon on the staff of this Institution, and he had been succeeded in this post by D. M. C. L. Argyll Robertson. By Argyll Robertson's discovery, about 1870, of the peculiar reactions of the iris in certain spinal diseases, the condition of the pupil called after him has become as classic a name in medicine as Bright's disease, or Pott's curvature of the spine. After lecturing on Ophthalmology for twenty years in the Extra-academical School, Argyll Robertson was appointed, in 1883, Lecturer in Diseases of the Eye to the University. In the same year George (later Sir George) Andreas Berry, who afterwards represented the University in Parliament, commenced to lecture on Diseases of the Eye in the Extra-academical School, and, in 1896, succeeded Argyll Robertson as lecturer upon this subject in the University. Later lecturers were George Mackay, William G. Sym, James V. Paterson, Arthur H. H. Sinclair, Harry M. Traquair and Ernest Hugh Cameron.

The teaching of Mental Diseases had, as mentioned elsewhere (p. 153), attracted attention at Edinburgh earlier than at any other medical school of Britain, and the first lecturer in a special department of Medicine had been created by the University, in 1879, in the person of Thomas (later Sir Thomas) Smith Clouston. This Lectureship naturally developed, not in connection with the Royal Infirmary, but with the Royal Asylum at Morningside, and its subsequent development is mentioned elsewhere (p. 154). Clouston and Argyll Robertson were the first two University lecturers on medical subjects, and these Lectureships were already in existence at the time of the Tercentenary celebration.

Diseases of Children formed the next subject to receive recognition from the University by a Lectureship. There had previously been in the Extra-academical School a long succession of lecturers on this subject, who had been members of the staff of the Royal Hospital for Sick Children, and, in 1885, the University appointed James Andrew and James Carmichael, Physicians to this Institution, to be University lecturers, an honorary position which was from 1900 accorded to the whole senior staff of this hospital.

The special department of Diseases peculiar to Women and Children had from an early date received attention from lecturers in the Extra-academical School, and, so far back as 1851, Alexander Keiller, one of the ordinary Physicians to the Royal Infirmary, had arranged with his colleagues that he should institute a course of clinical teaching on the diseases of women. A few years later, an extra ward was set apart for Keiller's course on this subject. James Matthews Duncan had been definitely appointed Physician for Diseases of Women to the Royal Infirmary in 1861, and, in 1870, Thomas Keith, who had attained great eminence for his special operation of ovariotomy, was appointed Extra Surgeon for Ovarian

Disease to the Royal Infirmary, a post which he retained till 1888.

From about 1875, the Professor of Midwifery in the University was regarded as one of the Professors of Clinical Medicine, and was given charge of half a ward in the Royal Infirmary for patients suffering from diseases peculiar to women. Till the Gynæcological department of the Hospital was opened in 1900 it was the practice of the Managers to place one half ward, devoted to this purpose, under the charge of the Professor of Midwifery in the University, and another half ward, shared with one of the ordinary Physicians, under the charge of an Extra-academical Lecturer in Gynæcology. In 1905, when Professor A. R. Simpson resigned the Chair, the University appointed a Lecturer in Systematic and Clinical Gynæcology in the person of A. H. F. Barbour, separating Gynæcology from the duties of the Midwifery Chair, which was now occupied by Sir John Halliday Croom. When the latter resigned in 1922, and was succeeded by Benjamin Philp Watson, the two subjects were again united, and the Lectureship in Gynæcology in the University was abolished.

Mention should also be made of Angus Macdonald, Nathaniel T. Brewis, James Haig Ferguson, William Fordyce, James Young, Hugh S. Davidson and W. F. Theodore Haultain, who have acted as gynæcologists to the Royal Infirmary and taught this subject.

A special department in Diseases of the Ear and Throat was constituted by the Royal Infirmary, in 1883, with Peter McBride as Surgeon to this department and, in 1897, he was appointed a Lecturer in the University in Diseases of the Nose and Throat. He was succeeded by Robert McKenzie Johnston in 1903. Later teachers of the subject were A. Logan Turner, John Malcolm Farquharson, John S. Fraser, and John D. Lithgow.

The next institution of a special department by the Royal Infirmary was in 1884, when a department for Diseases of the Skin was opened, with William Allan Jamieson placed in charge of it. Since 1878 he had been lecturing on this subject in the Extra-academical School and, in 1899, he was appointed Lecturer in Diseases of the Skin to the University. He was succeeded in charge of wards and as lecturer by Norman (later Sir Norman) Purvis Walker in 1906, and he, in turn, by Frederick Gardiner, who had been junior physician since 1912, and by Robert Cranston Low in 1924.

A department of the Royal Infirmary which was initiated and has undergone great development within the past fifty years is that connected with the application of electricity in medicine. This therapeutic agent had gained prominence in France about 1850 and, in 1884, was attracting special attention on account of its use against uterine diseases and tumours by Apostoli in Paris. At Edinburgh the subject was taken up with enthusiasm by R. Milne Murray, who began a course of extra-academical lectures in 1866; he devised a considerable amount of electrical apparatus that was extensively used in the Royal Infirmary and elsewhere. In 1896 the Managers of the Royal Infirmary established an Electrical department, to which Milne Murray was appointed medical electrician, with Dawson F. D. Turner as assistant medical electrician. When Milne Murray was appointed to the gynæcological staff of the Institution in 1901, Dawson Turner succeeded him as medical electrician, with William Hope-Fowler and, shortly afterwards, Archibald McKendrick as assistants. Dawson Turner had been one of the first persons in this country to recognise the importance to Medicine of the Röntgen rays discovered about 1893, and his private installation, set up, in 1896, at his house in George Square, was the first of its kind in Edinburgh. In 1898, when radium was discovered, he at once secured a specimen, and for some years this was the only supply in Edinburgh, for medical purposes, which he placed at the disposal of the Royal Infirmary for the treatment of patients. From these small beginnings the Radiological and Radium departments of the Infirmary rapidly developed, and, in 1925, a new department was built and equipped by the Managers at a cost of about £50,000. This included a very completely equipped and staffed department for electrotherapy and massage. At this stage a whole-time Radiologist was appointed to the Institution in the person of John Miller Woodburn Morison, who held this appointment conjointly with that of Lecturer in Radiology in the University. He was succeeded in 1930 by J. Duncan White.

The physicians to the Royal Infirmary during this period who shared in the teaching of clinical medicine, and who have not been mentioned in some other connection, included the following: Claud Muirhead, D. J. Brakenridge, Andrew Smart, D. Chalmers Watson, Edwin Matthew, John Eason and Alexander Goodall.

The arrangements for clinical teaching in the Royal Infirmary have undergone considerable change during recent years.

The Corporations of Physicians and Surgeons of Edinburgh had been chiefly instrumental in the foundation of the Infirmary and, from an early period in its history, the Managers had resolved that only members of these bodies should be appointed to its staff. Before the end of the eighteenth century permission had been given first to the clinical professors and later to all the physicians and surgeons of the staff to deliver clinical lectures on the patients.

About the middle of the nineteenth century, the Physicians-in-Ordinary combined to give a joint course in Clinical Medicine and, as this proved very successful, a similar arrangement was later adopted between the various professors holding wards in the Infirmary. There thus existed for many years a University class and an Extra-academical class of Clinical Medicine. The same practice did not grow up on the surgical side where the surgeons continued to teach individually.

In 1913 an agreement was drawn up between the University Court and the Managers of the Royal Infirmary regarding clinical arrangements and Pathology as taught in the latter Institution. At this time certain changes, to which reference has already been made, were in contemplation regarding the appointment of a Professor of Clinical Medicine, the division of the Chair of Materia Medica, and the re-arrangement of the duties carried out by the Professor of Pathology. By this agreement it was proposed that the four senior ordinary physicians in charge of wards in the Royal Infirmary should, during their tenure of office, be appointed Senior Lecturers in Clinical Medicine in the University, while the assistant physicians should be appointed Lecturers in Clinical Medicine. This had, among other results, the effect of bringing to an end the competition of the class conducted by the Physicians-in-Ordinary with the University class.

With regard to Clinical Surgery, it was proposed that the four senior ordinary surgeons should similarly be appointed Senior Lecturers in Clinical Surgery in the University, and that the assistant surgeons should be Lecturers in Clinical Surgery.

It was further proposed that Clinical Gynæcology should be dissociated from Clinical Medicine and should form a separate department; as prior to this time the Professor of Midwifery and the Ordinary Physician for diseases peculiar to women had lectured in rotation with their colleagues in the University and Extra-academical classes of Clinical Medicine respectively.

With regard to remuneration for teaching, the general arrangement was that in each of these three departments, after deduction of a sum representing the amount of fees previously received by the clinical professors and certain other charges, the fees received from students should be divided among the senior lecturers, while the assistants in the various departments were to be paid honoraria by the University.

In the case of Pathology, it was arranged that the Professor of this subject, who now ceased to have charge of wards, should be appointed by the Managers Consultant Pathologist to the Infirmary, and that the Acting Pathologist to the Infirmary should be appointed Lecturer in Morbid Anatomy to the University.

A supplementary agreement, mainly necessitated by the introduction of facilities for the clinical teaching of women students, was drawn up, in 1917, between the University Court and the Managers of the Royal Infirmary.

Partly on account of changing circumstances, and partly because these agreements were found to have been ill-considered, they became gradually more irksome, and, by 1928, it was found necessary to discontinue the existing arrangement; and two new agreements were drawn up in 1929 between the Managers on the one hand and the University Court and the Governing Board of the School of Medicine of the Royal Colleges, as separate parties, on the other hand, with a proviso that these agreements should, at the request of either party, be reconsidered every five years. The arrangement in the agreement of 1913 that the members of the honorary staff, other than Professors, should be appointed by the Managers of the Infirmary on the nomination of a clinical committee of the Board was renewed.

This Clinical Committee consists of seven members of the Board of the Royal Infirmary, namely: the two members representing the University; one of the two members representing the Royal College of Physicians; one of the two members representing the Royal College of Surgeons; the representative of the College of Justice (chairman of the committee); and two other members of the Board. A Joint Committee of the University and Royal Infirmary was again set up for nomination of the Clinical Professors, whose election lies with the University Court (Clinical Medicine and Therapeutics); the Joint Committee consists of seven members, namely, the Principal of the University (chairman), three members appointed by the University Court, and three members appointed by the Board of the Royal Infirmary.

Clinical Boards from the staff in each of the Infirmary departments were also instituted for the purpose of regulating the conduct of study and similar objects.

The important principle was reaffirmed that there should be equality of status as between all physicians and surgeons, including the Professors, with precedence within the Infirmary in the order of seniority of appointment to that Institution.

With regard to finance, it was arranged that the fees of University students should be collected by the University; of students in the School of Medicine of the Royal Colleges by the School; and in the case of unattached students by the Infirmary, and that the total fees, along with a sum of £2500 paid by the University, should be placed in an Infirmary clinical account which, subject to certain deductions for the payment of honoraria to assistant physicians and surgeons, salaries to clinical tutors, and honoraria to examiners, should be divided equally in respect of all physicians and surgeons in the various departments. The provisions contained in these new agreements have greatly simplified the clinical teaching.

PSYCHIATRY

The subject of the treatment of mental disorder has always been regarded with special interest in Scotland, and many of the most noteworthy developments in this department of medicine have originated in this country. A course of lectures on Mental Diseases was commenced by Alexander (later Sir Alexander) Morison, in 1823, and this, the first course on the subject in Britain, was continued annually by him for a period of thirty years. When he retired, in 1852, the lectures were delivered by David Skae, Physician-Superintendent of the Royal Edinburgh Asylum at Morningside, under the supervision of the Royal College of Physicians of Edinburgh, and were given annually till his death twenty years later. After the death of Skae, in 1873, a similar arrangement was made by his successor in the asylum, T. S. Clouston. The Commissioners appointed under the Universities (Scotland) Act, 1858, had recommended that lectureships in Mental Diseases should be established in connection with the Medical Schools at Glasgow, Aberdeen, and Edinburgh, and, in 1879, the Senatus of the University of Edinburgh was the first to resolve that it was desirable to institute in the University a Lectureship in Mental Diseases. To this post Thomas (later Sir Thomas) Clouston was appointed. It may be remarked in passing that John Conolly, who did much to advance the humane treatment of the insane in the early part of the nineteenth century, had been a student at Edinburgh immediately after the opening of the Royal Edinburgh Asylum at Morningside, and that his graduation thesis had dealt with *The State of the Mind in Insanity and Melancholia.*

Sir Thomas Clouston held the Lectureship in Mental Diseases till 1910, when he was succeeded as Physician-Superintendent of the Royal Edinburgh Asylum and as Lecturer in Mental Diseases in the University by George Matthew Robertson. The increasing social importance of mental disease and the great development in its treatment led the Managers of the Royal Edinburgh Asylum to consider the desirability of instituting a Professorship in this subject. They accordingly presented the University with £10,000 on condition that the Professor of Psychiatry in the University and the Physician-Superintendent of the Royal Edinburgh Asylum should be the same person. To this post G. M. Robertson, who was already Physician-Superintendent of the asylum, was appointed, in 1919, and the arrangements were made that in future appointments the occupant of the combined post would be selected by a conjoint committee of the Managers of the Asylum and of the University representatives. On Professor Robertson's death in 1932, he was succeeded by David Kennedy Henderson.

The provision of this Chair has given a great stimulus to the study of Psychiatry by indicating its importance both to the public and to the medical student. The course for students now extends to fifty hours, embracing lectures on psychology and on mental disorders as well as clinical instruction in the Asylum, of which the name is now altered to the Royal Edinburgh Hospital for Mental and Nervous Disorders. It is the most complete course on this subject in Britain. A Diploma in Psychiatry was also instituted, in 1911, for graduates in Medicine. This Chair, since its institution, has attracted bequests, such as the Ryder bequest of £5300 by means of which the work of the department has been greatly improved, and the Walter Kay bequest of £4557 to the Chair for research purposes.

Important developments, both in the treatment of the mentally afflicted, and in the teaching of insanity, were instituted by Robertson. He was the principal leader in Britain in the hospitalisation of asylums for the insane, which had been begun by his predecessor, Sir Thomas Clouston, before 1892. Eight nursing homes for early mental cases were established in connection with the mental hospital, and were quickly imitated in other places. Jordanburn Nerve Hospital was organised for the treatment of the same type of case among the poorer classes of the community, and this hospital, together with the West House Hospital, provided clinical cases for the University class in Mental Diseases, and for an elaborate course of instruction extending over two terms, which was arranged there by Professor Robertson. A juvenile clinic was also established at Jordanburn Hospital by Professor Robertson in association with the Professor of Psychology, and this also has become a valuable factor in teaching.

CHILD LIFE AND HEALTH

The subject of disease in children as one requiring special consideration began to attract attention about the middle of the nineteenth century, and by 1860, as the result largely of an appeal by *The Scotsman*, a small hospital with 24 cots was opened in Lauriston Lane. In 1870 the accommodation of this hospital for sick children was increased to 72 beds, and a surgical department was inaugurated there, in 1887, under the care of Joseph Bell. The building of the present Sick Children's Hospital at Sciennes Road was commenced in 1890. From an earlier date the diseases of women and children had been included in the Obstetric course of Professor Alexander Hamilton and his successors, and in the 'sixties regular courses on this subject were given at Edinburgh by A. Keiller, T. Grainger Stewart, and William Stephenson. They were followed by a succession of lecturers in the Extra-academical School who were Physicians to the Royal Edinburgh Hospital for Sick Children and, in 1885, the subject was recognised by the University, James Andrew and James Carmichael, who were then physicians to this hospital, being appointed University lecturers in the subject.

The most celebrated of these was John Thomson, who began to lecture on diseases of children in 1891, and who perhaps did more than any other physician of his time to encourage the study of diseases peculiar to children, or showing characteristic differences when they occurred in early life. In 1898, he published one of the earliest text-books on this subject in his *Guide to the Clinical Study and Treatment of Sick Children*, a book which went through four editions and was translated into French and Spanish.

He also did much to further the interest which was arising about this time in a subject that recently has attracted much public attention, that of mental defect in children. His work, entitled *Opening Doors*, which he described as being "for the mothers of babies who are long in learning to behave like other children of their age," attracted great attention, and the notice of the medical profession was directed for the first time by him to several diseases occurring in children which up to that time had been little known.

In 1930, the trustees of the late Edward Clark, printer in Edinburgh, intimated to the University Court that they had decided to make a grant to the University out of the residue of the trust estate of the sum of £15,000 as an endowment for the foundation of a Chair in the subject of Child Life and Health. The University accordingly drew up regulations for the establishment of a Chair in this subject, with a salary of £600 per annum. To this post Charles McNeil, Physician to the Royal Edinburgh Hospital for Sick Children, was appointed.

TUBERCULOSIS

An important development of Edinburgh medicine in the later part of the nineteenth century was that connected with the control of tuberculosis. The Victoria Dispensary for diseases of the chest was established at 13 Bank Street, Edinburgh, by Robert (later Sir Robert) W. Philip, in November 1887, some five years after Koch's discovery of the bacillus responsible for tuberculosis. This dispensary aimed at the detection of the disease with its treatment and prevention in other members of the families of the affected persons. After a period of growing activity and usefulness, the dispensary was removed, in 1891, to 26 Lauriston Place, and at the same time the important step was introduced of visiting patients in their own homes, so as to trace other infected cases at an early stage among those who had come into contact with the patients. This principle has been followed in other tuberculosis dispensaries established in Britain and other countries, and has undoubtedly had a great effect both in the prevention and in the early diagnosis of infection, and has been largely responsible for the diminution of pulmonary tuberculosis in recent years.

In 1894 the further step was taken of securing Craigleith House, on the north side of the city, as a hospital for tuberculosis, which was named the Royal Victoria Hospital; in 1911, the increase in the dispensary's activity led to its removal to the large building which it now occupies in Spittal Street.

By this time 7000 visits were being paid annually by doctors and nurses to tuberculous families. This system of tuberculosis control was adopted by the Local Government Boards in Great Britain and Ireland, and became, in 1912, the accepted basis for that part of the National Insurance Act of 1911 which dealt with tuberculosis benefit. The Edinburgh organisation that had been erected by Sir Robert Philip, including a farm colony at Lasswade, which had been added to it in 1910, was accordingly taken over by the Corporation of Edinburgh in 1914. The Tuberculosis Trust had meantime been set up to continue the remaining duties of the former tuberculosis committee, and continued its activities by the establishment of a sanatorium colony at Southfield, and by other measures.

In the summer of 1914, this Trust approached the University with a proposal to found a Chair or Lectureship, and as a result handed over a capital sum of £18,000 to the University Court, along with the facilities which its various institutions could provide for teaching and research. In December 1917, the Chair of Tuberculosis was finally established, and Sir Robert Philip was elected as Professor of Tuberculosis in this the first Chair of its kind within the British Empire.

APPOINTMENT OF LECTURERS AND INSTITUTION OF LECTURESHIPS

About 1894 the University Court introduced the principle of conferring upon the chief assistant in each department the status of Lecturer upon some subject included in the duties of the Chair to which he was attached. In addition, lectureships were instituted in special subjects in which instruction and research were desirable. In 1894 the appointment was made of a Lecturer in Anatomy in the person of David Hepburn who, in 1903, became Professor of Anatomy at Cardiff; E. B. Jamieson then became the Lecturer.

In 1898 a Lectureship in Tropical Diseases was established and Andrew Davidson was made Lecturer. He also taught in the Extra-academical School in succession to E. W. Felkin. Davidson was followed in the University Lectureship by Major D. G. Marshall, I.M.S., and he, in turn, in 1924 by Lieut.-Col. E. D. W. Greig, I.M.S. In order to bring the lecturer into closer relation with clinical work the Managers of the Royal Infirmary, in 1930, made Greig Physician-Consultant on Diseases of Tropical Climates to that Institution.

A Lecturer in Applied Anatomy was appointed in 1903 with the object of bringing human anatomy into closer relationship with clinical surgery. Harold J. Stiles was elected to this post. When he became Professor of Clinical Surgery in 1919, Francis E. Jardine succeeded him as Lecturer in Applied Anatomy.

In 1904 a Lecturer in Infective Diseases was appointed by the University. It had been the practice up to this time of the senior visiting physician at the old fever hospital to deliver a clinical course on Infective Diseases to students in their final year. When the new Fever Hospital at Colinton Mains was erected it was felt that the time had come to appoint a Lecturer, and Sir James O. Affleck was elected. He was succeeded, in 1908, by Alexander James and by Claude B. Ker, Superintendent of the Hospital; upon the death of the latter, in 1925, Walter T. Benson, his successor as Superintendent, was appointed to the post.

In 1907 a Lectureship in the History of Medicine was established, it being the first Lectureship on this subject at any British University, and, in 1908, John D. Comrie was appointed to the post.

In 1912 it was decided to appoint a Lecturer in Neurology, and to this post J. J. Graham Brown was elected. He held it until 1920, when he was succeeded by Edwin Bramwell, who held the office till his election to the Chair of Clinical Medicine. In 1913, A. Ninian Bruce was made a Lecturer in Neurology within the department of Physiology.

In the same year Harry Rainy was made Lecturer in Physical Therapeutics, holding the appointment until 1920. There was no further appointment as Jonathan Campbell Meakins had, in 1919, been called to the newly established Chair of Therapeutics.

In 1913 the separation of Pathology from Clinical Medicine had been effected, and James Lorrain Smith, appointed Professor of Pathology in the preceding year, not having charge of wards in the Royal Infirmary as his predecessors had, became a consulting pathologist to this Institution. A Lecturer in Morbid Anatomy was accordingly appointed to be the acting head of the Pathological department in the Infirmary, and Theodore Shennan, who was already a Lecturer in the Extra-academical School, and who subsequently became Professor of Pathology at the University of Aberdeen, was appointed to the post. He was succeeded by W. Alister Alexander, and he in turn, on becoming an Assistant Physician to the Infirmary, by James Davidson.

In 1914 James M. Graham, who had for some years been delivering lectures on Surgical Pathology in connection with the Chair of Surgery, was appointed Lecturer in Surgical Pathology. He was succeeded by J. N. J. Hartley in 1924, and he in turn by K. Paterson Brown in 1928.

In 1916, considerable improvements were effected in the teaching of Clinical Midwifery, in which an extended course was now demanded of students, and the members of the staff of the Royal Maternity Hospital became Lecturers in Clinical Midwifery.

In 1919 a Lecturer in Venereal Diseases was appointed. A special department had existed in the Infirmary from an early date, and prior to that year the custom had obtained that the junior surgeon of the Institution should take charge of this department. Public attention had been forcibly drawn to their prevalence and to the insufficient treatment which these diseases often received; and after the war the public health departments of cities began to establish clinics for their more effective treatment. As a result a clinic was established in the Royal Infirmary, and at the same time a lecturer, in the person of David Lees, was appointed by the University Court for the instruction of students.

In 1920 the assistants to the Professors in other departments were raised to the status of Lecturers. This concerned the Chairs of Bacteriology, Pathology and Physiology. Lecturers were appointed in Bio-chemistry, Histology, Neurology and Bio-physics, and to the newly-erected Chair of Chemistry in Relation to Medicine.

In 1921 a Lecturer in Public Health was appointed, and James Buchanan Young, who had for many years been carrying out the reporting work which the John Usher Institute of Public Health performed for the Public Health Department, was elected to the post, and, in 1928, was succeeded by Lieut.-Col. John du P. Langrishe.

In 1924 a Lecturer in Neuropathology, who to a certain extent replaced the previous Lecturer in Neurology, was appointed, F. E. Reynolds, formerly Professor of Pathology in the Medical School at Cairo, being assigned to the post; this he held till 1932. In 1927 W. R. D. Fairbairn became Lecturer in the department of Psychology; in 1931 A. Ninian Bruce was made Lecturer in Psychiatry.

In 1925, in consequence of the changes in the teaching of Public Health, a Director of Instruction in Sanitary Administration was established, and William Robertson, Medical Officer of Health for the City, was appointed. In 1930 he was succeeded by John Guy.

In 1928, as increasing importance was becoming attached to diseases of the teeth, a Lecturer was appointed to give instruction in Dental Diseases. In 1928 also, Lecturers were appointed in connection with the Chairs of Therapeutics, Medicine and Surgery.

In 1929 the increasing public recognition of the social importance attaching to the control of mentally defective persons led to the appointment of a Lecturer in Mental Deficiency, Robert D. Clarkson, who for many years had been Superintendent of the Royal Scottish National Institution, Larbert (for mental defectives), being appointed.

In 1930 a Lectureship in Orthopædics was established. The Edinburgh Hospital for Crippled Children was in course of erection at Fairmilehead, and an arrangement was reached between the management of the hospital and the University Court that a conjoint appointment should be made of a surgeon to the hospital and Lecturer in Orthopædics in the University. To this post William A. Cochrane was appointed.

In 1933, Norman M. Dott was made a Lecturer in Neurological Surgery.

THE TEACHING OF WOMEN IN MEDICINE

The admission of women to the study of Medicine at Edinburgh and to graduation in the Faculty involved some friction. Women students of Medicine had nominally been admitted to Edinburgh University in 1869. The immediate difficulties which arose after that time and before 1883 have been described by Sir Alexander Grant in *The Story of the University*. In 1886 the Royal Colleges of Physicians and Surgeons of Edinburgh resolved to admit women to the examination for the Joint Qualification; and, with the help of numerous Extra-academical Lecturers, the School of Medicine for Women was founded. Women were still, however, excluded from classes in the Royal Infirmary, though clinical teaching for them had been provided in Leith Hospital from 1887; it was not till five years later that they were admitted to the clinical classes in the Royal Infirmary. The Universities (Scotland) Act, 1889, had by that time placed women on the same footing with men as regards the degrees in Medicine; and in October 1894, the University announced its determination to admit women forthwith to graduation in the Faculty. There were still some restrictions in regard to the teaching of men and women together, and for a number of years the wards of the Junior Physician and of the Junior Surgeon in the Royal Infirmary were set apart for the instruction of women in separate classes. These restrictions, however, gradually disappeared, and after the war all the physicians and surgeons had clinics for women students in rotation. This arrangement still exists in the surgical wards of the Infirmary; but in the other departments all differences have disappeared, and in all practical matters women are now on the same footing as the men students.

POST-GRADUATE TEACHING IN MEDICINE

An important activity of the Edinburgh Medical School which commenced about the middle of the period under review is that of post-graduate teaching. Individual lecturers had from time to time announced and delivered courses intended for graduates on new or specialised subjects; but before 1905 there had been no attempt to organise any combined course. In that year the University and the School of Medicine of the Royal Colleges agreed to take conjoint action; and a committee of representatives of these two bodies and of the Extra-academical Lecturers was formed which, under the Chairmanship of Professor D. J. Cunningham, drew up the outline of a course to be held in the long vacation. Arrangements were made with the Managers of the Royal Infirmary and of other hospitals, so that the necessary clinical facilities were available to the teachers and graduates attending the classes. This course for general practitioners consisted of clinics, lectures and demonstrations by a large number of the teaching staff in the Edinburgh School of Medicine.

After some years it became apparent that the course should consist of more specialised instruction, and before the war the post-graduate instruction had been divided into a medical and a surgical course during August, and the more general previous course for practitioners during September. The war put an end to these courses for five years and, on its conclusion, a reversion at first took place to the original simple arrangement for instruction, but within a few years the courses reached their present organisation, consisting of (1) a course on obstetrics, gynæcology and diseases of children, intended for practitioners beginning to specialise in these departments; followed by (2) a practitioner's course largely concerned with medicine; and by (3) a general surgical course intended for those commencing to devote special attention to surgery. The post-graduate committee also undertook to give the necessary publicity to special courses organised by individual lecturers, or groups of lecturers, and to provide instruction for graduates who might desire to study at Edinburgh at times other than the long vacation, or who might wish instruction in special branches of Medicine or Surgery.

In addition to these courses, two series of clinics (*a*) in Clinical Surgery and (*b*) in Clinical Medicine were arranged by the post-graduate committee. The surgical clinics are held every day over three terms, all the charges on the surgical side of the Royal Infirmary participating. The medical clinics are at present held during the summer term only, and in these all the charges on the medical side take part.

With regard to the number of graduates attending these courses and clinics, the following are the figures for the year 1930-31, viz.: (1) Obstetrics, Gynæcology and Diseases of Children, 13; (2) Practitioners' course, 28; (3) General Surgical course, 50. The course of surgical clinics showed the following attendance, viz.: Autumn term, 86; Spring term, 84; Summer term, 91. The medical clinics in the summer term were attended by 23. In addition to these, the graduates attending the various courses for limited numbers brought the total for that year up to 442 individuals.

Diplomas which were instituted in Tropical Medicine and Hygiene (1905), Psychiatry (1911), Public Health (1919), Radiology (1926) and Tropical Veterinary Medicine (1930), have attracted graduates in large numbers.

VI

THE FACULTY OF ARTS

No Faculty in the University has passed through a more complete transformation in the past fifty years than the Faculty of Arts. Its curriculum has been twice completely remodelled (by the Arts Ordinances of 1892 and 1908), and the present Arts Degree is hardly recognisable as a descendant of that of 1883; and those more general changes in academic conditions, which have affected the University as a whole, have operated more widely and deeply upon this Faculty than upon any other. Three such epochs stand out as of special importance: the admission of women to study for degrees, by the Commissioners' Ordinance of 1892; the establishment of the Carnegie Trust in 1901; and the Education (Scotland) Act, 1919. Each of these in turn, and in various ways, opened the University gates more widely, and the new influx of students was found to direct itself mainly into the Faculty of Arts. That Faculty has thus been called upon to provide for a multitude of new desires and needs, beyond those that have arisen from the natural development of the departments of learning with which it is specially concerned.

MEN AND WOMEN STUDENTS IN ARTS

To begin with, the changes in the mere number of students matriculated in the Faculty throughout the half-century are sufficiently striking, though it is far from easy to interpret them in relation to the wider developments of the period, educational, economic, social and even political. The old and honourable tradition of the Scottish University, that it draws its students from all classes of the people, has been maintained, but has undergone a significant change. The poor student of the nineteenth century depended mainly upon the self-sacrifice of his family, upon his own efforts to earn money by various kinds of work in his spare time and in vacations, and, if he was fortunate, upon one or other of the fairly numerous bursary foundations, many of them old and most of them small, which Scottish respect for learning and Scottish local or academic patriotism had provided. The poor student of the twentieth century still draws upon these sources, and University officers in the course of their work are constantly coming upon instances of courage, determination and self-denial on the part of parents and other relatives, as well as of students themselves, which show that the old spirit is still alive in Scotland. But in the course of the last generation, very large sums of money, from Mr Andrew Carnegie's great benefaction and from public funds, have been made available, and from these sources the young Scotsman or Scotswoman who can pass the minimum entrance test for a graduation course, but whose own means are insufficient to see him or her through it, can now claim help almost as of right. Within the last year, however, there has been a certain change in this respect. Both the Carnegie Trust and some, at any rate, of the County and Burgh Education Committees have found it necessary to require something more than the minimum entrance qualification of students who are to receive grants from them.

The statistics of enrolment during the half-century may be summarised as follows. During the period, nearly a decade, between the Tercentenary Year 1883-84 and the date when women were first admitted to matriculation—perhaps the most momentous epoch in the history of the University—the number of students matriculating in Arts (all men) fluctuated between about 1150 and about 950, with a tendency to decrease. The decline was hardly more than arrested by the admission of women in 1891-92, and two years later it had apparently become more marked; but this—a drop of about 160—was accounted for by the institution of a separate Faculty of Science, since, hitherto, students reading for the Science Degree, instituted nearly thirty years earlier, had matriculated in Arts, and the new Faculty drew off a number of men almost exactly corresponding to the difference. From about 1902, the Science Faculty began to rise steadily, and by 1913-14 had more than 400 students.

Meanwhile, the contingent of women in Arts was growing. Between 1895 and 1905 it more than doubled its strength, and reached a figure well over 300 in the latter year. The fall in the number of men had apparently ceased by then. In 1906-7, for the first time for nearly twenty years, the Faculty passed the 1000 mark.

The Carnegie Trust had now been at work for a full quinquennium, but so far it did not appear to have been "flooding" the Arts Faculty. During the five years preceding the institution of the Trust (1896-1901) the annual average had been about 800 students; for the next five years it was about 900, of whom less than 400 were Carnegie beneficiaries. It seems, therefore, as if a considerable proportion of those who were availing themselves of the Carnegie benefit were students who would probably have managed to come to the University without it. But from about 1906 to the beginning of the war, the increase became more pronounced. For that period the average annual enrolment was about 1200, and between 700 and 800 of these were Carnegie beneficiaries, divided about equally between the sexes. It follows that a larger proportion of the women than of the men in the Faculty were there with the assistance of the Trust; and this has continued down to the present. For the quinquennium 1925-30, the percentage of Carnegie beneficiaries in the whole number of Arts students was about 40; of the women it was 43, as against 36 of men. The difference is no doubt accounted for by the fact that the proportion of students coming from outside Scotland, and therefore ineligible for Carnegie benefit, is much larger among the men.

In the year 1914-15, when the numbers of men, and to some extent of women also, were affected by the war, there was a sharp decline. The lowest level was reached in 1916-17, with 288 men, most of them lads under age for military service, and 411 women. From 1918-19 the figures for both sexes rose rapidly, those of the men being swollen by the multitudes coming back from the Army to resume their studies. By 1923-24, this wave had largely subsided, and the numbers settled down to a normal level of a new kind. In that year, for the first time except in the war period, there were more women than men, and the women retained their majority for the next four years. The annual average, which before the war had been between 1200 and 1300, rose to about 1970 for the quinquennium 1925-30—an increase of over 50 per cent.

The new phenomenon, the preponderance of women over men, is much more evident if we take the figures of *the undergraduates studying for the M.A. degree*, rather than the total number matriculating in the Faculty; since the latter include a considerable and in recent years a growing proportion of graduates, many of them working for the Ph.D. Degree, some having taken their first degrees in other universities, and also students proceeding to the new Degree in Commerce instituted in 1918, the majority being men. The *Arts* undergraduates have during the last five or six years regularly shown a percentage of about 55 women to 45 men. In 1931-32 the figures were 636 men and 719 women. There are, however, signs that this preponderance of women over men may be coming to an end. In 1931-32, the number of women entering the first year was lower than it had been for more than ten years, and was smaller than that of men for the first time since 1919. This fact connects itself with the serious unemployment among graduates who have entered the teaching profession.

The increase in the aggregate numbers since the war has thus been much greater than in any earlier period, and has been mainly in women students. This increase has evidently been in large measure due to yet another new factor—the operation of the Education (Scotland) Act, 1919, often called the "Munro Act," since it was the present Lord Justice Clerk who, as Secretary for Scotland, steered its passage through the House of Commons. The power which the Munro Act gave to the new Education Authorities to make grants from the public rates, whether for maintenance or for travelling expenses, to students attending the universities, has been very generously exercised. And, as has been said, by far the largest proportion of the grantees have found their way into the Faculty of Arts, and the majority of these have been women. Further, probably at least 75 per cent. of these women students, and more than 50 per cent. of the men, have entered the University with the intention of becoming teachers under the Scottish Education Department. The proportion in the Arts Faculty of aspirants to the scholastic profession has always been considerable, but in the last decade it has enormously increased, since the possession of a University Degree has become essential as a qualification for men-teachers of all grades, and for women teachers desiring to enter the more highly paid grades. The Arts Faculty has thus tended to become a place of training for one particular vocation.

On the other hand, the effect exercised by the Carnegie Trust upon the numbers of students is probably smaller in proportion than before the war. The Trustees have found themselves since 1911-12 obliged to reduce the amount of their grants to individual students, and to pay only a part (now normally three-fifths in the Arts Faculty) of the total class fees; while the fees have been increased and are practically double what they were when the Trust came into existence; though their amount is comparatively a minor item in the whole cost of maintaining a student at the University. The Carnegie benefit is now restricted to those whose family resources are manifestly unequal to the strain.

CURRICULUM FOR THE DEGREE OF MASTER OF ARTS

In the year 1883-84, at which this History begins, the curriculum for the Arts Degree was governed by Ordinance 14 of the Universities Commission of 1858, which had come into operation in 1861. That Ordinance had made no essential change in the programme of subjects for the Degree, which remained almost as it had been since 1708, when the Faculty of Arts was constituted with six Professors. The seventh subject, Rhetoric, was at first included in the Chair of Logic, till a separate Regius Professor was instituted in 1762. This subject was somewhat modified in 1861 by the Commissioners' new regulation that candidates for the Degree must attend a course in English Literature, with which Rhetoric was now combined. The curriculum thus consisted of the well-known "seven subjects": Latin, Greek and Mathematics, each to be studied throughout the winter sessions of the first and second years; and Logic, Moral Philosophy, Natural Philosophy, and Rhetoric and English Literature, studied each for one winter session in the third and fourth years. But it was provided that students who came up to the University sufficiently grounded in any or all of the first three subjects might pass directly into the senior or second-year classes in these, so that it was possible, and became more and more common, to complete the Degree course in three winter sessions. The Commissioners further required that in each subject there should be a regular Degree examination at the close of the winter session, distinct from the class exercises performed throughout the session. The Ordinance did not lay down any condition for entrance to these examinations beyond requiring that the student must have "completed his attendance" at the corresponding classes; apparently the present requirement that he must not only have been present in the lecture-room, but have "duly performed" the class-work, was not yet imposed. This principle of regular Degree examinations was not altogether a new one, since in 1835 the Faculty, of its own initiative, had adopted a rule that no student should be admitted to graduation without passing an examination in each of his subjects. But it was given a fresh emphasis and prominence by the Commissioners.

Moreover, a new value was conferred upon the Degree by the 1858 Act which gave graduates membership of and suffrage in the newly constituted General Council. Indeed, one of the objects of the Commissioners evidently was to encourage students to take their Degrees at the end of the course, which hitherto had been rather the exception than the rule in Arts. At any rate, there had been a marked increase in the numbers of Arts graduates, which showed an annual average of about 70 in the twenty years from 1863, as compared with 12 or 13 in the preceding period.

A still more striking innovation made by the 1861 Ordinance was that it provided for graduation with Honours. A student who had completed his curriculum for the Ordinary Degree might now offer himself for a further or Honours examination in one of four departments—Classical Literature, Mental Philosophy, Mathematics (including Natural Philosophy) or Natural Science. The first three of these corresponded to the subjects of the old curriculum (Rhetoric, with English Literature, being reckoned as belonging to the Philosophical department), but the fourth was new, and its appearance on the list is significant. The subjects included in it were Chemistry, Geology, Zoology and Botany (the last being added by the supplementary Ordinance 18), and none of these was as yet included in the Ordinary Arts curriculum, though Chairs in these subjects already existed in the University, three belonging to the curriculum in Medicine. This meant that Natural Science, as distinct from Physical Science, was now for the first time definitely recognised as an element in a liberal education. The supplementary Ordinance also gave power to the University Court to require that one of the Natural Sciences should be included in the Ordinary curriculum, in addition to the original seven subjects. This power was not, however, exercised at Edinburgh, though the provision for Honours in Natural Science was put into force.

This scheme for the Honours Degree continued to operate for about thirty years, till it was superseded by the more elaborate scheme of the Arts Ordinance of 1892. During that period the numbers of Honours graduates in the several departments were as follows:—Classics, 103; Philosophy, 114; Mathematics, 78; Natural Science, 41; a total of 336, including one woman's name in 1893—the year when women were first admitted to graduation.

This is not the place to discuss the virtues and the defects of the old seven-subjects curriculum. It was the product of a long development, firmly based on a sound tradition. It had the merit—a great merit, especially from the point of view of the general public—of being definite and uniform: a Scots M.A. was one who had attended his classes and passed his examinations in seven subjects approved by long experience as cultural disciplines. But by the 'eighties, at any rate, the question was being asked, why these seven subjects and no others should be thus privileged. There was a demand for a wider *Lernfreiheit*, and for the recognition of some of those other disciplines, old and new, which had proved their value and importance; the Natural Sciences, which had, indeed, already been recognised as worthy of the attention of the Arts student, but had not yet found a place in the Ordinary curriculum; the various branches of History, a subject already represented in the curricula in Divinity and Law; Political Economy, with a Chair in the Arts Faculty since 1871; and the Modern European Languages and Literatures. The example of Oxford and Cambridge and of Continental Universities, especially those of Germany, was being cited to show how Scotland was falling behind the times in the scope and methods of her higher education.

THE ARTS ORDINANCE OF 1892

The opportunity to remedy these and other deficiencies appeared when, after a long series of abortive attempts, time was at last found to pass a new Scottish Universities Bill through Parliament in 1889, and a new Commission came into being. What was no less important, a new Parliamentary Grant of £42,000 a year was made available for distribution among the four Universities, and a further £30,000 was added by the Education and Local Taxation Account (Scotland) Act, 1892. From these sources the annual sum of £25,920 was allocated to Edinburgh; and provision was thus made for additions to the teaching strength of the several Faculties, as well as for other reforms.

In 1892, after long discussion, the Commissioners enacted their Ordinance 11 to regulate the Arts curriculum in all the four Universities. Some room was left for divergences in detail, according as each of the four already possessed, or might afterwards acquire, the means of teaching Arts subjects not provided for in the others ; but a certain kernel of obligatory subjects was retained for them all, so that the Scots M.A. Degree should still be of a definite and uniform type, approximating fairly closely to the traditional one, but allowing for the inclusion of new subjects.

The provisions of Ordinance 11 may be considered under three heads: (1) The revision of the subjects of the Arts curriculum, Ordinary and Honours; (2) the new regulations regarding its length, especially the institution of the summer session in addition to the winter session; and (3) the setting up of a uniform Preliminary Examination to be passed by all students before admission to the classes qualifying for the Degree.

(1) The Ordinary M.A. curriculum was to consist, as before, of not less than seven subjects. Of these, four must be (i) either Latin or Greek; (ii) either English or a Modern Language or History; (iii) either Logic and Metaphysics or Moral Philosophy; and (iv) either Mathematics or Natural Philosophy. The choice of the fifth subject was also restricted, so as to secure that of the three departments of the old curriculum at least one must be included as a whole; the student had to take either (*a*) both Latin and Greek, or (*b*) both Logic and Moral Philosophy, or (*c*) two of the three subjects of Mathematics, Natural Philosophy and Chemistry. The remaining two of his seven subjects he might choose at will from the list of those recognised by the Ordinance and provided for in the Faculty.

It follows that, of the seven subjects of the old curriculum, at least three must be included, and in the great majority of cases, at least four. The position assigned to English, as an alternative to History or a Modern Language, was doubtless the result of compromise; in the discussions which preceded the passing of the Ordinance, it was proposed at first that English should be an obligatory subject for all; but this in the end was abandoned in order to find a way of satisfying the claims of those newer subjects which were at the time most obviously in need of recognition, and for the teaching of which provision was about to be made by founding new Chairs or Lectureships.

The subjects which were thus for the first time admitted to places in the list of those qualifying for the Ordinary Edinburgh M.A. Degree, either immediately or in the course of the next year or two, as the new funds at the disposal of the Commissioners or the University Court were applied for this purpose, were the following:—(*a*) Subjects already established in Chairs in other Faculties than Arts: Hebrew and Semitic Languages, and Ecclesiastical History, in the Faculty of Divinity; Public Law, Roman Law, and Constitutional Law and History, in the Faculty of Law; and also the sciences of Astronomy, Zoology, Botany, Chemistry and Geology, some of which had been originally founded in the Medical Faculty, and all of which now belonged also to the new separate Faculty of Science—constituted by another Ordinance in 1893; (*b*) Subjects already provided with Chairs in the Faculty of Arts, but not hitherto included in the Degree curriculum; Sanskrit (founded 1862), Political Economy (1871), Education (1876), Fine Art (1880) and Celtic Languages and Literature (1882); (*c*) Subjects for which provision was now made for the first time by the creation of new Chairs or Lectureships: History (this being the only Chair founded in 1894 by Ordinance of the Commissioners), and French and German, as Lectureships established by the University Court in the same year. Thus the traditional seven subjects of the Arts curriculum were now increased to twenty-five, though the old subjects were all placed in positions of advantage over their new rivals.

The curriculum for the Honours Degree was also reconstituted. In place of the Honours examination in one of four departments, to be taken after completion of the Ordinary curriculum, a new scheme of eight Honours "Groups" was drawn up, three of them corresponding in scope to three of the departments of the old scheme—Classics, Mental Philosophy, and Mathematics and Natural Philosophy—and five being new, Semitic Languages, Indian Languages—though these two were not actually provided for at Edinburgh till 1918 and 1919 respectively—English (Language, Literature and British History), Modern Languages and Literature, in which as yet only French and German were recognised, and History. A ninth group, Economic Science, was added by a supplementary Commissioners' Ordinance in 1898. Natural Science disappeared from the list for Honours, probably because it was thought that students who wished to specialise in it should take their degrees in Science rather than in Arts. Candidates for Honours, instead of completing the whole of the Ordinary curriculum of seven subjects, were now required to study only five subjects, two within the Honours Group and three outside it. The whole curriculum had to include either Latin or Greek; and in the case of the new groups it also included either Logic or Moral Philosophy, and either Mathematics or Natural Philosophy. Evidently the Commissioners were anxious, while providing for more advanced study in the Honours subjects, to insure that the Honours Degree should retain something of the traditional breadth and comprehensiveness; they also kept to the sacred number seven as the minimum number of courses to be taken, of which four had to be courses in the Honours subjects.

(2) The new curriculum, whether for the Ordinary or the Honours Degree, was to be of a minimum duration of three winter sessions or of two winter and three summer sessions. This was an important new departure. Hitherto, all the courses recognised as qualifying for the Degree had been given only in the winter session, from October to March. In some of the seven subjects, and since 1886 in all of them, there had been classes in the summer (May to July), but these had been merely "tutorial"; they did not count as parts of the attendance required for the Degree, and nearly all of them were conducted not by the Professors themselves but by their assistants. Some of these summer classes were in the nature of revision-courses for students who had already attended the subjects in winter; others were introductory or elementary; and others were advanced courses, largely for the benefit of those intending to take the Honours examinations. All alike

were voluntary or optional addenda to the regular curriculum. The new Ordinance created a summer session of at least ten teaching weeks or fifty class meetings, which was to count, for purposes of the Degree, as the equivalent of half a winter session. It was for the University authorities to decide in which subjects summer classes of this kind were to be instituted, and at Edinburgh these were in practice restricted to Latin, Greek, Mathematics and Natural Philosophy. "Tutorial" classes of the old kind continued to be held; but their number gradually decreased and in 1904 the last of them was discontinued.

The institution of the summer session connects itself with another important development of teaching in the Faculty, which appears in the Commissioners' Ordinance 17, passed at the same time. This Ordinance provided for what, so far as concerned Arts subjects, was virtually a new academic office, that of University Lecturer. Since 1708, when the old system of Regents, each conducting his class through the whole curriculum, had given place to that of Professors of the several subjects, the only recognised rank of a University officer giving instruction for Degrees was that of Professor, and this state of things is still reflected in the common speech of Scotland, where the title "Professor" is often given to anyone who teaches in a University, or even to a medical or surgical specialist. But for long it had been customary for Professors in the larger classes to employ private assistants, who relieved them of part of the work, often very heavy, of correcting students' exercises, and might even deputise for them in illness or other necessary absence. This practice had, in the course of the nineteenth century, been to some extent recognised and regulated by the Senatus, whose sanction had become necessary for the regular employment of such teachers; so that there had come into being a more or less definite status of University Assistant, which in turn became a training ground for the Professoriate. And, as has been said, the tutorial classes which had come to be held outside the regular winter session were entirely conducted by Assistants. Further, in certain subjects which were not yet recognised as necessary parts of the Degree curriculum, and for which funds were perhaps not available to establish full Chairs, Lectureships had been instituted. These teachers, whose appointments were sometimes unofficially designated "Stools," were in full and sole charge of their subjects, but were not members of Faculty, and their courses were not qualifying courses. No such Lectureships had as yet been founded in what may be called pure Arts subjects; but there were several in Science, for instance, those in Agriculture (1890, Steven Lectureship) and in Forestry (1889), and others, of a different kind, in certain clinical or other special branches in Medicine.

These two institutions, that of the University Assistant who might have a tutorial class to conduct by himself, and that of the University Lecturer in a special subject not taught by any Professor, were retained, developed, and, to some extent, combined under the Commissioners' Ordinance 17. Lecturers might now be appointed, not only, as hitherto, in subjects not taught by Professors, but also in subjects already provided with Chairs, in which cases the Lecturer was the Professor's subordinate in his department, and was in fact in most cases also his Assistant. The new qualifying classes to be held in the summer session were placed in the charge of these Lecturer-Assistants, who thus obtained a much more important share in the teaching work of the Faculty. The first of such Lectureships to be created were, accordingly, those in the old subjects. On the other hand "independent" Lectureships in new subjects of the extended Degree curriculum began to be instituted. In 1894-95, French and German, recognised as subjects qualifying for the Degree under the new Ordinance, were each assigned a Lecturer in sole charge. These Lectureships and others founded later attained, in point of numbers of students and otherwise, an importance equal to most professorial departments. It was not, however, till 1919 that provision was made, by the University Court's Ordinance 33, for the admission of their holders to seats on the Faculty of Arts; whereas any subject, it might be of narrower scope, or attracting much smaller numbers to its classes, which had the good fortune to secure an endowment sufficient for a

From the painting by] [*William Nicholson*

SIR RICHARD LODGE, M.A., LL.D., LITT.D.

Professor of History
1899-1925

Chair, was entitled to representation not only on the Faculty but on the Senatus, with security of tenure for the teacher. In the years after the war, the most important of these Lectureships were erected into full Chairs, in most instances after an interval as Readerships:—French in 1918, German in 1926, and Geography and Psychology in 1931.

During the period when Ordinance 11 was in force, the following further additions to the Lectureships in the Faculty were made:—History (1900, Mackay Lectureship), Ancient Greek and Roman History (1900, Sir William Fraser's Foundation), Political Economy (1901), Military History (1904, now discontinued), Psychology (1906, partly provided by the Combe Trustees), and Statistics and Mathematical Economics (1907); and in several instances more than one Lecturer-Assistant was appointed in the same professorial subject. During the same period—after the Commissioners' foundation of the Chair of History, already mentioned—only one new Professorship was established, that of Ancient History and Palæography, by Sir William Fraser's bequest, which is in fact a Chair of Scottish History.

This increase in the teaching strength of the Faculty, continued and accelerated in later times, was connected especially with the development of the Honours work. New courses or half-courses in special departments within the Honours Groups were instituted; and a system of tutorial instruction, whether for individuals or for groups, was begun in certain subjects, especially in linguistic studies, though the adoption of this as a general practice, and for Ordinary as well as Honours students, came only after the Arts Ordinance of 1908. The principal instrument of tuition was still the formal lecture, and a full course must consist of "not less than one hundred meetings of the whole Class on separate days," which meant that Professors normally lectured on five days a week throughout the winter session.

The minimum length of the Honours curriculum was the same as the Ordinary—three years. In practice, however, it became usual for the Honours man to take a fourth year, attending twice over the advanced or Honours courses in the principal subjects of his Honours Group, in which he had already taken the Ordinary classes. He might, however, and frequently did, take one or more of the three subjects outside the Group by attendance on two half-courses in his summer sessions. Most, if not all, Honours students would attend a good deal more than the minimum number of classes required by the Ordinance. No maximum limit of time was laid down for study necessary for the Ordinary Degree ; the work may, in fact, be spread over many years, or interrupted by intervals of any length. But the Honours course must be completed within five or, in special circumstances, six years from the student's first matriculation.

(3) The third main change—which, indeed, was rather a development of an existing practice—introduced by Ordinance 11 was the adoption of a new uniform scheme for testing students before admitting them to study for the Degree. Under the former regime, as has been said, those who at their entrance were found to be sufficiently grounded in Latin, Greek and Mathematics, the subjects belonging to the first year of the four-years' curriculum, were allowed to omit the junior classes in these, and pass directly into the senior. There had thus grown up a regular Entrance Examination in these subjects, success in which saved a year of study. The Commissioners took over and extended this principle. They laid down that every student who desired to proceed to the degree must pass a Preliminary Examination in four subjects, a sufficient knowledge of which was thus assumed to be necessary as a foundation for academic study, whether of these subjects themselves or of others which he would begin at the University. The four items were (1) English ; (2) Latin or Greek ; (3) Mathematics ; and (4) Greek or Latin if not already taken, or a Modern Language—French or German or Italian—or Dynamics. Attendance on any class was to qualify for the Degree only if the whole Preliminary Examination had been passed, and attendance on any class in a foreign language only after passing the Preliminary Examination in that language, or an examination of equivalent standard. Certain further complications, which need not be

detailed here, arose from the fact that in three of the Preliminary subjects — Latin, Greek and Mathematics — there were two standards, a higher and a lower. A pass on the higher standard was necessary in at least one of these subjects; in one or both of the other two a lower would suffice, unless the candidate wished to take the subject selected as part of his Degree curriculum. The whole conduct of the Preliminary Examinations (for Arts and the other Faculties) was placed in the charge of a Joint Board representing the four Universities; and powers were given to the Board to accept passes in the Leaving Certificate Examination of the Scotch Education Department, or in such other examinations as they thought fit, as equivalent to passes in any part of the Preliminary. In course of time, indeed, the Leaving Certificate was to become the more frequented avenue of entry to the University for students who had their schooling in Scotland, though it was not till 1918 that it was finally recognised as the normal one.

The general intention of the scheme was clear: to insure, as far as possible, that all students admitted to the Degree course had had a good school education, and thus to reduce the amount of work of the school standard which had to be done in the University. It was, however, found necessary to retain for some years the old junior classes in Latin, Greek and Mathematics, though these were now taken out of the regular qualifying curriculum; the last of them, that in Mathematics, was discontinued in 1903.

These enactments of Ordinance 11 and the others mentioned obviously mark an epoch in the history of the Faculty. They were not revolutionary, and some of them were from the first criticised as too cautious and conservative. But on the whole, the period which they inaugurated was one of increased efficiency and success. Room had been found within the four corners of the curriculum for a much richer variety of subjects; but enough of the traditional requirements had been retained to preserve a family likeness to the old Degree. Better opportunities for advanced study were opened up by the new scheme of Honours Groups. The institution of the Lectureships offered prospects of a career in academic teaching to a larger number of men. And something had been done to raise the minimum level of education at which University study was to be allowed to begin.

THE ARTS ORDINANCE OF 1908

The Ordinance of 1892 remained in force for sixteen years; but long before the end of that period a movement for further reform had begun to show itself, in which three main currents may be distinguished.

First, it was desired to extend the teaching over a larger part of the year. The institution of the summer session, with its qualifying half-courses conducted by Lecturers, had already done this to a certain extent, and for a certain number of students. But the professorial teaching was still confined to the two periods of the winter session, which was of the normal length of twenty-two weeks—ten before and twelve after the Christmas vacation, as compared with eleven in the summer session. The Ordinary Degree Examinations were held at the end of the winter session, in March and April, and again before the opening of the classes in October; so that a student who had completed his attendance in any subject during two summer sessions had to wait to be examined in it till after the summer vacation following the second. The Honours Degree Examinations took place only at the end of the winter session. The work of the Professor and of his class was still, therefore, extremely congested. The Professors, or most of them, had, it is true, six months' continuous leisure from teaching, with the corresponding opportunity for travel, research and writing; but this was secured at a heavy cost in the output of physical and mental energy in winter, as the students were required to pass their Degree Examinations immediately after the end of the winter session. It was felt that a more leisurely rate of imparting and assimilating instruction would yield results more valuable to the learners and more satisfactory to the teachers; that the latter might be willing to sacrifice some weeks, or even months, of their summer freedom for this end, and thus lighten the excessive strain of the winter. The proposal, therefore, was to abolish the division between the winter and summer sessions, and to make one teaching year, continuous over the three periods—to which the English designation "terms" is now applied—of about equal length, from October to Christmas, from January to March, and from the Easter vacation to about the end of June. The whole teaching power of the Faculty, and all its students, would be actually at work during the whole of the teaching year.

It was not, however, proposed to increase, but rather to reduce, the number of lectures in each course. The student was to have more time to digest them and to read for himself; and other and more intimate methods of instruction—"tutorial" was the adjective used to indicate their character, in these discussions and in the subsequent legislation—were to be developed in the time thus released from lectures. It had long been felt that the formal professorial discourse, taken down in the student's note-book, was no longer an up-to-date instrument, was indeed a legacy from medieval times when books were scarce.* It was apt to induce a too passive and merely receptive temper in the student, which might be corrected by more discussion and catechetical teaching, and also by requiring him to cover some part of the ground in each subject in his independent reading, for which the lectures should be a supplement and stimulus rather than a substitute. Thus the plan of the three terms implied a considerable increase of the Faculty's equipment in at least three directions: teaching staff, accommodation for teaching students individually or in small groups, and library provision.

* The dictated lecture, which still has its hold upon students, has been a subject of censure from quite early times. In 1647 a representative Commission of the four Scottish Universities condemned the excessive "dyteing of notts" as "unprofitable and noxious paines," and half a century later a Parliamentary Commission—alas, too confident of its powers—ordered "the custome of dictating and writing of notes in the classes to be discharged from and after the month of October 1696." Of course, there are two sides to the question; the transcription of a good lecture by a student whose mind is awake may be a most effective medium. But the taking down of every word that falls from the rostrum as embodying the sole and final sound doctrine of the subject, and the consequent abstinence from any other reading or independent thought, are still the darling sins of the Scots undergraduate—of either sex.

In the second place, there was a demand for a still wider liberty in the choice of subjects in the Degree curriculum. As we have seen, a number of new subjects had already been admitted to it, and some of these were now pressing for recognition on a level more nearly equal to the older ones. Among these "modern disciplines," the claims of the Modern Languages, History, Political Economy, Psychology and Education, were specially prominent; and there was the prospect that yet more subjects, such as Geography, or departments of subjects, such as Economic History, would have provision made for them as new funds became available; and they in turn would demand places as items in a qualifying curriculum. Further, now that a satisfactory entrance standard had been set up in the Preliminary Examination, there seemed to be less need to insist on the same basis of subjects for the Degree itself. All subjects, it was now argued, might be recognised as of equal standing, and the student left free to make up his curriculum of those best suited to his tastes and aptitudes and to the needs of his future career. Some old-fashioned people, indeed, might be inclined to doubt whether the new subjects really had the same disciplinary value as the old. But it was a difficult position to maintain in controversy with colleagues representing the new subjects, or in debate before an outside public somewhat impatient of the slow rate of academic response to modern interests and needs. Much of the discussion, for instance, centred on the question of Latin and Greek, one or the other of which was still obligatory in the Ordinary curriculum.

Thirdly, it was felt that a curriculum of seven subjects, each of which was studied to a certain standard for a period of two terms, was not altogether satisfactory. It had breadth, no doubt, and variety, a variety which might be greatly increased; but it had little depth in any part. Some reduction might be made in the number of subjects, in order that those remaining, or some of them, should be studied more intensively, and for a longer time. Greater freedom in choosing the curriculum would thus be balanced by the requirement that some parts of it must be chosen for more advanced work.

These and other arguments, put forward with growing insistence, led finally to a fresh reconstruction of the Arts curriculum. When, after several years of discussion within the Faculty and the Senatus, and after repeated conferences with the other Scottish Universities, the time was ripe for new legislation, the principle of uniformity among the four Universities, which had been observed by the Commissioners' Ordinance of 1892, was abandoned. Each of the University Courts promulgated its own separate scheme. The main lines followed by the Glasgow, Aberdeen and Edinburgh Ordinances, which were finally approved in 1908, were alike; the St Andrews Ordinance, which was not passed till two years later, diverged in several important particulars.

The Edinburgh scheme was embodied in Ordinance 11 of the Edinburgh University Court; thus, by a curious coincidence, it bore the same number in this series as its predecessor of 1892 had borne in the series of Commissioners' Ordinances. It was framed to give effect to the proposals that have been indicated above: the institution of the three-term session; the increased freedom in the choice of subjects for the curriculum; and the application to the Ordinary Degree of the principle of specialisation, or more intensive study, in some part of the curriculum—though this last requirement, as will be seen presently, was to a large extent evaded, or rendered inoperative, in actual practice. The Ordinance, couched in much more general terms than that of 1892, left the adjustment of details to be made by the Senatus by way of additional regulations from time to time. This explains the fact that it has remained in force down to the present, though the actual working-out of the curriculum has undergone many changes within the rather wide limits of discretion allowed to the Senatus.

The provisions of the 1892 Ordinance regarding the Preliminary Examination were re-enacted, with one or two small modifications. As before, powers were taken to accept passes at the Leaving Certificate Examination (or other similar tests) in the Preliminary subjects. This part of the Ordinance, however, has been superseded by a new comprehensive scheme, common to the four Universities, and providing a uniform standard for admission to study in any Faculty, which was embodied in Ordinance LXX of 1918, and came into full operation in 1927. The effect of this upon the Arts Faculty will be discussed later.

The Ordinance, moreover, made the three following general enactments. In the first place, the academical year was to consist of at least twenty-five teaching weeks, divided into three periods. In practice, there are normally ten weeks in the autumn term, ten in the spring term and nine in the summer term; but the last week in each is mainly devoted to examinations, so that the effective teaching year is of twenty-six weeks. Secondly, a normal minimum of "seventy-five meetings of the whole Class on separate days" was fixed for a full lecture course, with "additional meetings for tutorial instruction where such is provided." Such a course is normally spread over the three terms, but in certain cases it may be completed in two. The Senatus may sanction full courses of less than seventy-five meetings, chiefly Honours courses of at least fifty meetings in the autumn and spring terms. Thirdly, the Ordinary Degree curriculum was to consist of five subjects, of which two were to be studied for two years and passed on a higher standard in the Degree Examinations. But the Senatus were given power to reckon one course in each of two "cognate subjects" as equivalent for this purpose to a "double course in a single subject," and to determine which subjects were to be combined in this way. Nothing was laid down in the Ordinance about the choice of the subjects to make up the curriculum, or the order in which they were to be taken. These questions were left to the Senatus to decide by way of regulations made and alterable from time to time.

The only considerable change in the rules for the Honours curriculum was that only two subjects were now required to be taken outside the Honours Group, instead of three, and the former limitations on the choice of these "outside subjects" were removed, though others might be imposed by the Senatus. The minimum duration of the curriculum, both Ordinary and Honours, remained as before, three years.

The new Ordinance thus left it almost entirely to the Senatus to determine the content and the general character of the Degree; and in framing their regulations the Senatus who were, of course, giving effect to the recommendations of the Faculty, exercised their new freedom to the full. The restrictions laid down in the 1892 Ordinance, in which, as has been said, a certain nucleus of subjects from the traditional seven had been retained, were abandoned. Instead, it was required that every curriculum for the Ordinary Degree "must embrace subjects taken from at least three of the four Departments of Study," Languages and Literature, Mental Philosophy, Science, and History and Law. Thus the subjects included in each of the four departments were placed on a footing of absolute parity. The list of those recognised as qualifying for the Degree now numbered thirty: nine languages, five "philosophical" subjects, eight sciences, and nine subjects under "History and Law." Geography, in which a Lecturer had been appointed in 1908, was classed both in the Science and in the History and Law department, but counted only in the latter for the purpose of the regulation requiring subjects from at least three of the four. The original seven subjects were thus deposed from their position of privilege: Latin, Greek and English, for instance, were now equal with Celtic; Logic and Moral Philosophy with Education or Psychology or Political Economy. It was possible to complete a curriculum without any linguistic or literary study, or without philosophy, or without any scientific subject.

Even more important for the working of the scheme was the application of the Ordinance requirements regarding subjects and courses. The effect of these was that while the curriculum must include at least seven *courses* (the same number as before), it might be made up of either five, or six, or seven *subjects*, according as the student chose to take two "double courses in single subjects," or one such course and one pair of "cognate subjects," or two pairs of "cognates." Further, the character of the "double courses" varied according to the provision which could be made in the several subjects. In some it was possible to institute a "Second Ordinary" or "Intermediate" course distinct from and more advanced than the first; in others (chiefly in language subjects, in which the programme of reading for the Degree Examination was changed every year) the student was allowed simply to attend the first course a second time, but was required to reach a higher standard in the Degree Examination after his second attendance. Altogether, in the first draft of the new regulation, fourteen subjects were made available for "double courses" in one or the other of these forms. In the rest, no such provision was made, and they could only be taken for one year.

The scheme of "cognate subjects" was still more complicated. In the first draft, forty-two different combinations were recognised: thirteen pairs of languages, five of philosophical subjects, ten of scientific, seven of historical, and seven of subjects belonging to different departments. Most of these pairs had to be studied in two separate years, but a few of them could be taken in the same year. In every instance the standard to be attained in the Degree Examination in both subjects was the same as if they had been taken singly; a student who made up his curriculum by taking two pairs of "cognates" and three single subjects could thus obtain his Degree by a bare pass in each of his seven examinations. As a result of the scheme the standard of the Degree was not necessarily higher in any part than under the old Ordinance, and there was an almost complete freedom of choice within the departments.

When the Ordinance was still in process of being drafted it was realised that this new freedom might prove very embarrassing to students. The Senatus, therefore, devised a new method for guiding, and to a certain extent controlling, the selection and arrangement of the courses. In 1907, a year before the new Ordinance was finally approved, two of the more senior Lecturers in the Faculty were appointed to act as

"Official Advisers." They were to interview students at the beginning of the session and assist them in drawing up their programme of classes. At first, it was optional for a student to consult an Adviser, but from 1909 consultation was made obligatory for all those desiring to complete the Degree. The Advisers' first duty was to see that the regulations were being followed—no simple matter under the new scheme, with its almost unlimited number of possible combinations and permutations of subjects; beyond that, they might advise against ill-balanced or otherwise undesirable schemes. They acted, under the authority of the Dean, as the agents in administering the policy of the Faculty. Their work increased in importance and in volume and complexity as the new regulations came fully into operation. In 1910 a third Adviser was appointed to direct students who were combining an Arts curriculum with one in Science; and in 1920 a fourth, for those taking the new Degree in Commerce. In 1926, when the Ordinary Arts Degree Regulations were revised, the original two M.A. Advisers were increased to four. In 1930 their title was changed to "Directors of Studies." They have now a more authoritative control of the curricula; every student reading for a Degree is assigned to one or other of them according to the course which he is following, and may not attend any class without his Director's permission. The Directors are consulted by students in any matter of difficulty; they meet from time to time in committee, with the Dean as chairman, so as to insure uniformity in dealing with the various kinds of cases, and report, where necessary, to the Faculty.

The effect of the first set of regulations made under the new Ordinance upon the subject-content of curricula is revealed in the annual reports presented to the Faculty by the Official Advisers from 1908 onwards, some of the results of which may be summarised. In the period 1911-14, in which the new regulations had come into full working order and conditions had not yet been disturbed by the war, the following facts emerge.

As between "double courses in single subjects" and pairs of "cognate subjects," the proportion was about 28 per cent.

to 72 per cent.; more than half the students who completed the Ordinary Degree in these years took two "cognate" pairs and no "double courses," and less than a quarter took two "double courses." It would thus appear that the original intention of the Ordinance, to secure that in some part or parts of the curriculum a higher standard should be exacted, was largely being evaded in the working of the scheme of "cognate" subjects. As regards the actual content of the curricula, most of the original seven subjects were still holding their own in equal competition with the newer ones: Latin, English and Mathematics were each taken by more than half the total number; Natural Philosophy, Logic and Moral Philosophy by more than a third; but Greek by less than one seventh. On the other hand, Political Economy with 54 per cent., British History with 52, and French with 37 had come into prominence. German, which was much less commonly studied than French in Scottish schools, had about 10 per cent. Education, which was taken almost entirely by students in training for the teaching profession, was included in more than a fourth of the curricula, and Geography, the most recently recognised subject, in nearly as many. Of the other sciences, Chemistry and Botany were attracting considerable numbers; Geology and Zoology fewer but still a fair proportion; and Psychology, which though it was classed in the Philosophical department, was more and more applying the methods of an observational science, was increasing its strength, especially among intending teachers. Those subjects which were common to the Arts and Law curricula—Constitutional Law and History, Public Law, Roman Law and Mercantile Law—naturally drew students who were to go on to a Law Degree, and had this further advantage from the student's point of view, that their classes could be completed in the two terms of the old winter session. So also could Political Economy, which was a class qualifying for the Law Degree, though the great majority of its members were purely Arts students. On the whole, these results were not unsatisfactory, as showing that the Faculty was giving full scope to the new subjects to assert their claims upon students.

Misgivings, however, might arise upon a closer scrutiny of the contents of some of the individual curricula pursued by students of these years. It might, for instance, be questioned whether it was desirable to include such specialised and professional subjects as Education or Mercantile Law in the undergraduate Arts course. And there was also the danger that in applying the principle of parity of subjects, the Faculty might allow the specific character of the Arts Degree, as a mark of academic attainment, to be impaired. In illustration of this, the following facts may be cited from the Official Advisers' Report of 1915, in which they analysed in detail the curricula of those students who had graduated Ordinary M.A. in 1914. Nearly one-fourth of them, it appeared, had taken their degrees without studying any foreign language, and nearly one-seventh without any literary subject at all. Almost half had omitted both Logic and Moral Philosophy. More than 40 per cent. had had no Science, and less than 30 per cent. had taken either Mathematics or Natural Philosophy; and, on the other hand, several of the curricula had been almost wholly scientific, five out of the seven courses being taken from that department. Even assuming the parity of subjects—and some doubt might be felt, for example, whether Mercantile Law or Military History or even Geography were really of equal value with Logic and Metaphysics or Mathematics or Latin, *as an academic discipline at the undergraduate stage*—it was not altogether easy to discover the academic principles underlying such M.A. curricula as the following, which were among those enumerated in the Report:—(1) Double courses in Mathematics and Natural Philosophy, single courses in Chemistry, Political Economy and Mercantile Law; (2) a double course in Mathematics, Political Economy and Geography taken as "cognates," single courses in Natural Philosophy, Constitutional History and Education; (3) Political Economy and Economic History as "cognates," British History and Ecclesiastical History as "cognates," single courses in Arabic, Constitutional History and Public International Law; (4) double course in Botany, Mathematics and Chemistry as "cognates," single courses in English, Political Economy and Economic History. In comparison with the old seven-subjects Degree, or even with the more varied Degree allowed by the 1892 Ordinance, these curricula lay open to objection as being either too heterogeneous or too narrow to provide a satisfactory basis for future professional study; especially when it is remembered that the great majority of the subjects were studied only for one year—in some cases only for two terms—and none for more than two years.

Reconsideration of the scheme, however, was interrupted by the war, and by the appearance of new and urgent problems after the war, especially the great increase in the numbers of students, to which reference has been made. That increase, as has been said, was caused partly by the return of men from military service, with claims for special facilities and exemptions to enable them to complete their Degrees, and, to a still greater extent, by the demand for larger numbers of graduates in the teaching profession, and by the work of the new Education Authorities in making grants to enable students to come to the University. The prospective teachers desired especially to take subjects which they would be able to teach in schools, or which were otherwise of direct professional value, such as Psychology and Education. Many of them were undergoing their period of professional training at the Edinburgh Provincial Committee's Training College concurrently with their Arts curriculum in a combined course of four years, and had therefore to work to a double time-table. Thus any new restriction that might be imposed on the choice of subjects for the Degree might cause difficulties to a large and growing section of the students. In any case, the work of teaching and examining these large numbers occupied the full energies of the Staff, and the flaws and weaknesses in the regulations were perhaps aggravated. There was, however, a growing opinion, both within and outside the University, that the Degree had become too indeterminate, and that something ought to be done to give it a more specific character.

The first move in this direction, indeed, was made by the

Faculty almost immediately after the war, in 1919-20. The amendments then adopted had reference chiefly to the scheme of "cognate subjects," which was felt to be the least satisfactory part of the system. Some of the pairs of subjects that had been recognised for this purpose had no very obvious organic connection as stages in a progressive study, and, in any case, there was no provision for testing whether the student had made more of his second subject as the result of having studied the first. To remedy this, the list was revised and reduced from forty-five to twenty-eight combinations; and power was taken, by the amending Ordinance 25, to require that the Degree Examination in the second of two subjects taken as "cognates" should be passed on a higher standard than if it were taken as a single subject. It was also laid down that when a single subject was taken in a "double course," the class to be attended in the second year should not be the same as the first, but a distinct and more advanced one—it might even be an Honours class. Lastly, a tentative and partial reversion was made to the principles of the 1892 Ordinance, by requiring that every curriculum for the Ordinary Degree should include either Philosophy (the new designation of the class formerly called "Logic and Metaphysics") or Moral Philosophy. But this requirement was relaxed in the case of students taking their courses in the University and the Training College concurrently; they were allowed to offer Psychology as an alternative to Philosophy or Moral Philosophy.*

In 1921 Education ceased to be recognised as a subject in the undergraduate curriculum, except for those students also attending the Training College, who were allowed to take it only after their third year. This change was connected

* This concession was at first open to a large number of students and was largely taken advantage of by them. But during the following decade the number tended to diminish and in the end almost disappeared. The practice of taking a four-years' "concurrent" course of University and Training College fell out of favour with students and with the Education Department, and was replaced, in the great majority of cases, by a three-years' course in Arts followed by one year of post-graduate professional training at the College.

with another important new departure, which will be described later, the institution of the Diploma (in 1914) and the Degree (in 1917) in Education. Some, indeed, of the members of the Faculty thought that when this special provision was made for the professional teacher, Education should be taken entirely out of the M.A. curriculum; but in the end the compromise above indicated was reached. In 1919, also, Mercantile Law, another mainly technical and professional subject, was removed from the Arts list.

On the other hand, several new subjects had been introduced since the new Ordinance, by the foundation of new Lectureships with funds from the Carnegie Trust, from Sir Donald Currie's Endowment (1905), and from other sources: Geography and Economic History in 1908, Arabic and Colonial and Indian History in 1912. In 1919 a whole series was added, as the Faculty extended its activities in the busy and hopeful atmosphere of reconstruction after the war: Italian, Spanish and Russian as regular subjects for the Degree the last, however, being discontinued after a few years, as the demand for it unfortunately fell off; English Language, Ancient Philosophy and Realistic Economics, as new subdivisions within the Honours schools of English, Philosophy and Economics; and Actuarial Mathematics, in which a Diploma had been instituted in 1918. In the same year a further development took place in the establishment of a new Degree in Commerce, to be administered in the meantime by the Arts Faculty, with Lectureships, afterwards raised to Chairs, in Accounting and Business Method, and in Organisation of Industry, besides a Lectureship in Banking which had been founded in 1909.

THE SCHEME OF TYPES FOR THE ORDINARY CURRICULUM

The Faculty, however, was not yet satisfied with what had been done to amend the condition of its most important charge, the Arts Degree. As the number of students continued to rise, and in prospect of a relaxation in the conditions of

GERARD BALDWIN BROWN, M.A., LL.D.
Professor of Fine Art
1880-1930

entrance, which had been under discussion since the passing of the new Entrance Ordinance of 1918, but had not yet been put in force, it was more and more felt that something further should be done to define the basis and the specific character of the Degree, which was now being taken by so many and in such an immense variety of ways. The suggestion had repeatedly been made, especially by the General Council, that though it might be neither practicable nor desirable to return to one single type of Ordinary curriculum such as that of the 1892 Ordinance, a number of alternative types should be drawn up, with their parts more thoroughly co-ordinated. This had recently been done by the Faculty of Science in working out the schemes under the series of new Ordinances for graduation in Pure and Applied Science, which had secured in every case a closely articulated curriculum, while leaving room for variation of emphasis on this or that group of studies.

Accordingly, in 1925, the Arts Faculty recommended, and the Senatus and Court approved, a further change in the Ordinary Degree Regulations, applying the principle of alternative types, to one or other of which every student must conform. Three types were defined, to meet the needs of three more or less clearly distinguishable groups of students. Each of them was to comply with the general requirements of the existing Ordinance as to the number of courses, single and double or "cognate," and with the existing regulations that one of the two main philosophical subjects, and subjects from at least three of the four departments, must be included. In addition, some study of science was to be required of all, and at least one foreign language.

Type A was to include (1) Latin or Greek or an "oriental classical language," *i.e.* Hebrew, Arabic or Sanskrit; this alternative was specially for the benefit of the considerable number of Eastern students, Indians and Egyptians; (2) English or History, *i.e.* the Ordinary class of British History; (3) Philosophy or Moral Philosophy; and (4) a subject from the Department of Science. Type B required (1) a modern foreign language, French, German, Italian, Spanish or Celtic, to be studied in a double course; (2) a second such language, in at least a single course; (3) Philosophy or Moral Philosophy; (4) a subject from the Department of Science. Type C required (1) Mathematics, in which the Second Ordinary Course must be taken; a student with a sufficient grounding in the subject might do this without attending the First Ordinary Course, in which case he would have an additional free choice for one of his remaining courses; (2) another subject from the Department of Science; (3) a foreign language, ancient or modern; and (4) Philosophy or Moral Philosophy.

Of these, Type A was intended, on the whole, to approximate to the traditional curriculum or, at any rate, to that of 1892, except that it allowed a Natural Science to be taken instead of Mathematics or Natural Philosophy. Those who were willing and qualified to include a classical language had, in fact, a somewhat wider freedom of choice in the rest of their curriculum; accordingly this type was the best suited for those who wished to specialise in Philosophy or History. Type B, also with a literary and linguistic basis, could be taken by those who were without a knowledge of Latin or Greek and Mathematics, but might compensate for this by more intensive study in modern languages. Type C was mainly scientific, with a mathematical basis.

These regulations were put in force for students entering on the Ordinary curriculum in 1926-27, and were found to be on the whole satisfactory and easy to apply. After five years' experience the Faculty, in 1931, made some further additions to them, which are now in operation. Type A remains in its original form, except that a second foreign language, ancient or modern, may be taken instead of English, and a number of other History classes instead of British History. In Type B, the student must take either English or else a second course in his second modern foreign language. In Type C, the requirement of the Second Ordinary Course in Mathematics has been so far relaxed that only the First Ordinary Course need be taken, provided *two* other courses from the Department of Science are also included; in addition, one of the four subjects, English, History—British or otherwise—Political

Economy and Psychology, is required. In each of the Types, at least one "double course in a single subject" must be taken, so that in every minimum curriculum, *i.e.* every curriculum that has included only seven courses, at least one subject has been studied for two years and up to a higher standard.

Students are allowed to take additional subjects or courses beyond the necessary minimum of seven, provided their Directors of Studies are satisfied that they are making good progress in their essential classes, and that the additional classes are suitable. These, up to a certain maximum, may be taken without further payment, as the charge for the whole curriculum is an inclusive fee.

The distribution of the students among the several Types has been approximately 50 per cent. in Type A, 20 per cent. in Type B, the great majority of these being women, and 30 per cent. in Type C. A scrutiny of the results of the Ordinary Degree Examinations held in the summer terms of 1930 and 1931 gives an approximate indication of the relative positions of the subjects in respect of numbers of students. In this calculation, it should be understood, there are included large numbers who would ultimately proceed to Honours. The subjects which in these two years were taken by over 100 examinees came in the following order: French, 664; English, 576; Philosophy, 447; Latin, 431; Mathematics, 421; Geography, 349; Psychology, 301; British History, 247; Moral Philosophy, 236; Political Economy, 215; Natural Philosophy, 172; German, 148.

The stages of development in the Ordinary curriculum sketched in the foregoing narrative are fairly clearly marked. There was first the movement of expansion, the admission of new subjects and their recognition as on an academic parity with the old ones, the removal of restrictions on the students' choice, and the consequent departure further and further from the old tradition of the Degree. This movement gained its first and partial victory in 1892, and advanced to complete triumph after 1908. Then came the perhaps inevitable reaction. It was realised that, especially with the vastly increased numbers of students—and these, in spite of the test imposed by the Preliminary Examination, of very various quality in respect of their school preparation—freedom of choice was tending to mere multifariousness and incoherence; and it was felt that some of the new subjects could hardly be profitably studied by undergraduates who had not been subjected to the training nor acquired the information and ideas supplied by the central disciplines, linguistic, philosophical and scientific. Continuity of tradition has been in a measure restored, but development has not been arrested, nor the final word spoken. We may hope that it never will be; the Arts curriculum, like a living organism, has to adjust itself ever anew to the changes in the national society and in the body of human knowledge.

THE DEVELOPMENT OF THE HONOURS CURRICULUM

Most of what has been said above has had reference to the Ordinary Degree. But the history of the Honours Degree is not less important. The scheme of Honours Groups laid down in the 1892 Ordinance has not been much altered in its general outline, but several important minor developments have taken place, and the volume of Honours work has steadily increased. The number of students who completed the Degree with Honours in the several groups in the twenty-year period from 1895—the year of the first graduation under the 1892 Ordinance—to 1914, was as follows: Classics, 290 men and 30 women; Mental Philosophy, 74 men and 7 women; Mathematics and Natural Philosophy, 165 men and 14 women; English, 89 men and 66 women; History, 49 men and 12 women; Modern Languages, which as yet consisted only of the combination of French and German, 44 men and 120 women; Economic Science (first appearing in the graduation lists in 1902), 37 men and 2 women. A new Group, Latin and French, instituted near the end of the period, was taken by 1 man and 3 women. The total, including a considerable number who had taken Honours after completing the Ordinary Degree (as had been the practice before 1892) was 673 men and 253 women; of these 22 men and 2 women had taken Honours in two, and one man in three Groups.*

The old Honours schools of Classics and Mathematics, it will be noted, retained their primacy. Philosophy had fallen back somewhat; and English and Modern Languages were making great progress, being specially in favour with the women, as was to be expected. The proportions of Classes awarded were:—Firsts, 42 per cent.; Seconds, 46 per cent.; and Thirds, 12 per cent. The proportion of Thirds was about the same in both sexes; the men had rather more Firsts than Seconds, and the women about two Firsts to three Seconds.

A comparison of these figures with the corresponding data for the decade 1922-31, that is, after the abnormal conditions of the war had ceased to affect the number of graduates, shows some significant changes. The totals were: Classics, 86 men and 28 women; Philosophy, 30 men and 2 women; Mathematics and Natural Philosophy, 155 men and 58 women; English, 88 men and 119 women; History, 102 men and 38 women; Economic Science, 32 men and 5 women; Semitic Languages, 5 men; Sanskrit and Indian Languages, 2 men (the two last groups first come into the lists in 1923); Geography (1931), 1 man. The Modern Languages Group was largely reorganised in the course of this period. The system in which two languages, French and German, or French and Latin, were taken concurrently throughout the course, and ranked as equal in the final examination, was discontinued. Instead, a number of new combinations was recognised, in each of which one of the two languages is subordinate, and is studied only to an Intermediate Honours standard, to the end of the second or third year. The principal language is continued for two years more, the penultimate year being usually spent in study at a university or other teaching institution in the country where the language is spoken; so that the student acquires not only a good command of it in speaking, but also a

* The late James Munro, afterwards for a time Lecturer in Colonial and Indian History, took a Second Class in English and First Classes in History and Economics.

most educative experience, at first hand, of the foreign society and culture. The statistics of this new curriculum, and the transition to it from the previous one, are as follows: Between 1922 and 1925, 2 men and 5 women took Honours in French and German under the old scheme, and 3 men and 8 women in Latin and French; from 1923 to 1931, French was taken as principal language (with Latin, German, Spanish or Italian as subordinate) by 38 men and 101 women; German (with Latin, French or Spanish) by 7 men and 31 women; Spanish (with French) by 4 men and 2 women; and Celtic (with Latin or French) by 3 men.

The aggregate numbers for all the groups during the decade were 555 men—3 with double Honours—and 418 women—2 with double Honours. The annual average of men graduating with Honours was thus higher by more than 60 per cent. than in the twenty years before the war, and the average of women was more than doubled.

One cause of this remarkable increase, apart from the general rise of numbers in the whole Faculty, was the new regulation of the Scottish Education Department, that only those who have graduated with Honours may be appointed as principal teachers of their subjects in secondary schools; so that the Ordinary graduate who enters the teaching profession is condemned for life to a lower rank and a lower scale of salary. On the other hand, as might be expected with these larger entries, the proportion of First Classes was markedly lower than in the previous period, being about 36 per cent. among the men, 23 per cent. of the women, and 31 per cent. of the total. The proportion of Thirds was about the same as before —a fact which may have been connected with another item of the Education Department's regulations, namely the refusal to recognise Third Class Honours as qualifying a graduate for admission to training for appointment as principal teacher. The Third Class man was thus in a position virtually inferior to that of the Ordinary graduate; and the examiners in those groups in which the majority of the students were intending to become teachers could not but have the fact in mind in awarding Classes. This is one of several points in which the work of the Faculty is complicated by the policy of the Department.

As regards the relative positions of the Honours schools, it will be noted that in the period after the war the Modern Language Group, with its new alternative combinations, was attracting the largest numbers, of whom about three-quarters were women; English came second, also with a feminine majority; and History had advanced to fourth place. Of the three oldest schools, Mathematics had maintained and increased its numbers, Classics and Philosophy had fallen behind. The liberal spirit in which the Faculty had welcomed and encouraged the newer subjects was, in fact, at least as evident in the working of the Honours scheme as in the Ordinary.

In the five years 1926-31, the number of students who graduated M.A. was 715 men and 1067 women. The number of Honours graduates among these was 277 men and 235 women —a percentage of 28 : 39 per cent. of the men and 22 per cent. of the women.

More important than these merely statistical facts is the development that has taken place within the Honours Groups. Under the 1908 Ordinance—as under that of 1892—the minimum number of classes to be attended in the subjects of the Group was four, of which two must be "Honours Classes under separate Professors or Lecturers"; but in practice hardly any student would venture to present himself for the Honours Degree Examinations without having taken much more than the minimum. In some Groups it became usual to take each of the two main Honours classes twice over. Under the new scheme in Modern Languages, as has been mentioned, a period of residence and study abroad, usually of one continuous session, during which the student is in constant effective touch with the teachers in Edinburgh, is now an essential part of the curriculum. In practically every Group, supplementary courses or half-courses in special subjects or departments of subjects have been instituted; and the programme of work prescribed for the final examination, whether as obligatory or in the form of alternative options, has been extended and diversified. Opportunity was thus given, not only to the students to widen and deepen their studies, but to the Professors and Lecturers to bring their own special researches into direct and fruitful relation to their teaching. Some, indeed, of the new Lectureships which were established within the main subjects came into being in this way. Thus a Lecturer who had specialised in some particular division of the subject might have a separate Honours course or half-course in it recognised; the provision of teaching was thus enriched, and a beginning was made in introducing students to methods of research.

Again, as this elaboration within individual subjects progressed, some of the composite Honours Groups were broken up. For instance, British History was originally included as a subject in the English Group; but as the teaching of English Language developed, History was removed from the Honours Examination and, instead, was required to be taken as one of the candidate's two "outside subjects," to be passed at an earlier stage and on the Ordinary standard. Similarly in the Economics Group, either Moral Philosophy or British History had at first to be taken along with Political Economy in the Honours Examination; but, after the separate Lectureship in Economic History was founded, that subject took its place alongside Political Economy, and the other two were dropped, though British History is recommended as an "outside subject." The History Group, again, became in course of time one of the most elaborately organised. It now embraces general British History, Constitutional Law and History, European History and Political Science as obligatory items, with one optional subject chosen from a long list of alternatives—Scottish, Ecclesiastical, Economic, Greek or Roman History, History of Art, Constitution of the British Empire, and Prehistoric Archæology, in most of which both Ordinary and Honours courses have been instituted.

Each of the Honours Groups has thus developed a more or less completely articulated scheme of classes, not indeed rigid or obligatory, but normally followed from stage to stage of the curriculum; and the practice has grown up of requiring a certain minimum standard to be attained in the class-work of the earlier years, as a condition of entry to the advanced Honours courses. This at least helps to keep the numbers within manageable limits, and lessens the chances of final disappointment for those who seem unlikely to reach a satisfactory level in Honours. It is seldom found possible for a student to attempt the Final Honours Examination before the end of his fourth year (though three years is the statutory minimum); and it is not uncommon to postpone it to the fifth.

This elaboration of Honours curricula raises the question of height or depth *versus* breadth. As we have seen, the 1892 Ordinance, while it separated the Honours curriculum from the Ordinary, sought to prevent the former from becoming a merely intensive study of one particular field. It was to include at least three courses in subjects outside the Honours Group, and the choice of these was so regulated that some, at any rate, of the traditional subjects must be taken by every student. The 1908 Ordinance removed these restrictions, and at the same time reduced the number of "outside subjects" to two, the Faculty and the Senatus having power to make special rules for each group. Thus, as has been mentioned, the Honours student in English is required to take British History; in Economics, British History or Moral Philosophy; and in the other Groups various regulations are in force which in most cases limit the choice of one of the two outside subjects, leaving the other free.

In some instances, the multiplication of the classes, obligatory or optional, systematic, "tutorial," or "practical," to be taken in the Honours subjects, has made it impossible for the student to fit in others which he would desire to take as outside subjects, simply owing to difficulties of time-table. In general, the development of the Honours scheme has tended to narrow the curricula in proportion to their greater intensiveness. The balance of loss and gain from this can hardly be ascertained. The ablest Honours students, no doubt, find in the intensive work upon their special subjects an awakening and training of the whole mind, and acquire principles and methods which they can apply in any field. It may be otherwise with many who, though competent and industrious, have a narrower range of intellectual curiosity. There is some danger, when such large numbers aspire to the Honours Degree—some of them mainly for the sake of its "market value" in one particular profession—that the broad foundation of the pyramid may be sacrificed to its height, and that students who might be benefited by a widening of their interests may become dulled and bewildered by too much specialised study.

The time-table difficulty, again, affects the Ordinary curricula no less than the Honours, and grows more serious every year with the addition of new subjects and new classes to a scheme which covers the whole day from 9 A.M. to 6 P.M.

THE TUTORIAL SYSTEM AND THE TEACHING STAFF

As we have seen, one of the main objects of the 1908 Ordinance had been to give room for the development of new methods of teaching by means generally and somewhat vaguely designated "tutorial" in supplement of, or even in substitution for, the formal lecture. The statutory minimum number of lectures in a full Ordinary course was to be 75 instead of 100, spread over a teaching year of 25 or 26 instead of 22 weeks. Ordinarily, therefore, not more than three lectures a week need be delivered, and two hours a week were available for "tutorial instruction," in whichever of the many possible varieties of method it was given. The common object was to give opportunity for more direct personal contact between teacher and student and for a larger and more conscious contribution from the student to their common task; to permit the student to define his difficulties and seek for their solution in discussion; and also to increase his sense of independence and responsibility. Less of the ground in each subject would now be covered by the lectures, and more time would be occupied in exercises of various kinds, such as writing and reviewing translations, compositions and essays in the humanistic subjects, working problems in mathematics, performing laboratory experiments in physics, and so on. The practice naturally varied, according to the nature of the subject, the number of students in the class, and the views of the individual teacher. But in practically every instance, the new system involved an increase of staff.

This was fully realised when the changes were under discussion before 1908. As early as May 1906 the Faculty presented a report to the Senatus on the subject, in which it was urged that additional Assistants should be provided in most or all of the larger subjects, and that the salaries of the existing Lecturer-Assistants, who would have to undertake much of the new teaching, should be augmented. But it was also made clear that the Professors themselves were to take a large share in what was expected to be an increasingly important part of the work of their Chairs. Funds for these developments were in prospect, from the increase of class fees. The expansion of the teaching staff then adumbrated has continued steadily throughout the period.

The creation of Lectureships, both "independent" and combined with Assistantships, under the 1892 Ordinance has already been mentioned. The "independent" Lectureships were those established in new subjects, the others were attached to existing Chairs; and there was also a growing number of Assistants below the rank of Lecturer, some of whom after a period of probation were raised to Lectureship status. The numerical result of these and other new appointments upon the teaching strength in Arts since 1908 may be briefly stated. In 1908-9, there were 16 Professors (with seats on the Faculty), 7 independent Lecturers, 10 Lecturers who were also Assistants, and 10 Assistants. In 1931-32, there were 25 Professors, 4 Readers, 13 independent Lecturers, 34 Lecturers in professorial departments, and about 30 Assistants—some of the latter serving on a part-time basis. These numbers include the teachers in subjects connected with the Degrees in Commerce and Education and the Diplomas in Actuarial Science and Social Studies, but not those in subjects which, though they may be taken in the Arts curriculum, belong primarily to the

Faculty of Science (such as Chemistry or Geology) or of Law. The status of Lecturer-Assistant has been discontinued for some years, and the whole staff has been more explicitly graded in rank, salary and security of tenure.

The most important change which has taken place in this connection has been the opening of membership of the Faculty to others besides the Professors. This was accomplished by a series of Ordinances, 33, 39 and 54, passed between 1919 and 1929. The first of these created the new status of "Reader," which may be conferred either upon a Lecturer in charge of a separate subject, or upon a Lecturer attached to a professorial department; it carries with it permanent tenure and membership of the Faculty. Under the second Ordinance, a Reader may be appointed to a seat on the Senatus. The third increased the number of teachers below the rank of Professor who may be admitted to the Faculty to one-third of the total membership, and made it possible to grant such admission to Lecturers as well as Readers. Thus the Faculty now includes nearly all the teachers responsible for separate subjects and a considerable number of other senior members of the staff.

No reform of recent years has had more valuable results than this. It has removed certain obvious anomalies, strengthened the corporate sense of the teaching body, and enabled a larger number of them to contribute effectively to the policy of the Faculty. Further, an important part of the Faculty's business consists in approving, or in rare instances amending, the recommendations of the Boards of Studies, which have charge of the detailed arrangements of courses in the several main subject-departments, Languages, Philosophy, and so on. Of these Boards all Lecturers are members; and though their business is largely a matter of formal routine, it brings the junior members in touch with the work in other subjects than their own, and from time to time gives them the chance of taking part in the discussion of larger issues.

Even this great expansion of staff has not kept pace with the growing number of students, at any rate in the major subjects. For example, a teaching strength in English Literature of 1 Professor, 3 Lecturers, and 3 Assistants, two of them part-time, has to deal with some 400 students in the several classes and years. For tutorial work, the huge First Ordinary class has to be divided into sections of about forty, and the teaching of these is apt to resolve itself into something like an additional lecture, under which the more backward members may remain merely passive and receptive. The labour of reading and commenting upon essays and other exercises written by them, even though only fortnightly, is enormous and exhausting. This is an extreme instance, but none of the larger departments and few of the smaller can yet be said to be adequately staffed.

The effects of the tutorial system upon the average quality of students' work, so far as it is possible to assess them, have no doubt been excellent. But on the one hand there are still too many—and these the most in need of stimulus—who fail to come into effective touch with the teachers; and on the other, the uniformity of methods which is inevitable with such large numbers may result in too much "spoon-feeding" of the abler students, who might safely be left to themselves to "*read* for the Degree" rather than be lectured into it. At any rate, it may be doubted whether the pressure of teaching work in the three-term system is now much lighter than in the old winter session. It becomes increasingly hard for teachers, and especially Professors, to find the time for their own independent research and writing. A great Englishman, who spent a long stretch of his enormously active and productive career in an Edinburgh Chair, has written of the Scottish professoriate of those earlier days as "an almost ideal combination of vocational employment, with varied residence and opportunities for *a*vocational work and play." The change to the new system after 1908 certainly meant a considerable sacrifice on the Professors' part; and though on the whole it has been justified by its results to students, there may still be room for such development as will give both them and their teachers more leisure to think.

OTHER DEGREES AND DIPLOMAS WITHIN THE FACULTY OF ARTS

While the Arts Faculty in 1893 ceased to be responsible for the Degree curricula in Science, it has since then been called upon to administer the Ordinances for two new Degrees, in Education and in Commerce.

DEGREE IN EDUCATION

The history of the Education Degree goes back ultimately to the establishment of the Chair of Education by the Bell Trustees in 1876, which was to provide, for students intending to become teachers, instruction during their undergraduate course in the "Theory, History and Practice" of their profession. In 1885, the University instituted a "Schoolmaster's Diploma"; this was open to graduates—at first of Edinburgh only, but of other Universities later—who had attended the class of Education and certain others and had completed a course of practical training. It was granted in two grades, General for Ordinary graduates and Secondary for Honours graduates, and was "recognised" as a professional qualification by the Scottish Education Department. This recognition was afterwards withdrawn and in 1907 the Senatus resolved to discontinue the Diploma, but awards were made from time to time till 1911.

In 1914, after prolonged discussion and negotiation with the Department and the National and Provincial Committees for the Training of Teachers, it was revived with a new title and a more fully articulated curriculum, which was again revised in 1917. The Diploma in Education is open to graduates in Arts or Science of any Scottish University or of any other University recognised for the purpose, who have completed a course of professional training as teachers. The curriculum consists of the University classes of Education and Psychology (of which the former must have been taken outside the M.A. Degree curriculum, but the latter may be included in it), and a further short course on Modern Educational Systems and Problems. It was from the first intended to make this Diploma course part of an extended curriculum for a Degree in Education, and this was carried out by a new Ordinance, 18, which came into operation in 1917. For the Degree of B.Ed. a further course and examination were added to those for the Diploma, to be taken not earlier than the fifth year of University study. The Degree is on an Honours standard, and the subjects are Advanced Psychology, Advanced Education, theoretical and experimental, and School Organisation and Administration. It is usually taken after a period of professional service in teaching following the Diploma stage. The number of students who graduated B.Ed. between 1918 and 1931 was sixty-eight.

In this connection, an important development in the relations between the University and the Edinburgh Training Centre at Moray House may be recorded. In 1925, when the Chair of Education had become vacant by the death of Professor Darroch, who had done immense service to both institutions and for the general good of Scottish education, the University Court made an agreement with the National Committee, in terms of which the tenure of the Chair was conjoined with that of the Directorship of Studies at the Training Centre. The work of the Chair is thus intimately associated with the work of professional training, and is in fact carried on at Moray House. Further, the special interests and needs of those Arts undergraduates who intend to enter the Training Centre are directly represented on the Faculty by the Professor.

DEGREE IN COMMERCE

The idea of a Degree in Commerce was born during the war. At the end of 1916, the Edinburgh Chamber of Commerce laid before the University the suggestion that, in prospect of the difficulties that would beset the country at the end of the war, and of the need for "a co-ordination of energy and intelligence" to maintain our commercial position, the University "should open to those who desire to occupy responsible positions in commerce a curriculum which would afford them a training designed to meet their needs, and that the successful completion of such a curriculum should be indicated by the bestowal of a Degree." The suggestion was at once taken up, and work was begun upon the drafting of a scheme, though it was not until more than a year later that the Ordinance 22 instituting the Degree of Bachelor of Commerce was finally approved. It came into operation in 1918-19.

The Commerce curriculum consists partly of subjects already established in the Arts and Science Faculties and partly of others, for which provision was now made for the first time. For the latter, funds were contributed by a number of public bodies, the Edinburgh and Leith Chambers of Commerce, the Merchant Company, the Leith Shipowners, the Accountants' Society and the Bankers' Institute. These provided endowments for the two subjects, Accounting and Business Method, and Organisation of Industry, both of which are now full Chairs. Seven full courses, or an equivalent number of half-courses, must be taken over a period of three years. Every candidate must attend full courses in Political Economy and at least one modern foreign language, which is studied on the same linguistic and literary standard as for Arts, and at least half-courses in Accounting, Organisation, Mercantile Law, Economic History and Economic Geography. The remainder is made up by various alternative options, including sciences with a bearing on industry, Industrial Law, International Law, Banking and certain advanced branches of Economics. The students are under the guidance of a special Director of Studies; and an endeavour has been made, on the whole with much success, to bring them into touch after graduation with industrial and commercial firms, banks and other possible employers. A considerable number of those who have taken the course have been men engaged in civil or municipal services. Between 1920 and 1931, the Degree was completed by nearly 300 students, and the number taking the curriculum has averaged about 140, with some 25 per cent. of women in recent years.

From an etching by] [*William Hole, R.S.A.*

JOHN STUART BLACKIE AND SAMUEL HENRY BUTCHER
1852-1882 1882-1903

Professors of Greek

OTHER DIPLOMA COURSES

The expansion of the Faculty's activities after the war is also indicated by the creation of several new Diplomas besides that in Education. The first was the Diploma in Geography. This subject, since its admission to the Arts curriculum in 1908, had been attracting large numbers of students, and, in addition to the class for the Ordinary Degree, an advanced course within the Honours Group of Economics had been instituted. The growing demand for specially qualified teachers of Geography in schools led to the provision of still further courses and, in 1919, a full Diploma curriculum was drawn up. It embraced various scientific, technical and historical branches of geographical study, and was to be completed either after graduation in Arts or Science or simultaneously with a Degree curriculum of at least four years. The Diploma remained until 1930, when it was superseded by the new M.A. Honours Group of Geography, with a scheme occupying a normal period of four years and including Geology, as well as the usual two "outside subjects." A dissertation based on original field-survey work is also required.

In 1919 also, the University, after consultation with the Faculty of Actuaries, who contributed funds for the purpose, instituted a Diploma in Actuarial Mathematics, with a two-years' curriculum. The students have to satisfy the normal conditions for entrance to study for Degrees, but are not required, as in the case of other Diplomas, actually to graduate before or at completion of the Diploma.

Another new branch of University work is the organisation of systematic training of workers for social service in the many forms, public, industrial and philanthropic, that have been developed in the last generation. This began with the formation, largely on the initiative of Professor James Seth, of the Edinburgh School of Social Study and Training in the years immediately after the war. The School was from the first "under the auspices of the University," which gave accommodation for its teaching and admitted its students to attend the appropriate University classes. Courses in ethical and economic theory, in industrial and social history and psychology, in hygiene and in local and national administration, were instituted (some being the existing Degree courses, in whole or in part), supplemented by practical work. Two curricula were drawn up, one qualifying for a Certificate for students not proceeding to a Degree, and a second for a Diploma to be taken after or along with a Degree curriculum. In 1928 the School was formally incorporated as a University Department, its Director received the status of University Lecturer in Social Economics, and a special Board of Studies was set up to administer its curriculum, under the authority of the Faculty of Arts.

A still further series of post-graduate Diplomas has been instituted in some of the language subjects. That in English Language is for those who have graduated with Honours in the English Group, including English Language on a subordinate or Intermediate Honours standard, and who spend a further year in advanced study of Old and Middle English, and write a thesis or dissertation. Other Diplomas in German, Spanish and French are for those who have taken Honours in two Modern Languages; one of these has been taken on a subordinate standard in the Degree curriculum, but is continued for a further year up to the full Honours standard for the Diploma.

POST-GRADUATE STUDY AND THE DOCTORATES

These Diplomas form part of a larger development which has made great advances during the period, especially in recent years, namely the organisation and recognition of post-graduate research work. This has been carried on in all the Faculties, most actively perhaps in Divinity and Science; but the Faculty of Arts has had a considerable share, direct and indirect.

In 1895 the Commissioners made an Ordinance, common to all the four Universities, instituting three new Doctoral Degrees, in Science, Philosophy and Letters. These were to be obtained by thesis, and to be open to Masters of Arts of any Scottish University, of at least five years' standing, with

First or Second Class Honours, in Mathematics and Natural Philosophy for the D.Sc. Degree, in Mental Philosophy for the D.Phil., and in any other Group for the D.Litt. Powers were also given to accept Degrees of other Universities, or in other Faculties, as equivalent for this purpose to an Honours M.A., and in particular a Scottish B.Sc. But in such cases the candidate was required to spend two winter sessions as a Research student in the University before submitting his thesis, whereas in the other cases the work might be done anywhere.

Two new principles were introduced by this measure. First, there was the general principle that the Universities ought to have means of testing and recognising advanced study; the thesis was to be "an original contribution to learning," or, in Science, "a record of original research," not a mere compilation. Secondly, the Scottish Honours Arts graduate was not necessarily required to do his work under supervision in the University where he had been an undergraduate, or even restricted to that University for his Doctorate. With few exceptions, however, the Edinburgh Arts Doctorates have been taken by Edinburgh Masters of Arts.

Various modifications have been made in the scheme by later Ordinances, especially those in which the curricula for Degrees in Science have been elaborated. In 1919, when the new Degree of Ph.D. was instituted for all Faculties (as will be described presently), the D.Phil. was discontinued; and instead the D.Litt. was opened to graduates with Honours in Mental Philosophy. The number of the Doctorates awarded up to that date was:—D.Phil., 18 men and one woman; D.Litt., 16 men and one woman. From 1919 to 1931, 19 men and 2 women graduated D.Litt., including some whose theses were on philosophical subjects. The standard of the Degree, always high, has naturally become more exacting in the later period, now that the Ph.D. is available for researches of smaller scope.

The system of higher Degrees was extended after the war, when there was a general demand for better organisation of post-graduate research. European and American examples were cited; and the British Universities were exhorted to make provision, not only for their own graduates but for those who might come from other countries. Legislation in this sense was at once put in hand by each of the Scottish Universities, all following the same general line of instituting a new Doctorate obtainable in any Faculty, by thesis submitted after a period of research carried out under supervision.

This new Degree bears the now general title of Doctor of Philosophy—not perhaps strikingly appropriate to all the varieties of subject-matter which may be treated in the theses. It is open to any graduate, with or without Honours, of any Faculty and any University. The candidate must specify his subject of research and satisfy the Senatus of his fitness to undertake it. He must spend at least two years upon it, during which his work is supervised by one or more of the Professors or Lecturers, and finally he submits a thesis embodying its results. Each applicant is assigned to the appropriate Faculty, and here only the practice of the Faculty of Arts need be described. It has become usual to require those who are not Edinburgh graduates to spend at least the greater part of their time actually in the University; Edinburgh graduates may be allowed, if the nature of their subjects makes it advisable, to carry on part of their research elsewhere, provided they keep in effective touch with their supervisors. If the student is engaged in professional or other work in addition to his research, he must spend at least three years. Between 1921 and 1931, the number of theses on subjects within the Arts Faculty's authority which were sustained for the Degree was 83, 58 by men and 25 by women. This represents a heavy addition to the work of the members of the Faculty who have been appointed as supervisors and examiners, especially Professors in the major subjects. No doubt many of the theses have been valuable pieces of research that might never have been done but for the incentive of the Doctorate. But opinion is by no means unanimous on the question whether the results of the system are fully commensurate to the labour, or whether it is really the best way of promoting higher studies in the Arts subjects.

This question suggests another concerning the Arts Degree which may be very briefly touched upon. The Scottish custom of awarding the Mastership as a first Degree in Arts is not in accord with the practice of any other University, and has not always been followed even in Scotland. In pre-Reformation times, before Edinburgh was founded, the three elder Universities had four grades: the Baccalaureate, which marked the completion of the third year of study; the Licentiate, *licentia ubique docendi*, at the end of the fourth; the Mastership, normally taken within the following year, which conferred full membership of the University as a teaching body, and was supposed to carry the obligation of teaching in it for a time; and the Doctorate, which was also a teaching Degree but in some particular subject, and which became in the end merely honorary. Thus the establishment in 1895 of the new Doctorates by thesis was in a sense a revival. In Edinburgh, the Licentiate at the end of the four years' course does not seem to have existed apart from the Mastership. But in certain periods in the eighteenth and the early nineteenth century instances occur in all four Universities of the granting of a Bachelor of Arts Degree. The Commission of Visitation of 1826 proposed to regulate this, both Ordinary and Honours, with a curriculum of four years and six of the seven subjects; the seventh, Natural Philosophy, was to be reserved for a further year of study for the Master's Degree, with others, such as Political Economy and Chemistry. These recommendations were not carried out; and the B.A., which continued to be given in a rather irregular and haphazard way, signified merely the completion of part of the M.A. course. It was abolished by the 1858 Commissioners, who made the M.A. the only Arts Degree. In 1892 the Edinburgh Senatus of their own authority instituted a new qualification of "Licentiate in Arts," which was simply the Baccalaureate without the name or standing of a Degree. It could be conferred on a student who had passed in any five of the seven subjects required for the M.A., and was thus of no particular character. It was taken only by a few, and in 1901 was abolished.

But the question of reviving the B.A. Degree has recently been reopened. It is urged that the Scottish Universities should conform to normal academic usage by reserving the title of Master of Arts for a status higher than that of a first Degree, or at any rate of a pass Degree completed in three years. The suggestion is either that the undergraduate course of three years should lead to the Baccalaureate, and the Bachelor should "proceed Master" after a further period of study; or else, that the M.A. Degree should be conferred only after a four-years' curriculum of more exacting standard or with Honours. A historical narrative like this, however, is not the place to discuss the merits of the question.

NEW REGULATIONS FOR ENTRANCE TO THE UNIVERSITY

The Joint Board of Examiners and the system of Preliminary Examinations set up by the Commissioners in 1892 continued to control the entrance of students to study for the Arts Degree (as for other Degrees) until 1918. At the end of that year an entirely new scheme came into force, which was embodied in Ordinance LXX (General No. 3) of the four University Courts.

The principle of the new Ordinance is thus stated in the preamble: "It is expedient that the normal test of fitness for admission to the Scottish Universities should be the production of evidence duly attested by a competent authority of the satisfactory completion of a suitable course of secondary education"—a formula whose most potent implications lie in the epithets, "normal," "satisfactory" and "suitable." Simple as the words might appear, the principle has not been found easy of application. Its main object was to bring the Universities into a more organic relation to the whole educational system of Scotland.*

In the scheme of the Preliminary Examination, as we have seen, the Universities' Joint Board, while requiring every

* The conception and the drafting of the Ordinance were largely the work of the late Viscount Haldane.

entrant to show his knowledge of certain subjects—the list varying according to the Faculty in which he desired to graduate—was empowered to accept passes in these subjects at the Scottish Leaving Certificate Examination (or other similar tests) in lieu of passes at the Preliminary. An increasing proportion of the students who came from schools in Scotland obtained their admission, in whole or in part, in this way. In 1918 it was decided that the Universities should be relieved altogether of the task of examining these students, and that the Leaving Certificate should be, not merely an alternative to the Preliminary Examination, but the normal avenue for Scottish entrants. The Preliminary would be taken only by those who were unable to take the Leaving Certificate, that is, mainly by students from outside Scotland, and by Scottish students who were not educated in schools presenting their pupils for the Certificate.

The Leaving Certificate was thus to be, for the great majority of Arts students, the "evidence of the satisfactory completion of a suitable course of secondary education." But the Universities were to be entitled to judge of the "satisfactoriness" and of the "suitability"; that is, they were to accept, not any and every form of Leaving Certificate, but only those which attested a satisfactory attainment in the kind of subjects required as a foundation for academic study, namely, Languages (including a good command of English), Mathematics and Science. In deciding these questions, they were to be represented by a new Entrance Board of sixteen members. It was not primarily an examining body like the old Joint Board. Its main function was to assess the value, for University purposes, of examinations conducted by other bodies; but it was also to provide examination tests for those students who could not present a sufficient certificate. The Preliminary Examinations, therefore, continued to be held as before; and since there is always a considerable number of Scottish students who have either failed to obtain a Leaving Certificate at school, or whose Certificates are lacking in subjects required for the Universities, it is usual to allow these, as well as others, to make up their deficiencies by passes at the Preliminary. This is perhaps contrary to the intention of the Ordinance, which purports to allow such entries only "in exceptional circumstances," whereas the cases referred to occur as a matter of course every year. But a strict interpretation of the rule would impose severe hardships, and would in fact place many Scottish students at a disadvantage in comparison with those from elsewhere.

Moreover, the Ordinance specifies that admission is to be granted "to enter upon a course of study *in any Faculty*." This, after much controversy, has come to be interpreted as meaning that the conditions of entry are to be *the same for all the Faculties*. Here serious difficulties arise, for the Faculties are not at one in their requirements regarding particular subjects and standards. For several years after the passing of the Ordinance the Entrance Board was labouring to produce a set of detailed regulations on these matters that would satisfy all needs. At one stage a scheme was drafted which would have differentiated, for example, between entrants for Arts and for Science; but this, though approved by all the Senates and by a majority of the Courts, was successfully opposed by the champions of uniformity. In the end, as late as February 1927, the present regulations were accepted and came into force.

Their main items are as follows:—Every student who is to proceed to a Degree must obtain from the Entrance Board an "Attestation of Fitness," the conditions of which are the same for all Faculties. The two principal alternative ways of obtaining it are (*a*) by the presentation of a Scottish Leaving Certificate (or, for students from outside Scotland, of another similar certificate) and (*b*) by completing the Preliminary Examination. There are certain differences in detail between the two, but the general requirements are the same in both, namely, that the student must show attainment in at least four subjects: (1) English; (2) Mathematics or Physical Science; (3) a foreign language, ancient or modern; and (4) a fourth subject, which may be one of the foregoing not already counted, or one of a number of others, including Natural Science. The general content of the qualification, as distinct from its form and standard, is thus very much the same as under the former system.

The difficulties arise especially from the fact that two standards are recognised for certain subjects, particularly in Latin, Greek, and Mathematics, and that two of the four passes may be on the Lower Standard. The effect of this for the Arts student is that he may now be admitted, say, with only lower passes in Latin and Mathematics, or lacking one or even both of these subjects altogether. Again, the Senatus have power to require that for attendance on any particular class—it may be one which is an essential part of the curriculum—some special qualification must be shown, either in the subject of the class itself or in some other which is needed for its study, for instance, Latin for advanced classes in English Literature or for Mediæval History. In such cases, and in others that could be cited, the student, though allowed to enter upon the curriculum, may find himself unable to complete it without passing in some further Preliminary Examination, and this is apt to impede his progress in his Degree classes.

The ideal procedure would be to admit no one until he is fully qualified to take all the classes necessary for his particular Degree; but this cannot be realised so long as the entrance test is a uniform one for all Degrees. Apart from this, the main principle of the Ordinance has been attacked on the ground that, by making the Leaving Certificate the normal qualification, the Universities have handed over the keys of their entrance-gate to an external authority, whose functions and interests, though closely touching their own, are yet essentially different.

These, however, are controversial issues, and are still under debate. The aim of the Entrance Ordinance, to make the Universities the crown and completion of a fully articulated national scheme, was unquestionably high and far-reaching, but it was formulated at a time when many of those who would have to operate it were pre-occupied with special duties and anxieties in war-time, and its difficulties were perhaps not fully realised. At any rate, it cannot be supposed that the final solution of this complex and vitally important problem has yet been reached.

UNIVERSITY OF EDINBURGH

NEW SCHEME FOR SCHOLARSHIP AND BURSARY ENDOWMENTS

The passing of the Educational Endowments (Scotland) Act, 1928, setting up a Commission with powers to frame new schemes for administering the many trusts which, in the course of generations, had been created for educational purposes throughout the country, suggested to the University Court and Senatus that they should take occasion to review and revise the conditions under which the University's numerous Scholarship, Bursary and Prize funds were administered. The Act expressly exempted University endowments—as also endowments for religious education—from the Commissioners' jurisdiction; but it was provided that any University which so elected might request the Commissioners to undertake the revision of any of its funds, in which case they would acquire the right to frame schemes for such funds at their discretion, subject to an appeal to the Scottish Universities Committee of the Privy Council, with whom the final decision would lie. The Court, after consulting the Senatus, decided to take the somewhat bold and hazardous step of making such a request to the Commissioners—a step which none of the other three Universities ventured to take, but which was fully justified by its results. These results are embodied in the Commissioners' "Edinburgh University Fellowships, Scholarships and Bursaries Scheme, 1931," which received the final approval of His Majesty in Council and came into force in July 1932.

It should be stated that the Scheme does not cover all the Scholarship and Bursary endowments of the University; a number of these, mostly of more recent origin, were not in need of amendment, and were not submitted to the Commissioners. These are still administered under their former governing instruments.

The Scheme is a highly elaborate and complex document. It deals with some eighty-five separate endowments, whose dates of foundation range from the reign of William III to the opening decade of the present century, and their incomes from £10 to £3000 a year. Their purposes are hardly less various, but for the present survey they may be arranged under two main heads: (*a*) Fellowships and Scholarships for students who have already completed, or are about to complete, their undergraduate curricula in the several Faculties; (*b*) Bursaries for undergraduates, mostly for award at entrance to the curriculum. A third category might be added, that of Prizes, but these present no special difficulty.

Before entering upon some of the details regarding these classes severally, one provision of the Scheme may be noted which applies to all the funds alike. The Commissioners under the Act of 1889 had made possible the admission of women to study for degrees. They had also (by their Ordinance No. 58) made some provision for admitting women to eligibility for Bursaries and Scholarships, but with a certain timidity. They gave power to the University Court to open to competition, without distinction of sex, any Fellowship, Scholarship or Bursary which had been in operation for twenty-five years before the date of their Commission (*i.e.* before August 1864); but they forbade women being accepted as candidates for any one of later date, unless it were expressly open to them in terms of the Deed of Foundation. This Ordinance was both difficult and vexatious in application, at any rate to foundations created between 1864 and 1892 (the date when women were admitted to graduation). After 1892, if a gift were made for the benefit of "students of the University," the term might be supposed to include women; before 1892, it could be argued, a founder could only have had men in mind and his benefaction ought not to be used for the behoof of women students.

The Senatus, however, had for more than twenty years, with the full concurrence of the University Court, ventured simply to ignore the cautious limits laid down by the 1889 Commissioners, and had allowed women to compete on the same terms as men for all these foundations. The legality of this action had never been challenged, and might be held to be now established by mere use and wont. But it was desirable to clear up the matter beyond doubt, and accordingly a clause was put into the new Scheme, that "Each of the

Fellowships, Scholarships, Bursaries and Prizes to be awarded under this Scheme shall be open to persons of both sexes." Statute was thus brought into harmony with practice.

(a) *Scholarship Funds.*—The University in the middle and later decades of the nineteenth century had been fortunate in receiving a considerable number of gifts or bequests of capital sums to be applied for the benefit of students who had distinguished themselves in their undergraduate studies. To these the term "Scholarship" is generally applied (a few, mostly of larger amount, are designated "Fellowships"). They vary in annual value from £75 or £80 to as much as £250. Most of them are assigned to particular subjects or groups of subjects: for instance, in the Arts Faculty, to one or other of the three main Departments of which the old fixed M.A. curriculum consisted before the changes made in 1892, namely, Classics, Philosophy, and Mathematics and Natural Philosophy. In some cases, the pursuit of advanced study or research, in Edinburgh or elsewhere, was made a specific condition of tenure by the Deeds of Foundation; and this condition had in practice been imposed by the Senatus in nearly every case. The Scholarships thus serve the vitally important purpose of enabling specially distinguished students, at the critical epoch after graduation, to devote themselves for a further period to strictly academic study. Many of the scholars from the Arts Faculty, for instance, have gone to Oxford or to Cambridge, or to Continental universities, for further degrees; others, in Medicine or Science, have undertaken research in the subjects of their future professions.

The Commissioners' Scheme made no change in the general principles of the Scholarship system, but was directed to their more effective operation. In some instances, groups of Scholarships in the same or kindred subjects have been "pooled" to form a series of consolidated funds—*e.g.* those for Classical, Philosophical and Divinity Scholarships—within each of which the several foundations retain their separate names and identities; but provision can be made for a more regular rotation, so that in each year about the same number will be available for award. Some changes have been made in the periods of tenure and the annual values. For example, the Scholarships on the Vans Dunlop foundation, the greatest of these funds (established in 1879), were fixed by the founder at the value of £100 a year for three years: under the new Scheme, power is given to the Senatus, while retaining the system of triennial awards, to decide that any Vans Dunlop Scholarship shall be of the value of £150 for two years. This in some measure restores the original relation between the amount of the Scholar's income and its purchasing power; while it is found that two years' post-graduate study or research is in most cases sufficient for his purpose.

Further, the "pooling" of the funds makes possible a more satisfactory method of dealing with unexpended balances of income. Under the former practice, such balances were automatically added to capital, and some of the funds, from which fewer awards had been made, had been largely augmented in this way, without a corresponding increase in their usefulness. Powers have now been taken to apply the balances of the new consolidated funds from time to time to purposes other than the mere accumulation of capital: such as the extension of the period of tenure of a specially meritorious Scholar, or the increase of the payments to one in special need; the making of grants for the expenses of Scholars' research work or the publication of its results; the provision of travelling allowances, or the award of an occasional Scholarship in the subjects proper to the fund, such as may be desirable in a year when the number of distinguished candidates exceeds that of the regular Scholarships available. In general, the Scheme, while observing the main purposes of the founders, has enabled the Senatus to apply the funds more effectively in accordance with changing conditions, financial and academic. In all cases, the power of the Senatus to require the Scholars to pursue approved study or research is explicitly asserted.

The aggregate income of all the Scholarship endowments included in the Scheme is nearly £10,000, the present number of Scholarships being 80.

(b) *Bursary Funds.*—The Bursary endowments were much more multifarious in their origins and conditions than the

Scholarship endowments. The aggregate income of those included in the Commissioners' Scheme is about £4700, from which 127 Bursaries are provided. The principle of "pooled" or consolidated funds has been applied to them even more generally than to the Scholarships; Bursaries are grouped according to the Faculty or Faculties in which they are tenable, their separate names and identities being preserved. In place of the varying periods of tenure hitherto in force—which caused arbitrary and inconvenient fluctuations in the number of Bursaries available for award from year to year—it is laid down that each shall be tenable for the period necessary to complete the Degree curriculum (Ordinary or Honours as the case may be). Provision is made for applying unexpended balances in the several funds, to extend tenures in special cases, to make additional payments to Bursars in special need, or to other appropriate purposes; the Senatus also have power to allow a Bursary of less than £25 to be held along with another by a student in necessitous circumstances.

The principal changes, however, have been in the direction of enabling the Senatus, first, to impose upon all holders some test of their fitness (beyond the possession of the minimum entrance qualification), and second, to use a wider discretion in the case of the "preferential" or "restricted" Bursaries. Many of the foundations were originally given primarily or solely for the benefit of students from a particular parish or county, or even of a particular name. In the changed conditions since the passing of the Education (Scotland) Act, 1919, which gave powers to the local Education Authorities to make grants to students coming to the University, these restrictions had become less necessary, especially in the rural areas; on the other hand, the number of Bursaries available for award in open competition was quite inadequate. There was also a number of "patronage" Bursaries which, though vested in the University, were tenable only by students presented by outside patrons, whether individuals or bodies.

The Commissioners have applied the following principles to all those Bursaries which are for award to students entering the curriculum. All candidates must present themselves at the Entrance Bursary Examination held each year, the subjects and conditions of which are determined by the Senatus. None of the Bursaries included in the Scheme may be awarded to any candidate unless his name is placed on the published list of those whose performance in the Examination is judged sufficient to merit an award. The various preferences or restrictions indicated by the founders have been so far retained that preferential Bursaries are open in the first instance to preferential candidates placed on this list; but if none so appear, the Bursary becomes, *pro hac vice*, an open Bursary, available for award to any candidate on the list. All preferences or restrictions referring to particular surnames have, however, been removed altogether. Patrons, again, are entitled to present candidates to compete, but not to secure Bursaries unless they show sufficient merit. A certain number of the Bursaries are specifically restricted to "students who require pecuniary aid in obtaining a University education," the determination of the requisite degree of need being left to the Senatus.

The effect of these provisions is to give the Senatus, from year to year, at once a larger and more evenly distributed number of Bursaries for award to entrants who show marked promise, while at the same time the interest of the localities favoured by original founders has been safeguarded. Above all, the desire of the founders to benefit individual students has been respected; none of the funds has been diverted to any other purpose. The Scheme is the outcome of much labour and frequent consultation between the University and the Commissioners, who throughout showed their desire to strengthen the hands and increase the freedom of the Senatus in carrying out these vitally important trusts.

BUILDINGS AND ACCOMMODATION

At the date when the present survey begins, the new buildings in Teviot Row were being finished, and the transference thither of the Medical departments, except Natural History, was completed in 1884. This greatly relieved the congestion in the Old College — the name officially adopted in 1920 to distinguish the building on South Bridge—which was left with only three Faculties to house. But the relief was far from sufficient even then and, as time went on, new departments and new methods in old departments demanded ever more room. Not only was the actual cubic space too small; it was occupied, apart from libraries and administrative offices, mainly by large class-rooms adapted only for lectures. The internal rearrangement of a structure with massive walls of Craigleith stone involved great technical difficulties and heavy cost; and though minor alterations were incessantly being made, no real solution of the problem could be achieved within the four corners of the Old College. The inevitable tendency was to overflow on to other sites.

The stages of this process are detailed elsewhere; but those of them which have chiefly concerned the Arts Faculty may be summarised here. Two of the main scientific departments were the first to migrate, Engineering in 1905 and Natural Philosophy in 1906, to sites a stone's throw to the east of the Old College. In 1914 Agriculture and Forestry moved to George Square, and in the same year Mathematics was housed in premises on the north side of Chambers Street. After the war, a further series of removals began. The inauguration, in 1919, of the scheme of building on the University's new land at West Mains, The King's Buildings, led in due course to the departure of Geology in 1923 and Natural History in 1929. In 1926 another property in Chambers Street, now restored to its historic name of Minto House, was acquired and adapted to take in English and the Modern Languages. In 1929 rooms adjoining the Mathematical Institute were provided for the new subject of Prehistoric Archæology. And in 1931 Geography went into occupation of the Engineering premises when that department was removed to The King's Buildings. Finally, the reunion of the Churches in 1929, to be followed by the union of the old Church of Scotland Divinity Hall with the New College of the United Free Church, has enabled part of the work of the Faculty of Divinity to be transferred to the latter building on the Mound.

From the painting by] [*William Nicholson*

GEORGE EDWARD BATEMAN SAINTSBURY, LL.D., D.LITT.

Professor of Rhetoric and English Literature
1895-1915

But the problem of accommodation of the Arts departments still remains difficult. The needs of the central Library and the many departmental and class libraries, both for shelf-room and for students' reading-rooms, are still inadequately supplied. Common-room accommodation for students and teachers is sadly lacking;* administration and examinations claim ever more space; and above all, there is an urgent demand for small rooms to be used for the intimate tutorial teaching of individuals or small groups, which cannot be properly given in large class-rooms. The Old College, noble in its outward architecture, has in the complicated recesses of its interior many unlovely and comfortless places, whose furnishings of desks and benches seem designed to humble the body without elevating the spirit. The situation itself, in the heart of a busy quarter of the city, with lines of increasingly noisy traffic on three sides, and exposed to dust and smoke and the familiar Edinburgh easterly *haar*, certainly keeps the University aware of the community in which it lives. This is no doubt a spiritual advantage and a vital element in the Edinburgh academic tradition. But it has its price.

THE DEANS OF THE FACULTY

In the first forty years of the half-century, the Faculty of Arts had only three Deans, each of whom made a notable contribution to its policy through the many changes that have been described. The first of them, Professor Alexander Campbell Fraser, had already been Dean for some twenty years when the period opened, and remained in office till his retirement from the Logic Chair in 1891. For almost the whole of his last decade (from Blackie's retirement in 1882), he was the senior member of the Faculty, and had an unrivalled authority among his colleagues. His figure, with venerable philosophic beard in which he would sometimes veil his face when wrestling with some metaphysical problem in class, was that of an ancient sage, aloof and absent-minded; but

* A Women Students' Common Room was opened in 1931.

he was a most competent man of business, in the stately and leisurely fashion of those times.

Campbell Fraser's successor in the Deanship was George Chrystal, Professor of Mathematics since 1879. He took office just when the new scheme for the Arts Degree, under the 1892 Ordinance, was about to be inaugurated; and he remained throughout its operation, and led the Faculty through the transition to the existing Ordinance in 1908. Those who were his colleagues during these twenty years remember him as one of the ablest administrators the University has ever had. He had a wide knowledge of the educational problems of the time in Scotland, a clear conception of how the University ought to deal with them, and a gift of lucid and persuasive argument. He was the champion of the newer subjects in their claim to fuller recognition in the Arts curriculum; and the generous measure in which these claims were provided for under the 1908 Ordinance was mainly due to him. If, as has been suggested, the momentum of the reform carried it rather too far in the direction of complete freedom of choice and equality of subjects, the value of Chrystal's work, at the time when it was done, remains beyond question. And in handling the mass of Faculty affairs from day to day, his cool and steady judgment, his power of rapid decision, and his unfailing thoroughness in detail were beyond praise.

When Chrystal died in 1911 of illness brought on by his unsparing devotion to work, his place was inevitably taken by Professor (now Sir Richard) Lodge. His thirteen years in the Deanship were again a critical period; for though no large change of policy, like those of 1892 and 1908, was mooted, the development under the latter scheme was in progress, especially in the Honours Groups. The expansion of the staff, the addition of new subjects, the rapid increase in the number of students, made the Dean's work ever more arduous; and the war brought its own special anxieties. Professor Lodge had also to preside over the creation of the Education and Commerce Degrees, and to guide the Faculty in the difficulties that arose in the working of the new Entrance Ordinance. In all this, in the large share which he took in general University administration as a member of the University Court throughout his Deanship and for a time as its Secretary, and in the many forms of his public work, he inspired the despairing admiration of his colleagues no less than their confidence.

Since Sir Richard Lodge's resignation in 1924, a year before he retired from the Chair of History, the Deanship has been held for shorter periods: from 1924 to 1927 by Professor Edmund Taylor Whittaker, who initiated the scheme of Types for the Ordinary Degree; from 1927 to 1929 by Professor Herbert John Clifford Grierson; and since 1929 by Professor Norman Kemp Smith. As the bulk and the variety of the Faculty's business grow, it becomes more and more difficult for any Professor to give more than a few years to service as Dean. And while the Faculty has unquestionably derived great benefit from the experience and authority of a Dean who has been long in office, there are compensating advantages in the other practice, which gives more members of the Faculty the opportunity of realising, by close contact, how its affairs are conducted from day to day, and its relations with other parts of the University.

THE MEMBERSHIP OF THE FACULTY

It remains to attempt some account of the *personnel* of the Faculty and of the work in its several departments and subjects during these fifty years. This must obviously be done in a very summary fashion, so many are the men, so various their gifts and personalities, and so immense the range of the Liberal Arts which they represent.

The Faculty of Arts as a distinct organ of the academic body dates from 1708. It consisted primarily of those Professors whose classes made up the Arts curriculum, who from 1762 numbered seven. But from the latter part of the eighteenth century it had been increased by the foundation of Professorships in subjects not belonging to any of the other three Faculties. Of these, some were ultimately to be transferred to the Faculty of Science: Astronomy (founded in 1786), Agriculture (1790), Engineering (1868), and Geology

(1871). The others were in humanistic subjects, though not yet recognised for the purposes of the Arts Degree: Sanskrit (1862), Political Economy (1871, also belonging to the Law Faculty), Education (1876), Fine Art (1880), and Celtic (1882). In 1893 the Commissioners, by their Ordinance 31, made a fresh arrangement; they constituted the separate Faculty of Science and reconstituted Arts with fifteen Chairs, including the Chair of History then about to be founded, and also those of Hebrew and Constitutional Law and History. Since that date, the professorial membership has risen to twenty-five. The new foundations are Ancient History and Palæography (1901, Sir William Fraser's Foundation), French (1918), German (founded in 1919, though the first appointment to the Chair was not made till 1926), Accounting and Business Method (1919), Natural Philosophy (a second Chair, founded in 1922 in memory of Professor Peter Guthrie Tait, and designed especially for the teaching of Mathematical Physics), Organisation of Industry and Commerce (1925), Prehistoric Archæology (by Lord Abercromby's bequest in 1927), Geography (1931), and Psychology (1931); and in 1908 the Professor of Ecclesiastical History was given a seat on the Arts Faculty as well as on that of Divinity. Under the University Court's Ordinances of 1919 and 1929, as has been mentioned, a number of Readers and Lecturers may also be admitted to seats, up to half the number of the Professors. The Faculty has thus much more than doubled its size during the half-century.

Of those who were members at the opening of this period there is one whose term of active service covered nearly the whole of it. Gerard Baldwin Brown was appointed the first occupant of the Watson Gordon Chair of Fine Art in 1880, and retired from it, but not from teaching and authorship, in 1930. His work for the University and for the cause of the fine arts in Scotland is too recent to be spoken of here. But it may be permitted to say that no Professor of his time has better represented "sweetness and light," or been more effective in opening new windows in the minds of Scottish students. He died in 1932, in his eighty-third year.

FACULTY OF ARTS

LANGUAGES AND LITERATURE

The Chair of Humanity, the old and gracious designation of Latin letters in the Scottish Universities, was occupied from 1863 by the stately and urbane William Young Sellar, remembered especially as the author of a series of volumes on the Roman poets which are still classics of classical criticism. In 1891 he was succeeded by Harry Chester Goodhart, a young Cambridge scholar of brilliant parts and winning personality, who died at the opening of his prime in 1895. William Ross Hardie, who then returned to his original University with a record of unsurpassed success as a Fellow of Balliol, was the most accomplished classic among the Edinburgh graduates of his century. His extraordinarily powerful verbal memory, combined with unerring taste in the choice of words, made him especially a master in composition and translation, whether from or into the ancient languages. He was conscientious to a fault in his preparation for even the simplest parts of his class-work, to which he brought all the resources of his learning. His output in print was thus smaller than it should have been, but all of it was informed by the same judgment, sincerity and thoroughness. At Hardie's death in 1916 the Humanity Chair was left vacant till after the end of the war, when Professor Oliffe Legh Richmond, then of Cardiff, was appointed.

At the opening of the half-century the Chair of Greek had just been vacated by John Stuart Blackie, who for thirty years had delighted and diverted his students with his exhibition of Hellenic versatility, not omitting some teaching of the Greek language. In 1882 Samuel Henry Butcher came from Cambridge *via* Oxford to make conquest of Edinburgh not less decisively, though in a different way. With a singularly attractive grace in bearing and speech, he appealed by sheer contrast to the rather unkempt Scottish undergraduate as an embodiment of Hellenism, at any rate on its aristocratic side. His books on the Aristotelian Poetic and on the *Aspects of the Greek Genius* perpetuate the charm, but cannot wholly convey its essence. He gave much service in general University affairs in the Court and in the Union as well as in the Senatus, and helped to fight the rearguard action of the older subjects in the debates preceding the change of the Arts curriculum.

The next Professor of Greek, appointed in 1903, was Alexander William Mair, a young Aberdeen and Cambridge man who had been Butcher's Assistant and had done the full work of the Chair for a time in his absence. Mair was master of the Greek language almost as familiarly as of his mother-tongue; he had a notable poetic gift and a remarkable power of getting into close touch with his students, in spite of, or rather because of, his unconventional ways as a teacher. His sudden and tragic death in 1928, in an outbreak of fire in his house, cut him off in the midst of strenuous literary labours, only part of which had been published. Much of them had been done in the more recondite regions of Greek poetry, such as the Alexandrines, in which his really profound learning had been exercised with most fruitful results. The Chair was filled by Arthur Wallace Pickard-Cambridge, formerly Fellow of Balliol, till he was appointed Vice-Chancellor of Sheffield University in 1930, when Professor William Moir Calder came from Manchester.

David Masson, Professor of Rhetoric and English Literature since 1865, was of all the Faculty perhaps the most outstanding and popular figure in the Tercentenary year. His immense vigour and gusto, the power of phrase that "made his lectures literature," and his wide personal acquaintance with the great Victorians, inspired his huge classes, increased as they already were by the large attendance of women prior to their admission as students for the Degree. George Edward Bateman Saintsbury, who succeeded him in 1895, came with an illustrious record of literary and political journalism in London, and continued for twenty years, while performing the whole duty of a Professor, that astonishing output of volumes that made his fame as the most learned and catholic, and withal one of the liveliest and wisest, of the English critics of the age. His writing was continued for many years after his retirement in 1915, when Professor Herbert John Clifford Grierson moved from the Aberdeen to the Edinburgh English Chair. Saintsbury died in 1933, in his eighty-eighth year.

Both the Classical and the English School already had long histories and well-established traditions, though it was not till 1892 that the latter attained the dignity of an independent Honours Group. Since then the principal new developments of teaching have been in certain special subjects in supplement of the main literature courses. In English, the study of English Language in its Old and Middle phases (with Middle Scots) has become an integral part of the Honours curriculum, and has had a separate Lectureship since 1919. The Classical school has added classes in Greek and Roman History, with a Lectureship created in 1901, which shares in the Fraser endowment for Ancient History; in Greek Philosophy with a Lectureship since 1919, which also belongs to the Philosophical Department; and in Classical Archæology which, till 1930, was taught by the Professor of Fine Art. Throughout the period, a number of the Honours graduates have gone on to further study at Oxford or Cambridge, in most instances with the help of the fairly numerous Classical Scholarships that were founded in the course of the nineteenth century.

The Modern European Languages, on the other hand, came in only in the last thirty years, from the establishment of the French and German Lectureships in 1894. The two Lecturers then appointed, Charles Sarolea and Otto Schlapp, continued in office till near the end of the half-century, and were both ultimately raised to professorial rank, when funds were at last available to found the two Chairs; by which time they were among the senior teachers in Arts. As has been said, these two languages soon advanced to importance in the curriculum—French in recent years has actually had the largest numbers of students of any subject in the Faculty—and each of the Professors, in different ways, has contributed notably to the understanding of European life and culture in Scotland. Professor Schlapp was succeeded in 1929 by Professor Walter Horace Bruford; Professor Sarolea in 1931 by Professor James Middleton Moore, formerly Lecturer, who died with tragic suddenness in 1932, after a life of most fruitful service to French teaching throughout the country. His successor is Professor John Orr, from Manchester.

Italian and Spanish were added after the war, and have still only the standing of Lectureships, though both have developed Intermediate Honours Classes, and Spanish full Honours, within the Modern Languages Group.

Two other languages had places in the Faculty from an earlier date. The Professorship of Sanskrit, founded in 1862, was held from 1875 by Julius Eggeling, who did eminent work in his subject in the cataloguing of MSS. in London and in the editing of oriental texts. He also gave service of vital value to the whole University for many years as Convener of the Library Committee, and was in fact the real organiser of the Library. Professor Arthur Berriedale Keith succeeded him in 1914. Celtic, established as a Chair in 1882, largely by the enthusiastic efforts of Blackie, has had two Professors, Donald Mackinnon, whose chief monument is his catalogue of Gaelic MSS. in Scotland, and the present holder, Professor William John Watson.

The Chair of Hebrew belongs primarily to the Divinity Faculty, but forms, with Arabic, an Honours Group in Arts. Arabic has had a Lectureship since 1912.

MENTAL PHILOSOPHY

Alexander Campbell Fraser, Professor of Logic and Metaphysics from 1856 to 1891, has already been spoken of as Dean. His chief philosophical work was done in the region and school of Berkleian metaphysics; and it was as a metaphysician of profoundly metaphysical cast that he most impressed his students. His colleague in the Moral Philosophy Chair from 1868 was Henry Calderwood, formerly a minister of the United Presbyterian Church, an effective teacher if somewhat limited in range and dogmatic in method. The middle decades of the half-century were filled by the partnership of two brothers, both students of their predecessors, Andrew Seth—who on succeeding to the lands of Haining in Selkirkshire took the name Pringle-Pattison—in the Logic Chair from 1891 to 1919, and James Seth, Professor of Moral Philosophy

ANDREW SETH PRINGLE-PATTISON, D.C.L., LL.D.

Professor of Logic and Metaphysics
1891-1919

from 1898 to 1924. In their complementary gifts, they made a remarkable pair of teachers. Pringle-Pattison's published work, both during and after his professoriate, earned him the position of the leading British exponent of theistic philosophy. The qualities of his mind were expressed in a literary style of rare clarity and beauty. James Seth, if a less profound and original thinker, was equally successful as a teacher, with a similar power of appealing to his students' love of literature. He also practised and preached with ardour the doctrine that the academic moralist should, above all things, be a good citizen. The elder brother continued to be a student and a writer for twelve years after leaving his Chair; but the younger died suddenly in the summer vacation of the year in which his resignation was to take effect. Their successors are Professors Norman Kemp Smith, who returned to Scotland from Princeton, and Alfred Edward Taylor, who came from St Andrews.

The first holder of the Lectureship in Ancient Philosophy was Robert Purves Hardie, who at his retirement in 1932 had served the Philosophy department for more than forty years, and had been appointed to Readership in 1920. He is known especially as a profound Aristotelian scholar.

Psychology till 1906 was taught from the Logic Chair, but in that year its growing importance and its development as a science were recognised by the creation of an independent Lectureship, held till 1919 by William George Smith, and since then by James Drever, who became Reader in 1924 and Professor when the Chair was established in 1931. The subject has benefited by generous grants from the Combe Trustees, which have enabled it to obtain a technical equipment and build up a reputation second to none in the British Isles.

The Philosophy School, like the Classical and the Mathematical, has a number of Scholarship endowments, which have enabled Honours graduates to proceed to English or Continental Universities for advanced study and research, and thus in many cases to prepare themselves for academic work.

Political Economy, which ranks in the Philosophical department of the Faculty, though it also has close connections with that of History, had Joseph Shield Nicholson as Professor from 1880. He was recognised as a master among British economists, a massive author, and a formidable debater in the many press-controversies that have arisen about his subject in recent decades. The number of his students steadily increased, and was for a time among the largest in the Faculty. Professor Frederick Wolff Ogilvie was appointed his successor in 1926. The Economic Group has been expanded by the creation of Lectureships in Economic History—the first holder of which was the late George Unwin, afterwards Professor at Manchester and leader of a fertile research school—in Statistics and in Realistic Economics.

The Professor of Education from 1876 to 1903 was Simon Somerville Laurie. With an unrivalled knowledge of the history and the needs of Scottish education he combined eminent gifts as a metaphysician and moral philosopher, and administrative aptitudes which were of general service to the University. He was followed by Alexander Darroch, who had been Assistant and Lecturer under him, after having begun on the lowest rung of the ladder as a pupil teacher and afterwards graduating with high Honours in Philosophy. Darroch, in his turn, became a powerful force in the University and in Scottish education; no member had greater weight in the Faculty's councils, where his keen and candid mind, with a certain rugged and humorous simplicity of speech, won the regard and affection of his colleagues. After his sudden death in 1924, the arrangement already recorded, by which the Professor of Education is also head of the Moray House Training Centre, was inaugurated by the appointment, in 1925, of Professor Godfrey Hilton Thomson.

SCIENCE

The subjects included in this Department in Arts belong also to the Faculty of Science, and their history is treated at length in that section of the volume. But Mathematics and Natural Philosophy have always been integral parts of the Arts curriculum, and their Professors among the most important members of the Faculty. Professor Chrystal's epoch-making tenure of the Deanship has already been mentioned. His work in the Chair of Mathematics was not less distinguished. He was great both as teacher and as original investigator; and he notably strengthened the reputation of Edinburgh as a centre of mathematical research. Professor Edmund Taylor Whittaker came from Dublin to succeed him in 1912.

Peter Guthrie Tait, Professor of Natural Philosophy from 1860, the friend and collaborator of Clerk Maxwell and Kelvin, was one of the giants of Victorian physics, and was honoured in his own University not less for the vigour and effectiveness of his teaching of the elements of his subject than for the long series of researches by which he extended its frontiers. James Gordon MacGregor, who came to the Chair from Canada in 1901, was one of the most distinguished of Tait's pupils and well maintained his tradition. He was succeeded, in 1913, by Professor Charles Glover Barkla, formerly of Liverpool. The new Tait Chair of Mathematical Physics was filled in 1922 by the appointment of Professor Charles Galton Darwin, grandson of the great biologist who was himself for a time an Edinburgh student.

HISTORY AND LAW

The 1889 Commissioners, as has been mentioned, founded only one new Chair in the Edinburgh Arts Faculty. To this they gave the comprehensive title of "History," though there were already two others that could claim authority in that great territory. The older, that of Ecclesiastical History, dating from 1702, belonged to the Faculty of Divinity, and was not brought into Arts till 1908. The other had come into existence in 1719 as a Chair of "Universal History," and was reconstituted in 1722 as "Universal Civil History and Greek and Roman Antiquities," and again in 1862 as "History" *simpliciter*. Under this title it remained, even after the creation of the new Professorship by the Commissioners, until 1909, when it became in name what it had been in fact for half a century, a Chair of "Constitutional Law and

Constitutional History." The class was a necessary part of the curriculum for the Degree in Law, but from 1892 was recognised also for that in Arts. The Commissioners' Professorship was thus left, so to say, with the title of the metropolitan see in the province of History. The subject of its Ordinary class has from the first been general British History, but the Professor may deal with other branches in his Honours classes. The first occupant, appointed in 1894, was George (later Sir George) Walter Prothero, who after five years left to take up the editorship of the *Quarterly Review*. Richard Lodge, who had been the first Professor of History at Glasgow, then came east to enter upon a quarter of a century of service to Edinburgh in many parts, among which the work of his Chair in teaching and writing had always the first share of his abounding energy. Its record is too lately closed to call for eulogy here. In 1925 he was succeeded by Professor Arthur Frederic Basil Williams.

Yet another Professorship was added when Sir William Fraser, the noted Scottish antiquarian, bequeathed a large sum to the University, among other purposes to endow a Chair of "Ancient History and Palæography." It was clear, from Sir William's own record in historical investigation, as well as from certain other passages in his will, that what he had had in mind was Ancient *Scottish* History, though "Ancient History" *sans phrase* might naturally be taken to mean that of Greece and Rome. Fortunately, the bequest was large enough to make some provision for the latter also. The Fraser Chair has for its province Scottish History, with special attention to its ancient written records; and a Lectureship was created (as noted above) in Greek and Roman History, which serves both the Classical and the Historical School. The first occupant of the new Chair, appointed in 1901, was Peter Hume Brown, who was already a foremost authority in the subject though he had not yet taught in a University. His classes were at first confined to Honours work on Scottish History before the Union of the Crowns, but later their scope was extended to modern times, and the subject was made available for the Ordinary Degree. Hume Brown continued to write during his professorship, producing both his large *History of Scotland* and a series of volumes on smaller parts of it, especially on the period of Queen Mary. After his sudden death in 1918, Professor Robert Kerr Hannay succeeded to the Chair.

The expansion of the History School by further Lectureships has already been noted; those in Modern History—founded by the will of Sheriff Æneas James George Mackay, formerly Professor—in Political Science, in Greek and Roman History, in Economic History, and in European and Medieval History. Military History, first introduced in 1904, was discontinued soon after the war, and Colonial and Indian History was changed to a course on the Constitution of the British Empire.

The successive occupants of the Chair of Constitutional Law and History are mentioned under the Faculty of Law, to which they were primarily attached, though the importance of their work in the Arts curriculum has grown with the development of the whole Group of historical studies.

The creation, by the will of Lord Abercromby, of a Chair of Prehistoric Archæology in 1927, added still another province of learning to the department—a vastly wider field, indeed, than any other, in the range of time which it covers. The first Professor is Vere Gordon Childe. Professor Herbert Read succeeded Baldwin Brown in the Chair of Fine Art in 1931.

Geography has a place in the departments both of History and Science. The first holder of the Lectureship, from 1908, was George Goudie Chisholm, an Edinburgh man who was already a veteran teacher and author on the subject. He soon brought it to an important place in the curriculum, and was one of the first Lecturers to receive the rank of Reader. It was not, however, till some years after his retirement that the necessary endowment for the Chair could be completed. It is occupied by Professor Alan Grant Ogilvie who, in 1923, had succeeded him as Lecturer and Reader.

The only change that has hitherto occurred in the personnel of the Faculty in the new department of Commerce was by the death in 1927 of Thomas Patrick Laird, the first Professor of Accounting and Business Method. He was a man of recognised eminence in his profession of Accountant, and served the University not only in guiding the development of the new branch, but as a member of the University Court. He was succeeded by Professor William Annan. A year or two earlier, the Lecturer in Organisation of Industry and Commerce, William Oliver, had been raised to the professoriate.

VII

THE FACULTY OF SCIENCE

ALTHOUGH Edinburgh has produced from very early times distinguished workers in Science, the University itself was slow in giving official recognition to branches of Science other than those which grew out of the department of Mathematics, or were accessory to the teaching of Medicine.

Of these two groups the subject of Natural Philosophy, given for the first time the status of a Chair in 1708, provided opportunity for the work of John Playfair, who was not only distinguished in his own special line of Applied Mathematics, but became famous in the history of Geology because of his *Illustrations of the Huttonian Theory*; while, in the second group, the Chair of Chemistry and Medicine, founded in 1713, was adorned by Joseph Black, famous especially for his discovery of "fixed air," which is now well known as carbon dioxide. This discovery was made, however, before Black came to the University as Professor and, although still young, his failing health made it difficult for him to undertake research work in addition to his teaching duties.

The Chair of Natural History, founded so long ago as 1770, was mainly devoted to the biological subjects that were required by medical students; and, although it covered Geology nominally, there was no organised study of that subject until late in the eighteenth century, when James Hutton laid the foundation of geological science in its modern sense. At that time the Professor of Natural History was indifferent to, and his successor, who retained the Chair for the next fifty years, was definitely opposed to, the new doctrines, even for many years after the general acceptance elsewhere of the Huttonian theory and of Charles Lyell's *Principles* on which they were built.

The atmosphere of the University thus seemed far from

bracing for the growth of science, which was nevertheless cultivated by extra-academical workers in Edinburgh and still more so south of the Border. It was only after the middle of the nineteenth century that science became seriously recognised in the University through the individual influence of a remarkable group of outstanding men—Edward Forbes, who came to the Chair of Natural History in 1854; Lyon Playfair, appointed to the Chair of Chemistry in 1858; P. G. Tait, following James D. Forbes as Professor of Natural Philosophy in 1860; Archibald Geikie, in the newly-established Chair of Geology in 1871; and Fleeming Jenkin, the first professor to occupy the Chair of Engineering, instituted in 1868 as one of the measures tardily adopted to repair the blunder of establishing, in 1855, through Government intervention, a hybrid Professorship of Technology.

In the 'sixties and 'seventies the University possessed a formidable contingent of distinguished scientific workers; but even then the departments which they had made famous were administered only by a committee of the Faculty of Arts for some thirty years before a separate Faculty of Science was established in 1893. It is an interesting incident to record that, for the first nine years of this critical period, from 1859 to 1868, the office of Principal was held by Sir David Brewster, a past-President of the British Association and a renowned figure in the world of scientific optics.

Edinburgh, nevertheless, for many years before 1893 contributed most substantially and with distinction to the growing body of scientific knowledge; for, in addition to the names mentioned already, the University had as Professors, Isaac Bayley Balfour (1888-1922) in Botany; George James Allman (1855-70), Wyville Thomson (1870-82), and James Cossar Ewart (1882-1927) in Zoology; Alexander Crum Brown (1869-1908) in Chemistry; William Turner (1867-1903) in Anatomy; and James Geikie (1882-1914) in Geology.

Looking back on this list of Professors, all distinguished Fellows of the Royal Society, London, it is surprising that the University hesitated so long in giving formal recognition to Science as a separate Faculty. The city itself had for long been the scene of active work in Science; its Royal Society was established so long ago as 1783, being still twelve years younger than the Royal Physical Society; the Geological Society had been active since 1834, whilst the British Association had met at Edinburgh four times before the Faculty of Science was instituted, the last occasion being in 1892 when Sir Archibald Geikie was President.

When the new Faculty was at last created by Ordinance in 1893, it numbered only eleven members, but has since grown to thirty-three, partly by the introduction of Readers and Lecturers, partly by admitting some Professors whose teaching was confined either to the Faculty of Arts or Faculty of Medicine; and, finally, by the institution of new Chairs in Applied Science—Forestry in 1920, Mining in 1924 and Animal Genetics in 1928.

Degrees in Pure Science, Engineering, Agriculture and Public Health were governed by special ordinances before 1893; but in 1895 the Degree of D.Sc. was established and the B.Sc. was afterwards granted for Forestry, Mining and Metallurgy, Veterinary Science and Technical Chemistry. Diplomas for post-graduate studies are also now given in Agriculture and Technical Chemistry.

Throughout its history the Faculty of Science has elected only two of its members to fill the office of Dean; James Geikie was elected annually from 1893 until he resigned his Chair in 1914, and Sir Thomas Hudson Beare has filled the office since that time.

BOTANY

The record of John Hutton Balfour, Professor from 1845 to 1879, was not included in Grant's *The Story of the University*. He was then Professor-Emeritus and died in 1884. Born in Edinburgh in 1808, he was the eldest son of Andrew Balfour, surgeon in the Army. After a period in the Arts Faculty at Edinburgh and later at St Andrews—with the intention of taking a subsequent Divinity course—he returned to Edinburgh to study Medicine. After graduating as M.D., in 1831, he went to Paris to work under Dupuytren, Lisfranc and

Manec. Returning in 1834 to practise in Edinburgh, he was for a time assistant to Sir George Ballingall, Professor of Military Surgery. Associated also with Professor Graham, he continued his botanical studies especially in the field and, in 1840, established himself as an Extra-academical teacher of Botany. Elected in 1842 to the Glasgow Chair of Botany, he was appointed at Edinburgh in 1845 as Professor of Medicine and Botany.

A man of untiring industry, Balfour, in addition to the duties of his Chair and of the Keepership of the Royal Botanic Garden, was for many years Dean of the Faculty of Medicine and Secretary to the Royal Society of Edinburgh. His teaching energies were devoted to Botany and the title of Professor of Medicine became a nominal one.

Balfour's long tenure of office of thirty-four years was distinguished by a marked advance in teaching methods in his subject. For a considerable time—and especially under Graham—Field Botany had been a characteristic part of the student's training. Balfour was particularly interested in this aspect of his subject and greatly extended it. Excursions were made regularly on Saturdays throughout the summer session, and these sometimes were prolonged into several days in the field—frequently in the Highlands. On one occasion the last excursion of the session was to Switzerland. Of wiry build—was not his byname "Woody Fibre"?—he was able to outdistance the fittest in his class. These excursions gave him intimate opportunities of influencing and guiding his many students. His teaching in the field was not merely a classification of plants but embraced much which would now be termed Ecological Botany. In that direction he was a pioneer, as he was in his more formal teaching—for he introduced practical laboratory classes with demonstrations of microscopic objects and physiological experiments. Adequate laboratories were not yet available, but he had his "microscopical room" and the beginnings of a museum, of which students could avail themselves. Contributory to the success of these new developments was the enlargement of the Botanic Garden during his tenure of office. It was trebled in size and, during his administration, showed a very great increase in the number of species cultivated—many contributed by his pupils from all over the world. Encyclopædic in his knowledge of his subject—as is well indicated in his text-books—Balfour was a lucid expositor and, apart from his University lectures, was much in demand for popular discourses. He was always on the alert to absorb the new for the benefit of his students, though the evolutionary doctrines of Darwin and his successors did not meet with ready acceptance at his hands.

Alexander Dickson, his successor from 1879 to 1887, was born in Edinburgh in 1836, the second son of David Dickson of Hartree. Educated at home he began the study of Medicine in 1855 and, before graduating in 1860, had worked under Kölliker at Würzburg and Virchow at Berlin. Dickson settled in Edinburgh with a view to practise medicine, but did not pursue it as he had become, on the death of his elder brother, the proprietor of the family estate in Peeblesshire. He was devoted to biological research and, even before graduation, he had written on botanical subjects. In 1862 he acted at Aberdeen for Professor Dickie who was in ill-health, followed Harvey as Professor at Dublin in 1866, was appointed to the Glasgow Chair in 1868 in succession to Walker Arnott, and returned to Edinburgh on the retirement of Hutton Balfour.

Dickson's interest in research is manifest in his numerous papers—a record far exceeding that of any of his predecessors. He wrote widely on flower-morphology, embryogeny and teratology. He was particularly efficient in the artistic drawings illustrative of his investigations—a gift of which he made full use in his lectures. It is on record that Dickson's inclination was not towards teaching; nevertheless, his lectures were models of scientific presentment, while his geniality and kindliness made him adored by his students. During his tenure of office a new and enlarged lecture hall was built at the Botanic Garden, capable of accommodating more than 500 students.

Dickson's health was far from robust and he had to spend

much of his time on his country estate. Afflicted by a physical ailment which he characteristically concealed to avoid causing anxiety to his friends, he suddenly expired in December 1887 on the curling pond at Hartree.

Sir Isaac Bayley Balfour, Professor from 1888 to 1922, the most distinguished occupant of the Chair of Botany and a botanist of world-wide reputation, was born in Edinburgh in 1853, son of John Hutton Balfour. His school was Edinburgh Academy. He began his studies at the University in 1870, graduating B.Sc. in 1873 with First Class Honours, and M.B., C.M. in 1877. Unsuccessful in his endeavour to join the *Challenger* Expedition in 1872, he was a member of the *Transit of Venus* Expedition to Rodriguez in 1874. A thesis compiled on the botanical results of this voyage gave him his D.Sc. in 1875. The arrangements of the medical curriculum enabled him to combine the duties of assistant to Thomas Henry Huxley, temporarily in charge of the Chair of Natural History, and to Sir Charles Wyville Thomson, as well as to act, in 1878, as substitute for his father, absent through illness. He was also for a time a dresser and assistant with Lister.

After a winter of study with De Bary at Strassburg and with Sachs at Würzburg, he was appointed Professor of Botany at Glasgow in 1879. The winter of the same year saw him in Socotra where he secured material for his important work on the flora of that island. In 1884 he was transferred to Oxford as Sherardian Professor of Botany. During his tenure at Oxford he played a prominent part in the founding of the *Annals of Botany* (1887) and, for one term, was deputy for the Professor of Geology. It is thus an index to the breadth of his attainments that he had already taken a share in university teaching of Botany, Zoology and Geology, as well as in medical work with Lister.

After Dickson's death Balfour was recalled to Edinburgh—to the posts his father had held for thirty-four years—a length of tenure which he was to equal exactly. His influence on all departments under his control was profound. Great improvements were effected. The development of the Botanic

Garden rendered it still more advantageous for university teaching. The extensive Arboretum was now incorporated in the Garden, and the whole made one unit, vested in the Crown; the ranges of plant-houses were almost entirely rebuilt and enlarged; the number of species in cultivation was more than trebled, for Balfour's enthusiasm for horticulture did not rest until the Garden was one of the richest in the world.

He was also successful in securing gradually the complete renovation of the buildings used for university purposes. Laboratories, museum and research rooms were provided on a generous scale to keep pace with the demands for extension of scientific work. With these were associated the gradual acquisition of an adequate herbarium and other equipment necessary both for research and for teaching.

His tenure of office coincided with the development of the Faculty of Science to its present outstanding position. Previous holders of the Chair devoted themselves almost entirely in their teaching to the medical student. Science students were few and their opportunities for study limited. When Balfour demitted office Honours students had a course of four years; instruction in Botany for Pure Science was given separately from the course for students of Medicine; additional subjects, such as Forest Botany, Forest Mycology, Agricultural Botany and Agricultural Mycology were added to meet the needs of the new Science curricula, entailing increase in staff and equipment in accordance. He was, moreover, the first to establish, in 1891, in this country an adequate instruction course for foresters and gardeners.

In addition to his high quality as a man of science and as an administrator, Balfour was recognised as a very fine lecturer and teacher. Large classes seemed to appeal to him, and he was at his best when his classroom was filled with several hundred students. But lucid as was his exposition in lecturing, he ever regarded the excursions and the practical work as the best means of evoking their interest in things biological. The methods he employed to secure this end marked a very real advance in the teaching of his subject.

From boyhood he was in close touch with the practice of horticulture and forestry and joined in the excursions made by his father throughout Scotland; he had early opportunities of botanical exploration abroad—all these experiences influencing his teaching and giving it a practical bearing. During his last twenty years he devoted himself again to his systematic studies and became an authority on the flora of Eastern Asia, and especially on that of China. He visited Japan and China in 1909-10. Systematic Botany no longer holds a prominent place in university curricula owing to the needful development of many newer aspects of the botanical field. But Balfour was careful that the pendulum should not swing too far, and wisely retained a measure of systematic botany as a valuable part of his teaching, while taking full advantage of the new developments.

An acknowledged leader for forty years in his Science, he was compelled by ill-health to retire in 1922; he died in November of the same year. Excessive labours during the war gravely affected a constitution naturally sound. In the absence of nearly all his regular staff, he took upon himself the bulk of the teaching in his department and the administrative duties in the Botanic Garden.

Two projects which he had in view on his retirement have since been carried through. A further area has been added to the Botanic Garden, bringing its extent up to sixty acres—beyond which city conditions do not permit of extension. But in the west of Scotland, through the generosity of Harry Younger, the estate of Benmore, near Dunoon, has been gifted to the nation, chiefly for the development of forestry and a forestry school. At Benmore, areas have been allocated for botanical and horticultural work under the control of the Regius Keeper of the Botanic Garden, while a part of the mansion-house has been reserved as a hostel for university students, especially for those engaged in biological research.

The present occupant of the Chair of Botany is Professor Sir William Wright Smith.

FACULTY OF SCIENCE

NATURAL PHILOSOPHY

In Peter Guthrie Tait, Professor of Natural Philosophy from 1860 to 1901 and the successor of James David Forbes, the University gained a Professor who was an outstanding man of science, an incomparable teacher and a striking personality. Tait was the only son of John Tait, secretary to the fifth Duke of Buccleuch, and was born at Dalkeith in 1831. When he was six years of age his father died, and the family moved to Edinburgh. After a few years at a preparatory school Tait entered the Edinburgh Academy in 1841, amongst his class-mates being Fleeming Jenkin, who afterwards became the first occupant of the Chair of Engineering in the University: Clerk Maxwell was his senior at the Academy by a year. Tait was dux of his class in each of the six years of his attendance. Although good in classics, he showed special aptitude for mathematics and, in the competition for the Academical Club prize in 1847, he was second in mathematics, Maxwell being first. Tait enrolled in the same year as a student of the University in the senior classes of Mathematics and Natural Philosophy but, after one session, went to Peterhouse, Cambridge. He became Senior Wrangler in 1852 and was elected a Fellow of his College, where he remained in residence until 1854, when he was appointed Professor of Mathematics at Queen's College, Belfast. Amongst his colleagues was Thomas Andrews, famed for his work on the Critical State. Tait entered into collaboration with the older man and gained valuable experience in experimentation during a series of investigations on ozone. Tait's real interest was on the side of Applied rather than Pure Mathematics and, in 1860, he became a candidate for the Chair of Natural Philosophy at Edinburgh. Amongst the other candidates was his old school-fellow, James Clerk Maxwell, who had then achieved a reputation as one of the most remarkable men in the scientific world. Despite this, Tait was chosen by the curators who, doubtless, in making their choice gave weight to his gifts as an expositor. The choice was indeed a happy one for the students of the University. For forty years he instilled the principles of physical science into successive generations of students in lectures which could not well be surpassed for clearness of presentation, easy utterance and incisive phraseology. His tall figure and commanding presence added to the effect produced by his words, and, although a certain aloofness prevented intimate contact between professor and students, few of them could ever forget his sustained effort to provide them with "a common-sense view of the universe we live in."

In the Natural Philosophy department no practical teaching was done until 1868, when Tait obtained from the University Court a small grant for equipment, and a room in the attic of the Old College as a teaching laboratory. For research work the Professor had still to be satisfied with the space provided by the lecture theatre, the museum and his private room, with the addition later of a small cellar in the basement. After 1880, consequent on the removal of the Anatomy department to the New Buildings, it was then possible to make some expansion. A suite of four rooms became available in the attic for the teaching of practical physics, while several cellars in the basement were made to serve for research purposes. The new teaching laboratories were placed in the charge of Cargill G. Knott and, later, of William Peddie.

Practical work in physics was not required for graduation, so that only those whose inclination lay in that direction attended the laboratory. There was at first no set course, and Tait, after trial, gave promising young men the opportunity of working at some research problem, suggested by himself, in any branch of natural philosophy which claimed their interest. During the 'seventies he was in the habit of publishing in the *Proceedings of the Royal Society of Edinburgh*, short papers which embodied their main results under the title of "Laboratory Notes."

At the time of the Tercentenary celebration Tait was beginning the second half of his tenure of the Chair. Attendance on laboratory courses still remained voluntary, but the gradual change of conditions affecting education,

From the painting by] [*Sir George Reid, P.R.S.A.*

PETER GUTHRIE TAIT

Professor of Natural Philosophy
1860-1901

and with it university courses, made its influence felt. The practical work became gradually systematised, more of an adjunct to lecture work, and less identified with research. The Science Faculty was still in its infancy, and it was almost entirely from the few students who were enrolled in it that the research workers were drawn, and these were very largely participators in his own investigations.

Tait's experimental work formed only the minor part of his scientific output, but much of it was of significant import. The researches on thermo-electricity and the construction of the thermo-electric diagram; the investigations of the effect of pressure on water and other liquids, undertaken to determine the error of the deep-sea thermometers used in the *Challenger* expedition; and the work on impact and ballistics, begun primarily to explain points in connection with the flight of a golf ball, may serve as examples. All Tait's practical work was characterised by simplicity and elegance of method and apparatus. His real eminence, however, lay in the field of Applied Mathematics. At the age of twenty-five he wrote, with W. J. Steele, a treatise on the *Dynamics of a Particle* and, in 1861, he had arranged to publish a work on mathematical physics. To his great delight, William Thomson, on hearing of this scheme, offered to collaborate, and six years of this fruitful collaboration produced the celebrated *Treatise on Natural Philosophy*, Volume I. The work was never completed owing to Thomson's many other activities, but Tait followed it later with separate smaller volumes dealing with various branches of physics. Tait was profoundly convinced of the great value of Hamilton's quaternions as an instrument of research in mathematico-physical science and published a treatise on the subject. He did not, however, succeed in impressing this view on his contemporaries, although he laboured constantly to that end. He was a prolific writer as well as thinker and contributed about 180 scientific papers on a great variety of subjects to the *Proceedings* and *Transactions of the Royal Society of Edinburgh*, his favourite medium of publication. In the 'eighties Tait's papers on the foundations of the kinetic theory of gases stand out pre-eminently in the record of his work. His collected scientific papers were published by the Cambridge University Press—Volume I. in 1898 and Volume II. in 1900.

Although averse to theological dogmatism, Tait had marked religious sensibility, and he joined with Balfour Stewart in an endeavour to overthrow materialism by a purely scientific argument. They published anonymously, in 1875, a volume with the title *The Unseen Universe, or Physical Speculations on a Future State*, which greatly stirred public opinion. The authorship was acknowledged in the fourth edition, issued in the following year.

Outside the University, Tait gave much of his time to the affairs of the Royal Society of Edinburgh. He became a secretary in 1864 and held the post of general secretary from 1879 till his last illness. His health became impaired in 1900, and he retired from the duties of his Chair in the spring of 1901. In the summer he died, after a life of constant endeavour to extend our knowledge of the universe.

A memoir of Tait, uniform with and supplementing the two volumes of scientific papers, was prepared by Professor Cargill G. Knott, formerly his assistant, and published, in 1911, by the Cambridge University Press.

James Gordon MacGregor, Professor from 1901 to 1913, had been one of a band of enthusiastic research workers whom Tait gathered round him in the early 'seventies. He was born in 1852 at Halifax, Nova Scotia, where his father, the Rev. Peter MacGregor, was a well-known minister of the Presbyterian Church. His early education was obtained in his native town. On leaving school, he entered Dalhousie and graduating, with every possible distinction, as B.A. in 1871, he was awarded the Gilchrist Scholarship which enabled him to study in Europe. He accordingly entered the University of Edinburgh in that year and pursued his favourite sciences of physics and chemistry. In 1872, he was associated in Tait's laboratory with James Alfred Ewing in a research on the electric conductivity of saline solutions, an investigation which determined the line of much of his later work. From Edinburgh he went to Leipzig to continue under Wiedemann the study of the electric conductivity of solutions. He graduated as B.Sc. of the University of London in 1874 and as D.Sc. in 1876. From 1877 to 1879 MacGregor was Physics Master at Clifton College, but was recalled to Halifax in the latter year as the first Professor of Physics at Dalhousie. Here, in spite of very limited resources, he taught for twelve years with remarkable success and carried out numerous researches. In the earlier years of his professorship he was in the habit of spending his summer vacations in Edinburgh, where he had the freedom of the physics laboratory for his investigations, so that he was well known in the University when he succeeded Tait as Professor.

The inevitable amplification of mechanism for teaching had begun in Tait's time, but its full development had to be faced by MacGregor. His logical mind, great energy and high capacity for detailed labour were precisely the qualities required for the onerous task of reorganising the Natural Philosophy department, of moving it from the Old College and establishing it in the new Surgical Hospital at High School Yards as a well-equipped physical laboratory on modern lines. The new department was opened in October 1906. In it provision was made for the practical teaching of all classes of students, and for the pursuit of research in the various branches of physics. He was assisted in its conduct by George A. Carse. MacGregor did not long enjoy the reward of his unstinted labours. There is little doubt that his devotion to the task during the strenuous years of reorganisation and reconstruction had much to do with the shortening of his life, for, although intensely active bodily and mentally, he was never robust. He died suddenly in May 1913.

MacGregor's researches were concerned largely with what is now commonly known as physical chemistry. He dealt *inter alia* with the electric conduction and the volumes of solutions, with ionisation in saline solutions and its effect on the freezing point. In papers on a different line of thought he discussed the foundations of dynamics. During his Edinburgh period he found little time for personal research, but he encouraged and supervised many young workers in carrying out investigations on mechanical, electrical, magnetic and optical problems. An admirable teacher, he inspired his students with something of his own zeal for knowledge, and his own incapacity to accept half-truths. He had no need to make himself accessible, for he was that by nature.

A project which latterly claimed much of his attention and energy was the development of a Memorial Fund which had been initiated by many of Tait's pupils and friends. Tait himself had felt that his Chair should be duplicated, and it was suggested by MacGregor that the memorial should take the form of an endowment for a second Chair of Natural Philosophy, co-equal with the first, and devoted especially to the teaching of the mathematical side of Physics. The scheme did not come to fruition in MacGregor's lifetime, but, in 1922, sufficient funds were available to institute the Tait Chair of Natural Philosophy, Charles Galton Darwin being appointed its first incumbent in the following year.

MacGregor was succeeded in 1913 by Charles Glover Barkla, the present Professor of Natural Philosophy.

ZOOLOGY

At the time when this history opens James Cossar Ewart occupied the Chair of Natural History. His tenure of office extended from 1882 to 1927, a period during which great expansion took place both in the teaching of Zoology and in the range of research in the subject.

Fifty years ago instruction in Zoology was almost entirely by means of a course of lectures given in the summer session and repeated in the following winter session. Classes in Practical Zoology were introduced in the early 'seventies, but were not compulsory and attended only by a small proportion of the students. Laboratory instruction was rapidly developed from 1883 onwards, and soon became an essential part of the course of Zoology for medical students and for students taking this subject for the Degree of M.A. or B.Sc., a more advanced practical course being established for some of the science students. One of the difficulties of the Professor was the absence of a collection of museum specimens to illustrate his teaching. Three Natural History collections had been formed in the University—the first, the Sibbald Museum, had disappeared by 1770; the second was removed on the death of Professor Walker in 1804, being regarded by his family as private property; and the third series of specimens "second only to those of the British Museum" was transferred, about 1861, to the Museum of Science and Art. For some years the loan of specimens from this Museum for use in connection with the classes of Zoology was denied, but, later, the Museum authorities agreed that, so far as was possible, specimens should be lent for teaching purposes. But this arrangement was not satisfactory either to the Professor or to the Museum, and the formation of a teaching collection in the department of Zoology was undertaken, the Museum of Science and Art aiding by the permanent loan of certain duplicates from their collections. Thus the cases in the University Natural History Museum, which had been standing empty for more than twenty years, were once again put to their original use. This room, a fine example of Adam-Playfair architecture, was fitted with benches to accommodate eighty students for practical work, and it served, until 1929, as the principal laboratory of the department.

A Lecturer in Embryology was appointed in 1885, and George Brook held the post for about eight years. He was succeeded by John Beard who, in 1890, had begun a course of more advanced lectures and practical work on vertebrates. There does not appear to have been a corresponding course of lectures on invertebrates, although some practical instruction on these animals was given, chiefly by Gregg Wilson. On his resignation in 1900, Wilson was succeeded by James H. Ashworth who, in 1901, was appointed Lecturer in Invertebrate Zoology. In addition to the purely scientific side of this branch of Zoology, a course in Entomology and Protozoology in connection with the newly established Diplomas in Tropical Medicine was instituted, in 1905, at the request of the Faculty of Medicine. This course, which was extended later to include instruction on parasitic worms, has been given usually twice each year and has brought to the department a succession of medical graduates, many of whom held important posts in the Tropics. In 1916 the course was extended to meet the needs of men studying for the Degree of B.Sc. in Veterinary Science, and was still further extended, in 1930, when the Diploma in Tropical Veterinary Medicine was instituted.

Professor Cossar Ewart's long connection with, and keen interest in, animal breeding led to extension of the work of the department in another direction, namely the institution, in 1911, of a Lectureship in Genetics and Heredity, the first occupant of which was Arthur D. Darbishire who died in December 1915. The Lectureship was in abeyance until the appointment, in 1921, of Francis A. E. Crew, then an assistant in the department of Zoology, under whom work in genetics and animal breeding rapidly developed into a separate department.

In February 1919 the University Court decided to institute a new Chair to which James Hartley Ashworth was appointed. The Professor of Natural History, J. Cossar Ewart, continued to be in charge of all work appertaining to the vertebrates, while the new Professor of Zoology was entrusted with the work on invertebrates, including entomology and parasitology, along with the supervision of the laboratories. At this period, the return of the men to the University at the conclusion of the war made a demand on the accommodation in the department, which was met with the greatest difficulty. Temporary structural alterations were made in the Old College so as to extend the space available as far as was possible; but it was abundantly clear that, even when the number of students was again normal, the premises would not provide the accommodation required for the varied kinds of work comprised within the limits of modern zoology. This was no new discovery, as the inadequacy and unsuitability of the accommodation for practical work and research had been the subject of communications to the University Court from 1906 onwards.

FACULTY OF SCIENCE

It may be recalled that the Natural History department on the west side of the Old Quadrangle was represented by the Museum, used also as a laboratory for first-year students, by a large and a small lecture theatre, a temporary laboratory, installed in 1920 in the south-west corner, and four rooms, inconveniently situated, used by the staff and the research workers. No alteration of these premises could provide either the amount or the quality of working space needed for teaching and for the staff and post-graduate workers. The adverse conditions under which the practical classes and research were being conducted made so deep an impression on the late Laurence Pullar of Bridge of Earn, when he visited the department in 1923 that, soon afterwards, he gave £20,000 towards the cost of a new department of Zoology. In their allocation of grants in 1926 the Trustees of the Carnegie Trust for the Universities of Scotland set aside a sum of £18,000 for the same purpose. At this stage the defects of the old department and the contributions in hand towards a new one became known to the International Education Board, founded by John D. Rockefeller, junior, in 1923. In May 1926 Professor Augustus Trowbridge of Princeton University, then Director for Europe of the Biological Section of the Board, called on Professor Ashworth and inquired into the financial position and the estimated cost of the erection and equipment of new premises adequate for their purpose. With his sympathetic co-operation a statement was submitted to the Board and, at the end of the year, the gratifying reply was received that the Board had authorised an appropriation of £74,000 to complete the sum required for the building and equipment, and to provide an endowment fund of £26,000. The income of this fund enabled two additional lectureships—Helminthology and Cytology—to be established, and made possible the additional technical staff required in the new building. The University Court, in accepting this generous gift, gratefully recognised that it would be able to establish a department more effective as a School of Zoology and centre of research than would have been possible with the resources otherwise at its disposal.

Early in 1927 Professor Cossar Ewart intimated his resignation of the Chair of Natural History from which he retired at the end of September of the same year. Professor Ashworth was translated to the Chair of Natural History and the Chair of Zoology remained vacant.

The new department of Zoology was erected during the years 1927 to 1929 upon the site of The King's Buildings and was formally opened by H.R.H. Prince George in May 1929. The architects, Sir Robert Lorimer and John F. Matthew, co-operated with the Professor to produce a building which is thoroughly practical for its purpose. Especially noteworthy are the laboratories for teaching and for research with their large windows affording light from the north or north-east, particularly suitable for microscopical and other fine work.*

The remarkable contrast between the teaching of zoology at the University fifty years ago and at the present time is sufficiently indicated by a consideration of the courses of instruction. Formerly, the Professor gave a course of lectures in the summer term to first-year students—repeated in the winter session—while the corresponding practical classes required the services of one assistant with help from student-demonstrators. Now, the course of lectures and practical work for students of the first year extends throughout the academical year, but students in Medicine and in Agriculture and Forestry are required to attend only during the first two terms. The course of instruction in zoology in the Science Faculty includes three further years of study and comprises courses of lectures and laboratory work in the comparative anatomy and embryology of vertebrates and invertebrates, in experimental zoology, in cytology, in genetics, and, for the B.Sc. in Veterinary Science, in entomology and parasitology. Courses in the two last subjects are also given in connection with the Diplomas in Tropical Medicine, in Tropical Veterinary Medicine and in Public Health.

The ten-year period immediately preceding that under review, from 1872 to 1882, was notable for the succession of

* A brief account of the department, with photographic illustrations, was published in the *University of Edinburgh Journal,* vol. iii., No. 2, October 1929.

students who afterwards made their mark in zoology. The roll-book of the department for this period contains the following names:—John (later Sir John) Murray of the *Challenger* Expedition; R. Ramsay Wright, afterwards Professor of Zoology at Toronto University; W. A. Haswell, who became Professor of Zoology at Sydney; W. A. (later Sir William) Herdman, the first Professor of Zoology at the University of Liverpool; Sir J. Arthur Thomson, Professor Emeritus of Natural History at Aberdeen; J. R. Henderson, Professor of Zoology at Madras Christian College; and a number of men who, after passing on to graduation in Medicine, took up work in which their interest in natural history played an important part, *e.g.* David Bruce, afterwards Major-General Sir David Bruce; Wemyss Fulton, late Director of the Scottish Fishery Board's Laboratory and H. B. Guppy. Among the members of the class, during this period, who completed their zoological education elsewhere were Professor D'Arcy W. Thompson, R. F. Scharff and H. O. Forbes.

Since 1882 the department of Zoology has continued to contribute its quota to the filling of Chairs and other posts. Philip J. White, J. D. F. Gilchrist and Gregg Wilson left to become Professors of Zoology respectively at the University College of North Wales, the University of Cape Town and Queen's University, Belfast; Major Patton to be Professor of Entomology at the Liverpool School of Tropical Medicine, and F. A. E. Crew to be head of the department of Animal Genetics at Edinburgh; Professor J. Graham Kerr of Glasgow, Professor J. P. Hill of University College, London, and Professor F. J. Cole of Reading laid the foundations of their subsequent work while at Edinburgh; and Honours graduates of the department have been appointed to important posts at Edinburgh and at other universities, in the British Museum (Natural History), in the Marine Laboratory at Plymouth and as entomologists in the Dominions.

One of the two Edinburgh graduates on the staff of the Marine Laboratory at Plymouth—Charles M. Yonge—was appointed, in 1927, head of the Expedition (June 1928 to July 1929) for the exploration of the Great Barrier Reef of Australia, the scientific results of which are being issued in four quarto volumes by the Natural History department of the British Museum. In January 1933 Charles M. Yonge was appointed Professor of Zoology at the University of Bristol.

ASTRONOMY

In 1883 Charles Piazzi Smyth was still Professor of Astronomy and continued to occupy the Chair for a further six years. The only observatory in Edinburgh at that time was the one erected in 1818, on the Calton Hill, by the Edinburgh Astronomical Institution, the accommodation in which was inadequate and little suited for serious work. Piazzi Smyth was a man of many ideas, who had shown enterprise and foresight, as we now see, in more than one direction, but a series of rebuffs and disappointments discouraged him, and the latter part of his tenure of office was not inspiring. He resigned the Chair in 1889. After some anxiety as to the future, a new chapter was opened by the gift by Lord Crawford, the 26th Earl, of his great collection of instruments, books, manuscripts and pictures, relating to astronomy, as the foundation of a truly National Scottish Observatory.

A site was found on the Blackford Hill, and the Government erected a handsome and roomy building to house the bequest, together with the residences for the astronomers. The Professor was also Astronomer Royal for Scotland as heretofore. Lord Crawford's astronomer, Ralph Copeland, was appointed Professor in 1889, holding the Chair till 1905. Much of his time was naturally occupied at first in arranging the new building, a task in which he was extremely zealous. He died in 1905, and was succeeded by Professor Frank (later Sir Frank) Watson Dyson, who still found work to do at Blackford Hill; this he had hardly completed when he was called back to Greenwich, in 1910, to become Astronomer Royal.

He was followed by the present Professor, Ralph Allen Sampson. During the twenty years of Sampson's tenure of the Chair, a period which has seen immense advances in the science of astronomy, both in its significance in ordinary life and in other branches of learning, it cannot be said that its status in the University has shown a corresponding, parallel development. Many reasons may have contributed to this. Astronomy is not the only science that has shown great growth. Other sciences and other vocational trainings can claim the same or more. Moreover, there is a well-marked trend among students to abandon the idea of a general cultural course of study, and to follow one which offers assured and wide avenues for future employment. The connection, however, with the Royal Observatory remains what it was, as well as the facilities in that connection offered to students. Indeed, the latter are greatly improved, as the equipment of the Observatory has been elaborated step by step until it is now second to none of its scale, either in this country or abroad.

AGRICULTURE

From the foundation of the Chair of Agriculture in 1790, no further provision was made for agricultural teaching at the University for a century. Agricultural students could, and frequently did, take the ordinary classes in subjects such as Botany, Chemistry, Natural History and Economics, but there were no courses relating these sciences to the practice of agriculture.

Professor Robert Wallace, who had succeeded Professor John Wilson in 1885, set himself to remedy this defect. In 1890, largely through his efforts, the Steven Lectureship in Agriculture was endowed. A wide discretion was allowed as to the branch of Agricultural Science in which the lectures should be given, but, in fact, the endowment has been devoted throughout to the provision of a course in Agricultural, and later, also Forest Zoology. In 1892, he co-operated with a number of extra-academical teachers in forming the Edinburgh Incorporated School of Agriculture—with a Board of

Directors—which offered courses in the principal branches of Agricultural Science.

The avowed object of the formation of the Incorporated School of Agriculture was to establish a body to whom Government grants could be made payable, and it was so far successful in its purpose that the English Board of Agriculture gave official recognition to Edinburgh as an agricultural teaching centre. A fundamental part of the policy of the Board, however, was to encourage the development of teaching centres which would serve wide areas and be responsible for the organisation and co-ordination of agricultural instruction of all grades within these areas, and which would secure the co-operation of County Authorities who had funds at their disposal for promoting technical education. The Board, therefore, while continuing to make grants to the University, suggested that the University Court should consult with the Highland and Agricultural Society regarding the consolidation of the agencies in Edinburgh engaged in the teaching of agriculture and kindred subjects; and further, that the co-operation of Local Authorities be invited with a view to the establishment of a centre for systematic agricultural study, for the training of agricultural teachers and for the organisation of extension work.

Action by the University on these lines resulted in the setting up, in 1895, of a teaching organisation known as the Edinburgh School of Rural Economy which made provision for a two-year curriculum for day students, for a considerable evening class programme and for a limited amount of extension work in agricultural instruction.

In 1901 a conference, which included representatives from the University, the Town Council of Edinburgh, the Highland and Agricultural Society, the Edinburgh School of Rural Economy and the County Councils, agreed on a scheme of agricultural education and research, embracing a central college at Edinburgh and extension teaching in the associated counties. Hence, in July 1901, there came into being the Edinburgh and East of Scotland College of Agriculture, in which was merged the Edinburgh School of Rural Economy.

The College of Agriculture is administered by a Board of Governors representative of Local Authorities, of the University and of various other interests. It exercises functions which, in the main, are distinct from those of the University Department of Agriculture. It makes provision for central instruction of a standard definitely lower than that given at the University while, perhaps, its most important function, which operated as the principal motive in its formation, is its programme of Extension Agricultural Education. The two, however, work in close *liaison*, and the establishment of the College has made good various deficiencies which existed in the University provision for agricultural education. Thus, the College has developed departments of Agricultural Chemistry, Agricultural Bacteriology, Agricultural Engineering and Veterinary Hygiene, which provide graduate courses for university students; while on the College experimental farm are found facilities for the practical instruction of university students and for the conduct of research by the university staff. The assistance rendered by the College in these directions has enabled the University to concentrate on strengthening the other departments of agricultural study for which it is directly responsible.

In 1888 the University, apparently on the authority of the Senatus, instituted the Degree of Bachelor of Science in Agriculture, the first to take the Degree being the late Sir William Somerville, afterwards Sibthorpian Professor of Rural Economy in the University of Oxford.

Formal provision for conferring the ordinary B.Sc. Degree in Agriculture was made in 1892; but the Ordinance made no provision for conferring a Degree of Doctor of Science in Agriculture, a Bachelor of Science in Agriculture, however, having the right to proceed to a D.Sc. in Pure Science.

The increase in the number of students and the development of teaching which took place in the early years of the present century rendered wholly inadequate the accommodation of the department of Agriculture in the Old College. The University acquired a site at No. 10 George Square in immediate contiguity to the College of Agriculture, and in

1914 a modern and commodious building was completed there to accommodate the departments of Agriculture and Forestry.

The regulations governing graduation in Agriculture were amended in 1922. The subjects of study prescribed for the Ordinary Degree of Bachelor of Science in Agriculture underwent substantial modification, and provision was made for conferring a Degree of B.Sc. with Honours in any one of certain specified subjects, the Degree being intended to qualify graduates for specialised work as Agricultural Chemists, Agricultural Economists and the like.

Professor Wallace, whose tenure of the Chair had been associated with a notable development in the department and in the general provision for agricultural education at the University, retired in 1922 and was succeeded by Professor James A. Scott Watson. The latter, in turn, retired at the end of 1925 on his appointment to the Chair of Rural Economy at the University of Oxford. Following this vacancy in the Chair, the University Court and the Governors of the College of Agriculture, with the avowed object of achieving a more intimate relationship between the University and College, entered into an agreement for the appointment of the Principal of the College as University Professor of Agriculture, and Principal Ernest Shearer of the College of Agriculture was appointed to the Chair. This agreement was to be subject to review at the end of the first seven years.

In the present year (1932) the University Court has approved the institution of a post-graduate Diploma in Agricultural Science. The diploma course, which extends over one academical year, is designed primarily to provide the opportunity for instruction in Agriculture and the related sciences in the case of the Honours graduate in Pure Science who wishes to qualify as an agricultural scientific specialist. It aims, therefore, at the same ultimate qualification as that provided by the course for the Bachelor of Science Degree in Agriculture, with Honours.

FACULTY OF SCIENCE

FORESTRY

The University of Edinburgh was the first British University to institute regular courses of lectures on Forestry. On 18th July 1889, the University Court, acting on a resolution of the Senatus, decided to establish a Lectureship, and William (later Sir William) Somerville was appointed first Lecturer. He was required to deliver one hundred lectures each winter session, and the first course was given during the winter of 1890-91. Somerville, however, held the Lectureship only for one year, as he resigned, in May 1891, to accept the Chair of Agriculture at Armstrong College, Newcastle-on-Tyne.

His successor, Colonel Frederick Bailey, Royal Engineers, appointed in 1892, developed considerably the School of Forestry, the teaching being strengthened by the appointment of special lecturers in such subjects as Forest Botany, Forest Engineering and Forest Zoology.

Colonel Bailey retired at the end of the winter session 1909 - 10, and was succeeded by Edward Percy Stebbing of the Indian Forest Service. The department had now developed to such an extent as to justify the University Court in promoting, in 1911-12, an Ordinance for the institution of a Degree in Forestry.

So long as the work of the department was merely confined to courses of lectures, the necessary accommodation could be provided in that portion of the ground floor of the Old College which faced Chambers Street; but the growth in the number of students which followed immediately after the institution of the Degree made it imperative that the department of Forestry should have additional lecture rooms, properly equipped laboratories and museums. These were required not only for the subject of Forestry itself, but also for the allied subjects of Forest Zoology and Forest Engineering. The University Court therefore decided, in 1911, to erect a new building on the north side of George Square large enough to provide accommodation for the departments of Agriculture and Forestry.

The Court appealed to the Development Commissioners for financial help; and the Commissioners eventually decided to make a capital grant equal to fifty per cent. of the cost of the building, in so far as it was allotted to Forestry, up to a maximum of £4500. At the same time the Forest Commissioners gave annual grants, extending over a period of five years (1) for the purchase of a site for, and the laying out of, a forest garden, and (2) for the salary of assistant lecturers and for laboratory expenses.

The building in George Square, with a frontage of 100 feet to the Square, gave provision in the basement for a machine room, tool rooms and laboratory, and on the ground floor for a large museum, class rooms, staff rooms, etc.; while the upper floors were utilised for the needs of Forest Zoology and Agriculture.

In 1919 the University Court decided that the time had come to establish a Chair of Forestry, and the Development Commissioners agreed to make a grant of £7000 towards the sum required for the endowment of the Chair, the remainder being contributed by donors and the Carnegie Trust for the Universities of Scotland. The necessary Ordinance was obtained, and the Lecturer, Edward Percy Stebbing, was appointed as first occupant of the Chair.

The Ordinance of 1911-12 provided only for an Ordinary Degree in Forestry and for the Doctorate. As the work of the department grew and the number of students increased, it was considered advisable to amend the original Ordinance and obtain authority to grant an Honours Degree. The new Ordinance was approved by Order in Council on 9th October 1924. This Ordinance provided that for an Ordinary Degree the course of study should extend over three academical years, but a candidate desiring to obtain the Degree with Honours was required to spend an additional year at the University, taking advanced courses in certain special groups of subjects.

CHEMISTRY

William Gregory's successor, Lyon Playfair, occupant of the Chair of Chemistry from 1858 to 1869, although of high distinction as a chemist, was much more widely known for his eminent public services. He was the son of George

Playfair, a surgeon of the East India Company, and was born in 1818 at Chunar in Bengal. His youth was spent at St Andrews. He attended the parish school and grammar school of the town, and at the age of fourteen entered the University of St Andrews where his grandfather, James Playfair, had been Principal at the beginning of the century. His father intended that he should follow a mercantile career and sent him to live with an uncle, a merchant in Glasgow. Playfair soon grew tired of office life and, in 1835, began medical study. He spent two years in attending medical classes at Glasgow, but was chiefly interested in chemistry, taught at that time in the Andersonian College by Thomas Graham. When Graham left to fill the Chair of Chemistry at University College, London, the chief attraction of Glasgow in Playfair's eyes was gone, and he came to the University of Edinburgh to complete his medical course. He had neglected anatomy and surgery by a too exclusive attention to chemistry; but his pursuit of these subjects had to be abandoned altogether, because the atmosphere both of the dissecting-room and the hospital produced in him a violent and uncontrollable eczema, so that, to his grief, his medical advisers ordered him to discontinue the study of Medicine. Amongst the medical professors at the University he made the acquaintance of Sir Robert Christison and James Syme, who remained his life-long friends. Stranded in his profession, he was advised by his father to look to India for a career; but after a short and uncongenial period with a mercantile house in Calcutta, he returned to England and resumed his chemical studies with Thomas Graham in London. To widen his outlook, Graham sent him, in 1839, to study organic chemistry with Liebig at Giessen. He became a favourite pupil of Liebig, whose great work on agricultural chemistry Playfair translated into English.

After graduation as Ph.D. in 1841, he took a position as chemical manager of calico-printing works at Clitheroe in Lancashire, but, in 1843, he resigned this post and accepted that of Honorary Professor of Chemistry at the Royal Institution of Manchester, whose president was the veteran chemist, John Dalton. Playfair soon organised a teaching laboratory which was attended by numerous students. Regarded now as one of the most promising young chemists in the country, he was fortunate in attracting the attention of the Prime Minister, Sir Robert Peel, by whom he was appointed, in 1844, as a member of the Royal Commission on the Health of Towns. This was the beginning of a public service which continued, practically without intermission, during his life. In the same year he was a candidate for the Chair of Chemistry at Edinburgh, but was unsuccessful in his candidature, William Gregory receiving the appointment. In 1846 he was appointed Chemist to the Geological Survey and Professor of Chemistry in the School of Mines. A small temporary laboratory was provided for him in Duke Street, Westminster. Here he collaborated with Joule in researches on the atomic volume of salts, and here he discovered and investigated the nitro-prussides, a new class of salts. He had as assistants Hermann Kolbe and Edward Frankland who were, later, chemists of world-wide celebrity. His work gradually drifted into applied science. He had made along with Robert Bunsen, in 1845, an enquiry into blast-furnace gases, which led to great economies in working, and he was now employed by Government on all sorts of practical enquiries, ranging from the insanitary condition of Buckingham Palace to explosions in coal-mines. His work in connection with the Exhibition of 1851 was perhaps the most useful of all the tasks to which Playfair devoted his energy and talents. He was appointed a member of the Executive Committee and "Special Commissioner," and there is no doubt that his personal influence, practical good sense, and "drive" had much to do with converting a scheme which threatened failure into an educational, industrial and financial success. From it there originated the great museum site in South Kensington, the Royal College of Science, and the Science and Art Department, of which Playfair was appointed Secretary in 1855.

On Gregory's death in 1858, Playfair was elected to the Chair of Chemistry in the University. At Edinburgh he created, practically out of nothing, a useful teaching laboratory. The rooms then available were very ill-suited to the purpose, and the funds quite inadequate. He spent on his department the whole of his professorial income during the first year of his tenure, and a large part of it during the remainder of his term of office. He found the classes at Edinburgh too large for effective teaching and introduced a tutorial system into the class of Chemistry, the tutors following the course of lectures, and drilling the students in practical exercises on the subjects discussed. He introduced in his class-examinations the system of merit certificates which soon became general in the University. When the Prince of Wales and Prince Alfred, Duke of Edinburgh, attended the University, Playfair was entrusted with the supervision of their studies.

Although possessing a truly scientific mind, Playfair, as he stated in his opening address, now regarded himself as "a sort of missionary to bring chemistry into relation with the industries of the country, which have too long been carried on by rule of thumb." The purely academic life proved too uneventful for him, and after entering Parliament in 1868 as member for the Universities of Edinburgh and St Andrews, he resigned his Chair in 1869. His parliamentary career brought him many duties and many honours, culminating in his elevation to the peerage, in 1892, as Baron Playfair of St Andrews. He died in London in 1898 and was buried at St Andrews, his family town.

Alexander Crum Brown, Professor from 1869 to 1908, who occupied the Chair at the time of the Tercentenary celebration, was in many ways a contrast to his predecessor. He was a keen scientific thinker, and his interests, though varied, were rather speculative than practical.

He was born in Edinburgh in 1838 and came of a distinguished family of divines and theologians, his father being John Brown, a prominent Edinburgh minister. His half-brother, John Brown, physician, was the author of *Rab and His Friends*, and a maternal uncle, Walter Crum, was a chemist of note in his day. Crum Brown had thus connections with literature, medicine and science which, if they did not account for his versatile gifts and catholicity of taste, at least contributed to their development.

He was educated at the Royal High School, Edinburgh, and Mill Hill School. In 1854 he entered the University as a student, first of Arts and then of Medicine. He was gold medallist in the classes of Chemistry and Natural Philosophy, and graduated as M.A. in 1858. Continuing his medical studies, he received the Degree of M.D. in 1861. During this period he read for the Science Degree of London University and, in 1862, had the distinction of being the first candidate on whom the Doctorate of Science of the University of London was conferred. He continued the study of chemistry in Germany, at Heidelberg under Bunsen, and at Marburg under Kolbe.

In 1863 he was licensed as Extra-academical Lecturer in Chemistry by the University, and succeeded Playfair in the Chair in 1869, his application receiving the support of nearly every prominent chemist in the country.

Crum Brown's scientific work bore a markedly individual stamp. His mind was essentially logical and philosophic, and he was especially interested in symbolic representation. His thesis for the medical doctorate, written at the age of twenty-three, showed the outstanding position of the man as an original thinker. It bore the title "On the Theory of Chemical Combination," and displayed remarkable insight and width of vision. In it was contained a system for the graphic formulation of organic compounds in all essentials identical with that universally adopted at the present day. His formulæ were the first to represent clearly both the valency and the linking of atoms in organic compounds and were in current use a few years after their publication in 1864. His later chemical work had much of a pioneering character and often anticipated the state of the science years afterwards. For example, in his article "Molecule," written in 1883 for the *Encyclopœdia Britannica*, he displayed views of crystal structure which were a generation ahead of the time. A theory of optical activity of organic compounds, the electrosynthesis of dibasic acids, and the "Crum Brown-Gibson Rule" for replacement in the benzene nucleus illustrate the nature of his chemical investigations in divergent fields.

His researches were by no means confined to chemistry. In conjunction with Thomas (later Sir Thomas) R. Fraser, a younger medical colleague, he made an investigation of fundamental importance on the connection between chemical constitution and physiological action. Physiological problems dealing with the senses also engaged his attention, amongst others, the movements of the eye, the function of the semicircular canals, and the analysis of vowel sounds. Several published papers show also his serious interest in certain branches of mathematics. In literature his reading was extensive and his knowledge of languages, ancient and modern, was altogether exceptional.

A man of Crum Brown's great and varied gifts could scarcely prove other than a stimulating teacher, although to the average elementary student his lectures were somewhat of a trial. An old pupil has written: "Chemical formulæ grew like magic on the blackboard. The casual limp-minded listener found Crum Brown's quick, vivid style much too strenuous; but the student who really wished to learn could not fail to experience keen intellectual delight from the masterly manner in which the whole subject was presented." His advanced lectures on organic chemistry were revelations of the working of scientific method. He delighted in analogies and parables, and exercised the greatest ingenuity in seeking from familiar life parallels to the scientific lesson he wished to inculcate.

About fifty years ago the department of Chemistry was moved from the Old College to the New Medical Buildings, where ampler accommodation for advanced students was provided. The laboratories were mainly equipped for the purposes of analytical chemistry, but gradually the requirements of other branches of the science were met. The number of students taking chemistry as a special study progressively increased, and twenty years after the new laboratories were opened it was necessary to make an extensive addition by adding a floor above the main apartments. This new extension permitted the separation of the students taking an elementary chemistry course for Arts or Science from the students of Medicine, to the great advantage of the former, the nature and character of whose practical work had been much hampered by overcrowding. Another twenty years elapsed before the medical students enjoyed similar advantages. Crum Brown was assisted in the development of his department by John Gibson, Leonard Dobbin, and Hugh Marshall, who were active in the conduct of the new laboratories. Amongst other assistants for shorter periods were James Walker and Alexander Smith.

Although Crum Brown did not, strictly speaking, found a school of chemistry, many of his pupils became heads of departments in universities at home and abroad, and as teachers imparted to younger generations the sound principles they had received from their master.

Crum Brown was not without a distinct turn for business. He acted as convener of the Science Committee of the Senatus before a Faculty of Science was established, and was also for many years a member of the University Court. Outside the University, the United Presbyterian Church and the Royal Society of Edinburgh claimed his chief practical interests. Witty, humorous and a born *raconteur*, he shone in social gatherings, especially at his own hospitable table.

He retired from the Chair in 1908 at the age of seventy and died in Edinburgh in 1922.

Crum Brown was succeeded by his pupil, James Walker, who was for a time Professor of Chemistry at University College, Dundee. The science branch of the department was still expanding and, in 1913, the University Court allocated a site at High School Yards for the provision of new laboratories, plans for which were nearing completion when war broke out. The scheme was necessarily suspended and, on the conclusion of the war, was altogether abandoned, as it had become evident that it could not meet post-war requirements.

FACULTY OF SCIENCE

A new elementary lecture course for students of Science had been instituted in 1909, which permitted the general course then existing to be better adapted to the special needs of medical students and, in 1912, Walker had urged in a Memorandum the foundation of a new Chemistry Chair for the tuition of students of Medicine. It was seen in the period of demobilisation that the establishment of this Chair would greatly ease the burden of teaching in the crowded years impending, and the University Court consequently promoted, in 1918, an Ordinance for the foundation of a Chair of Chemistry in Relation to Medicine, George Barger becoming its first occupant in the summer of the following year.

The immediate provision of new laboratories was also imperative, and the Court authorised the erection of a Chemistry department for students of Science, on the newly acquired site of The King's Buildings, near Liberton, the former department in Teviot Row then becoming available for the purposes of the Faculty of Medicine.

Work on the new site was begun in November 1919, A. F. Balfour Paul having been appointed architect. The building was erected in three sections, arranged so as to accommodate the abnormally large classes as the students progressed from year to year. The Foundation Stone was laid by King George V. on 6th July 1920.

The last section was finished in 1924, the completed department being opened by the Prince of Wales in December of that year. The total cost of the building, fittings and accessories was £182,000.

The department is unlike the usual style of academic building; it is essentially a one-storey brick structure which forms a rectangular block of 220 feet frontage and 320 feet depth, with a northern exposure. A central corridor and two side corridors, connected by a cross corridor in front, run back the whole length of the building. The main laboratories, five in number, are situated between the central and side corridors, and are built on a factory plan, being lit with well-distributed north light from a saw-tooth roof. The smaller research and other laboratories are placed in the front block and on the outer aspect of the side corridors. They are lit by ordinary windows. A small technical laboratory is equipped with miniature plant for manufacturing processes. The front block of red brick and stonework is of two storeys, the upper floor housing the library, administrative offices, staff room and special research rooms. There are two large and two small lecture rooms, all served from the same preparation room and museum.

The laboratories, which are planned for easy expansion, afford accommodation for 400 undergraduate workers, with ample provision for post-graduate research. At the present time (1932) there are, in addition to the permanent staff, over thirty research workers in the department.

Leonard Dobbin, who joined the staff in 1880, retired from the Readership in Chemistry in 1924, and was succeeded by John E. Mackenzie.

Sir James Walker retired from the Chair in 1928, and was succeeded by James Kendall, Professor of Chemistry at New York University, who had enrolled as an Edinburgh student in the year preceding Crum Brown's retirement.

ENGINEERING

The appointment of George Wilson to the Professorship of Technology in 1855 may be considered the initial step in the introduction of the study of Engineering at the University of Edinburgh. This Chair was abolished, however, in 1859; and it was not till 1868, when the Chair of Engineering was founded by the gift of £6000 as an endowment by Sir David Baxter, Bt., that Engineering took a definite place in the subjects of study at the University.

Under the agreement entered into between the University and Sir David Baxter, the first presentation to the Chair was placed in the hands of the founder. An understanding was entered into with H.M. Treasury, who were to make an annual contribution of £200 towards the salary of the Chair, under which the subsequent patronage reverted to the Crown.

From the painting by] [*Henry Lintott*

SIR JAMES ALFRED EWING, K.C.B.

Principal and Vice-Chancellor
1916-1929

Sir David Baxter selected as the first occupant of the Chair, Henry Charles Fleeming Jenkin, who was then Professor of Civil Engineering at University College, London. Owing to the lack of funds for the establishment of a laboratory, it was not possible to give any practical training in the newly established Engineering department, except drawing office instruction, a condition of affairs which remained till the death of Professor Fleeming Jenkin in 1885, and during the first few years of the tenure of the Chair by his successor, Professor George Frederick Armstrong.

The first degree conferred on a student in the Engineering department was in 1873, and the records of the department show that during the winter session of 1871-72 the prizeman in the class of Engineering was James Alfred Ewing who, in 1916, became Principal of the University.

Professor Armstrong was inducted in October 1885 and occupied the Chair until his death in 1900. In 1889 the University Court decided to allot a bequest of £3000 from John Fulton for general purposes to meet the cost of equipping an engineering laboratory, to be known as the Fulton Engineering Laboratory; and this was opened during the session 1890-91. It was housed on the ground floor of the Old College, on the Chambers Street front, but the lecture-rooms and drawing office of the department still occupied their old quarters on the top floor of the south-west corner of the Old College.

This inconvenient method of housing the department was still the only one possible when the present occupant of the Chair, Professor Sir Thomas Hudson Beare, was appointed in 1901. In his inaugural address in October of that year he urged upon the Senatus and the University Court the imperative need of better accommodation for the department, but, owing to lack of funds, nothing could be done for a few years.

When Sir William Turner became Principal of the University in 1903 he and Professor George Chrystal induced the Senatus to draw the attention of the University Court to the clamant need of providing better equipped and larger laboratories and lecture-rooms for the two departments of Natural Philosophy and Engineering. In 1905, by means of funds provided by the Carnegie Trust, the necessary money was obtained to enable these two departments to be moved to two reconstructed buildings at High School Yards, previously part of the old Royal Infirmary and of the City Hospital for Infectious Diseases. The building, reconstructed for the Engineering department, had been, prior to its use for hospital purposes, the High School of Edinburgh until 1829, when the present High School on the Calton Hill was opened.

The improvement in the accommodation and equipment was followed by the rapid increase in the number of students in the department. This fact in association with the institution of lectureships in various branches of Engineering Science, such as Hydraulics, Strength of Materials, Engineering Design and Drawing, soon made imperative more laboratory and lecture-room accommodation than the original scheme provided. This demand could only be very inadequately met in the building at High School Yards. Temporary relief to the overcrowded drawing office was obtained by the erection of a wooden hut behind the main building in the year 1920, when the department was overcrowded on the demobilisation of young men whose University training had been interrupted by military service. How great was the pressure upon the resources of the department during this period may be gathered from the fact that, in June 1922, no less than one hundred candidates were presented for the Degree of B.Sc. in Engineering, as contrasted with seven at the end of the session 1905-6, the first year in which the department had occupied the building in High School Yards.

Although the University Court was fully aware of the necessity of increasing the accommodation allotted to the Engineering department, there seemed little hope of finding the necessary money, as a large sum would be required not only for the purchase of a site and the erection of new buildings, but also for their adequate equipment. In 1927, the University Court received the welcome intimation that under the will of the late James Sanderson of Galashiels, a member of the firm of Messrs R. & A. Sanderson & Co., one of the oldest established firms in the Scottish tweed trade, a sum of about £50,000 would eventually be available for the needs of the departments of Chemistry and Engineering. After consultation with the University Court, the trustees of James Sanderson's estate decided that, as Chemistry had been provided for by the erection of the Science Buildings on The King's Buildings site, the main part of this handsome bequest should be devoted to the construction and equipment of a new building for Engineering in the same locality. Plans were prepared: the late Sir Robert Lorimer and John F. Matthew were appointed architects by the University Court and, in November 1929, the work was commenced.

The new buildings, facing Mayfield Road, are oblong in plan, the front extending to a total length of 200 feet, with a depth of 144 feet from east to west. The two-storeyed front portion of the building accounts for practically half the total area, and provides accommodation for the necessary lecture-rooms, drawing office, library, staff-rooms, etc. The laboratories occupy the one-storey back portion of the building—separate laboratories being provided for Strength of Materials, Heat Engines, Hydraulics and Mechanics. All these laboratories have been equipped with the necessary experimental apparatus for teaching work and research. The buildings were opened on 28th January 1932 by the Prime Minister, the Right Hon. J. Ramsay MacDonald.

The Commission, appointed under the Universities (Scotland) Act, 1889, promulgated the first Ordinance dealing specifically with Degrees in Engineering. Under this Ordinance every student pursued practically the same course of study, and provision was made for the granting of a Doctorate of Science in Engineering. Powers were taken in 1924 to confer an Ordinary Degree and a Degree with Honours, and the subjects of study were so arranged that specialised training could be given in Civil, Mechanical and Electrical Engineering.

An important improvement in the curriculum for

Engineering degrees was made in 1902-3 on the suggestion of Professor Chrystal, when an independent Lectureship in Technical Mathematics was instituted by the University Court. The Lecturer was to be responsible for the courses required under the Ordinance for the Degree of B.Sc. in Engineering. Later, he also undertook the third year course in Applied Mathematics (Dynamics).

It is an interesting coincidence that both the first occupant of the Chair of Engineering at Edinburgh and the present holder had previously occupied the Chair of Engineering at University College, London, while the present occupant of the Chair at University College, London, Professor Coker, took his Degree in Engineering in 1892 at the University of Edinburgh.

GEOLOGY

It is by observation of what takes place on the earth's surface to-day that we interpret what has taken place in past ages. By the use of this principle, now universally recognised as furnishing the key to the record of the rocks, geological studies were raised to the dignity of a science as the outcome of the labours of a brilliant band of observers in Edinburgh, near the end of the eighteenth century. Among them, James Hutton was pre-eminently the leader. The results of his observations were first published by the Royal Society of Edinburgh; and at a later date—1795—were expanded into a volume entitled *Theory of the Earth with Proofs and Illustrations.* Hutton's work was slow to attract attention, owing partly to the condensed and obscure style in which it was presented, but, fortunately, an able expounder was found in his friend, John Playfair, Professor of Natural Philosophy at the University who, after Hutton's death, published his now classic *Illustrations of the Huttonian Theory.*

Although the foundations of geological science in its modern form were thus laid at Edinburgh, the University for many years hindered more than helped in the construction of the superstructure. Even when Hutton's ideas became generally accepted, the subject remained in a subordinate position under the Professor of Natural History; and it was not until 1871 that a separate Chair was established through the influence of Sir Roderick Murchison who himself made a substantial contribution towards its endowment.

Archibald Geikie, who had had a brilliant career at the University as a classical student before turning to Science, was then Director of the Geological Survey of Scotland, and arrangements were made for him to combine both offices, until, eleven years later, he was transferred to London as Director General. He was then succeeded as professor by his younger brother James who carried on and extended, during the next thirty-two years, the school which had already attained a position of high standing.

Professor James Geikie's name will always be especially identified with the elucidation of the glacial history of Europe. During the later years of his tenure of the Chair he gave a series of Munro lectures on *The Antiquity of Man in Europe*. In this and in his earlier works he demonstrated the intimate connection between the early history of man and that of the Ice Age. He showed that the Pleistocene period was marked by alterations of epochs of cold and genial climatic conditions. Following the traditions of the Scottish School, Professor Geikie devoted much attention to the evolution of the surface features of the land. He was one of the founders of the Royal Scottish Geographical Society and for several years served as its president. During the last years of his life he held also the position of President of the Royal Society of Edinburgh.

On his retirement in 1914, Thomas John Jehu was appointed to the Chair. New laboratory methods in petrology, palæontology and economic geology demanded facilities that could not be obtained in the Old University buildings. At the close of the war, owing to the great influx of students, the department became congested to such an extent that the practical classes had to be conducted in relays of students under very difficult conditions. As a temporary makeshift, the University Court utilised some wooden huts which were used by troops during the war, but efforts were made to provide a more adequate building. This was a matter of great difficulty owing to the financial position; for the only sum available at the time was £1000—a gift from Sir John Findlay, Bt., of Aberlour, to the Geological department. But, in 1929, Sir Alexander Grant, Bt., of Logie, generously offered £50,000 for the erection of a new building.

Sketch plans, prepared by Professor Jehu and his staff, were placed in the hands of Sir Robert Lorimer and John F. Matthew, who had been appointed architects, and it was decided that the new building was to be called "The Grant Institute of Geology," which now forms part of The King's Buildings. It was formally opened on 28th January 1932, by the Right Hon. J. Ramsay MacDonald, Prime Minister.

The University is now provided with a building worthy of the metropolis of Scotland. The departmental library is one of the best equipped in the University, due largely to the gifts of books and papers by the two Geikies. The museum contains mineral collections gifted by Thomas Brown of Lanfine; the collection of minerals, rocks and fossils lent by Sir Charles Lyell and presented by the late Lady Lyell of Kinnordy; also the collection of the late James Currie of Leith, generously given to the University by Mrs Currie and family.

Many former students of the department have gone out to occupy positions of distinction. Among these may be mentioned Sir John S. Flett who, graduating in 1892, became the first Lecturer in Petrology under Professor James Geikie, and is now Director of the Geological Survey of Great Britain; Robert Charles Wallace, who became Professor of Geology at Winnipeg and is now President of the University of Alberta; John D. Falconer who, graduating in the same year, followed Flett as Lecturer in Petrology and afterwards became Director of the Geological Survey of Nigeria; the late G. S. Corstorphine, Principal of the Witwatersrand University; Robert B. Young, Professor of Geology in that institution, and his brother Andrew Young, Professor of Geology at Cape Town; Alexander M. Heron, who joined the Geological Survey of India in the

DEPARTMENT OF ZOOLOGY, GRANT INSTITUTE OF GEOLOGY
AND DEPARTMENT OF CHEMISTRY
West Mains Road

SANDERSON DEPARTMENT OF ENGINEERING LABORATORIES
AND DEPARTMENT OF ZOOLOGY
Mayfield Road

THE KING'S BUILDINGS

year following graduation in 1906, is now one of its Superintendents; William T. Gordon, also graduating in 1906, is Professor of Geology at the University of London and Secretary of the Geological Society; and William F. P. McLintock, a graduate of 1907, is Curator of the Geological Survey Museum in London.

MINING

An Ordinance of the University Court, giving power to confer the Degrees of Bachelor and Doctor of Science in Mining and Metallurgy, was approved by Order in Council on 27th May 1921. At that time there were no courses in either Mining or Metallurgy at the University. The Court, therefore, on the advice of the Senatus, acting under powers conferred by Section vi. of the Ordinance, allowed candidates to attend approved courses in these subjects at the Heriot-Watt College.

In 1923, James A. Hood, a well-known Midlothian Colliery owner, intimated his desire to found a Chair of Mining at the University with an endowment of £15,000. The University Court gratefully accepted this gift, and an Ordinance was obtained in 1924, authorising the foundation of a Chair to be known as the James A. Hood Chair of Mining.

In making this gift James Hood expressed the hope that the University Court would secure the co-operation of the Governors of George Heriot's Trust in the teaching of Mining. In July 1928, an agreement was reached between the University Court and the Governors of the Trust under which (1) the University Professor of Mining should also be the Professor of Mining at the Heriot-Watt College—the salary to be provided jointly by the two institutions; (2) the Governors of the Trust should require to find accommodation for the Professor and his staff, to continue to supply the necessary equipment and to meet the existing current expenditure of £700 per annum. Under this agreement, Henry Briggs, the Professor of Mining at the Heriot-Watt College, was appointed to the new Chair.

In 1925, the Governors of George Heriot's Trust intimated to the University Court that they proposed to provide new quarters for the Mining department by reconstructing certain buildings they owned in the Grassmarket. They therefore asked the Court to join them in an appeal to the Miners' Welfare Committee for a grant of £8000 towards the estimated cost of this reconstruction. The Welfare Committee agreed, provided that the remainder of the money needed was obtained from local sources. The University Court gave £1000 to the local fund, and eventually the whole of the necessary money was obtained and the reconstruction work was at once commenced. The building was opened on 23rd November 1928 by the Right Hon. Viscount Chelmsford.

In view of the fact that the annual expenditure upon the maintenance of the department in the new buildings would exceed the £700 a year fixed by the agreement made in 1928, the University Court entered into an arrangement with the Governors of George Heriot's Trust to provide—up to a limit of £600—one-half of any additional annual expenditure above the original £700. All matters concerning the staffing of the Mining School and similar questions are, by a later agreement between the University Court and the Governors of the Heriot-Watt College, referred in the first instance to a Joint Committee of ten members to which each authority appoints five. Three of the five, in each case, must be men of practical experience in the Mining industry.

In February 1931, a new Ordinance came into force, amending the title of the Degree by omitting the word "Metallurgy," and giving power to confer the Bachelor's Degree either as an Ordinary or as an Honours Degree. The new Ordinance retains the original condition that the period of study shall be four academical years, both for the Ordinary and the Honours Degree, and the further condition that every candidate must have spent at least six months in practical work in Mines.

FACULTY OF SCIENCE

ANIMAL GENETICS

The origin of the study of Genetics in Edinburgh is to be found in the period and in the work of Professor J. Cossar Ewart in his experimental investigations in telegony. The records of these are preserved in "The Penycuik Experiments," 1899. Professor Cossar Ewart then turned his attention to questions relating to the origin of the larger domestic animals and, thereafter, to the improvement of the fleece of the sheep by the application of genetic principles to the practice of breeding.

In 1911, a Lecturer in Genetics was appointed within the Department of Zoology, Arthur D. Darbishire being chosen for the post. Before his death, in 1915, from cerebro-spinal fever contracted while on military service, he had inscribed his name in the history of the science of Genetics. He is remembered especially for his work on the waltzing mouse, and for his attempt to reconcile biometry and Mendelism.

In the same year in which Darbishire was appointed, the Development Commissioners formulated a comprehensive scheme of education and research in agriculture. This included the creation of a number of research centres where the sciences which contribute to the advance of agriculture may be studied. It was the Commissioners' stated policy to nourish the existing rather than to create something entirely new and, in consonance with this policy, to Edinburgh was allocated research in animal breeding. Edinburgh was indeed the obvious centre for such an investigation. It was the scene of Professor Cossar Ewart's life work; associated with him was A. D. Darbishire and, as early as 1905, the University appointed a lecturer in the physiology of reproduction. This post was occupied until 1908 by Francis H. A. Marshall. In 1913, a committee representative of the University and of the College of Agriculture was called into being and became responsible for the affairs of the future Institute. War, however, relegated this and many other projects to the limbo of the indefinitely postponed. Not until 1919 were the activities of the committee resumed. In the interval A. D. Darbishire had died. Francis Albert Eley Crew, then an assistant in the department of Zoology, was offered the post of Director of Research, and instructed to draw up a scheme for the organisation and development of the Institute. It was a difficult task. No capital was available for buildings, the annual budget was small, and there was no existing Institute of a similar kind which might be used as a model. But the difficulties were overcome. An old block of buildings at High School Yards was handed over to him by the University; his plan of organisation was approved by the committee, and three post-graduate workers were attracted to the new Institute in its first year. In the second year this number was increased to eleven.

The years which succeeded were years of rapid expansion and, in 1924, the department had grown too large for its quarters at High School Yards. Seven rooms were placed at its disposal in the Chemistry department at The King's Buildings, and some thirty acres of the surrounding grassland were made available as an experimental farm. At last it had become possible to use farm animals as experimental material, though the opportunity was still very limited.

The year 1926-27 was a notable one in the history of the department. In that year the International Education Board of America approved of a grant of £30,000 towards the building and equipment of the department and the endowment of a Chair of Genetics in the University. A like sum was raised through the generosity of various private individuals and public bodies, notably Lord Forteviot, the Development Commission, the Empire Marketing Board and the Highland and Agricultural Society. Lord Woolavington contributed half the sum necessary for the endowment of the Chair. Plans were prepared by Sir R. Lorimer and J. F. Matthew, and building operations were commenced in 1928 on the site occupied by The King's Buildings. The new Institute has been built to the west of the Chemistry department, taking the form of a T with the cross-bar facing east. The building, four storeys in height, has been planned so as to provide for the possibility of future extension; to its western end another

DEPARTMENT OF ANIMAL GENETICS

The King's Buildings, West Mains Road

wing can be added. In addition to the main block there are other buildings. Thus, to the south-west is a building for sheep, provided by the Empire Marketing Board; this is equipped with operating theatre, sterilising and instrument rooms, food store and sheep pens. Accommodation is also provided by the department of Agriculture for Scotland for a number of other domesticated animals.

In March 1930 the new department was ready for partial occupation and the opening ceremony took place on Monday, 30th June. It was appropriate that Sir Edward Sharpey-Schafer should declare the building open; his long life devoted to experimental science had been an inspiration to the workers in the new department and his active interest a great encouragement to them.

While building operations were still in progress, the department received further support and encouragement from a Canadian source. In 1929, Thomas B. Macaulay, a Canadian with strong Scottish interests, gave practical expression to his sympathy with the aims of the department. With a generosity that was of more than financial importance, he endowed within the department a Research Lectureship and three Associated Assistantships. He endowed also a Research Fellowship in Human Genetics and contributed a sum for the purchase of the Experimental Farm of Shothead, Balerno.

From its inception the department's activities and interests have continued to widen. The earliest papers published from it were almost prophetic of its subsequent development. In 1922 evidence was given in its publications that the interests of the department embraced not only Genetics both formal and physiological, but also Animal Husbandry and Sex Biology. Each one of these subjects is now studied by a staff exceeding in number the total personnel of the department of 1920; and the whole intervening period of ten years has shown a continuous growth and expansion which more than justifies the high endeavour and adventurous independence that characterised the plan of organisation submitted in 1919 to the governing body.

VIII

THE FACULTY OF MUSIC

SIR HERBERT STANLEY OAKELEY (1830-1903)

Reid Professor of Music, 1865-1891

WITH the election in November 1865 of Herbert Stanley Oakeley as successor to Professor Donaldson, the Reid "Chair of the Theory of Music" entered upon a new and happier phase of its somewhat chequered history. The new Professor came with high credentials. The second son of Sir Herbert Oakeley, Baronet, he had been educated at Rugby and Christ Church, Oxford, graduating as B.A. in 1853, and as M.A. in 1856. His musical gifts had early attracted attention. In the Memoir of him, *The Life of Sir Herbert S. Oakeley*, which was written by his brother, reference is made to his remarkable delicacy of ear even as a child. It is related of him that "when four years old, being shown the notes on the piano and told what to call them, he could, without seeing the keys, name any note or combination of notes which was sounded." Making rapid progress in organ and pianoforte playing, he studied Harmony and the Theory of Music under Stephen Elvey.

In 1855 he went to Leipzig, then renowned through the genius of Mendelssohn and the Conservatorium founded by him. Here he studied under Moscheles and Plaidy. Here, too, he made acquaintance with Clara Schumann, Hauptmann, David, Röntgen (the elder) and others. In Berlin he played before Paul Mendelssohn, brother of the great composer, and interviewed Meyerbeer, then engaged in the composition of his opera *Dinorah*. In 1863 he was again on the Continent. At Dresden he worked with the famous Dresden organist, Johann Gottlieb Schneider, who had numbered among his pupils Mendelssohn, Schumann, Liszt, and other musicians scarcely less illustrious. Munich, where he met Franz Lachner, and Vienna were also visited and, later, Rome in which capital he stayed for several months. In Rome he had the privilege of intercourse with Liszt to whom he submitted some of his compositions, and of whose playing and remarkable gifts he has left an interesting account.

When, in 1865, Oakeley was elected to the Edinburgh Professorship he had established himself in the esteem of musicians of high rank, both in this country and on the Continent, as a talented organist and composer and also as the possessor of a remarkable faculty of improvisation. His powers in this direction were sometimes in demand on the most unexpected occasions. At the close of his Inaugural Address, delivered in the Music Classroom, several of the students, according to the *Edinburgh Courant* of that time, expressed a strong desire to hear the organ. Professor Oakeley accordingly played General Reid's *Garb of Old Gaul*, "with specimens of varied harmony, followed by an extempore fugue on the opening subject of the March, in which he introduced inversion of the subject and other contrapuntal devices. In one of the variations the subject was taken on the pedal organ."

In the course of his Inaugural Address the Professor said: "I shall deem it my duty to take anxious care that the benefits contemplated in this magnificent foundation shall never be lost through any fault or remissness of mine." If to some of his listeners, mindful of the vicissitudes through which the Chair of the Theory of Music had already passed, the words of Dante recurred with peculiar significance—

> "Per me si va nella città dolente
> Per me si va nell' eterno dolore
> . . . .
> Lasciate ogni speranza, voi, chi entrate."

no such thoughts troubled the mind of the speaker. He suggested rather, in pleading for thoroughness in musical training, that over the door of the Music Classroom there might be inscribed the motto that he had observed in the music room of the Leipzig Gewandhaus: *Res severa est verum gaudium.* He incidentally mentioned the possible use of the organ in the services of the Church; a remark "that was received with loud cheers and hisses." He also looked forward to the time when graduation in music at Edinburgh would be an accomplished fact.

Oakeley's first care was to raise the artistic standard of the annual concert enjoined by the terms of the will of General Reid. At that time little orchestral music of any artistic importance could be heard in Edinburgh. The supply, however, was about equal to the demand, and not the least onerous of the new Professor's tasks was, if not the creation, at least the widening of the basis of intelligent artistic appreciation of, and love for, the rich treasures of orchestral and even of chamber music. This work, during the whole of his regime of twenty-six years, he carried on with zeal and enthusiasm, undaunted by criticism that was frequently ill-informed and even the reverse of generous. One writer objected to the "Reid Festival"—as it came to be known—because it represented nothing better than the glorification of the professional musician; while Professor J. S. Blackie, whose eccentricities, however, never wounded those who really knew him, described it as sheer "west-end flunkeyism."

For his first Reid Concert, on 13th February 1866, Professor Oakeley brought together an orchestra composed of players from Edinburgh, Glasgow and London. Alexander C. Mackenzie, afterwards Principal of the Royal Academy of Music, London, led the second violins. The soloists included Teresa Tietjens and Alfredo Piatti. During the years 1867 and 1868, when Clara Schumann played Beethoven's E♭ major Pianoforte Concerto, the Crystal Palace Orchestra, with August Manns as conductor, was engaged, and, in 1869, Charles (later Sir Charles) Hallé's Manchester Orchestra. At this concert were performed Beethoven's A major Symphony, overtures by Weber and Cherubini, and the entr'acte music from Schubert's *Rosamunde*. Sims Reeves was the principal vocalist. Hallé played Mendelssohn's pianoforte Concerto in D minor, No. 2, and solos by J. S. Bach, Schumann and Chopin. The impression made by this and subsequent Reid Concerts was such, and the demand for admission tickets before long became so great, that the Professor organised two supplementary concerts on the same scale as the "Reid." The "Reid Festival" consisted, therefore, for a considerable number of years, of three concerts, each with full orchestra and soloists, given on successive evenings. The trouble as to the right of free admission to the concerts, rampant in Professor Donaldson's time, now for the most part disappeared. By giving free admission not only to the members of the University Court and of the Senatus, but also to the fourth-year students and the leading musicians of the city, and admitting the rest of the audience by payment, Professor Oakeley was successful in satisfying both "town and gown."

From 1869 to 1891, that is for a period of twenty-two years, Sir Charles Hallé's renowned orchestra was engaged for the Reid Concerts. During this period were performed all the Beethoven symphonies, most of them several times; all Mendelssohn's and Schumann's; the three greatest of Mozart; and symphonies by Haydn, Schubert, Brahms, Dvořák, Spohr, Goldmark and other composers; eighty overtures; ninety-three concertos—including repetitions—and other orchestral pieces. Among the soloists, instrumental and vocal, were Clara Schumann, Sir Charles Hallé, Ernst Pauer, Norman Neruda (Lady Hallé); Piatti, Sainton, Carrodus; Tietjens, Nordica, Trebelli, Sainton-Dolby; Sims Reeves, W. H. Cummings, Edward Lloyd, Foli, George Henschel, and others equally celebrated. The superb quality of the orchestral playing and the great educational value of the Reid Concerts were on all sides freely admitted.

It was in his organ recitals that Professor Oakeley came into most intimate contact with the students. To these recitals any student was entitled to admission on presenting his matriculation card. They were much appreciated; indeed, many of the students had never heard an organ before coming to the University. Between 1866 and 1891 Professor Oakeley gave altogether 200 recitals on the Music class-room organ. This splendid instrument, one of the finest in the country, was erected by Hill & Son, London, in 1861 for Professor Donaldson, nineteen stops being added later under the direction of Professor Oakeley. The old tracker action was taken out and replaced in 1907 by the more modern tubular pneumatic action, during the Professorship of Frederick Niecks. It is interesting to note that in its present form the instrument earned the high approval of Albert Schweitzer when, in 1932, this well-known Bach scholar visited Edinburgh.

During his first year at Edinburgh Professor Oakeley founded the Edinburgh University Musical Society. From 1869 to 1890 the programmes of the annual concerts comprised glees and madrigals, overtures and symphonies, and pianoforte solos by the Professor. He himself attended or conducted the rehearsals, was active in the arrangements and composed part of the music. Although many of the students, when they first came, knew little of music and nothing of musical notation, they were generally able to give a good account of themselves at the annual concert in March, and the concerts were well patronised.

A course of lectures was given each year on the music of different countries, and a class in Harmony was formed in connection with the Association for the Education of Women. The chief part of Professor Oakeley's work at the University, however, was done in connection with the Reid Concerts and the organ recitals.

Among his compositions are many anthems, songs and hymn tunes, including the familiar and popular *Abends* and *Edina,* and the "Edinburgh" Festal March and Students' Song; his "Jubilee" Cantata; Morning and Evening Service; Suite for the orchestra in the Olden Style; and his "Carmen Seculare," written for St Andrews University. Twenty of his songs were published in a *Jubilee Album* and dedicated to Queen Victoria. In 1876 he received the honour of knighthood, and in 1881 was created Composer of Music to Her Majesty in Scotland. The Honorary Degree of Mus.D. was conferred on him by several universities: in 1871 by the Archbishop of Canterbury; in 1879 by the University of Oxford; and in 1887 by the University of Dublin. In 1881 he received the Degree of LL.D. from the University

SIR THOMAS HENRY HOLLAND, K.C.S.I.

Principal and Vice-Chancellor
1929

of Aberdeen, and in 1876 Trinity College, Toronto, conferred on him the Degree of D.C.L.

An accident while on holiday in Switzerland resulted in permanent lameness which affected to some extent his organ playing, or at least his bodily comfort when playing. On the recommendation of his medical adviser he resigned from the Chair of Music in 1891. His resignation was received with regret by the University Court. In presenting him for the Honorary Degree of LL.D., on 17th April 1891, Professor Kirkpatrick, after enumerating his distinguished services to the University, said: "This University owes him cordial gratitude, and she grieves to be about to part from a most distinguished member, and a beloved friend." In 1899 he also received the Honorary Degree of Mus.D.

In the interval between the resignation of Sir Herbert Oakeley in 1891 and the appointment of his successor, a local musician, John Greig, was deputed by the University Court to carry on the duties of the Chair.

In the meantime some agitation had arisen in certain quarters with regard to the actual and positive results that had so far accrued from the Reid Foundation, as compared with its potential musical and educational possibilities. While the high standard of playing of Sir Charles Hallé's orchestra and the æsthetical and educational value of the Reid Concerts were freely recognised, it was argued that the real function of the Chair was to teach, not to amuse. The whole sphere and method of the Chair, it was thought, ought to be liberated and enlarged, so as to bring it into close and intimate connection with the musical life of Edinburgh and of Scotland. Properly organised, the Reid Foundation might be made to yield the most beneficial results. The terms of the will of General Reid were scrutinised afresh, and it was, or was thought to be, discovered that, to General Reid, the institution of the annual concert was but an afterthought, seeing that it was conveyed in a codicil to his will: further, that the real intention of General Reid, in founding the Chair, was the establishment at Edinburgh of a great Musical School, similar to the well-known Conservatoires of the Continent, or the Colleges and Academies of England. Such a School, with the Reid Professor at its head, would be supported by the best teaching ability in the city. As regarded the practical working of such a scheme, it was suggested that the £200 devoted to the Reid Concerts would suffice to secure for the University the services of ten highly-qualified teachers of music in its various branches, including instrumental music.

Others, however, were of opinion that such a liberal interpretation of the terms of General Reid's will might quite conceivably involve the Senatus in another lawsuit similar to that already brought against it by the late Professor Donaldson, but for a somewhat different reason; that by no stretching of terms was it possible to identify a Conservatoire or Music School of the kind contemplated with the "Chair of the Theory of Music" prescribed by General Reid, who was not only a gallant officer and a man of culture, but possessed of no mean attainments as a musician and composer. The chief function of such a Chair was not so much to give instruction in instrumental or vocal technique, as to give enlightenment concerning the higher and more intellectual aspects of music; the majority, indeed, of those aspects which raise the art of Music to at least as high a plane as that of other University subjects.

In November 1891, Frederick Niecks was elected to succeed Sir Herbert Oakeley as Reid Professor of Music.

FREDERICK MATERNUS NIECKS (1845-1924)

Reid Professor of Music, 1891-1914

Born in Düsseldorf in 1845, Niecks evinced so decided a talent for music that while only a boy of thirteen he made his public *début* as a violinist at a concert of the Musikverein in Düsseldorf, where he played De Bériot's Second Concerto. His systematic instruction in the Elements of Music and violin playing began when he was six years of age, at first under the care of his father, who was himself a violinist and conductor; later, under the masters, W. Langhans, who afterwards attained eminence not only as violinist, conductor, and teacher, but as a writer on musical history and æsthetics; and Leopold Auer, who rose to fame as a violinist and as the teacher of famous violinists, among whom may be mentioned Mischa Elman and Jascha Heifetz. Niecks studied composition and pianoforte playing under Julius Tausch. The organ, too, he studied. After successful public appearances, strenuous years of teaching and varied orchestral experience, his health became seriously affected, and compelled him, when little more than twenty, to relinquish the career of a violin virtuoso. About this time the Edinburgh musician, Sir Alexander C. Mackenzie, then revisiting Germany, induced him in 1868 to settle in Scotland, where he became viola player in Mackenzie's string quartet, and organist and teacher in Dumfries. In 1877 he proceeded to Leipzig University where he engaged in the study of philosophy, and especially of psychology and æsthetics. Returning to this country, he became a naturalised British subject, and Scotland henceforth became his home.

In 1875 Professor Prout had engaged him to write a series of articles for a musical journal, and from this time up to the end of his life, Niecks was a constant contributor to this and other periodicals on subjects relating to the Art of Music. These articles constitute not the least important part of his life-work, and are of the most varied character. Some are critical or biographical studies; others are the fruit of analytical or historical research; others, again, deal with educational problems and psychology as applied to the teaching of Music. A series of articles on the life and music of Chopin led to the completion and publication in 1888 of his work, *Frederick Chopin as a Man and Musician.* A German translation appeared in the following year. This established its author's reputation in the world of music and letters and has long been recognised as a standard work, one indeed pre-eminent in several respects, and not least for its painstaking research and accuracy, as well as its literary style. He had already published a *Concise Dictionary of Musical Terms, to which is prefixed an Introduction to the Elements of Music,* and, in 1890, had lectured before the Royal Institution of Great Britain on the Early Development of Instrumental Forms.

In December 1891 Professor Niecks was inducted to the Chair of Music. He had been elected as successor to Sir Herbert Oakeley only after considerable opposition and much hostile criticism. In the following February he delivered his Inaugural Address in the Music Classroom. In this address, entitled *Musical Education and Culture,* Professor Niecks referred at the outset to some of the difficulties that had confronted his predecessors, and remarked that he found himself in the position of a traveller to a much-sought but never-reached land. He felt, however, confident of success. His confidence arose "chiefly from the changed conditions that now partly exist, and partly may be easily called into existence. The more favourable conditions already existing are the more developed and diffused taste for music, and the fuller perception of the requirements of musical training and of the importance of musical culture; the more favourable conditions yet to be attained are regulations that will make the musical teaching in the University available to a wider circle of students."

After a tribute to the work and services of Sir Herbert Oakeley, he proceeded to examine the essential elements of a true musical education. To most people music differed from perfume only in its affecting the ear instead of the nose. To some it was an emotional excitement. To few did it present itself as an art, a something that appealed to the ear, mind and heart alike. Only when music was studied, comprehended and enjoyed intellectually and emotionally, as well as sensuously, did it become a means of culture, a purifier of character, a refiner of manners, and an enlarger of our whole being.

Again, music had an æsthetical as well as a technical side. Each of these sides was twofold—physical and psychical. "These various constituents—the æsthetical and technical, with their physical and psychical subdivisions—should receive attention throughout the course of a musical education." One of the causes of an imperfect musical education was "the general belief that the object of learning music is to be able to perform in company. Just as there are still fathers and mothers who think the drawing lessons are a failure unless their child brings home pictures to be framed." Instruction in music was nearly always instrumental, aiming for the most part at finger drill, a method that produced, not musicians, but machines. The æsthetical side of music ought not to be neglected, nor those departments that are generally classed as theory, although indeed they are to a much larger extent practical than theoretical. What would one say of the study of English "if it were confined to spelling, pronunciation, and a little reading, and did not also include grammar, composition, rhetoric and the history of the language and its literature?"

What was wanted was not so much an increase in the number of frequently indifferent executants, but the raising of the standard of musical culture. It was a common thing to hear of the success of this or that music-school, a success, however, which often meant nothing more than a commercial success—namely, a great number of pupils. One might have a school numbering thousands where yet the artistic result might be *nil.*

The nature of a University Music Chair was quite distinct from a music-school. Nevertheless, an extra-academical music-school might be founded, unencumbered by the machinery of a university administration, but connected with the Chair of Music in such a way as to enable the pupils to come to the university for the study of certain subjects and finally, if so disposed, for a degree. In this way the usefulness of the Chair would be increased, and the teaching in the music-school perfected, the supplemental instruction of the Music Chair being exactly that in which music-schools were deficient.

Professor Niecks, on his appointment, set himself to establish in the most thorough manner the Faculty of Music. Already during Professor Oakeley's regime, the Faculty of Arts had submitted a scheme of Graduation in Music, which was approved and transmitted to the University Court. The Court, however, having in the meantime obtained the opinion of the Chancellor of the University that under the present Statutory powers it was doubtful if the University had the power of conferring degrees in Music, and having in view the prospect of early legislation as to the Universities of Scotland, resolved to delay for the present further procedure in the matter. In 1891, a Draft Ordinance (Regulations for Degrees in Music) was remitted to the consideration of the Music Committee, and through the University Commissioners was submitted for the approval of Professor Niecks. The Professor, however, found himself obliged respectfully to recommend its rejection, as being too ancient in its provisions, for although it followed the lines of honoured tradition, it did not take into account the changed and changing conditions of the present, nor the contingencies of the future. He himself stated that "in explaining to the Commissioners my objections to the earlier document, and in advocating the ideas which I wished them to substitute for it, I met sympathetic and understanding listeners." A new scheme was thereupon drawn up. This scheme, eventually approved, has been eulogised by Professor Tovey, the present Dean of the Faculty of Music, as having had "no parallel in Europe at the time of its foundation," and as still remaining (1920) "in advance of current ideas as to the ways in which a University can teach music."

The new features in the scheme were especially these:—

(1) Tests in ear capacity and training.

(2) Performing, including singing and playing at sight, and playing from score.

(3) Harmony, Counterpoint, Fugue, and Instrumentation, Form, etc., theoretical and practical, and with a view to artistic production.

(4) Musical Analysis—*i.e.* the intelligent study of musical works of art with regard to structure and content, technique and æsthetics. For musical analysis the study of literary and especially poetical analysis is of the greatest importance.

(5) History of music, especially regarding what most matters—development and style.

(6) Acoustics in so far as bearing on the art of music.

(7) Last, and most important—the teaching professor, without attendance on whose previous prelections the candidate may not present himself at the Degree Examinations.

The new Ordinance was finally approved, and from this point the Faculty of Music, as a definitely constituted body, began to exist. Hitherto the Reid Chair had been under the *ægis* of the Faculty of Arts. In August 1893 the Ordinance was laid by the University Commissioners before Parliament; and in January 1894 it was intimated that it had been approved by Her Majesty in Council. The Faculty of Music now constituted consisted of the Principal, the Reid Professor of Music, and such other professors, not exceeding three, as the Senatus might from time to time appoint to be members of the Faculty.*

* In organising the Faculty of Music, Professor Niecks from the outset broke down all Philistine opposition by inducing the Principal of the University to accept membership *ex officio*. At its inception, part of the strength of this arrangement lay in the very fact that Principal Sir William Muir never regarded his own pretensions to an interest in music as anything more than a joke. On the other hand, his acceptance of the position showed that Niecks had, for the first time in the history of the Chair of Music, convinced an experienced administrator that music was a subject of solid knowledge and that its Edinburgh Professor was a member of the Senatus whose judgment deserved respect. In the meetings of the Senatus too, Professor Niecks violated the traditions of his Chair by not crumpling up at the first sign of opposition, and his courage was signally rewarded by the Professor of Rhetoric and English Literature, David Masson, who finally ended the anti-musical tradition by severely denouncing those who would "discourage a man who wants to do good work."

"The *ex officio* membership of the Faculty of Music has been endured by four Principals, each of whom has, in various ways, earned the gratitude of the Chair of Music. The fourth holder, Sir Thomas Holland, has gracefully abdicated this anomalous musical position, but not before he had continued the tradition of his predecessors in giving the Faculty substantial help in its business.

"The constitution of the Faculty of Music, as arranged by Niecks, permits of the inclusion of five members of the Senatus. The Professor of Music is usually, for convenience, Dean of the Faculty. Under Niecks, the Faculty consisted of himself, the Principal *ex officio*, and Professor (now Sir James) Walker. Latterly the Faculty has been increased to its full legal complement of five, selected from members of the Senatus without any formal restrictions."—(D. F. T.).

Under the Ordinance—Regulations for Degrees in Music—two Degrees in Music might be conferred by the University, viz., Bachelor of Music (Mus.B.) and Doctor of Music (Mus.D.). Every candidate for the Degree of Bachelor of Music must pass a Preliminary Examination, and must attend at the University of Edinburgh a course or courses of instruction extending in all to not less than eighty lectures, including a course in the History of Music, which was made obligatory for all candidates. The candidate may thereafter proceed to the First Professional Examination, and thence, not less than one year after passing the First, to the Second Professional Examination. The extent and standard of examination shall be fixed by the Senatus. Bachelors of Music of Edinburgh University, of not less than three years' standing, and not less than twenty-five years of age, may present themselves for the Degree of Mus.D. as (1) Composers, (2) Executants, or (3) Theorists or Historians.

In thus insisting on a residential qualification, Professor Niecks was several years ahead of his time, and set an example which has since been followed by other universities. At that time Oxford and Cambridge exacted no residence at all from music students, but were mere examining bodies in relation to musical degrees. Further, even at the present day, after the lapse of nearly forty years, and notwithstanding the developments that have taken place during that time, the Edinburgh Doctorate in Music still retains its unique character, being entirely unlike any other musical degree. The requirements for the Degree in its several departments are as follows :—

I. (1) Candidates for the Degree of Doctor of Music as composers shall submit a prescribed number of Vocal and Instrumental Compositions in the larger forms (such as Oratorio, Opera, Cantata, Symphony, Sonata, Overture). Each work shall be the original and unaided composition of the candidate and shall be accompanied by a declaration to that effect signed by the candidate.

(2) Candidates shall also be examined in the following subjects :—

(*a*) The more advanced Contrapuntal Forms—Fugal Writing in more than four parts, etc.

(*b*) Instrumentation.
(*c*) The works of the great composers from Palestrina onwards.

II. (1) Candidates for the Degree of Doctor of Music as Executants shall be required to show their special skill in the execution of solo and *ensemble* works in different styles. The works shall be selected partly by the candidates and partly by the Examiners.

(2) The candidates shall be examined in sight-reading, and shall give evidence of their power of playing Orchestral Scores, and shall be required to invent Transitions and to modulate from one key and piece to another. They shall further be required to pass an Examination on the History and Music of their special instrument, and on the method of teaching that instrument.

III. (1) Candidates for the Degree of Doctor of Music as Theorists or Historians shall present one or more treatises on theoretical subjects which shall be the result of research and original thought, not mere abstracts or compilations of existing works. They shall be accompanied by a declaration signed by the candidate that they are his own unaided work.

(2) Candidates shall also be required to pass an Examination (*a*) in the Theory, and (*b*) in the History of Music. The Examination shall be on a higher standard in the subject which the candidate selects as his specialty.

IV. The Degree of Doctor of Music (Mus.D.) may be conferred *honoris causâ tantum.*

A Curriculum, providing for regular instruction, and leading up to the Degree in Music, was now instituted; a scheme drawn up by Professor Niecks having been approved by the Senatus and University Court. The Syllabus comprised courses of lectures on the History of Music; Formal and Æsthetical Analysis; and Harmony, Melody and Rhythm. Later, other courses, comprising both practical and theoretical instruction, were added, including classes in Counterpoint and Composition, and Musical Form; also, a class in Aural Training and several Tutorial classes. The new Curriculum met with success from the outset and, modified and added to from time to time, was continued throughout the whole of Professor Niecks's regime. Until 1902, the work was carried on entirely by him.

Already, and before the institution of the new Curriculum, the Professor had taken a decidedly advanced step in obtaining the admission, through the University Court, of women students to the Music classes. He had also made a plea that non-graduating music students should be admitted to the classes on payment of an entrance fee of 5s. This plea was opposed by the Senatus, but finally carried the day, strongly supported as it was by Professor Masson, who said: "I am delighted to see that next winter we shall have a regular course of musical lectures—this is the first time, and the University will be the richer for it. We therefore ought to do all we can to make the difficult position of Professor Niecks as easy as possible for him."

One of the most difficult of the problems confronting the new Professor was the determination of the future of the Reid Concert or Concerts. During the last years of Sir Herbert Oakeley's tenure of the Chair the old trouble as to the distribution of tickets had again emerged. For this and other reasons the attendance at the Reid Concerts had seriously declined. Sir Charles Hallé had definitely refused to return with his orchestra to Edinburgh. He had stated publicly that "his players were not accustomed to perform to empty benches." Other and new conditions, also, had arisen, which had an adverse influence on the Reid Concerts. An efficient local orchestra consisting of professional musicians had been organised, and a series of Subscription Orchestral Concerts, given weekly throughout each winter, was meeting with much public favour. It seemed impossible that the Reid Concerts could continue in the form they had assumed for so many years under Professor Oakeley.

The Gordian knot was simply and effectively dealt with by Professor Niecks. He proposed that the Reid Festival in the form in which it had been held should be discontinued, and that in *lieu* thereof a series of Historical Concerts should be given in the Music Classroom during each winter. A scheme was drawn up and approved, providing for a series of four Historical Concerts during each winter session, one of the concerts to be held in February of each year in honour of General Reid, and at which part of the Reid music should be performed. To these concerts all music students had the privilege of free admission, the general public being admitted by payment. Tickets were also issued to the University staff and to professional musicians in the city. The concerts covered a wide range and were of the most varied character. Some exemplified the development of early instrumental forms, some the development of the opera from Monteverde to Wagner, or of the overture and the symphony. Others consisted of String Quartets (two seasons under the Professor's leadership), Quintets, Octets for wind instruments, and other usual and unusual forms of chamber music; also concerts of early Italian or English instrumental music, performed on instruments of the period, old viols and such historically important, although seldom heard, instruments as the lute, viola d'amore, viola de gamba, harpsichord, etc. The Scottish Orchestra was engaged on several occasions, as well as noted musicians, among whom may be mentioned Arnold Dolmetsch and party, the Verbrugghen quartet, Wanda Landowska, Fanny Davies, Frederick Lamond, Sir Walter Parratt, and many others.

These recitals of music of various historical periods, almost indispensable to students of musical history, met at first, strange to say, with severe criticism in certain quarters. They were denounced as being little more than ancient and fossilised art-products of no interest except to the musical antiquarian. The concerts, however, attracted and continued to attract throughout their existence large audiences, and soon acquired a reputation which extended considerably beyond the city of Edinburgh, indeed a more than European reputation. The programmes of these concerts, dating from 1892 to 1914, containing many technical and analytical as well as æsthetical and historical annotations, constitute an important and valuable work of reference.

The University Musical Society was continued under the Presidency of the Professor, with James A. Moonie as chorus-master and conductor. Under his able *bâton* the Society continued to flourish with greatly increased numbers. A concert was given annually in the McEwan Hall and almost invariably attracted a large audience.

In 1895 the Honorary Degree of Mus.D. was conferred on Professor E. Prout and Sir A. C. Mackenzie; and in 1898 the Degree of Mus.B., by examination, the latter for the first time in the history of a Scottish University. By the will of Théophile Bucher, who died in 1871, his trustees were enjoined (on the death of a liferentrix) to pay over the residue of his estate to the University of Edinburgh for the purpose of providing one or more Scholarships in Music. Bucher also gifted to the University an important collection of music and books on music. The Scholarship was first awarded in 1896. There are at present two Bucher Scholarships, each of the annual value of £120, tenable for three years, with a possible extension of two more years.

Among the services rendered by Professor Niecks to musical education was his foundation, in 1901, of a *Musical Education Society*, which met in the Music class-room and attained a membership of between seventy and eighty. In 1909 he initiated a series of Concerts for Young People, and in 1910 a scheme was launched. Of much educative value, largely owing to the guidance and explanatory remarks of the Professor, the concerts were greatly appreciated. In many other ways he identified himself with the musical interests, activities and organisations, such as choral and orchestral societies, of the city of Edinburgh. Towards the end of 1913 he began to feel that his health was unequal to the wear and tear of public life that the Reid Chair brings with it. He also felt that the time had come for changes. Already he had made three attempts to form a Music School in Edinburgh. The first two attempts failed for lack of adequate support; the third, which was supported by the town, might have succeeded, had not the war intervened. After twenty-three years of professorial activity he sent in his resignation in the spring of 1914.

In 1915 he received from the University the Degree of

LL.D. In presenting him for the Degree, the Dean of the Faculty of Law said: "Professor Niecks came here with an established reputation as a man of rare accomplishment in the theory and practice of music. His tenure of the Reid Chair has been marked by a strenuous mobilisation of all its resources for a definite educational purpose; the Music room, with its valuable appliances, became a living centre of efficient instruction." In 1898 Dublin University had already honoured him with the Degree of Mus.D. In appreciative references from many quarters he was recognised as a great musical scholar and a man of wide erudition, well read in the literature of various languages; one who "by his character and his personality, as well as by his writings, had exercised a profound influence on the development of musical taste and culture in this country."

In 1907 he published *Programme Music in the Last Four Centuries: a Contribution to the History of Musical Expression.* Much of this work first appeared in the form of lectures delivered in the Music classroom. His last years were occupied in writing a Life of Schumann, in which he was greatly assisted by his wife, a daughter of the late Professor Sir John Struthers. The "Life" first appeared as serial notes intended for eventful book-form. He did not live to complete the originally planned full-scale work, but the series was posthumously published in book-form—*Robert Schumann, a Supplementary and Corrective Biography.*

A memorial plaque, the work of his friend and colleague, Professor Schlapp, has been placed in the Music class-room, and a sum of money presented by the contributors to the Frederick Niecks Memorial Fund has endowed an annual Prize in Musical History.

DONALD FRANCIS TOVEY, *b.* 1875

Reid Professor of Music, 1914.

In 1914 Donald Francis Tovey was elected as successor to Professor Niecks.

Taking up his professorial duties in 1914, the year of the outbreak of war, Professor Tovey did not at first find the conditions, mainly owing to the nation's call on its young manhood, too favourable for the immediate carrying into effect of the schemes he had formed for the development of the Faculty of Music. From the outset, however, he energetically exerted himself to explore every possibility whereby the Music Course might be made increasingly attractive to students, and the efficiency and thoroughness of the University training not only maintained but rendered as complete as possible; he insisted on the importance and value of the "residential" classes, and the desirability and even necessity of extending the time devoted to actual training at the University.

In 1915 he inaugurated a new class in Musical Interpretation, and soon thereafter other classes in Orchestral Practice and Orchestration, History and Analysis, Thoroughbass, Score-reading and Advanced Counterpoint and Composition. Since 1918 the number of music students has continued steadily to increase, and there has been a corresponding increase in the number of those graduating in Music.

In 1916 Professor Tovey organised the Reid Orchestra, the personnel of which was drawn from professional players in Edinburgh and students of music sufficiently advanced in the technique of orchestral instruments. The rehearsals are held in the Music class-room, and students of Orchestration have a valuable opportunity of gaining a practical knowledge of the orchestra. From 1917 onwards a series of orchestral concerts has been given annually by the Reid Symphony Orchestra. The educational value of these concerts is considerably enhanced by the copious and important æsthetical and analytical annotations contributed by the Professor and incorporated in the concert programmes. These programme notes have now accumulated to several volumes, and it is the intention of the Professor to utilise their material as the basis of text-books for the use of students.

In addition to the new classes already referred to, one in Acoustics and several of a tutorial character have been formed. The additional work entailed has necessitated an increase in the teaching staff. In 1929 a new Draft Ordinance (regulations for Degrees in Music) proposed that several alterations should be made in the regulations for Degrees in Music. Already a change had been made in the regulations for the Second Degree Examination for Mus.B., the "literary" part—Rhetoric and English Literature, and one of the languages not already taken in the Preliminary Examination—being excluded from the subjects of examination. The new Ordinance was approved by the University Court, and later by His Majesty in Council, and is now in force. The new regulations ordained that the Degree of Bachelor of Music may be conferred with Honours. The subjects are the same as those for the Ordinary Degree, but the examination is separate and the papers are different. Honours students must attend the complete musical curriculum of the University of Edinburgh during the autumn and spring terms of not less than three academical years. Two classes of Honours are given, viz., First and Second Class. For the Ordinary Degree the University still retains the power to confer it after the minimum term of an autumn and spring residence in special cases, but it is now becoming more widely understood that the course for the Mus.B. will normally take three or four years.

In 1930, through the generosity of Isabella Wells Fraser, a Scholarship of the annual value of £120 was founded, in memory of her son, for the purpose of enabling a young student of Scottish parentage to prosecute his studies in Music abroad. A Medal will be given to the successful candidate, bearing on one side—"The Andrew A. Fraser Scholarship in Music," and on the other the name of the holder and year. There are now four Scholarships available for students in Music.

In addition to the Reid Orchestral Concerts, the Historical Concerts, instituted by Professor Niecks, have been, and are being continued under the direction of Professor Tovey. During the early development of the Reid Orchestra these concerts took the form of pianoforte recitals by the Professor, including a notable series of the pianoforte works of Beethoven.

IX

THE LIBRARY

In the course of the last half-century the importance of libraries in the economy of academic institutions has become more and more fully recognised. Universities have no doubt always been proud of their libraries, but in the older days, and perhaps particularly in Scotland, they tended to regard them more from the professional scholar's point of view than from that of the ordinary undergraduate. For this the lecture system, which flourished so hardily in the Scottish Universities, may have been partly responsible. But with the modern developments of scholarship and science, the inevitable growth of specialisation, and the increasing domination of the book, it became obvious that oral teaching had to be more and more largely supplemented by the printed word and, as a result, the libraries began to be more extensively used. The change of outlook may be noted in the emphasis repeatedly laid, in recent years, by the University Grants Committee upon the "profound importance of the library in the academic life of the University."

One of the first results of this wider conception of the functions of a University library has naturally been an endeavour to secure increased accommodation both for books and readers. Here many of the older universities found themselves in something of a dilemma, as their buildings had been planned without sufficient prevision of subsequent needs, and the problem of expansion has often been extremely difficult to solve. It has been so in Edinburgh University. The Library buildings, designed by Adam and Playfair, and finished rather more than a hundred years ago, have always been deservedly admired for the imposing dignity of their architecture; and they have also notable merits from the librarian's point of view; but they could not be extended at either end without encroaching upon other departments of the University, and extension on the west flank had been rendered impossible when the Town Council, in 1854, appropriated the free ground there for civic purposes. So far as its actual premises are concerned, therefore, the demand of the Library in recent times has always been for more space; and, in one way or another, the demand has been or is being successfully met.

The first large scheme proposed for dealing with the problem was to instal steel shelving in place of the heavy, old-fashioned wooden shelves in the lower portion of the Library. As far back as 1899 the Library Committee considered the advantages of the American system of shelving; and a few years later, in 1903, it definitely recommended that the ground-floor of the Library should be refitted according to plans submitted by the Art Metal Company. The recommendation was accepted and the work was carried through in the course of the next year or so. It may be noted that the energetic support given to the scheme by Principal Sir William Turner was largely responsible for its adoption and its rapid execution.

In 1923 a further installation of steel shelving was secured for the Library after the department of Agriculture, which was situated at the western end of the Library buildings, had been removed to its new quarters in George Square, and the space it had hitherto occupied was set free. The lower section of the book-store thus provided is known as the Turner Room, and in it most of the newer accessions are housed.

More recently still, when the Natural History department was about to be removed to The King's Buildings, it was realised that the premises to be vacated would provide a really adequate extension of the Library; and in 1928 the Library Committee made a strong recommendation to the University Court that all the available space should be utilised for that purpose. It was not, however, until a comprehensive scheme for dealing with the problem of accommodation in the Old College was under consideration, a couple of years later, that any definite plans for the extension of the Library could be submitted; indeed the scheme finally approved is only now in course of execution. It is being carried out in three stages; and it should keep at bay for a very long time to come that fear besetting all anxious-minded librarians that their book-accommodation may run short. The first stage, which was completed in the course of 1932 has, along with other structural changes, converted the old Natural History Museum into a much-needed enlargement of the Students' Reading-Room.

An important extension of the Library outside the Old College has quite recently been obtained by establishing a Central Medical Library at the New Buildings in Teviot Row. A reading-room for medical students was opened there as far back as the year 1885 and constant and increasing use of it has been made ever since. But for a considerable time the teaching staff of the Medical Faculty found themselves handicapped by the want, in their immediate proximity, of a central library where the most recent medical literature, and especially the periodicals, might be available for consultation. The creation of such a library was favourably considered by the Library Committee in 1921; but the lack of suitable accommodation in the New Buildings delayed its realisation. In 1929, however, when the extensive scheme for the reconstruction of the Medical departments was taken in hand, it became possible to secure library accommodation in the department of Forensic Medicine and, thanks to the generous financial support given by the trustees of Sir William Dunn and by the Rockefeller Foundation, the Central Medical Library became a substantial fact by the end of 1930.

Finally, a word must be said about the numerous departmental and class libraries which have been instituted in the course of the last fifty years. Such libraries are a distinctive feature in the economy of the modern university; for, though they are apt to make somewhat formidable depredations on the main library, they are obviously indispensable where, as at Edinburgh, a number of departments are situated at a great distance from the central building and from each other. There are between twenty and thirty departmental and class libraries in different parts of the University, some of them very extensive, and others quite modest. The Library Committee has always adopted a sympathetic attitude towards them, giving them all the support in its power and allowing them to develop, so far as possible, on their own lines.

CATALOGUES OF BOOKS AND MANUSCRIPTS

Another of the chief problems of the Library in the course of its recent history has been the provision of catalogues of its printed books and manuscripts. Nothing hampers the student more in his use of a library than the lack or the inadequacy of these indispensable aids; and such of them as the University Library possessed had, for the most part, become patently insufficient before the close of last century. This was frankly recognised by the Library Committee with regard to the old manuscript catalogue of the printed books, which had grown congested and disordered beyond redemption; and it was clear that nothing less than a new and comprehensive catalogue was required. In 1895 the Committee had considered the possibility of printing such a catalogue. In the course of the next two or three years it drew up a provisional scheme for its preparation, appointing a Catalogue Sub-Committee, of which James Burgess, formerly Director General of the Archæological Surveys in India, was the head; and the actual work of cataloguing was begun. It was not, however, till 1899 that a substantial fund for the purpose became available from the residue of the bequest made to the University by Sir William Fraser, the well-known Scottish genealogist, and the recataloguing of the Library was then energetically taken in hand by a temporary staff under the supervision of Burgess. After six or seven years the Fraser Fund had been more or less exhausted; and the plan of printing the whole catalogue had to be postponed, though not before it had been found possible to issue, in 1906, a hand-catalogue, containing a selection of the more modern books in the Library likely to be of use to students. At length, in 1912, the University

Court was in a position to set aside a sum for the completion of the catalogue. The work of revising it and bringing it up to date occupied the next three years, and in the autumn of 1915 a beginning was made with the printing. It went on steadily till the first volume was completed, when war conditions brought about a temporary suspension. Fortunately, this did not last very long, for printing was resumed in 1919. The second volume was issued in 1921, the third and final volume in 1923.

Some hesitation had been felt about publishing so large a catalogue in book-form, but undoubtedly the Library Committee has been justified in its decision to do so. The printed catalogue has not only lightened the work of the Library staff and proved of incalculable service to readers but it has made known to scholars and research students, in all parts of the world, the existence of items of importance which they would otherwise almost certainly have overlooked.

Apart from its printed books the Library possesses various collections of manuscripts, and it was obviously desirable that these also should be catalogued as far as possible. David Laing's magnificent bequest to the University of his manuscripts and charters had brought a mass of documents to the Library in 1878, many of them of great historical value. These awaited the experts who could and would prepare catalogues or calendars of them—for love rather than for money, since such work has generally to be its own reward. The first to volunteer for this task was the Rev. John Anderson, afterwards Curator of the Historical Department in H.M. General Register House, who, in the year 1881, offered to catalogue the charters in the Laing Collection for a nominal sum. The Library Committee gladly accepted his offer; and he carried on his laborious work for many years before bringing it to a close. In 1896 the University Court, on the recommendation of the Library Committee, agreed to have Anderson's catalogue printed. It was published in 1899 in a substantial volume, and was at once recognised as an extremely valuable contribution to Scottish history and genealogy.

The charters formed only a portion, but by no means the

largest portion of the Laing collection. There was also a number of early manuscripts and a multitude of miscellaneous documents, mainly historical. Fortunately, an opportunity of having the more important items in this part of the Collection calendared and abstracted presented itself in 1902 when the Rev. Henry Paton, on behalf of H.M. Commissioners on Historical MSS., informed the Library Committee that he had examined the Laing material and had been asked by the Lords of the Commission to request the permission of the University authorities to have a report of it prepared and printed. Permission was given with alacrity. The first volume of Henry Paton's Report, issued as one of the publications of the Historical Manuscripts Commission, appeared in 1914; the second was kept waiting for a full decade—it was the period when strict governmental economy in such matters might claim to be a virtue—and was not published until 1925.

An adequate catalogue of the medieval Western manuscripts in the Laing Bequest and other collections of the Library had for long been a desideratum, and here again the University was fortunate in obtaining the services of a skilled and scholarly palæographer. In 1911 Catherine R. Borland was granted a Carnegie Research Fellowship in History to enable her to prepare such a catalogue; and to this task she devoted herself whole-heartedly for the next few years. Thanks to special grants made by the University Court and the Carnegie Trust, her work, *A Descriptive Catalogue of the Western Medieval Manuscripts in Edinburgh University Library*, was published in 1916, in a form worthy of its matter and of the care that had been bestowed upon it.

Cataloguing enterprises seem to be peculiarly subject to delays and interruptions; and the next undertaking of the kind that has to be recorded here confirms that generalisation very forcibly. The Library possesses a notable collection of Oriental manuscripts, the most important section of which belonged originally to Lieut.-Col. John Baillie of Leys, by whose grandson, John B. Baillie, it was presented to the University in 1876, with a stipulation that a descriptive catalogue of its contents should be prepared in due course.

The initial difficulty here was to find a competent person to undertake the work; and the Library Committee pursued a Fabian policy in the matter until 1904, when the visit to Edinburgh of a young Persian, J. K. M. Shirazi, induced it to take action. It commissioned him to make a beginning with the cataloguing; and shortly afterwards it secured the services of an Indian student, Mohammed A. Hukk, who was then at the University, and suitably qualified, to continue the work. The major part of the Arabic and Persian manuscripts had been dealt with by the end of 1905; and in the course of the following year the catalogue, as prepared by Hukk, was actually set up in type, though its publication had to be deferred. Subsequently, a considerable number of Oriental manuscripts, found to have been overlooked, were sent by instalments to Professor Hermann Ethé of Aberystwyth to be catalogued. By the summer of 1914 the catalogue seemed ripe for publication. But with the outbreak of the war, fate once again intervened, and seven years passed before a final revision of the work was entrusted, in 1921, to Edward Robertson, at that time Lecturer in Arabic in the University. Even then further delays were caused by Robertson's departure from Edinburgh, and it was not till 1925 that the *Descriptive Catalogue of the Arabic and Persian Manuscripts in Edinburgh University Library* at last made its appearance.

It will be seen from this brief summary that in the matter of printed catalogues, at any rate, the Library can boast of a very creditable record for the past half-century.

LIBRARIANS

This brief sketch of the later history of the Library would be incomplete without a short notice of the librarians who have held office. The first of these was John Small, though his long reign as Librarian extended only into the first few years of the half-century. In his case, as in that of his most notable predecessor, Robert Henderson, the office descended from father to son and, in both instances, the virtues of the hereditary principle were certainly well exemplified. John Small, who was born in 1828 and graduated M.A. at the University in 1847, was appointed in the latter year to the post of Acting Librarian, recently made vacant by the death of his father. In 1854 he was raised to the position of Chief Librarian, remaining in office until his death in 1886. He was not only a distinguished librarian—he acted as President of the Librarians' Association in 1880, when its annual conference was held in Edinburgh—but a good scholar, who did much valuable work in editing a number of the early Scottish poets. The shelf catalogues of certain portions of the Library, written in his not too legible hand, are still in use and testify to his industry and accuracy.

An interval of some months elapsed after Small's death, during which the Library was temporarily supervised by Professor Julius Eggeling. In 1887 a new Librarian, Hugh Alexander Webster, entered upon office. Webster, who had been an Edinburgh student, was a man of exceptional gifts, a good linguist, with a very wide range of general information, which qualified him to act, and apparently with credit, as one of the sub-editors of the admirable ninth edition of the *Encyclopædia Britannica.* His warm-hearted and generous nature gained him many friends, in whose service he was always prepared to sacrifice his own interests. It was perhaps unfortunate that he should have adopted a profession which calls for a somewhat stricter method and a somewhat readier acceptance of routine than he could easily bestow. At any rate he found, as time went on, that his library duties by day, his journalist work by night, and the many outside calls made upon time and energy were more than he could undertake. In July 1900 he resigned his post owing to ill-health and went to London. After he had more or less recovered, he returned to Edinburgh, where he died in 1926.

After Webster's resignation the Library Committee decided that it would be a mistake to fill the vacant post until the preliminary cataloguing of the printed books, then under the supervision of James Burgess, should be completed. It agreed, however, that someone must be appointed provisionally to act as the responsible head of the Library and chose one of its own members, Professor Julius Eggeling, who had always taken a keen interest in the Library and had supervised it during the interregnum between Small's death and Webster's appointment. Subsequently, Eggeling's association with the administration of the Library was placed on a more permanent footing and he became Curator until 1913, when he retired from an office which was henceforth discontinued. Eggeling had been appointed to the Chair of Sanskrit in 1875. His interests were and always remained primarily those of the scholar; but he did good service to the Library and was excellently qualified to act as Curator, no less by his extensive knowledge of literature than by his personal qualities. He represented the finest type of the German scholar of an older day, combining a wide culture with a charming simplicity of character and a charity which endeared him to all who had dealings with him.

Although the post of Librarian had thus been left vacant since 1900, the Committee after some years recognised the desirability of filling it again; and in 1905 it elected a member of the Library staff, Alexander Anderson, usually distinguished from others of that name by his epithet "Surfaceman." Anderson, who was born in 1845 in the village of Kirkconnel, had worked as a surfaceman or plate-layer in his earlier days, had discovered a vein of poetry in himself, and had made a name as a writer of Scottish songs. In the year 1880 he had been appointed Assistant Librarian in the University Library. He gave up this post in 1883 to act as Secretary to the Edinburgh Philosophical Institution; but in 1886 he returned to the Library. In 1901 he was made Head Assistant, and in 1905 Librarian, which office he held for the brief residue of his days. It may be doubted whether Anderson, who had been accustomed to an active, open-air life, ever found an academic environment congenial: certainly his linnet-songs became much less frequent after he was immured in the Library. He died in 1909 after a long and painful illness. The present holder of the office is Frank C. Nicholson, appointed in 1910.

LIBRARY

BEQUESTS

While the Library (thanks very largely to the generous support of the Carnegie Trust) has had during the past few decades a much more liberal allowance for the purchase of books than it enjoyed in earlier days, it continues to be, as it has been from the beginning, heavily indebted to private benefactors. Without the bequests and gifts made by Clement Litil, William Drummond of Hawthornden, J. O. Halliwell-Phillipps, David Laing and others, its estate would be woefully reduced; and in the course of the last fifty years it has continued to receive many valuable donations. A mention, however cursory, of the chief benefactions is certainly called for in such a sketch as this.

A collection, important on account of the Celtic books which it contains, was received in 1899, when William Mackinnon of Ballinakill, Ireland, purchased the library of the Celtic scholar Alexander Cameron of Brodick and presented it to the University. Up to that time Celtic Literature and Philology had been very scantily represented in the Library, and the Cameron Collection, as it is called, did much to supply the deficiency.

A valuable bequest from a former Professor in the University, Æneas J. G. Mackay, who held the Chair of History from 1874 to 1881, came in 1911. It consisted of the greater portion of his library, some four thousand volumes, mainly of historical and literary interest. Part of this collection was handed over to the Kirkpatrick History Library, which had been founded in 1891 by Professor John Kirkpatrick; part of it was reserved to form the nucleus of the English Departmental Library which was established in 1920; and the remainder has been retained in the general Library.

A small but valuable collection of books on the Philippine Islands and their history was left by Daniel Mackintosh Forbes, who died in December 1916, and whose generous bequest of his fortune to the University is recorded elsewhere.

The next considerable gift was the scientific library of William Spiers Bruce, the well-known Polar explorer, who died in 1921. It consisted of about a thousand volumes, together with a very extensive collection of pamphlets, mostly on oceanographical subjects.

A further important addition to the Celtic section of the Library was made in 1924, when the greater portion of the library of Donald Mackinnon, who held the Chair of Celtic in the University from 1882 to 1914, was bequeathed by Roger McNeil, Medical Officer of Health for the County of Argyll, and a graduate of Edinburgh. This collection contains, in addition to about 1700 printed books, two or three valuable, early Irish manuscripts.

In 1925 the Library was enriched by a notable collection of some 2500 volumes, mostly on archæological, ethnological and philological subjects, bequeathed by John, Lord Abercromby, to whom the University owes the foundation of its Chair of Prehistoric Archæology. The Abercromby Collection bears witness to its donor's archæological and linguistic erudition, for his hand has marked and annotated a large number of the volumes, the contents of which represent a surprising range of interests and a surprising variety of languages.

Finally, mention should be made of the books, mainly on English literature, bequeathed by Gordon Hislop, Lecturer in English at the University, whose death in 1929 at the early age of forty removed a fine scholar, a most engaging personality, and a keen and discriminating book-collector. The greater part of the Gordon Hislop Collection was left expressly to the English department and is housed in the Departmental Library.

There is something a little cold and business-like in this rapid enumeration of gifts and bequests. It would have been pleasant to describe them and their special features in greater detail.* But space does not allow, and the innumerable donations of smaller compass, though often of the highest value, must be left without any individual record here. It must suffice to make the most compendious of acknowledg-

* In 1910 David Cuthbertson, a member of the staff, published a short account of *The Edinburgh University Library*, with a number of interesting facsimiles and illustrations.

ments and say, like the King in *Hamlet*, "For all, our thanks!"

A record, however brief, of the treasures of the Library would be incomplete if no reference were made to the valuable gift bequeathed to it, in 1912, by Lord Lister. In a letter dated 25th July 1907, to his old friend, Principal Sir William Turner, Lister indicated his anxiety as to the safe custody, after his decease, of some of his most cherished possessions, and expressed the hope that the University of Edinburgh might place them under her care.

The Lister bequest was gratefully accepted by the Court and is now exhibited in the Upper Library. The Collection includes the caskets containing the Scrolls of the Freedom of three cities, Edinburgh, London and Glasgow, the gold medals and decorations, including the Order of Merit and the Prussian Order "Pour le Mérite," and the diplomas and certificates received from nearly one hundred universities and learned societies throughout the world. His portrait painted by John H. Lorimer, in 1895, adorns the wall of the principal staircase of the Old College.

[Lister Letter.

12, PARK CRESCENT,

PORTLAND PLACE.

27 July 1907

My dear Turner

Since I wrote to you on the 25th, I have decided that, if the University should approve of my proposal made in that letter, I would add the gold casket conveying the Freedom of the City of London to the things which I offered to bequeath to the University of Edinburgh.

My sympathies have never been with a merely examining body like the College of Surgeons, but with a teaching University, and above all with that of Edinburgh. It was thanks to its very liberal and wise policy regarding the extra-academical school that I was induced to teach Surgery when a very young man; and this led to my work on Inflammation which was the essential preliminary to that on the Antiseptic Principle. And I need hardly say how near my heart Edinburgh became during the professorship of Clinical Surgery.

Hence though at first it seemed natural that the casket referring to the London Freedom should remain in London, I should much prefer that it should go to Edinburgh.

This of course would be in case my proposal should be acceptable to the University authorities; and I can quite understand that the arrangement may not be thought a suitable one.

Believe me
very sincerely yours
Lister

X

THE UNIVERSITY PORTRAITS

WHILE the portraits belonging to the University of Edinburgh have come together more by chance than choice, and represent no settled policy in the commemoration of those who have made its history illustrious by their fame, or who have been specially helpful in its expansion, the series includes likenesses of many who have contributed notably to its development. Moreover, even with regrettable blanks, especially in the early years, they form an interesting commentary not only upon its own annals, but upon the progress of learning and culture in Scotland during the past three hundred and fifty years. At the same time, the pictures and busts offer material for a connected survey of portraiture in Scotland, and include admirable examples of some of the most gifted Scottish painters and sculptors. Placed in the Senate and Court rooms, the Library, staircases and elsewhere in the Old College, the collection has, however, been arranged on no related plan. Yet in a few cases the grouping possesses definite appropriateness. For example, the Raeburn portraits in the Senate room form a group connected with the University about the time the College buildings were being erected, and in the Music Classroom the portraits of Professors Donaldson, Oakeley and Niecks are associated with that of General Reid, the founder of the Chair of Music. In this article it is preferable to discuss the portraits as a sequence, more or less related.

From the old donation book, begun in 1667 by William Henderson, it would seem that the University possessed a number of portraits prior to 1695 when Robert Henderson—who had succeeded his father as librarian—made the list, headed "Icones Virorum Illustrium," at the end of the MS. catalogue of the library compiled by him. In July 1689 the wife of Provost Prince presented portraits of the six Jameses, Queen Mary and Queen Anne, Charles I and Charles II and "there royall consorts," and of "our learned countrymen Mr Ramsay" for "the ornament of the Library." From the catalogue *Auctarium Musaei Balfouriani e Musaeo Sibbaldiano* (printed Edinburgh, 1697) nine portraits, perhaps collected by Sir Andrew Balfour, who died in 1694, were presented by Sir Robert Sibbald, botanist and physician (1641-1722). In addition to likenesses of Charles I, Charles II and James II, portraits of James Drummond, Earl of Perth; William Drummond of Hawthornden, Sir George Mackenzie, George Buchanan, Mark Alexander Boyd and Robert Boyd of Trochrig came from that source. But, amongst the portraits still in the University, there is none which can be said with certainty to be one of those given either by the Provost's lady or by Sibbald. Indeed, except James VI and his Queen, in very feeble and unconvincing pictures, Catharine of Braganza perhaps, and George Buchanan, not one of these personages is now represented in the collection. Even of the fifty-nine portraits mentioned in Henderson's list few survive. Those of Buchanan, Principal Rollock and Napier of Merchiston, and some of the effigies of protagonists of the Reformation seem to exhaust the list. Amongst the last which include representations of Calvin, Zwingli, Melanchthon, Beza and Knox, the last a poor version of the more than doubtful Torphichen likeness, there is nothing with much claim to be an original or with any pretensions to artistic merit.

THE EARLY PORTRAITS

In these circumstances, the University series may be said to begin with two portraits of George Buchanan (1506-82), whose reputation, as a great scholar and the greatest Latinist of his time, was European when the University was founded.

These portraits, of which that painted on panel is probably a contemporary work and the other a somewhat later adaptation, have been so long in the possession of the University that no record seems to exist of how they came there.

Obviously related to the engraving by Jacques Granthomme in Boisard's "Icones Virorum Illustrium," published at Frankfort only sixteen years after Buchanan died, the former—after comparison with the skull said to be that of Buchanan (also in the possession of the University)—was accepted by Sir William Hamilton as genuine. Later, when investigating the portraits of Knox and Buchanan, James Drummond, R.S.A., came to the same conclusion. But a few years ago, Professor Karl Pearson, bringing all the resources of scientific examination to bear upon the problem, yet perhaps not allowing enough for the vagaries of archaic portraiture, rejected it in favour of the portrait attributed to Frans Pourbus (1548-81), in the rooms of the Royal Society, London. Still, it may be recalled that a portrait of George Buchanan was painted in Edinburgh in 1579, by one Adrianc Vaensoun, painter to the King, and was sent by Sir Peter Young to Beza at Geneva along with the likeness of Knox, which was engraved for the latter's *Icones*, published during the following year.

There is no doubt about the next portrait—that of John Napier of Merchiston (1550-1617), the inventor of logarithms. It was painted in the year preceding its sitter's decease and was presented by his great-granddaughter Margaret, Baroness Napier who, in 1686, succeeded to the title in her own right. Less entertaining in its accessories than the print by Francesco Delaram, dated 1620, in which "Napier's bones"—as the calculating machine with the little ivory rods which he invented was called—is introduced, it is much more convincing as a likeness and, in addition to the date "1616" and "Aetatis 66," bears his arms and several mottoes associated with him. On the other hand, the portrait of Robert Rollock (1555-99), first Principal of the University, cannot be accepted as a quite contemporary record. But it is confirmed as a likeness by the existence of other versions of about the same date (early seventeenth century), including one in the Scottish National Portrait Gallery. George Heriot (1563-1624) also appears in a copy, a considerably later version of that made by John Scougall in 1698 from the now lost original by Paul Van Somer. This is all that is left, except an indifferent picture of him at the age of twenty-six, to recall the founder of one of Edinburgh's oldest and most important educational institutions and the "Jingling Geordie" of Sir Walter's *Fortunes of Nigel.*

A portrait of William Drummond of Hawthornden (1585-1649) was included in the Sibbald gift; but, like the other portraits there, it has disappeared. Some years ago, however, the Library acquired an elaborate and delicately painted cabinet picture of the poet. On an old oak panel and dated 1633, it bears a very close resemblance to the fine head attributed to Jansen and engraved by Finlayson. Yet somehow, although charming and interesting, the craftsmanship is not quite convincingly contemporary. Some dubiety also exists about the admirable half-length said to represent the "Sainted Leighton," perhaps the most lovable figure in the troubled history of the Kirk in Scotland. Robert Leighton (1611-84), who was a Presbyterian and Principal of the University from 1652 to 1661, when he became Bishop of Dunblane upon the establishment of Episcopacy in Scotland following the Restoration, is known best from the little print by Robert White (1645-1703), executed either during the sitter's life-time or soon thereafter. Comparison with that scarcely confirms this picture. Of the portrait of Andrew Cant, Principal from 1675 to 1685, little need be said. It was presented in 1710 by his daughter, Mrs White, "in compliment to the Library," but it is considerably repainted.

Fortunately the portrait of William Carstares (1649-1715), perhaps the most famous Principal of them all, is completely authenticated. Painted by William Aikman (1682-1731), the most notable Scottish painter of the period, it is a good example of his somewhat formal but quietly accomplished and frequently well-characterised portraiture, and represents Carstares about the age of sixty. He is shown three-quarter length, seated, wearing Geneva gown and bands and with his hand placed on the top of a great folio standing upright upon a table at his side. Yet despite the clerical costume and the open volume, he appears to be, as he was, even more a statesman than a cleric or scholar. Looking at it one understands how he earned the name of the "Cardinal" from his Jacobite opponents, and exercised such an influence on the policy of Dutch William in Scotland and on the negotiations for the Union in 1707. It was Queen Anne, however, who appointed him Principal in 1703.

A friend of poets, James Thomson and Allan Ramsay, Gay, Somerville and Mallet, and a protégé of statesmen like Walpole and Argyll, Aikman, who had sold his ancestral acres in Forfarshire to become an artist, is one of the interesting if minor figures of the Augustan age. He painted the well-known portrait of Thomson, which Pitt thought "beastly like," but the likeness which belongs to the University is a copy made by the third Medina in 1774 from that by Patoun, of which the most vital version is in the Scottish National Portrait Gallery. Shown in a case in the upper Library, beside a first edition of *The Seasons* there is, however, a very interesting drawing of Thomson by Aikman, vouched for by Anne Forbes, the artist's granddaughter and a good portrait painter herself.

As Aikman returned in 1712 from the East, to which he was one of the earliest artist visitors in more modern times (he went at the conclusion of his studies in Italy), Carstares's portrait must have been painted between that time and the Principal's death three years later. It was engraved very indifferently by R. Cooper (1705-64) before the middle of the century, the prints being sold by "Gavin Hamilton, bookseller, opposite to the Parliament Close, Edinburgh."

There is unfortunately nothing painted by the next important Scottish portrait painter, Allan Ramsay, junior, the poet's son, a charming artist, who combined excellent characterisation with refinement and elegance in a very exceptional way. This is the more surprising as Allan was a man of culture and learning and on intimate terms with the literary circle of his day, including Robertson, Hume and Adam Smith among his friends. But his favourite pupil, David Martin (1737-98), who was in turn, if only in slight degree, Raeburn's master, heired some of his characteristics and is represented by two mature works. The head and shoulders of the Rev. Hugh Blair (1718-1800), Professor of Rhetoric and celebrated as a preacher—one of his volumes of sermons went into nineteen editions in his life-time—is a good, though not exceptional specimen of Martin's indeterminate, if sometimes graceful, art. The portrait of Joseph Black (1728-99), one of the founders of modern Chemistry and Professor of that science in Edinburgh, is also by him.

THE RAEBURNS

Painting in Scotland throughout the greater part of the eighteenth century had been confined to portraiture. There was no demand for anything else and, with the exception of Runciman's interesting essays in decoration and imaginative design and conventionally decorative landscapes, executed in the Norries's workshop for overmantels, little else was attempted. The last twelve or fifteen years of the eighteenth century and the first decade of the nineteenth saw the beginning of greater activity in the Arts in Scotland. This followed the splendid expression of nationalism in the vernacular poetry of Burns, and was coincident with the awakening of a sense of the past and the passion for the romantically picturesque which accompanied the advent of Sir Walter Scott's poems and novels. Yet it probably owed even more to the expansion of industry and commerce, improving social conditions, and to the coming of a more liberal conception of culture. Portraiture was now more extensively practised and a beginning was made in genre and landscape. This gradually developed until these three branches assumed a form so definitely influenced by racial tendencies, in respect of the way in which subject-matter was regarded, and by technical preferences in handling, tone and colour, that painting in Scotland may be said to have attained a distinctive character of its own.

In portraiture this advance was marked very conspicuously by the work of Sir Henry Raeburn (1756-1823). As it happens, too, the University owns a series of examples which reveals the essential character of his gift and, at the same time, illustrates the development of his distinctive style and technical qualities in a rather remarkable way. The earliest of these five portraits represents the Rev. William Robertson (1721-93), celebrated as an historian, influential as a leader of the "Moderates" and one of the most notable of the Principals. According to the legend "H. Raeburn Pinxit Edingh. A.D. 1792" in the left-hand corner of the canvas, this portrait was painted a few years after Raeburn's return from his sojourn in Italy, and if, as seems likely, that inscription was put there by the painter, it is probably the only canvas ever signed by him. Technically, too, this picture is very interesting. It shows the painter emerging from the rather thin and starved paint surfaces and greenish grey tones which had characterised his earlier work. The general colour remains grey, but more definite colour appears in passages and, while the design is cramped and crowded, pictorial effect is beginning to assert itself more.

Painted five years later, the seated three-quarter length of Lord Provost Thomas Elder (1737-99), though still somewhat thin and surfacy in handling, exhibits a noticeable improvement in freedom of touch and breadth of pictorial ensemble. If the effect is still level in tonality, the tones are richer and fuller in themselves and the actual design is freer in a linear sense and more richly decorative. The feeling for appropriateness in accessories, which was part of Raeburn's sense of character and is apparent in the introduction of the University Mace—presented by the City in 1789—and the volumes in the Robertson, is here expressed by putting the sitter into his Lord Provost's robes, and by placing on the table at his side the plans for the new University buildings, in the erection of which he took a very prominent part. These two portraits were commissioned by the Professors of the University.

Although separated by a few years only from that of the Lord Provost, the portraits of Professor Adam Ferguson (1724-1816) and Professor John Robison (1739-1805) mark, in their different ways, a very noticeable advance. Of its kind, the former is one of Raeburn's finest works. With an air of unconsciousness, as if the sitter were unaware that he was being painted, or even looked at, it is an admirable and unusually serene example of that self-contained quality which informs Raeburn's art at his best, and differentiates it, on the one hand, from the more dramatically conceived and richly inventive portraiture of Reynolds and, on the other, from the spontaneous and self-expressive grace in idea and execution alike, which gives that of Gainsborough a special fascination of its own. Raeburn was more content than either of his rather older English contemporaries to allow the sitter's looks and character to speak for themselves. It is this, combined with his remarkable gift for direct and powerful painting, which makes his rendering of men and women more personal and intimate—as of an individual rather than of a social type—than was habitual in his time. These qualities are clearly, if very quietly, evident in the Adam Ferguson, in which the head is particularly refined and sensitive in handling while retaining its due place in the total effect.

The Robison, however, is in some ways the culmination of the elements in Raeburn's middle style on which his ultimate development was based. Gradually, from a rendering of form to a great extent secured by a combination of simple tones and little shadow with admirable draughtsmanship, more linear but perhaps more truly constructive than later, he had evolved a method which conveyed, through simplification of the more salient planes—summarised by directness and squareness of touch—his impressions of reality in a manner at once suggestive and emphatic. Of this masterly directness and expressive emphasis the Robison is probably the supreme example. It justifies up to the hilt the claim made by R. A. M. Stevenson and Sir Walter Armstrong in the big Raeburn book, in which Sir James Caw was associated, that Raeburn's was the most conspicuous and successful use of direct painting between Velázquez and modern times. Yet, quite apart from the splendid bravura of its handling and the triumphant audacity of its colour scheme, this is a wonderful portrait, full of that vitality which issues from the capacity of expressing easily and surely a profound and searching conception of character.

Having attained a remarkable power of expression, through

simplification of form and a hand disciplined and quickly responsive to a trained and penetrating observation, Raeburn now built upon that a manner which, adding chiaroscuro to shape, enlarged his resources and enriched the pictorial effects at his command. It may be that structure suffered a little and that mastery issued in a certain tendency to formula; but the sense of mass seen in atmosphere was heightened in his later work, the modelling was fuller and rounder, and the pictorial effect richer, while his feeling for character remained undimmed and his skill in expressing it through appropriate accessories or by simple arrangements of light and shadow was perhaps more noticeable.

Of these changes in his style, the seated three-quarters of Professor John Playfair is typical. Playfair, who had been Professor of Mathematics previously, succeeded Robison in the Chair of Natural Philosophy in 1805, and Raeburn painted his portrait some eight or ten years later. Marked by all the characteristics of his fully developed manner, penetrating in characterisation, rich in tone and chiaroscuro, dignified in design and painted with masterly assurance, this picture completes the representation of Raeburn's art in the Senate Room in a way that makes the quintette there specially interesting. A Principal, who was also famous as an historian and a Church leader; a moral philosopher, who exercised a great influence on the thought of his time; two professors of Natural Philosophy, whose contributions to science remain of some importance; and one of the most conspicuous of the City fathers who have made the town's relationship to the College a real factor in its development—these five portraits by the most famous Scottish portrait painter mark very clearly and in a distinguished manner an important epoch in the history of the University.

RAEBURN'S SUCCESSORS

Succeeding developments in Scottish portrait painting were founded to a great extent on Raeburn's practice. Some eleven years younger, George Watson (1767-1837), the first President of the Scottish Academy, if not in any true sense a rival, was perhaps the best alternative to Raeburn available in Scotland. Of his able and forcible, if undistinguished, art, the portrait of Thomas Brown (1778-1820) is a more than usually pleasing example. Perhaps the half-length of the founder of the Chair of Music, General John Reid (1721-1807) as an old man, represented in military uniform with flute in hand and music before him, may also be by Watson.

Raeburn's most important successor, Sir John Watson Gordon (1788-1864), while influenced by and carrying on the tradition of soberly handsome portraiture founded by him, possessed a definite personality of his own. Less masterly in craftsmanship and less rich in pictorial effect than Raeburn's, though related to them, his pictures are more frankly realistic in spirit, more intimate and individualistic in characterisation, and cooler and more atmospheric in colour. His essential qualities as an artist appear near their best in the more than admirable head and shoulders of Professor Alexander Monro *tertius* (1773-1859), third of his family in the Chair of Anatomy and Surgery as well as in name. Exhibited at the Royal Scottish Academy in 1861, it is a very fine example of the work of the artist's late maturity—sympathetic in characterisation, simple and quiet in design, reserved in colour, and very accomplished, yet entirely free from showiness, in actual handling. He was not, however, always very happily inspired when designing full lengths, as those of Principal the Rev. John Lee (1779-1859) and the Right Hon. John Inglis (when Dean of Faculty) show. Other professors painted by him were Andrew Duncan, senior (1774-1828), the Rev. Dr Brunton (1772-1854), George Dunbar (1807-51), Professor of Greek, and Sir James Young Simpson (1811-70). Of these, the last, which hangs in the retiring room of the Professor of Midwifery, is the most important, for portraits of the discoverer of chloroform are few in number. Executed in the late 'fifties and suggesting the alertness of mind of the sitter without minimising the bulk of his body or the massiveness of his head, it is perhaps the most convincing of his portraits. Mention should also be made of the pleasing and spiritedly touched cabinet full-length of H.R.H. the Prince of Wales (King Edward VII.) painted in 1859 when he was a student in Edinburgh. This is almost certainly the complete study on which the life-size, painted by command for Oxford University, was based.

Colvin Smith (1795-1875), another competent but much less gifted and personal successor, was the author of the rather dull bust of Robert Graham, Professor of Botany, if it is not a copy. But probably the admirable half-length of Daniel Ellis is that shown by him at the Academy of 1841. Although dating as late as 1879, Sir Daniel Macnee's portrait of John Hutton Balfour (1808-84), who succeeded Graham in the Chair of Botany, may also be mentioned here as Macnee (1806-82) was perhaps the last able exponent of the direct Raeburn tradition.

Sir David Wilkie as a portrait painter is not represented, except by a small copy of his portrait of the Natural Philosopher, Sir John Leslie (1766-1832); nor is that charming artist Andrew Geddes represented, except by a copy of his fine half-length of the Rev. G. H. Baird (1761-1840), who was appointed Principal in 1793.

A few Scottish painters of that period showed qualities in portraiture somewhat alien to the prevailing tendencies, though of course not escaping them entirely. Amongst these, Robert Scott Lauder (1803-69) and William Dyce (1806-64) were prominent. Both had ambitions towards high art and historical painting, and each of them did their more notable work in these directions. Here they, of course, appear as portrait painters. The very striking full-length of Professor John Wilson, who with his alert leonine head and habited in dressing-gown and slippers looks more like the "Christopher North" of the *Noctes Ambrosianae* than a Professor of Moral Philosophy, is by Scott Lauder. It was presented by the sisters of William Edmonstoune Aytoun who had married a daughter of Wilson. Not inappropriately the portraits by Dyce, in view of his wide culture, are of two University librarians, Nicholson Bain and John Small (Librarian, 1847-86), the latter accompanied by his young son. The former, though refined, is a quite ordinary performance. The other possesses some notable qualities. While the formal informality of the design is quietly arresting, the relationship of the figures almost implies a story, the expression on the man's finely drawn face being aloof and intense, and the boy's instinct with that charm of youth which the artist occasionally rendered with peculiar felicity.

Of the contemporary English painters, H. W. Pickersgill, a competent enough likeness-maker of mediocre technical gifts, seems alone represented. His half-length of Sir Roderick Impey Murchison (1792-1871) places a distinguished Scottish geologist on the list of the University portraits ; and his head and shoulders of the first Lord Playfair (1818-98) records, in not very conclusive terms, the likeness of a well-known chemist, who gave up a professorial chair to follow a brilliant career as a publicist. The subject of Pickersgill's third portrait, a slim man of serene aspect, is probably less familiar to most people. At first sight the claim of Captain Thomas Drummond (1797-1840) for representation seemed probably to be based upon the scholarship mentioned on the tablet, but he was a distinguished engineer and a resourceful inventor and, what is rarer, an almost uniquely successful administrator of Irish affairs.

MORE RECENT PORTRAITS

As the University possesses no portraits by Orchardson or Pettie, Chalmers or McTaggart, the charming and distinctive phase of Scottish pictorial art associated with the pupils of Scott Lauder calls for no comment here, and one passes on at once to those by Sir George Reid (1841-1913) who, as Academician and later as President, occupied for many years the outstanding position in Scottish portraiture. Executed with a fine appreciation of character, notable, if not specially subtle, technical power, and a sound and well-balanced sense of design, Reid's portraiture is in some ways in the line of descent from Raeburn and Watson Gordon, and at the same time more tonal in quality and quite personal in feeling. Of these gifts both the boldly designed and powerfully coloured three-quarter length of Professor Alexander Campbell Fraser, seated in flaring robes of scarlet yet looking the philosopher, and the very quiet and sympathetic head and shoulders of Professor Robert Flint, which is perhaps exceptional in its approach to subtlety and one of his best works, are typical. The standing three-quarters of the Earl of Balfour, from 1891 until his death Chancellor of the University, is scarcely so successful. Begun at Whittinghame in the 'nineties, the sittings were interrupted and it was never quite completed.

Although John H. Lorimer was Sir George Reid's junior by some fifteen years, three of the five portraits by him in the collection pre-date those by the older artist. The earliest is that of his father, Professor James Lorimer (1818-90), who in 1862 was appointed to the Chair of Public Law. Painted in 1878, when the artist was only twenty-two, it is a very accomplished and remarkable work for so young a man. The seated three-quarter length of Professor John Stuart Blackie (1881), ardent Grecian and more ardent and picturesque Gael, showing his fine profile but without his plaid, is more mature in handling. Already one sees in it the union of delicately observed detail and tonal envelopment which was to characterise the artist's subsequent and very individual work as a genre painter. And in the portrait of Lord Lister the tonality is characteristically fused on an atmospheric, if somewhat dark, basis, and the reading of character is at once restrained and convincing, the hands as well as the head being admirable. Painted for presentation by his former colleagues and pupils on his retirement in 1895, it was bequeathed to the University by the sitter.

In order of date, except for the portraits by Reid already discussed, two works by Fiddes Watt succeed the Lorimers. That of Simon S. Laurie, first Professor of Education, was shown in the Scottish Academy of 1907, and that of Professor Malcolm C. Taylor followed ten years later. Each of these, especially the latter, is excellent in its way, which is that of a frank, if rather slight treatment of the Raeburn convention.

Of the more recent portraits that of Principal Sir William

Turner by Sir James Guthrie (1859-1930), who succeeded Sir George Reid as President of the Royal Scottish Academy in 1902 and resigned in 1919, is the most notable. Admirable as a likeness, at once searching in form and sympathetic in conception, sumptuous, yet restrained in colour, rich in chiaroscuro and noble in design, it is one of that rarely gifted artist's subtlest and most powerful achievements. Moreover, it combines individuality of personality in the sitter, aged yet keenly alert, with a grave dignity in presentation and a significance in accessories (Vice-Chancellor's robes of black and silver, the crimson hood of the D.C.L., Oxford, the red ribbon of K.C.B., the silver mace of the University), which make it very remarkable as an official portrait. Yet with all, the purely pictorial aspect of the design is preserved quietly and the rich harmony of the whole is quite unforced. Painted in 1912, it was shown in the Royal Scottish Academy during the following year and, in 1914, attracted much attention at the Royal Academy, where Guthrie had not exhibited for thirty years.

Later portraits of interest are of James Walker, who for twenty-one years acted as Honorary Treasurer to the University Union, by David Alison (1919); of Sir Ludovic Grant, Professor of Public Law from 1890 to 1922, after Glyn Philpot (1924); of Sir Richard Lodge, Professor of History from 1899 to 1925 by William Nicholson (1925), a quaintly designed and rather witty cabinet full-length; and of Principal Sir J. Alfred Ewing, represented in Vice-Chancellor's robes with the blue hood of the LL.D. Edinburgh, by Henry Lintott (1929).

PORTRAITS IN MARBLE

This summary of the more interesting of the University portraits, when considered on grounds of personal distinction or artistic quality, having been confined hitherto to paintings, some account must now be given of the more important busts. Arranged beside the columns and in the bays of the Upper Library, which they embellish handsomely, if in a somewhat inconvenient way, forty-seven busts represent many well-known scholars, scientists and doctors. But, with one exception, none of them dates earlier than 1800. Portraiture in Scotland during the eighteenth century was practically confined to painting. The exceptions were the drawings by John Brown, suggestively described as "the draughtsman"; the charming and admirably modelled miniature medallions, associated chiefly with the name of James Tassie; and engravings founded for the most part on paintings, and so without independent existence.

Roubiliac and one or two other sculptors in London executed a few works for Scottish patrons, but, north of Tweed, the only workers in the round seem to have been William Gowan, the author of the interesting bust of Professor William Cullen which is classic yet, in some degree, picturesque in conception and well massed in shape; and R. Cummings, who about 1790 executed a bust of one of the founders of the *Encyclopœdia Britannica*, the Edinburgh printer William Smellie (1740-95), of which there is a plaster cast in the Queen Street gallery. Cullen (1710-90), who was Professor of Chemistry before he became famous as a physician and teacher of Medicine, was exceedingly popular with his students who subscribed for this bust and presented it to the University.

A bust of Alexander Monro *primus* (1697-1767) also suggests the eighteenth century by reason of the costume depicted; he was Professor also from 1720 to 1754. But it bears the signature of John Flaxman (1755-1826) and was probably founded upon Allan Ramsay's portrait of the subject. With it might be grouped the finely expressive and incisively, if smoothly, carved head of Professor John Playfair, by Chantrey (1781-1842), which, modelled in 1814, must be almost coincident with the Raeburn portrait in the Senate Hall. The Chantrey, however, is much more vital in characterisation and far subtler in its nuances of form and surface than the Flaxman.

Later English sculptors represented are Thomas Woolner, Christopher Moore, E. H. Bailey and T. E. Jones. By the first who, poet and painter as well as sculptor, was one of the original pre-Raphaelite Brethren, there is a marble bust of

Thomas Carlyle (1795-1881), carved in 1866 and admirable in its way, though less illuminating than the shaven-face profile medallion he modelled in 1851; and, by the second, a bust of Henry, Lord Brougham (1778-1868), Chancellor of the University of Edinburgh from 1859. These portraits of two of the most distinguished *alumni* of the University are placed in the students' reading-room.

When portrait sculpture began in Scotland the later phase of the picturesque and baroque had passed. It had produced some fine work of its kind in Italy and France and by a few foreigners working in England. It was now the age of Canova (1757-1822) and Thorwaldsen (1770-1844) and pseudo-classicism was the fashion. Men were modelled as Greek philosophers or Roman senators, with towels or swags of drapery round naked shoulders, and women as Greek goddesses, with what were considered classically dressed hair and clinging antique gowns. As it happened, Scotland had for some years (1821-29) in the first quarter of the century, one of the ablest practitioners of this mode. Samuel Joseph (1791-1850), son of the Treasurer of one of the Cambridge Colleges, showed some fine qualities and, within the limits set by the convention, distinct individuality. He possessed a real grasp of character, a rather unusual sense, for his time, of the qualities of marble as a material, and he used the prevailing style with taste and discretion. These characteristics appear in several busts in the Library. Those of Professor James Gregory (1753-1821), Professor Dugald Stewart (1753-1828) and Professor Sir John Leslie (1766-1832), the last, a very interesting treatment of an overfat physiognomy, may be referred to because of the combination of character with smoothly finished but expressive modelling and a fine eye for the mass and balance of the whole design. This gives them a certain dignity to which none of his successors in Scotland attained, despite an equal subservience to classicism.

Sir John Steell (1804-91) was the earliest purely Scottish sculptor of modern times apart from a few self-taught men who, prior to his advent, did some powerful, if rude work, of a popular genre kind in freestone. He had studied in Rome, but his work was done at home and he is said to have executed the first marble statue carved in Scotland since the Reformation. His portraiture, of which the University possesses at least seven examples, was accomplished in a conventional way, but is deficient in animation and too obviously subdued by neo-classicism. Most of his busts had the usual antique drapery about the neck and when they had not, as in the Edward Forbes (1815-54), or the Professor John Thomson (1765-1845), showed naked shoulders, which after all was a more natural and becoming mode than the other. Perhaps that of the Rev. Thomas Chalmers (1780-1847), whose work as Professor of Divinity was quite eclipsed by his influence as man, Church leader and orator, is the most important. Although dated 1875, it is a repetition by Steell of the bust modelled in 1845, and fuller of individual character than most of his work. It was difficult to miss character when modelling such a head.

While classic in the same sense as Steell, Patrick Park (1809-55) produced some work marked by a more distinguished feeling for style. Such is the almost heroic head and shoulders of Professor W. E. Aytoun (1813-65), in which the voluminous draperies support rather than detract from the animation of a head carried with a fine air of distinction. Born in the same year as Park, J. P. Slater, whose modelling and carving possessed no individual quality, was evidently in favour in University circles. Of five busts by him probably those of Professor Macvey Napier and Professor James Pillans are the most interesting. But William Brodie (1815-81) with eight or nine portraits outnumbers all the others. To him we are indebted for likenesses of James Syme, Sir Robert Christison, Sir J. Y. Simpson, and Sir William Hamilton. Perhaps the last is the finest in rendering of character and in design. In these respects at least it is one of the best things in the collection. John Hutchison (1833-1910), who in 1889 modelled the bronze statue of the Torch-bearer which forms the finial on the University dome, came next. As is evident from his busts of Sir Douglas Maclagan (1882) and Sir Wyville

Thomson (1883), he carried on the pseudo-classic convention which Brodie had followed. It was also practised by D. W. Stevenson (Professor Goodsir, 1867), F. J. Williamson (Professor John Wilson, 1888), George Webster (Alexander Anderson, the "Surfaceman" poet, who was Assistant Librarian, 1888), and other rather younger Scottish sculptors. Yet it is noticeable that, after the middle of the century, a more naturalistic treatment gradually came into vogue, and men were represented in academic robes and even in collars and ties and frock-coats—more in the manner as they lived. The later works of Brodie and Hutchison reflected this more realistic tendency, although the coats were close-buttoned, creaseless and without texture. But marble continued the one possible material for portrait sculpture, and the modelling and the carving and surface texture of the stone remained smooth and dull. Although informed by no specially vital talent, several busts by Charles McBride illustrate this transition. In his rather grandiosely designed, but delicately carved, rendering of Sir Alexander Grant, Principal of the University from 1868 to 1884 and its historian, he used a semi-antique drapery to envelop the shoulders (much as Steell or Brodie would have done in the heyday of classicism); in the bust of the Right Hon. John Inglis, Lord Justice-General, the robes of his office of Chancellor are rendered with considerable fidelity; in that of Sir William Muir, Indian Administrator and Principal from 1885 to 1902, the clothes below the open robe are such as were worn everyday by professional men of his time.

More recent developments in sculpture appear in no more than three or four busts. Yet during the last thirty or forty years sculpture in Scotland has widened in scope. It has become more decorative in effect and more intimate in characterisation, as well as freer and more varied in handling, and materials, as beautiful to look at and more comfortable to live with than cold white marble, are being used. Much of this has been due to the example of Pittendrigh MacGillivray, who is here, however, represented by a work in marble. This bust of David Masson (1822-1907), whose occupancy of the Chair of English Literature remains memorable to his pupils—and to no one more than the present Chancellor of the University—was modelled in 1895 or 1896, just after the sitter's retirement, and was one of the first works of the sculptor after he settled in Edinburgh. It has an animation and a sense of personality, a movement of silhouette and a rhythm of mass, and a feeling for style very rare in previous Scottish sculpture. Executed some five years later, the University has also in the larger-than-life bust of the donor, which stands in the McEwan Hall, an admirable example of MacGillivray's spirited and expressive modelling transferred immediately and without loss in vitality into bronze. A bust by Edward Lanteri, for a long time sculpture-master in the Royal College of Art, also bears the marks of this more modern realism, associated, as in MacGillivray's case, with respect for the past. Inscribed 1916, it represents Sir Archibald Geikie (1835-1924), Professor of Geology from 1871 until 1882, and is remarkable for the rather subtle way in which a quaint and somewhat whimsical expression plays through the polished accomplishment of its craftsmanship. If a somewhat amateur performance and a little empty in the modelling of the shoulders, the bronze-relief of Professor Frederick Niecks (1845-1924), which takes something of the form of a mural monument upon the wall of the Music class-room, is an admirable likeness. The work of his old colleague, Professor Otto Schlapp, it is dated the year after Niecks's death.

The last addition to the University series of portraits is, as it happens, a bust of the first occupant of the Chair of Fine Art, which bears the name of the well-known Scottish portrait-painter, Watson Gordon. Gerard Baldwin Brown (1849-1932), who was appointed in 1880 and lectured for fifty years, had a great reputation as an exact scholar and a learned historian of the Arts, and it was very largely due to him that art was eventually recognised as a phase of culture which ought to be given a place in the graduation course of the University. This bronze, the only bust not in marble in the collection, was modelled by C. d'O. Pilkington Jackson and was presented in commemoration of the Professor's academic jubilee.

XI

THE LIFE OF THE STUDENT COMMUNITY

UNDERGRADUATE SELF-GOVERNMENT

THE STUDENTS' REPRESENTATIVE COUNCIL

THE story of the constitutional development by which the undergraduate body was introduced effectively into the corporate life of the University coincides with the birth, adolescence and manhood of the Students' Representative Council, the pioneer of all other University Representative Councils.

It is remarkable that the idea of such a council should have originated at Edinburgh. The origin and foundation of the College were different from those of the other Scottish Universities. It was a "Tounis College" and was regarded as the least democratic. At its foundation, it is true, it was more or less residential, and it had a semblance of organisation. But it had none of the social sentiment which was associated with the more ancient religious and papal foundations. Nowhere was the personal independence of the Scottish student more pronounced; nowhere was student life more individualistic, and a real corporate organisation of the student body, constitutional or otherwise, was never a reality until 1884.

It was at a general meeting of students held within the University on the 17th January of that year that the first Council was elected. To Robert Fitzroy Bell, one of its first Presidents, belongs the credit of conceiving the idea. While on a visit to Strassburg in the summer of 1883, he had discovered the existence at that University of a "Studenten Ausschuss." Inspired in all probability by this example, and impressed by the anomaly that, while at Edinburgh the student element was strong, there was no concentration of University life, and at best but a very occasional and haphazard unity, without the slightest approach to representative government, he summoned, shortly after his return, the presidents and secretaries of all University societies to his room at 30 Walker Street, and framed a Constitution.

The year in which the first Council was elected witnessed the Tercentenary of the University, and the first task undertaken by the new body was that of co-operating with the Senatus in arranging for the celebrations, and entertaining, on behalf of the students, the guests from many nations who thronged to Edinburgh. The success of the Council's efforts on this occasion was recognised by the Rector, the Earl of Iddesleigh, and by the Senatus, which expressed in their minutes the hope "that this most historical occasion may be the commencement of a new corporate life amongst the students of the University, and that out of it arrangements will follow which will tend to increase the comfort and convenience of students, and to draw them more closely to each other in social and intellectual relations." With the expression of such goodwill on the part of the authorities, it was easy to see that the Council was not to prove a creature of the hour. Such was, in fact, its success that before five years had elapsed it obtained recognition and sanction from Parliament in the Universities (Scotland) Act, 1889—a remarkable achievement in so short a time.

The aims of the Council, though wide in scope, are simply told. They were, first, to represent the students in such matters as permanently or from time to time affected their interests; secondly, to afford a recognised means of communication between the students and the University authorities; and thirdly, to promote social life and academic unity among the students. It was towards the fulfilment of the last-mentioned aim that the Council first devoted its energies; but before very long it was given an opportunity of carrying out the first and second of its functions by representing the general body of students in a matter affecting them very materially. The same Universities Act which recognised the

Council gave full and important powers to the University Commission, the result of whose deliberations has influenced greatly the development of the Scottish Universities. The Council was not slow to recognise its responsibility, and before the Bill was introduced into Parliament, during its passage, and afterwards during the sitting of the Commission, deputations were appointed to give expression to the wishes of the students and their claim to be heard on questions of University administration, such as the changes in the curriculum and in the requirements for graduation which were then urgently demanded. These deputations received from the Commissioners equal attention with those of the other University bodies.

Meanwhile, the example set by the students of Edinburgh had been swiftly followed by those of St Andrews, Glasgow and Aberdeen and, before the passing of the 1889 Act, a Students' Council existed in each of these Universities. Between four such bodies, founded to meet a common need, and confronted by problems similar in nature, signs of co-operation were soon apparent. Before the reprinting of the Bill a deputation from the four Students' Representative Councils of Scotland had an interview with the Lord Advocate in order to press the claims put forward by them in a memorial addressed to the members of Her Majesty's Government. This joint deputation first suggested the holding of Inter-University Conferences.

These conferences, held annually in rotation at each of the Scottish Universities and attended at first by four, now by eight delegates from each, have been for many years among the most important of the Councils' activities. The numerous recommendations which they have passed are a sufficient reply to the question one used to hear, "What good do these conferences do?" For at least 80 per cent. of them have been accepted and put into force by the authorities to whom they have been addressed. The meetings have, moreover, a higher value than that of successful recommendation, for just as the individual Council set itself to develop the academic spirit and foster academic unity within its own sphere, so the

Conference of the four Universities extended and broadened these principles. This same process was, in 1921, carried into an international sphere, when the Students' Representative Councils of Scotland entered as a national Union La Confédération Internationale des Etudiants (C.I.E.), an organisation which was founded in 1919, and now embraces almost the whole of Europe, together with the United States, Canada, South Africa and New Zealand, with affiliations in many other states, and which numbers in its constituent organisations over a million students. The Council meetings of the Confederation, held annually in European capitals, have been attended during the last ten years by numbers of Scottish students.

While the C.I.E. provides an organisation for national representation, the needs of individual Edinburgh students going abroad to study and of foreign students coming to Edinburgh are met by the International Academic Committee of the Council. This Committee finds its sphere of labour in the establishment of contact with the student bodies of foreign universities, and its duties are to maintain relations with, and arrange for the reception of, delegates from abroad; to supply information concerning the curricula and social organisations of British and foreign universities; and to furnish to students travelling abroad such introductions as may be in its power.

It was, however, in its aim to promote social and academic unity that the Council achieved its first, and probably its most notable, success. Corporate life had come; but it might very well be incomplete if the social side were to be left untouched or undeveloped. The very first matter remitted to the Executive by the Council was a proposal to establish a University Union. The Executive reported most favourably on the proposal, general meetings of students were held and, amid much enthusiasm, the scheme was unanimously approved. A letter pointing out the grave need for a social centre of academic life was sent to the Chancellor, Lord President Inglis, whose approval and support the Committee strongly desired, and a large number of noblemen and gentlemen were invited to form a general committee. By 1886 about £5000 had been collected by public subscription and other methods, and towards the end of that year it was decided to hold a Fancy Fair. The work of organising this enterprise was undertaken largely by the young Council, and upon its magnificent result the whole student body could afford to look with justifiable pride. The Fair brought in the sum of £10,000, and a success, literary as well as financial, was gained by the Committee which produced and edited the Journal of the Fair, entitled *The New Amphion*, containing original contributions from many eminent authors and artists, including Robert Browning, Andrew Lang, George Macdonald, Robert Louis Stevenson, and the present Chancellor of the University, Sir James M. Barrie.

The remainder of the sum necessary for the completion of the Union was raised by a Dramatic Festival, concerts, debates and lectures.

Apart from the University Union, probably the most important task undertaken by the Council for the benefit of the student body was the acquisition of the fine Athletic Field and pavilion at Craiglockhart. The Students' Representative Council felt that a great university should provide adequate opportunity for athletics. The problem was faced promptly and dealt with energetically. A field was chosen as eminently suitable in everything but cost; for to buy, equip and maintain it necessitated the raising of £13,000. But here was an opportunity to remedy a grave defect in the equipment of the University. The effort was made with great enthusiasm; students and professors worked loyally, and in one session £6000 was collected. The campaign extended to London when the Right Honourable A. J. Balfour convened a meeting of Scotsmen resident there, and inspired them to give generously towards the scheme. At length, in 1896, the new field was ceremonially opened.

Though the construction of the Union and the acquisition of the Athletic Field were during this period the main objects to be carried out, the Council never forgot the power which its representative nature gave it to deal with other student

Sir DAVID ORME MASSON, K.B.E.

First Senior President, Students' Representative Council
1884

interests. It saw and successfully met the many little difficulties which so large a body of men must have laboured under when there was no organisation. Its activity was manifold in such matters as the post-office, the library, class-room accommodation, class-hours, the inauguration and control of amusements, torchlight processions, the stewarding and organising of public receptions to great men, the arranging of University Services—now held twice each term in St Giles's Cathedral—in suggestions for new classes and for the institution of new Faculties, and the biennial Final Examination in Medicine—to mention only a few.

In 1889 it was announced that one of the main achievements of the Council during the previous year had been the establishment of a University magazine to be the permanent interpreter of real student opinion, and a regular medium of student thought and interests, social, intellectual and physical. A glance at the history of the University periodicals shows that a journalist fever broke out among students every now and then and produced a few stray numbers. Of these, possibly the greatest interest centres round the *Lapsus Linguæ* (1823), the *New Lapsus Linguæ* (1824), and *The University Maga* with amusing sketches of certain members of the Professoriate. It was not given to any of these attempts to outlive the span of three years. There was no guarantee of continuity; for these papers were run by a few friends or by a club and, when the friends went down, or the club broke up, no successors were left to carry on. The great advantage which accrued from the Council's control of the University magazine was the guarantee which it gave of continuity in name and, to some extent, in policy. This advantage has been secured without in any way limiting that editorial freedom which is essential in a topical journal. While responsible ultimately to the Students' Representative Council, and nominally assisted by a large staff, the Editor, in reality, stands supremely and almost bewilderingly alone. It is a tradition that no good word should be said for *The Student* by anyone at the University, and a wise editor soon makes up his mind that, as he cannot possibly satisfy his critics, he must attempt rather to satisfy himself. As a consequence, *The Student* can to-day successfully challenge comparison with the magazine of any British University.

To meet the needs of "freshers," the Council, in 1895, decided to publish a "completely new Handbook," containing information about university life and institutions likely to be useful to students. By this the freshman is at once carried, as it were, into the swim of affairs. There is little of interest to him connected with the University that is not treated; how to attach himself to the various societies and unions, guidance as to his course of study and his recreations, notices of important dates during the session, and much more that is interesting and useful.

The Scottish Students' Song Book, the best of its kind, should not be forgotten. As was natural, the Councils of the Scottish Universities found great difficulty in its compilation, but it did appear at last, in April 1891, with remarkable success. In addition to fulfilling its primary purpose beyond expectations, it has the merit of being profitable financially to the Councils interested.

The Council—to pursue its history into more modern times—benefited greatly, along with the other undergraduate organisations, from that remarkable renaissance of student activity which took place in the years immediately succeeding the Great War. The return to interrupted careers of men who had spent two, three, or even four years in the trenches, and the arrival as freshers of those who had been "called up" straight from school, and whose appearance and manners most clearly belied the term, united to make the University Matriculation roll during this period the largest upon record; and by men grown accustomed to military life the promotion of corporate student activity was unlikely to be forgotten in the pursuit of purely academic study. The chief material effect of this revival, so far as the Council was concerned, was the institution of the Students' Representative Ceenium, a student entertainment, partaking largely of the nature of a *revue*, which was produced annually in aid of the Royal Infirmary. The first few performances, which were held in the Lauriston Hall, had an immense success, and did much to produce, if only once a year, an appearance of academic unity among the students. The sketches were mainly concerned with University topics; prominent University figures, not excluding professors, were the objects of the jests; and although the general public was generous in its support, the audience had a pronounced student character. After some years, however, the increasing success of the performances induced the Council to transfer the production to the Synod Hall. It was decided at the same time to devote the profits to the funds of the Council. Produced on a more ambitious scale, the *revue* tended to lose that essentially student quality which had been its chief merit; in the larger hall the undergraduate element of the audience was no longer so pronounced and the sketches and "turns," though still of a high quality, were less concerned with topics of a purely University interest. The Synod Hall Ceeniums were continued until 1930. In the following year the Council, convinced that, at different times throughout the session, much unnecessary time and labour were being spent on the organisation of individual charity efforts which, if co-ordinated, would both involve less trouble and produce a better financial return, decided to organise a grand Charities' Week in the summer of 1932, and to divide the proceeds among the various charities which were considered to have a claim upon student support. In view of this decision, it was decided to abandon the 1931 Ceenium in favour of a *revue* to be produced during the Charities' Week. The 1932 Charities' Week was well supported by the students and brought in gross receipts of over £4000, a sum considerably in excess of the total raised in any previous year by the individual efforts. It is hoped that this enterprise will in future years bring in an even larger amount.

Before the session 1930-31 the Council, which had till then suffered from cramped and insufficient office accommodation, was given the use of a commodious apartment formerly occupied by the Non-Associated Societies. Suitable furnishings and equipment for this new office were supplied through the generosity of Thomas Cowan, who presented the sum of

£250 to the Council in recognition of its services in organising student volunteer assistance during the General Strike of 1926.

Any survey of the Council's work and achievements would be gravely incomplete without a tribute to one whose advice and assistance were throughout the first thirty-eight years of its life continually at its disposal. By the death, in 1922, of James Walker, the Council lost its greatest friend. He was largely responsible for securing, in 1884, the annual grant from the University Court to the Council funds, and from then up to the time of his death he did much, not only to ensure the stability of its financial position, but to assist it in its various departments of administration. His interest in the University was by no means limited to the Council. To successive committees of the University Union, whose accounts remained for many years under his charge, he proved a valuable friend, and both the provision of a Union branch at The King's Buildings, and the settlement of the Women's Union in its present situation were due largely to his efforts. In the office of Rector's Assessor on the University Court, to which he was nominated in 1907 and which he occupied until his death, he gave loyal service to the University authorities as well as to the students whom he represented. By conferring on him, in 1919, the Honorary Degree of Doctor of Laws, the Senatus chose the best method in its power of honouring one whose highest ambition had always been to promote the interests of the University.

A tablet recording James Walker's services to the Students' Representative Council was, shortly after his death, erected within the Council Hall.

THE RECTORIAL ELECTIONS

Before passing from the administrative organisation of the student body to those associations which are mainly social and intellectual in their aims, it is necessary to give some account of an official whose functions and position form a vital factor in the whole system of undergraduate government, and whose election, ever since it was placed upon a democratic footing,

Photo by] [*Ian Smith*

"THE BATTLE FOR THE STEPS"

Rectorial Election, 30th October 1920

has been a matter not only of the very keenest concern to succeeding generations of students, but of wide public interest.

The office of Rector of the University is in itself one of considerable antiquity. For over two hundred years the Lord Provost of the city was *ex officio* its holder; but by the Universities (Scotland) Act, 1858, which carried out extensive and important changes in the constitution of the University, the election, at three-year intervals, of a Rector who was to preside at meetings of the University Court, and who, in turn, was to nominate an Assessor on the Court, was handed over to the students.

The very nature of the office of Rector clearly suggested that its occupant should be a man of high public distinction, able by his influence to forward the interests of the University, and, from the very first, the tradition was laid down of nominating for the office distinguished politicians of rival parties. This tradition prevailed from the first Rectorial Election in 1859 until after that of 1929. At the first Students' Conference, it is true, a motion was tabled that the Councils should interfere in the Rectorial Elections of their respective Universities by putting up candidates of local standing; but the motion was defeated and, although in 1865 Carlyle owed his victory over Disraeli less to political distinction than to eminence in the Republic of Letters, the election itself was conducted upon the customary political basis.

From the first, too, the Rector was expected to deliver an Address during his term of office. In course of time, as he was almost invariably, by reason of political duties, resident in London for the greater part of the year, and thus seldom fulfilled his statutory function of presiding over the University Court, the delivery of an Address came to be regarded as his most important function. As elections were triennial, every student who completed a graduation course was able at some time during his University course both to participate in a Rectorial Election and to hear a Rectorial Address; and of all the memories of student life which remain with the Scottish graduate throughout his after-life it is improbable that any are so vivid as those of the particular Rectorial Election and the particular Rectorial Address which fell within his own University career.

To the election of the Rector the entire student body always brought the very keenest partisan spirit, and, even after the foundation of institutions calculated to encourage academic unity, the most notable signs of corporate activity among students were found during Rectorial campaigns. In the words of Sir William Turner: "At each triennial period, as soon as the Rector was appointed, the students became dormant in regard to the public life of the University, and did not awake to activity until the preparations for the next election made a fresh demand on their vivacity and energies."

The Rectorial campaign extended, as a rule, over some fifteen days. During its earlier stages publicity was given to the rival candidates by means of placards (sometimes draped at dead of night around the higher pinnacles of the University buildings), pamphlets, election papers, addresses, and social meetings of all kinds. Attacks were made by the rival factions upon their opponents' headquarters, and great was the success of any party which succeeded in kidnapping an opposing leader and removing him to a safe distance until the election was over. The campaign culminated in the famous "Battle of the Standard," held in the Old Quadrangle on the morning of the poll. This struggle, ending, as it often did, in indescribable confusion, always began with due formality. The party whose candidate had been victorious in the last election entered the Quadrangle and took up a position at the top of the broad flight of steps at its west end, where, grouped around their standard-bearer, they awaited the assault of their opponents. Within a few minutes after the issue had been joined, not only was the region immediately surrounding the standard-bearer the scene of a dense and ferocious struggle, but throughout the whole Quadrangle a kind of guerilla warfare was in progress. The ammunition sacred to the occasion was the all-pervasive and highly effective pease-meal which, discharged in volleys, produced effects similar to those both of a smoke-screen and of lachrymatory gas. On the announcement of the poll, a large placard bearing the result of the election was, by time-honoured ritual, lowered from the south-east balcony and torn to pieces by the students below. Thereafter, the leaders of the various parties ascended a conveyance and drove in state through the city to declare the victorious candidate.

With the decision to discontinue the traditional fight arrived at by the various political associations of the University before the election of 1929, much of the excitement, as well as the picturesqueness of the election, disappeared, and loud were the complaints among graduates throughout the country concerning the degeneracy of the modern student. The chief reason for the decision was, however, the increasing insecurity of the balustrades in the Old Quadrangle, which constituted a danger to the lives and limbs of electors rather greater than that to which their predecessors had been subjected in previous elections.

Partly, perhaps, because of the cancellation of the "fight" the 1929 election was a failure, and the poll was the smallest upon record. Throughout the whole University, including the political associations, there appeared a feeling of dissatisfaction with the traditional political basis of the election. Beyond this feeling, opinion among students was divided, some pointing a jealous finger to the distinguished list of Rectors displayed by the neighbouring University of St Andrews and calling for candidates whose sole qualification should be high distinction in a sphere of life not limited to politics; while others raised the demand for a "working Rector" who should, at all costs, perform his statutory function of presiding at meetings of the University Court. An agreement not to put forward candidates, to be renewed before each Rectorial Election, was signed by the representatives of the political associations, and a committee from the associations and the Representative Council was appointed to draw up regulations for the conduct of the election. These, when amended and approved by the University Court, were brought into force. Their main provisions are that any twenty students shall be sufficient to nominate a candidate and that the conduct of the election, including the consideration of nominations, shall be entrusted to a Rectorial Elections' Committee, with the Senior President of the Students' Representative Council as its Convener, and composed of officials of the Council and the Unions, the Rector's Assessor, a representative of the Senatus on the University Court, and a representative of the General Council nominated by the Students' Representative Council. It is probable that the functions of this committee and the general regulations for the conduct of the election will undergo some alterations before the present Rector demits office, though any return to the old political system is unlikely. Meanwhile, the record poll in the 1932 election affords some justification for the change.

THE UNIVERSITY UNION

In any University town the Union forms a natural centre of student life. But the Edinburgh Union has differed from similar societies in other parts of the kingdom, both in its method of foundation and in its subsequent development. Its avowed purpose has been the "provision and maintenance of means of social and academic intercourse for its members"; but in neither of these specified directions has this aim been wholly realised. The academic aspect has been represented mainly by Union debates, and, while University debating shared to a remarkable degree in the revival of student activities after the war, the record in general has been one of failure. Various reasons have been suggested for this and, among them, that, in accordance with the Union constitution, the organisation and control of debates have constantly been entrusted to committee members who have had neither knowledge of nor interest in such matters. But a truer explanation is probably to be found in the admission that, save in exceptional years, serious debating has seldom found much support at Edinburgh outside the select circle of the Associated Societies.

The Union has always claimed the right to entertain the guests of the University and its office-bearers have a place in the student hierarchy on a par with that held by the dignitaries of the Students' Representative Council itself.

Professor James Mackintosh. Professor E. T. Whittaker. Professor Sir T. Hudson Beare. Bedellus. Professor W. P. Paterson. Professor J. Lorrain Smith. Professor Sir James Walker. W. A. Fleming, *Sec. to the University.*

John L. Somerville, *Treas. U. Union* H. S. Kirkaldy, *Hon. Sec. S.R.C.* Sir James Alfred Ewing, *Vice-Chancellor* J. B. Colquhoun, *Pres. S.R.C.* Rt. Hon. Stanley Baldwin, *Rector* J. Senter, *Pres. U. Union* Rt. Hon. the Earl of Balfour, *Chancellor* J. P. Bannerman, *Hon. Sec. U. Union* Hon. Lord Constable, *Rector's Assessor*

THE OCCASION OF THE INSTALLATION OF THE RT. HON. STANLEY BALDWIN AS RECTOR, *6th November*, 1925.

THE WOMEN'S UNION

The foundation, in 1905, of the Women's Union was a natural consequence of the admission of women to the University, and was a result of the activities of the women themselves. Mrs Baldwin Brown and Elsie Inglis were prominent among those who launched the venture. Till 1920 the Union occupied small and inadequate premises in Lothian Street, but this prolonged period of probation has been valuable to the women students of to-day in so far as it has made it possible for their present premises in George Square to be thoroughly up-to-date, and suited in every way to the needs of a modern age. Rapid increases in membership have necessitated a further extension.

THE OFFICERS' TRAINING CORPS

The University contingent of the Officers' Training Corps, composed of four units, the Battery (the oldest Artillery O.T.C. in the kingdom), the Engineers, Infantry and the Medical Corps, has always attracted to its ranks a large number of undergraduates, and though unable to exercise much influence upon student corporate life except during the short periods of its annual summer camps, yet it occupies an important place among University organisations. Each of the units has, on many occasions, distinguished itself in competition with the contingents of other universities. A particularly notable success was gained in 1907 at Bisley when the Battery won the King's Cup, open to all the Volunteer Units in Great Britain. In an age when the disbanding even of territorial contingents is frequently demanded, the O.T.C. continues to attract its annual quota of recruits, for the truth of the matter is that, quite apart from its purely military training, to which the average student is inclined to pay but little attention, it provides a valuable discipline both for mind and body, and opportunities, during a fortnight of every year, for a companionship which other University organisations are unable to supply. To the student who is rather fagged after Final or Degree Examinations nothing could be more beneficial than the open-air life at camp, with its comparative immunity from mental strain.

At an impressive ceremony on 19th February 1923, the University War Memorial, situated at the west end of the Old Quadrangle, was unveiled by the Chancellor of the University, the late Earl of Balfour. The Memorial, which was designed by Sir Robert Lorimer and carried out by C. d'O. Pilkington Jackson, bears the names of 944 of the University's alumni—many of them former members of the O.T.C.—who fell in the Great War.

THE STUDENT SOCIETIES

"Essentially as important in any university as the regular apparatus of the teaching arrangements are the voluntary groupings of the students among themselves for mutual acquaintanceship and stimulation, and for the prosecution of special kinds of knowledge." "The University of Edinburgh has been conspicuous even to excess for the number of such societies that have figured in her annals." These two statements, which formed the opening paragraph of the Presidential Address delivered to the Associated Societies of the University by Professor Masson in 1896, are clearly as true to-day as in the year when they were made. That the first, which is a general observation applicable to any university in any age, is particularly true of the University of Edinburgh is amply testified by the remarkable influence which debating and social societies have always exercised upon the nature of her student life. The second, if true in 1896, must be still more so to-day, for the last quarter of a century has seen a great increase in the number of University societies. *The Students' Handbook* for 1932 contains notices of as many as 61 and, within the years immediately previous, the total was probably even larger. For some at least of the societies are but ephemeral phenomena and their number varies from year to year. The zeal and ingenuity displayed by the Edinburgh student in organising new societies, and in devising functions for them to perform, has always been remarkable. Too often the new

THE ROLL OF THE FALLEN

1914-1919

The War Memorial—The Old Quadrangle

association has proved unable to survive the academic careers of its enthusiastic founders. Launched in a blaze of gaudy and attractive posters, it for a time entices the fresher and gives temporary hospitality to that restless element among senior students which is ever flitting, like the honey-bee, from one society to another; for a few years its notices flutter on the boards within the Quadrangle entrances, until, forsaken by its founders and supplanted in popular esteem by some more youthful body, the Society quietly expires, surviving perhaps for a session as a small handful of office-bearers—the last, like the now proverbial sea-captain, to forsake the sinking vessel.

The University societies, apart from the Royal Medical Society—the oldest Royal Medical society in the kingdom—which has functions differing widely from those of the others, fall into the two broad groups of Associated and Non-Associated Societies. Of these, the Associated Societies, which now comprise the Celtic, Diagnostic, Dialectic, Philomathic and Scots Law, differ from the others in their greater antiquity; in their aims, which are mainly literary and debating; and in their organisation as a definite body governed by a Council of delegates. This Association, which dates from the session of 1833-34, was the outcome of co-operation in the session 1831-32 between the five original constituent societies—the Scots Law, Plinian, Hunterian Medical, Dialectic and Diagnostic—in resistance to the Town Council, then the governing body of the University, which, in the course of a long quarrel with the Senatus, ordered all the University societies, with the exception of the Speculative (which then, as now, enjoyed special privileges), and probably the Theological, to quit the University buildings. The five societies which thus co-operated were fortunate in securing the help of Henry Cockburn (later Lord Cockburn), then Solicitor-General for Scotland, who gained for them the use of a room in the old janitor's house. From then onwards, the Association has enjoyed the exclusive use of a hall within the University buildings, and though attempts have been made on more than one occasion to curtail its liberties, particularly in the matter of "early closing," the members have always shown themselves capable of guarding their own privileges.

The office of Honorary President of the Associated Societies, founded in 1853, partly with the intention of supplying for Edinburgh students an office similar to that of the Rectors who were then in other Scottish Universities elected by the students, has been occupied by some of the most distinguished lawyers, politicians, and men of letters of this and the last century. The position, like that of Rector, is now triennial, and its occupant delivers an Address during his term of office.

The individual societies which form the Association, though differing widely in their essential qualities—their manner of debating and their time-honoured ceremonies—have much that is in common; and, to those students who have belonged to a society and have succeeded in capturing even a small part of its spirit, it will always remain the quintessence of University life.

The hall of the Association, like that of the Representative Council, is situated in the nethermost parts of the Old Quadrangle, and to the casual observer there is in the appearance of the learned debaters, as they pass one by one through the half-lighted entrance to the Quadrangle and slip down the opening of their dark and apparently subterranean passage, something reminiscent of the Early Christians on their way to meetings in the catacombs.

The Associated Societies, which were the earliest home of serious debating in the University, are now providing almost its only refuge. The Non-associated Societies, in contrast, are a mushroom growth and also a very prolific growth. Some of them are inevitable components of the modern University. The Musical Society, for instance, has filled a place which could have been occupied by no other. The Cosmopolitan Club, founded in 1930, has been valuable in binding together widely varied personalities and in reflecting the world-wide scope of our University; while the Political Club, the most recently founded of all, has given a new outlet for the energies once lavished on Rectorial battles. Among the Faculty and departmental associations, the English Literature Society claims particular mention by its production annually of sixteenth and seventeenth century plays, which would not otherwise be placed upon the stage. The Classical Society, also, has performed a number of Greek and Latin comedies with marked success. The vast bulk of these societies, however, have often been criticised as somewhat narrow and parochial in their range of interests, tending in some ways towards disintegration, rather than towards any kind of academic unity. Nevertheless, true though such criticism may be, it must be remembered that many worthy students of both sexes have found their own little Utopia in the company of kindred souls gathered within the four walls of a territorial or departmental society.

The preceding pages have given some account of the varied institutions which have played a prominent part in the student life of the last fifty years. But student life in its essence goes deeper than any of its organised institutions, and in student life itself the period has seen many deep and extensive changes. The foundation of numerous new departments, particularly those at The King's Buildings; the provision of greater facilities for reading and study within the University precincts; and the appearance of new amusements within the city are only a few of the influences that have united to alter both the habits and the outlook of the undergraduate. In this connection it would be futile to ignore the tremendous change which has come upon student life in consequence of the advent of women to the University. Twenty-five years ago the position of the woman student was still anomalous and uncertain. To-day it is in some ways superior to that of the male majority. Many years of planning and importuning have at last secured for the women an attractive and much-used common-room within the walls of the Old Quadrangle itself, while the men must still converse with their acquaintances in the open air.

HALLS OF RESIDENCE AND HOSTELS FOR STUDENTS

The construction of an increasing number of Halls of Residence or Student Hostels has been a notable feature during the last forty years. As early as the end of last century University Hall, the first men students' hostel, which now comprises Ramsay Lodge, Blackie House, and St Giles's House, was founded by the late Professor Sir Patrick Geddes. More recently, with the opening in 1929 of Cowan House, founded and endowed by Thomas Cowan, accommodation has been provided for over a hundred students. Though the part played by the older Halls in the life of the University at large has never been pronounced, and though the newer establishment has not yet existed long enough to assert its influence to the full, these residences have undoubtedly done much in the past and will, in all probability, do still more in the future to produce, if only among a limited number of students, a feeling of corporate unity.*

Of the women's hostels, Masson Hall, founded in 1897, and Muir Hall, instituted primarily for the use of the women in Medicine, have provided many leaders for an ever-growing community of women students. Five other large and well-equipped hostels founded more recently at Craigmillar Park provide accommodation for over 250 residents. The institution of such residences is an indication of the methods by which the student life of the future must inevitably be developed, and, while the cessation of the life in lodgings which by its nature plays an important part in the education of the student, and round which so many Edinburgh undergraduate traditions cluster, would be in the highest degree regrettable, the value of the residences in promoting communal student activity is undeniable.

* The University Hall residences are owned and administered by a body independent of the University; Cowan House is the property of the University, its warden is appointed by the University Court, and its administration is supervised by a special Committee of the Court. In addition to his generous provision of the house and endowment, Thomas Cowan also established a fund for Cowan House Scholarships, awarded each year for periods of two or three years to a number of students entering the University.

In spite of the changes bred by the appearance in the University of new institutions and new ideas, there yet remains about the habits of her students much that is essentially unaltered. Still the continuous stream across the Meadows to nine o'clock classes, sober-clad lawyer mingling with more gaily-apparelled medical student; still within the Old Quadrangle—itself a symbol of what is permanent in student-life—the same phenomena are apparent at those regular intervals when the lecture-rooms, like Charybdis of old, swallow and disgorge their victims; the animated throng which increases steadily from ten minutes to the hour until the hour itself; the perceptible swirling about the steps at five minutes past, the few hurrying latecomers, and then solitude unrelieved, except for a few lonely figures, for another fifty minutes. Still the eternal need, presenting itself as acutely to the student of to-day as to those of an older generation, for some diversion in which to spend the odd hour between morning classes, and which occasionally results in the encroachment of the "odd hour" upon the lecture-hour itself. The modern solution of this problem is found in two establishments conveniently situated, the one for the Old, the other for the New Quadrangle, known respectively as the "Old Quad" and the "Medical" Martin's. Of these, the New Quad establishment—for that of the Old has about its atmosphere something of distance, reserve and decorum, which leads the more sociable Arts student to fare, if time permit, further afield—presents on a morning during Term a fairly adequate picture of modern Edinburgh student-life in its lighter aspect.

UNIVERSITY ATHLETICS

In the year 1876 the teams of students engaging in Rugby and Association football, in cricket, golf, cycling and cross-country running, received their first impetus towards real consolidation as an Athletic Club by the acquisition of a University field at Corstorphine. Many students, then as now, chose to support the former pupil clubs of the City schools, and various groups within the University continued their independence for several years after the new field was in use. Thus, the Australasians were able to put two good cricket teams in the field, and the South Africans were represented by both Rugby and cricket teams. The West Indians remained separate, and even the Dumfries and Galloway Cricket Club had a considerable reputation, which was closely rivalled by the Medical Jurists.

The possession of a University field, however, served to strengthen gradually the position of the official teams, and an extension of the Inter-University matches attracted a growing number of the best players to the official side so that, in 1887, on the first appearance of a Cambridge Rugby team on Scottish ground, Edinburgh University were able to defeat them in a hard-fought game at Raeburn Place.

In 1889 the first challenge in racing and field events was issued to a team of students in England, and the University in an encounter with the teams of the United Hospitals of London were defeated at Powderhall, Edinburgh, by six events to three.

The players of shinty formed a new section in 1891. In their appeal for new members the game was described as "a combination of the leading qualities of football, cricket and golf." This initial enthusiasm has been maintained in spite of the small membership of the section and the difficulty of obtaining match fixtures.

The slow means of transport in the 'nineties and the attraction for students of clubs possessing playing fields within the City were responsible for the movement towards securing a better and more convenient ground than Corstorphine. By 1896 the sum of £10,000 had been subscribed towards the purchase of the fine field at Craiglockhart. It was formally opened in that year by the Marchioness of Tweeddale. In raising this sum, Principal Sir William Muir gave a valuable lead to the staff and other supporters of University Athletics, many of whom were members of the Extra-academical School of Medicine. It included a grant of £2000 from the University Court in official recognition of the place of athletics in University life. The grant was followed by the establishment of the University Field Committee, which held its first meeting in June 1896, with Professor Annandale as Chairman and C. E. W. Macpherson as Honorary Secretary and Treasurer. In 1898 the Pavilion was opened by General Wauchope of Niddrie.

In 1908 Sir Joseph Montagu Cotterill became Chairman and continued in this post until 1929, when the functions of the Field Committee were taken over by the University Court's Committee on Athletics. This body contains representatives of the University Court, the Senatus, the Students' Athletic Clubs — men's and women's — the Pavilion Section — a group of graduate supporters of the Athletic Club—and the Association of University Teachers. The Secretary of the Athletics' Committee is Colonel Ronald Bruce Campbell, Director of Physical Education, a post which was established in 1929 when the first organised effort was made to provide free medical examination for all students and to offer good facilities for physical training other than games. John L. Somerville is Treasurer of the Athletic Club.

The playing facilities were increased in 1925 by the acquisition of a second field at Craiglockhart.

The sections of the Club are now as follows:—Rugby, Shinty, Hockey, Association, Cricket, Boxing, Tennis, Boating, Hare and Hounds, Sports, Golf and Swimming.

During the past fifty years there have been inevitable changes of fortune in the position of the University teams and in the popularity of the various sections.

Rugby reached a very high level in the famous team of 1900-01 under Andrew B. Flett. With eight internationalists in the side, the *Student* critic seemed to be justified in his statement that "Our representation in international matches this season has never been equalled by any other team and, we make bold to say, never will." Nevertheless, in the following year no fewer than nine members of Alfred N. Fell's team were awarded international caps, including the whole of the back division. Among them the outstanding name of Ernest David Simson appears for the first time.

The Association section has been well maintained, but during the early years of the period of this history it began to suffer, like other amateur clubs, from the steady growth of professionalism which has made a front-rank position virtually impossible for an amateur team in the East of Scotland.

Hockey was started in 1900 and has made steady progress in popularity and strength, with good international representation.

The Tennis section has changed its grounds on several occasions and is now well accommodated on eight first-class courts at The King's Buildings. From 1898 to 1902, in 1911, in 1921 and again in 1932, the first team held a leading position in Scottish tennis. The outstanding event in the history of the Golf section is probably the feat of A. J. Travers Allan in winning the Amateur Golf Championship in 1897, the year after his graduation and only a short time before his death at the early age of twenty-five.

The membership of the other sections has been well maintained on the whole, and all may be said to have succeeded in their object, not of winning championships, but of providing healthy sport and exercise for those who have the wisdom to take advantage of their opportunities.

The Sports section has attained a special distinction in providing several champions and, in particular, has had the honour of sending two such fine runners as Eric Henry Liddell and Frederick Payne Reid to the Olympic Games. Liddell won the 400 metres race at Paris in 1924 and when, in the same summer, he graduated B.Sc., the ceremonial was interrupted in order that the Principal might crown him with a wreath of wild olive, after the manner of the Olympic victors of Ancient Greece.

The Women's Athletic Club may be said to have taken origin in 1898, when the women students of Medicine formed the first Hockey Club in the University. Two years later the Club was formally started and sections for walking and cycling were formed. The Hockey Club ceased to be a purely medical combination. The Women's Club has shown an excellent record of progress. It now possesses a fine playing field at Peffermill, and tennis is played in the combined club on the courts at The King's Buildings. Active sections engage in boating, golf, hockey (four XI's), lacrosse, tennis, sports, swimming and badminton.

The history of each section could be written in full and read with interest by the participants in the various games which go to make up the sound organisation of the two Athletic Clubs. The cycle of events is also of interest—the Assault-at-Arms in the Waverley Market in 1880, reproduced by the Assault in the McEwan Hall in 1929—the gymnasium in the offices of the Students' Representative Council moved to the University Union and now restored again as a University gymnasium, properly planned and equipped in the building adjoining Minto House in Chambers Street. The Athletics' Committee of the Court and the Athletic Club Committee have further schemes in contemplation and, with an increasing number of members taking part in University athletics, a prosperous future is assured for the Club.

APPENDIX I

THE FOUNDATION OF THE COLLEGE OF EDINBURGH

Table of References

1. Knox, *History*, ii., 210.
2. *Extracts from the Burgh Records*, iii., 70.
3. *Extracts*, iii., 105.
4. *Extracts*, iii., 145.
5. Register of Privy Seal, xxx., f. 47: Jan. 23, 1561-2.
6. *Extracts*, iii., 158, 163, 171, 182.
7. *Extracts*, iii., 132, 145.
8. Register of Privy Seal, xxxi., f. 84: March 16, 1562-3.
9. *Extracts*, iii., 182.
10. Sederunt Book of Session (Reg. Ho.), June 14, 1561.
11. Edinburgh Commissary Decreets (Reg. Ho.), i., f. 53: June 10, 1564.
12. *Register of Privy Council*, i., 528: May 4, 1576.
13. Knox, *History*, ii., 298, 311.
14. Calderwood, *History*, ii., 242.
15. *Extracts*, iii., 174, 191.
16. Calderwood, *History*, ii., 287.
17. *Extracts*, iii., 207.
18. Register of Privy Seal, xxxiii., f. 110: Oct. 4, 1565.
19. *Extracts*, iii., 208, 210.
20. Calderwood, *History*, ii., 498.
21. *Register of Privy Council*, i., 487, 494: Calderwood, *History*, ii., 329.
22. *Register of Privy Council*, i., 497.
23. Register of Privy Seal, xxxvi., f. 71 ff.
24. Register of Privy Seal, xxxvi., f. 25.
25. Register of Privy Seal, xxxv., f. 95.
26. Collector-General's Account (Reg. Ho.), Jan. 1567-8.
27. *Wodrow Miscellany*, i., 326.
28. *Glasgow Charters*, Jan. 26, 1572-3.
29. *Report of University Commissioners* (1837), iii., app. 187.
30. *Extracts*, iv., 10, 46, 56.
31. Acts and Decreets (Reg. Ho.), lxvi., f. 342: *Extracts*, iv. 27.
32. *Book of the Universal Kirk*, April 1576.
33. *Register of Privy Council*, ii., 528.

34. *Extracts*, iv., 63, 74-5.
35. *Extracts*, iv., 109.
36. Calderwood, *History*, iii., 446.
37. *Acts of Parliament*, iii., 178.
38. *Extracts*, iv., 103.
39. *Registrum Magni Sigilli*, iv., 1802.
40. Calderwood, *History*, ii., 399.
41. *Extracts*, iv., 105.
42. *Extracts*, iv., 127, 136.
43. *Acts of Parliament*, iii., 137.
44. City Charters.
45. Register of Presentations to Benefices (Reg. Ho.), ii., f. 26.
46. *Extracts*, iv., 557, 200.
47. *Extracts*, iv., 198.
48. *Extracts*, iv., 200.
49. Register of Presentations to Benefices (Reg. Ho.), March 18, 1580-1: Town Council Minutes (MS.), March 30, 1581.
50. Register of Privy Seal, xlvii., f. 99.
51. *Extracts*, iv., 211, 230.
52. Acts and Decreets (Reg. Ho.) lxxxviii., f. 257.
53. *Extracts*, iv., 562.
54. *Acts of Parliament*, iii., 214. There was a bill about a college in Orkney, possibly concerned with a bequest by Reid.
55. Calderwood, *History*, iii., 577-8. Craufurd did not investigate these facts with any care. He was wrong in supposing that the Crown made a grant or promise in 1580, and in connecting Clement Litil's bequest of his books in that year with the inception of the College. The library was given to the Town and kirk (*Extracts*, iv., 181), accommodated in Lawson's house, and transferred to the College in September 1584, when Lawson had gone (*ibid.*, 349-50; *cf.* 382), but intended in 1588 to be replaced in the ministers' lodging (*ibid.*, 518). No doubt Lawson had much to do with the College scheme; but he was certainly not a *persona grata* at court when the charter was obtained.
56. Craufurd, *History*, 85: according to a royal letter (City Charters, July 25, 1617) it is to be King James's College, "as we gave the first being and beginning thereto."
57. *Register of Privy Council*, iii., 472.
58. *Extracts*, v., 90. For the complicated fortunes of the Strathnaver property, see *The Book of Mackay*.
59. The signature, in vernacular, is in the Register of Presentations to Benefices (Reg. Ho.), ii., f. 72.
60. *Registrum Magni Sigilli*, v., 688.

61. In 1587, when James came of age, the burgh had a charter (City Charters, July 29) ratifying mortifications as excluded from the royal revocation and from the Act of Parliament annexing Kirklands to the Crown.
62. Grant, *The Story of the University*, i., 107-121.
63. Town Council Minutes (MS.), Nov. 7, 1582.
64. Acts and Decreets (Reg. Ho.), lxxxviii., f. 257.
65. Town Council Minutes (MS.) Nov. 7, 1582: Feb. 20, 1582-3.
66. Town Council Minutes (MS.), March 29, 1583; *Extracts*, iv., 571.
67. Register of Privy Seal, xlix., f. 158 (Aug. 18, 1583): cf. *Extracts*, iv., 331: *Acts of Parliament*, iii., 318.
68. *Extracts*, iv., 457, 466, 478: 305.
69. Register of Presentations to Benefices (Reg. Ho.), ii., f. 101: signature for Trinity College on f. 134.
70. *St Andrews University Publications*, vii., 102.
71. *Extracts*, iv., 499.
72. Papers on pecuniary affairs of Session (Reg. Ho.).
73. Sederunt Book of Session (Reg. Ho.), Jan. 16, 1588-9: *Extracts*, iv., 535.
74. *Extracts*, v., 15.
75. McCrie, *Melville*, ch. v., note DD.
76. *Schediasmata* (Waldegrave, 1590). In his *Du Bartas* (Edin. 1600) Damman describes himself as of Fairhill and as *regium in Scotia historiæ et humanitatis professorem.*
77. Register of Deeds (Reg. Ho.), lxi., Jan. 4, 1597-8.
78. *Scottish Historical Review*, xxiii., 209.
79. *Extracts*, v., 10: *Letters, etc., of James VI.* (Abbotsford Club), 23.
80. Sederunt Book of Session (Reg. Ho.), July 26, 1591.
81. *Extracts*, v., 115-6, 131, 134.
82. Register of Deeds (Reg. Ho.), lxi., Jan. 4, 1597-8. In 1648 (Sederunt Book of Session, June 18, 1687) owing to increased cost of living and excessive number of bursars, the interest of £3000, now £240 instead of £300, was devoted entirely to a Regent of Humanity.

APPENDIX II

BIOGRAPHICAL NOTES OF THE PROFESSORS, READERS, LECTURERS

1883-1933*

Adams, David Laird, Professor of Hebrew, 1880-92; *b.* Woodside, Blairgowrie, 18th Feb. 1837; *educ.* Blairgowrie Parish School, Church of Scotland Training Coll. Edinburgh, Edin. Univ., and in Germany; M.A. Edin. 1870; B.D. Edin. 1870; ordained to St David's Chapel in Parish of St Cuthbert, Edin., 1871; Minister of Monimail, Fife, 1875; conducted Divinity classes in Edin. Univ., 1874-76; *d.* 2nd Aug. 1892.

Affleck, Sir James Ormiston, Lecturer in Infective Diseases, 1904-08; *b.* Edinburgh, 1840; *educ.* Edin. Univ.; Kt. 1911; M.B., C.M. Edin. 1867; M.D. Edin. 1869; LL.D. Edin. 1908; F.R.C.P. Edin. 1875; Assistant to Sir Douglas Maclagan (*q.v.*), 1869; Assist. Physician, Physician 1885, and Cons. Physician, Roy. Infirm., Edin.; Cons. Physician, City Hosp. for Infective Diseases, and Roy. Maternity Hosp., Edin.; *d.* Edinburgh, 24th Sept. 1922.

Ainsworth, Alfred Richard, Lecturer in Greek, 1903-08; *educ.* Dulwich Coll., King's Coll. Cambridge; B.A. 1902; appointed to Board of Education, London, 1908; now Principal Assistant Secretary.

Aitken, Andrew Peebles, Lecturer in Agricultural Chemistry, 1894-1904; *b.* Edinburgh; *educ.* Edin. and Heidelberg Univs.; M.A. Edin. 1867; B.Sc. Edin. 1871; D.Sc. Edin. 1873; F.I.C.; Assistant to Professor Crum Brown (*q.v.*) and Demonstrator in Practical Chemistry; Professor of Chemistry and Toxicology, Roy. (Dick) Veterinary Coll., Edin., 1875-1904; *d.* Edinburgh, 17th Apr. 1904.

Aitken, Henry, Lecturer 1908-22, Reader 1922-28, in Mercantile Law; *b.* 1851; *educ.* Ayr Acad., Univs. of Edin. and Glasg.; qualified as law agent, 1876; Partner of Wright, Johnston & Mackenzie, writers, Glasgow, 1881; Advocate, Scots Bar, 1889; K.C. 1903; *d.* Edinburgh, 18th Sept. 1931.

* This list does not include present holders of office, nor does it contain former lecturers who are at present members of the Clinical Teaching Staff of the Royal Infirmary.

APPENDIX II

Allen, Herbert Stanley, Lecturer 1919-20, Reader 1920-23, in Natural Philosophy; *b.* Bodmin, Cornwall, 29th Dec. 1873; *educ.* Kingswood School Bath, Trinity Coll. Cambridge; B.A. Camb. 1896, M.A. 1900; B.Sc. Lond. 1896; D.Sc. Lond. 1909; F.R.S. 1930; Superintendent of Blythswood Laboratory, Renfrew, 1900-5; Lecturer in Physics, King's Coll., London, 1905; Professor of Natural Philosophy and Director of Physics Research Laboratory, St Andrews Univ., since 1923.

Anderson, John, Lecturer in Logic and Metaphysics, 1920-27; M.A. Glasg. 1917; Professor of Philosophy, Sydney Univ., since 1927.

Andrew, James, Lecturer in Clinical Instruction on Diseases of Children, 1885-88; *educ.* Edin. Univ., Vienna, Berlin; M.B., C.M. Edin. 1866; M.D. Edin. 1868; M.R.C.P. Edin. 1869; F.R.C.P. Edin. 1870; Physician, Roy. Dispensary, Roy. Blind Asylum, Roy. Hosp. for Sick Children, Edin.; *d.* Edinburgh, 19th Sept. 1911.

Annandale, Thomas, Regius Professor of Clinical Surgery, 1877-1907; *b.* Newcastle-on-Tyne, 2nd Feb. 1838; *educ.* Bruce's Acad. Newcastle, Edin. Univ.; M.D. Edin. 1860; Hon. D.C.L. Durham 1902; M.R.C.S. Eng. 1859; F.R.C.S. Edin. 1863; F.R.C.S. Eng. 1888; House Surgeon to Professor Syme, 1861 and 1862; Junior Demonstrator in Anatomy, Edin. Univ., 1863; Lecturer on principles of surgery in the extra-academical school, Edin., 1863-71; Lecturer on clinical surgery, Roy. Infirm., Edin., 1871; Assist. Surgeon 1865-71, Acting Surgeon (latterly Senior) 1871-1907, Roy. Infirm., Edin.; *d.* Edinburgh, 20th Dec. 1907.

Armstrong, George Frederick, Regius Professor of Engineering, 1885-1900; *b.* Doncaster, 15th May 1842; *educ.* privately, King's Coll. London, Jesus Coll. Cambridge; M.A. Camb. 1864; M. Inst. C.E.; Fellow of King's Coll. London, 1889; on Engineering staff, Great Northern Railway, 1863-68; Engineer for Isle of Man railways, etc., 1868-71; first Professor of Engineering, McGill Univ., Montreal, 1871-76; first Professor of Engineering, Leeds Univ. Coll., 1876-85; *d.* Grasmere, 16th Nov. 1900.

Bailey, Frederick, Lecturer in Forestry, 1892-1910; LL.D. Edin. 1912; military service in Bhutan, India, 1864-65; attached to Indian Forest Service, 1871; in charge of the Survey Branch of the Department till 1884; Conservator of Forests, 1878; organised the Central Forest School, of which he was the first Director till 1884; in charge of English students at the French Forest School at Nancy, 1884-87; Conservator of the Punjab Forests, 1887; twice appointed Inspector-General of Forests; returned to this country owing to illness; Secretary of the Roy. Scottish Geographical Soc., 1892-1903; *d.* 21st Dec. 1912.

Baillie, Donald Macpherson, Lecturer in Moral Philosophy, 1911-13; *b.* Gairloch, Ross-shire, 5th Nov. 1887; *educ.* Inverness High School, Inverness Roy. Acad., Edin. Univ., New Coll. Edin., Marburg and Heidelberg Univs.; M.A. Edin. 1909; D.D. St And. 1933; ordained

Minister, United Free Church of Scotland, 1918; Minister of U.F. Church, Bervie, Kincardineshire, 1918-23, of St John's Church, Cupar, 1923-30, of St Columba Church, Kilmacolm, since 1930; Kerr Lecturer, United Free Church of Scotland, 1924-27.

BAKER, Bevan Braithwaite, Lecturer in Mathematics, 1920-24; *b.* 1890; *educ.* Sidcot School, Somerset, Univs. of London and Munich; M.A. Lond. 1914; B.Sc. Lond. 1909, 1912; D.Sc. Edin. 1923; Assistant in Mathematics, Univ. Coll., London, 1918-20; Professor of Mathematics, London Univ., and Head of the Dept. of Mathematics, Roy. Holloway Coll., London Univ., since 1924.

BALFOUR, Sir Isaac Bayley, Regius Professor of Botany, 1888-1922; *b.* Edinburgh, 31st Mar. 1853; *educ.* Edin. Acad., Edin. Univ., Univs. of Strassburg and Würzburg; K.B.E. 1920; B.Sc. Edin. 1873; D.Sc. Edin. 1875; M.B., C.M. Edin. 1877; M.D. Edin. 1883; LL.D. Edin. 1922; Fellow of Magdalen Coll., Oxford, 1884; on *Transit of Venus* Expedition to Rodriguez, 1874; on expedition to Socotra 1880, to Japan and China 1909-10; Professor of Botany, Glasgow Univ., 1879-84; Sherardian Professor of Botany, Oxford, 1884-88; King's Botanist for Scotland; *d.* Haslemere, 30th Nov. 1922.

BALLANTYNE, John William, Lecturer in Midwifery (to women), 1916-23; *b.* Eskbank, Dalkeith, 4th June 1861; *educ.* Bonnington Park School Peebles, George Watson's Coll. Edin., Edin. Univ.; M.B., C.M. 1883; M.D. 1889; F.R.C.P. Edin. 1888; Senior Assistant in Midwifery, Edin. Univ., 1885-90; Lecturer on midwifery and gynæcology in the extra-academical school, Edin., 1890-1916; Assist. Physician 1900-4, and Physician 1904-19, Roy. Maternity Hosp., Edin.; *d.* Edinburgh, 23rd Jan. 1923.

BALSILLIE, David, Lecturer in Chemistry, 1918-22; D.Sc.

BARBOUR, Alexander Hugh Freeland, Lecturer in Systematic and Clinical Gynæcology, 1906-22; *b.* Edinburgh, 7th Jan. 1856; *educ.* Edin. Instit., Collegiate School Edin., privately, Edin. Univ.; M.A. Edin. 1874; B.Sc. Edin. 1877; M.B., C.M. Edin. 1879; M.D. Edin. 1883; LL.D. Toronto 1906; LL.D. Edin. 1925; F.R.C.P. Edin. 1883 (Pres. 1914-16); Gynæcologist, Roy. Infirm., 1906-21, and Obstetric Physician, Roy. Maternity Hosp., Edin., 1899-1914; *d.* Edinburgh, 11th June 1927.

BARTHOLOMEW, Mary (Mrs Widdowson), Lecturer in Botany, Apr.-Dec. 1921; *b.* Duntarvie, West Lothian, 17th Dec. 1887; *educ.* Edinburgh Ladies' Coll., Edin. Univ.; B.Sc. 1910; Botany Mistress, West Leeds High School, 1911 to Dec. 1914; Senior Science Mistress, St George's High School, Edin., Jan. 1915 to Dec. 1916; Lecturer in Botany, City of Leeds Training Coll., 1917-20; Senior Lecturer in Botany, West of Scotland Agricultural Coll., 1920-21; *m.* Dec. 1921; Matron of Kingswood Training School, Bristol, since 1925.

APPENDIX II

Beard, John, Lecturer in Comparative Embryology, 1894-95, in Embryology and Vertebrate Zoology, 1895-1910, in Comparative Embryology and Vertebrate Morphology, 1910-20; *b.* 1858; *educ.* Owens Coll. Manchester, Roy. Coll. of Science London, Univs. of Würzburg and Freiburg; D.Sc.; Ph.D.; Naturalist at the Scottish Fishery Board's Laboratory, Dunbar; Assistant in Zoology, Edin. Univ., 1890-94; *d.* Edinburgh, 4th Dec. 1924.

Beattie, James Martin, Lecturer in Pathological Bacteriology, 1901-7; *b.* Alexandra, New Zealand, 31st May 1868; *educ.* Alexandra Public School, Arthur St. Public School, Dunedin, Otago Univ., Edin. Univ., Univ. Coll. London; M.A. N.Z. 1889; M.B., C.M. Edin. 1894; M.D. Edin. 1901; M.R.C.S. Eng. and L.R.C.P. Lond. 1899; Second Assistant in Pathology, Edin. Univ., 1898; Univ. Clin. Tutor, Roy. Infirm., 1899; Senior Assistant in Pathology, Edin. Univ., Feb. 1901; Assist. Pathologist, Roy. Infirm., Edin., 1902-5; Professor of Pathology and Bacteriology and Dean of the Medical Faculty, Sheffield Univ., 1907-12; Professor of Bacteriology (and Dean of the Faculty of Medicine, 1914-17), Liverpool Univ. and City Bacteriologist, Liverpool, since 1912.

Berry, Sir George Andreas, Lecturer in Diseases of the Eye, 1896-1905; *b.* Leith, 1853; *educ.* Edin. Acad., Marlborough, Edin. Univ., London, Paris, Vienna, Copenhagen, and Giessen; Kt. 1916; M.B., C.M. Edin. 1876; LL.D. St And. 1911 and Edin. 1931; F.R.C.S. Edin. 1881 (Pres. 1910-12); Pres., Ophthalmological Soc. of the United Kingdom; Ophthalmic Surgeon, Roy. Infirm., Edin., 1890-1905; Hon. Surgeon Oculist to H.M. in Scotland; Member of Edin. Univ. Court, 1911-23; M.P. (Conservative) for the Scottish Universities, 1922-31.

Bews, John William, Lecturer in Plant Physiology, 1908-10; *b.* Kirkwall, Orkney, 16th Dec. 1884; *educ.* Kirkwall Burgh School, Edin. Univ.; M.A. 1906; B.Sc. 1907; D.Sc. 1912; F.L.S.; F.R.S.S.A.; Lecturer in Economic Botany, Manchester Univ., 1907-8; Professor of Botany, Armstrong Coll., Durham Univ., Newcastle-on-Tyne, 1926-27; Professor of Botany, Natal Univ. Coll., Pietermaritzburg, South Africa, 1910-25 and since 1927, and Principal since 1930; Dean of the Faculty of Science, 1921, Chairman of the Senate, 1922-24, Univ. of South Africa.

Borthwick, Albert William, Lecturer in Plant Physiology, 1898-1908, in Forest Botany, 1908-15; O.B.E.; B.Sc. St And. 1895; D.Sc. St And. 1904; Chief Research Officer and Education Officer to the Forestry Commission; Professor of Forestry, Aberdeen Univ., since 1926.

Boyd, Francis Darby, Moncrieff Arnott Professor of Clinical Medicine, 1919-22; *b.* Edinburgh, 19th Oct. 1866; *educ.* Edin. Acad., Edin. Univ., Berlin and Prague; C.B. 1919; C.M.G. 1901; M.B., C.M. Edin. 1888; M.D. Edin. 1893; M.R.C.P. Edin. 1891; F.R.C.P. Edin. 1892; Assist. Physician 1899, Physician, Roy. Infirm., Edin., 1913-22; Lecturer on materia medica and therapeutics in extra-academical school, Edin.; Physician Deaconess Hosp., Edin.; Senior Lecturer in Clinical Medicine, Edin. Univ., 1913-19; *d.* Edinburgh, 4th April 1922.

BIOGRAPHICAL NOTES

Brennan, Hugh George, Lecturer in Russian, 1919-24; *b.* Plymouth, 21st June 1873; *educ.* privately, London Univ., Petrograd; B.A. Lond. 1911; M.A. Lond. 1914; L. ès L. Petrograd 1913; B.Sc. Imperial Oriental Acad., Petrograd, 1910; Professor of English Literature, 1910-17, and Professor of French Language, 1912-17, Imperial Alexander Lyceum, Petrograd; Professor of English Language and Literature, Imperial Oriental Acad., Petrograd, 1912-17; Lecturer in Russian Language and Literature, Glasgow Univ., since 1917, Glasgow and West of Scotland Commercial Coll., Glasgow, since 1919.

Brewis, Nathaniel Thomas, Lecturer 1913-17, Senior Lecturer 1917-21, in Clinical Gynæcology; *b.* Northumberland, 1856; *educ.* Edin. Instit., Edin. Univ.; M.B., C.M. Edin. 1882; F.R.C.P. Edin. 1887; F.R.C.S. Edin. 1899; extra-academical lecturer on obstetrics and gynæcology, Edin., 1889-1921; Gynæcologist, New Town Dispensary and Leith Hosp.; Gynæcologist, Roy. Infirm., Edin., 1906-21; *d.* Edinburgh, 1924.

Brink, Raymond W., Lecturer in Mathematics, 1919-20; M.A.; Ph.D.

Broadwood, Robert Grant, Lecturer in Forest Engineering, 1922-25; *b.* Edinburgh, 1895; *educ.* George Heriot's School Edin. 1904-13, Edin. Univ. 1913-15, 1918-19; B.Sc. 1919; Indian Forest Service, United Provinces, 1919-22; Forestry Commission, Forest of Dean, since 1925.

Brook, George, Lecturer in Comparative Embryology, 1885-93; *b.* 1857; *educ.* Owens Coll. Manchester; F.L.S.; Scientific Assistant to the Scottish Fishery Board, 1884-87; *d.* 1893.

Brown, Alexander Crum, Professor of Chemistry, 1869-1908; *b.* Edinburgh, 26th Mar. 1838; *educ.* Roy. High School Edin., Mill Hill School, Univs. of Edin., Heidelberg and Marburg; M.A. Edin. 1858; M.D. Edin. 1861; D.Sc. Lond. 1862; LL.D. (Aberd. 1893, Glasg. 1905, Edin. 1909 and St And. 1911); F.R.C.P. Edin. 1865; F.R.S. 1879; F.C.S.; F.I.C.; extra-academical lecturer on chemistry, Edin., 1863-69; Member of Edin. Univ. Court, 1889-1908; *d.* Edinburgh, 28th Oct. 1922.

Brown, Gerard Baldwin, Watson-Gordon Professor of Fine Art, 1880-1930; *b.* London, 31st Oct. 1849; *educ.* Uppingham School, Oriel Coll. Oxford; M.A. Oxf. 1876; LL.D. St And. 1924 and Edin. 1930; Hon. D.Litt. Durham 1931; F.B.A. 1924; Hon. R.S.A.; Fellow of Brasenose Coll., Oxford, 1874; Hon. Fellow of Oriel Coll., Oxford; Munro Lecturer in Archæology, Edin. Univ., 1926; *d.* Edinburgh, 12th July 1932.

Brown, John James Graham, Lecturer in Neurology, 1912-20, and Senior Lecturer in Clinical Medicine, 1913-19; *b.* Edinburgh, 1854; *educ.* Begbie's School Edin., Edin. Acad., Edin. Univ., Paris, Berlin, Vienna and Prague; M.B., C.M. Edin. 1875; M.D. Edin. 1878; F.R.C.P. Edin. 1882 (Pres. 1912-14); began to practise 1878; Member of the Commission sent to Spain to study the cholera epidemic, 1885; Assist. Physician 1897, Physician 1912-19, Roy. Infirm., Edin.; *d.* Edinburgh, 28th Feb. 1925.

APPENDIX II

Brown, Peter Hume, Sir William Fraser Professor of Ancient History (Scottish) and Palæography, 1901-18; *b.* Tranent, 17th Dec. 1849; *educ.* Prestonpans Free Church School, Edin. Univ.; M.A. Edin. 1878; LL.D. Edin. 1896 and St And. 1906; D.D. Geneva 1909; F.B.A. 1909; Historiographer Royal for Scotland, 1908-18; Rhind Lecturer, Edin. Univ., 1903; *d.* Edinburgh, 1st Dec. 1918.

Brown, William, Lecturer in Plant Physiology, 1910-12; *b.* Dumfriesshire, 1888; *educ.* Annan Acad., Edin. Univ.; M.A. Edin. 1908; D.Sc. Lond. 1916; engaged in research at the Imperial Coll. of Science and Technology, London, and for the Department of Scientific and Industrial Research, and for the Ministry of Agriculture; Assistant Professor of Plant Pathology, London Univ., at the Imperial Coll. of Science and Technology, 1923, and Professor since 1928.

Browne, Francis James, Lecturer in Clinical Midwifery, 1923-27; *b.* 1st Oct. 1879; *educ.* Roy. School Raphoe, Foyle Coll. Londonderry, Aberdeen Univ.; M.B., Ch.B. Aberd. 1906; M.D. Aberd. 1919; D.Sc. Edin. 1925; F.R.C.S. Edin. 1914; in general practice in Wales, 1906; Research Pathologist (and Assistant Physician, 1923), Roy. Maternity Hosp., Edin., 1919-26; Professor of Obstetric Medicine, Lond. Univ., Director of the Obstetric Unit, Univ. Coll. Hosp. Medical School, Obstetric Surgeon, Univ. Coll. Hosp., since 1927.

Bruce, William, Lecturer in Agriculture, 1920-22; B.Sc. 1900; M.A.

Buchanan, George, Lecturer in Bacteriology, 1925-26; *b.* Edinburgh, 1882; M.B., Ch.B. Edin. 1918; M.D. Edin. 1925; D.P.H. Edin. and Glasg. 1924; Superintendent, South African Instit. for Medical Research, Johannesburg.

Burn-Murdoch, Hector, Lecturer in English Law, 1912-23; *b.* Edinburgh, 30th Mar. 1881; *educ.* Merchiston Castle School 1892-96, Trinity Coll. Cambridge; B.A. Camb. 1902; LL.B. Camb. 1903; LL.B. Edin. 1905; Advocate, Scots Bar, 1905; Barrister-at-Law, Inner Temple, 1907; Advocate-Depute in the Sheriff Court, 1923; Extra Advocate-Depute, 1924; Advocate-Depute, 1926; Sheriff-Substitute of Berwickshire at Duns since 1927.

Burn-Murdoch, Thomas Monck, Lecturer in Clinical Instruction on Diseases of Children, 1900-1907; *b.* Edinburgh, 1855; *educ.* Begbie's School Edin., Bryce's E. Coll. School Edin., Edin. Univ.; M.B., C.M. Edin. 1877; F.R.C.P. Edin. 1899; Physician 1889-1906, now Cons. Physician, Roy. Hosp. for Sick Children, Edinburgh.

Burnet, George Wardlaw, Lecturer in International Private Law, 1894-99; *b.* 1853; *educ.* Collegiate School, Glasgow Univ., Edinburgh and Heidelberg; M.A.; B.L. Glasg. 1876; Advocate, Scots Bar, 1878; Sheriff-Substitute of Aberdeen, Kincardine, and Banff, at Aberdeen, 1898-1901; *d.* Aberdeen, 31st Jan. 1901.

BIOGRAPHICAL NOTES

Burrage, J. H., Lecturer in Plant Physiology, 1898-99; M.A.; Assistant in Botany, Edin. Univ., 1894-98.

Butcher, Samuel Henry, Professor of Greek, 1882-1903; *b.* Dublin, 16th Apr. 1850; *educ.* Marlborough, Trinity Coll. Cambridge; B.A. Camb. 1873, M.A. 1876; Hon. D.Litt. Camb. 1907 and Dublin 1892; Hon. Litt.D. Manchester 1906; Hon. D.Litt. Oxf. 1903; LL.D. (Glasg. 1885, Edin. 1904, and St And. 1906); F.B.A. 1902; Fellow of Trinity Coll., Cambridge, 1874-76; Fellow of Univ. Coll., Oxford, and Lecturer, 1876-82; Hon. Fellow, Univ. Coll., Oxford; Member of the Scottish Universities Commission, 1889-96; Member of the Roy. Commission on University Education in Ireland, 1901; Member of the Roy. Commission on Trinity Coll., Dublin, 1906; Unionist M.P. for Cambridge University, 1906-10; Trustee of the British Museum, 1908; Member of Edin. Univ. Court, 1891-1901; *d.* London, 29th Dec. 1910.

Caird, Francis Mitchell, Regius Professor of Clinical Surgery, 1908-19; *b.* Edinburgh, 1853; *educ.* Roy. High School Edin., Edin. Univ., Strassburg; M.B., C.M. Edin. 1877; LL.D. Edin. 1920; F.R.C.S. Edin. (Pres. 1912-14); Demonstrator of anatomy, extra-academical school, Edin., 1879-82; Assistant in Surgery, Edin. Univ., 1882-85; Lecturer on systematic surgery, extra-academical school, Edin., 1886-1908; Assist. Surgeon 1885-1903, Surgeon 1903-19, Cons. Surgeon 1919-26, Roy. Infirm., Edin.; *d.* Edinburgh, 1st Nov. 1926.

Calderwood, Henry, Professor of Moral Philosophy, 1868-97; *b.* Peebles, 10th May 1830; *educ.* Circus Place School, Edin. Instit., Roy. High School Edin., Edin. Univ., United Presbyterian Church Theological Hall; LL.D. Glasg. 1865; Minister of Greyfriars' Church, Glasgow, 1856-68; Chairman of Edin. School Board, 1873-77; Member, Edin. Univ. Court, 1892-97; *d.* Edinburgh, 19th Nov. 1897.

Cameron, Archibald, Lecturer in Latin, 1927-31; *b.* 4th Jan. 1902; *educ.* Glasgow Univ., Sorbonne, Balliol Coll. Oxford; M.A. Glasg. 1921; Diplôme d'Études Supérieures, Sorbonne, 1922; B.A. Oxf. 1925; Assistant in Latin, Aberdeen Univ., 1924-27; Regius Professor of Greek, Aberdeen Univ., since 1931.

Cameron, Thomas Wright Moir, Lecturer in Helminthology, 1929-32; *b.* Glasgow, 29th Apr. 1894; *educ.* Allan Glen's School Glasg., Univs. of Glasg., Edin. and London, Roy. (Dick) Veterinary Coll. Edin.; M.A. Edin. 1921; B.Sc. Edin. 1921; Ph.D. Edin. 1923; D.Sc. Edin. 1927; M.R.C.V.S.; engaged in research, 1921-25; Lecturer and Milner Fellow in the Dept. of Helminthology, London School of Hygiene and Tropical Medicine, 1925-29; Professor of Parasitology and Director of Research Instit. of Animal Parasitology, McGill Univ., Montreal, since 1932.

APPENDIX II

CANO, Baldomero Sanin, Lecturer in Spanish, 1919-20; *b.* Rionegro, Colombia, 27th June 1861; *educ.* Normal School of Antisquia, Colombia; Professor at Normal School of Antisquia; Under-Secretary of Finance in Colombia, 1905-9; Member of the National Assembly, Colombia, 1905 and 1907; Consul-General for Colombia in London, 1911; Member of Congress, 1923; General Representative for La Nación of Buenos Aires in Spain.

CARLIER, Edmond William Wace, Lecturer in Experimental Physiology and Histology, 1894-96, and in Advanced Physiology, 1896-99; *b.* Norwich, 1861; *educ.* King Edward the Sixth's School Norwich, Lycée de Valenciennes France, Edin. Univ.; B.-ès-S. Univ. France 1882; M.B., C.M. Edin. 1886; M.D. Edin. 1891; M.Sc. Birm. 1901; F.E.S.; Assistant in Physiology, Edin. Univ., 1886-94; Professor of Physiology, Birmingham Univ., 1899-1927; Emeritus Professor since 1927.

CARMICHAEL, James, Lecturer in Instruction on Diseases of Children, 1885-99; *b.* Edinburgh, 23rd Aug. 1843; *educ.* Edin. Acad., Edin. Instit., Edin. Univ., Berlin, Vienna; M.D. Edin. 1864; Physician 1882-98, and Cons. Physician, Roy. Hosp. for Sick Children, Edinburgh; *d.* Edinburgh, 24th July 1933.

CARROTHERS, William Alexander, Lecturer in Political Economy, 1920-21; B.A. Manitoba 1916; Ph.D. Edin. 1921; Professor of Economics, Univ. of Saskatchewan, Saskatoon, Canada, 1921-31.

CATHCART, Charles Walker, Senior Lecturer in Clinical Surgery, 1913-17; *b.* Edinburgh, 1853; *educ.* Edin. Collegiate School, Loretto, Edin. Univ.; C.B.E. 1919; M.A. 1873; M.B., C.M. 1878; L.R.C.S. Edin. 1878; F.R.C.S. Eng. 1879; F.R.C.S. Edin. 1880; Lecturer in Anatomy, Surgeons' Hall, Edin., 1881-85; Assist. Surgeon 1884, Surgeon 1901, Cons. Surgeon, Roy. Infirm., Edin.; Conservator of the Museum of the Roy. Coll. of Surgeons, Edin., 1887-1900; Lieut.-Col., R.A.M.C. (T.F.) at 2nd Scottish General Hosp., at Edin. War Hosp., and at Edenhall Hostel for Limbless Sailors and Soldiers, 1914-19; *d.* Edinburgh, 22nd Feb. 1932.

CHARTERIS, Archibald Hamilton, Regius Professor of Biblical Criticism, 1868-98; *b.* Wamphray, 13th Dec. 1835; *educ.* Wamphray School, Edin. Univ., Tübingen, Bonn; B.A. Edin. 1852; M.A. Edin. 1854; D.D. Edin. 1868; LL.D. Edin. 1899; D.D. Aberd. 1906; licensed by Edinburgh Presbytery, 1858; Minister of St Quivox, Ayrshire, 1858, of New Abbey, 1859, of Park Parish, Glasgow, 1863; one of Her Majesty's Chaplains for Scotland, 1867; Chaplain in Ordinary to the King in Scotland, 1901; Moderator of the General Assembly of the Church of Scotland, 1892; Dean of the Faculty of Divinity, Edin. Univ., 1875-84; *d.* Edinburgh, 24th Apr. 1908.

BIOGRAPHICAL NOTES

Chiene, John, Professor of Surgery, 1882-1909; *b.* Edinburgh, 25th Feb. 1843; *educ.* Mr Hunter's School Edin., Edin. Acad., Edin. Univ., Paris, Berlin, Vienna; C.B. 1900; M.D. Edin. 1865; Hon. D.Sc. Sheffield 1908; LL.D. Glasg. 1901 and Edin. 1910; F.R.C.S. 1868 (Pres. 1897-99); Demonstrator in Anatomy, Edin. Univ., 1866-70; extra-academical lecturer on surgery, Edin., 1870; Assist. Surgeon 1871, Surgeon 1878, Roy. Infirm., Edin.; *d.* Edinburgh, 29th May 1923.

Chisholm, George Goudie, Lecturer 1908-20, Reader 1920-23, in Geography; *b.* Edinburgh, 1st May 1850; *educ.* Roy. High School Edin., Edin. Univ.; M.A. Edin. 1870; B.Sc. Edin. 1883; LL.D. Edin. 1924; University Extension Lecturer, London, 1895-1908; *d.* Edinburgh, 9th Feb. 1930.

Chisholm, John, Lecturer in English Law, 1923-29; *b.* Perth, 1857; *educ.* Perth Acad., Madras Coll. St Andrews, Univs. of Edin. and Leipzig; M.A. Edin. 1878; LL.B. Edin. 1881; Advocate, Scots Bar, 1881; Barrister-at-Law, Middle Temple, 1883; K.C. 1904; Advocate-Depute, 1896-98; Sheriff of Chancery (Scotland), 1898-1905; Interim Sheriff of Fife and Kinross, 1900; Sheriff of Roxburgh, Berwick and Selkirk, 1905-29; *d.* Edinburgh, 31st Jan. 1929.

Chrystal, George, Professor of Mathematics, 1879-1911; *b.* Aberdeenshire, 8th March 1851; *educ.* Aberdeen Grammar School, Aberd. Univ., Peterhouse Cambridge; M.A. Aberd. 1871; B.A. Camb. 1875, M.A. 1878; LL.D. Aberd. 1887 and Glasg. 1911; Fellow (afterwards Hon. Fellow) and Lecturer of Corpus Christi Coll., Cambridge; Professor of Mathematics, St Andrews Univ., 1877-79; Dean of the Faculty of Arts, Edin. Univ., 1890-1911; first Chairman of Edinburgh Committee for Training of Teachers till 1909; *d.* Edinburgh, 3rd Nov. 1911.

Clark, Archibald Brown, Lecturer in Economics, 1901-10; *b.* West Linton, Peeblesshire, 1864; *educ.* West Linton Public School, Heriot School (Abbeyhill) Edin., Edin. Univ.; M.A. 1890; Assistant in Political Economy, Edin. Univ., 1899-1910; Professor of Political Economy, Manitoba Univ., Winnipeg, since 1910.

Clark, Robert James, Lecturer in Physics, 1927-32; Ph.D. Camb. 1927.

Clouston, Sir Thomas Smith, Lecturer in Mental Diseases, 1879-1910; *b.* Orkney, 22nd Apr. 1840; *educ.* Aberdeen, Edin. Univ.; Kt. 1911; M.D. Edin. 1861; LL.D. Aberd. 1907 and Edin. 1911; L.R.C.S. 1860; F.R.C.P. Edin. 1873 (Pres. 1902-3); Assist. Physician, Morningside Asylum, Edin., 1861; Superintendent, Cumberland and Westmoreland Asylum, Carlisle, 1863-73; Physician Superintendent, Roy. Edin. Asylum, 1873-1908; *d.* Edinburgh, 19th April 1915.

Coldstream, John P., Lecturer in Civil Procedure in the Courts of Law, Scotland, 1884-95; Writer to the Signet, 1866; Principal Clerk of Session, Scotland; *d.* *c.* 1908.

APPENDIX II

Cook, John James, Lecturer in Procedure and Evidence, 1895-1901; *b.* Pittenweem, 1864; *educ.* Pittenweem School, Edin. Acad., Edin. Univ., Freiburg Univ.; M.A. Edin. 1883; LL.B. Edin. 1887; Advocate, Scots Bar, 1889; Secretary, Boundary Commission for Scotland, 1891-95; *d. c.* 1901.

Copeland, Ralph, Regius Professor of Astronomy, 1889-1905; *b.* near Woodplumpton, Lancashire, 1837; *educ.* Kirkham Grammar School, Göttingen Univ.; Ph.D. Göttingen 1869; F.R.A.S.; went to Australia and spent several years on a sheep run where he began his study of astronomy; returned to England, 1858, and became apprenticed to a firm of engineers; went to Göttingen University, 1865; Assistant at Göttingen Observatory, 1867; served on Second German Arctic Expedition, 1869-1870; after being Astronomical Assistant to Lord Rosse at Birr Castle, Ireland, for three and a half years, became Assistant at the Observatory of Trinity Coll., Dublin, in 1874; Assistant to Lord Crawford at Dunecht, Aberdeenshire, 1876; Astronomer Royal for Scotland, 1889-1905; *d.* Edinburgh, 27th Oct. 1905.

Copson, Edward Thomas, Lecturer in Mathematics, 1923-30; *b.* Coventry, Warwickshire, 21st Aug. 1901; *educ.* King Henry VIII School Coventry, St John's Coll. Oxford; B.A. Oxf. 1922, M.A. 1926; D.Sc. Edin. 1928; Lecturer in Mathematics and Applied Mathematics, St Andrews Univ., since 1930.

Cotterill, Denis, Lecturer in Clinical Surgery, 1913-18; *b.* 1881; *educ.* Edin. Acad., Cambridge Univ., Edin. Univ. 1902-6; M.B., Ch.B. Edin. 1906; F.R.C.S. Edin. 1910; War service, France, 1914-18; *d.* Bohain, France, 2nd Dec. 1918.

Cotterill, Sir Joseph Montagu, Lecturer in Clinical Surgery, 1908-13; *b.* Brighton, 23rd Nov. 1851; *educ.* St Andrew's Coll. Grahamstown, Brighton Coll., Edin. Univ.; Kt. 1919; C.M.G. 1917; M.B., C.M. Edin. 1875; F.R.C.S. Edin. 1878 (Pres. 1907-10); House Surgeon and House Physician, Roy. Infirm., Edin., 1875-78; Assist. Surgeon 1883, Surgeon 1897, Cons. Surgeon, Roy. Infirm., Edin.; Lt.-Col., R.A.M.C.(T.); Senior Surgeon, Craigleith Military Hosp., during the Great War.

Cottrell, Allin, Lecturer in Technical Chemistry, 1921-26; *b.* Yorkshire, 20th Apr. 1886; *educ.* Oldham Secondary School, Manchester Univ.; B.Sc. 1907; M.Sc. 1910; F.I.C. 1919; M.I.Chem.E.; Assist. Lecturer in Chemistry in Dewsbury Technical Coll., 1909, and later Head of the Chemistry Department; during the War he was successively Chemist with the Cotton Powder Company, Faversham, with Chance & Hunt, Oldbury, at H.M. Factory, Queen's Ferry; Manager of the Acids Dept. at H.M. Factory, Gretna, 1916-19, and Chief Chemist, 1919-1920; *d.* 18th Aug. 1926.

BIOGRAPHICAL NOTES

CRAIB, William Grant, Lecturer in Forest Botany, 1915-17, and in Forest Botany and Indian Forest Trees, 1917-20; *b.* 10th March 1882; *educ.* Banff and Fordyce Academies, Aberdeen Univ.; M.A. Aberd. 1907; F.L.S.; F.R.H.S.; Officiating Curator of Herbarium and Library, Roy. Botanic Gardens, Calcutta; Assistant for India, attached to the Roy. Gardens, Kew; Regius Professor of Botany, Aberd. Univ., and Keeper of the Cruickshank Botanic Garden, Old Aberdeen.

CRAMER, William, Lecturer in Chemical Physiology, 1907-15; *b.* Brandenburg, 2nd June 1878; *educ.* Univs. of Munich, Berlin and Edin., Univ. Coll. Hosp. London; Ph.D. Berlin 1900; D.Sc. Edin. 1907; M.R.C.S. Eng., L.R.C.P. Lond. 1917; Assistant in Pharmacology, Berlin Univ., 1900-1; Assistant, Imperial Cancer Research Fund, London, 1904-5, and since 1915; Assistant in Physiology, Edin. Univ., 1905-7.

CRAWFORD, Samuel John, Lecturer in English Language, 1931; B.A. Belfast 1906, M.A. 1919; B.Litt. Oxf. 1912; D.Phil. Oxf. 1930; Tutor in English, Oxford Univ.; Professor of English Philology, Madras Univ.; Head of Language and Comparative Philology Dept., Univ. Coll., Southampton; Dean of the Faculty of Arts, London Univ.; *d.* Edinburgh, 27th Dec. 1931.

CROOM, Sir John Halliday, Professor of Midwifery, 1905-22; *b.* Sanquhar, Dumfries, 15th Jan. 1847; *educ.* Roy. High School Edinburgh, Edin. Univ., London and Paris; Kt. 1902; M.B., C.M. Edin. 1868; M.D. Edin. 1882; Hon. M.D. Dublin 1912; LL.D. Edin. 1922; F.R.C.S. Edin. 1873 (Pres. 1901-3); F.R.C.P. Edin. 1880; extra-academical lecturer on obstetrics and gynæcology, Edin., 1878; Gynæcologist, Roy. Infirm., Edin., 1886-1901; Obstetric Physician, Roy. Maternity Hosp., Edin.; Pres., British Gynæcological Soc., 1902; Chairman, Central Midwives Board for Scotland; *d.* Edinburgh, 27th Sept. 1923.

CUMMING, Alexander Charles, Lecturer in Chemistry, 1908-19, in Technical Chemistry, 1919-21; *b.* Melbourne, 12th Aug. 1880; *educ.* Caulfield Grammar School, Melbourne Univ., Univ. Coll. Dundee 1904-5, Breslau 1905-6, Univ. Coll. London 1906-7; O.B.E. 1918; B.Sc. Melb. 1902; D.Sc. Melb. 1905; F.I.C. 1917; Lecturer in Chemistry, Birkbeck Coll., London, 1907-8, Cons. Chemist, 1921-24; Managing Director of Macfie & Sons, Ltd., Sugar Refiners, Liverpool, since 1924.

CUNNINGHAM, Daniel John, Professor of Anatomy, 1903-9; *b.* Crieff, 15th April 1850; *educ.* Crieff Acad., Edin. Univ.; M.B., C.M. Edin. 1874; M.D. Edin. 1876; Hon. M.D. 1885 and D.Sc. Dublin 1891; D.C.L. Oxf. 1892; LL.D. St And. 1891 and Glasg. 1901; F.R.S. 1891; Demonstrator in Anatomy, Edin. Univ., and Professor of Physiology, Edin. Veterinary Coll., 1876-82; Professor of Anatomy, Roy. Coll. of Surgeons, Ireland, 1882, of Trinity Coll., Dublin, 1883-1903; Dean of the Faculty of Medicine, Edin. Univ., 1904-8; *d.* Edinburgh, 23rd June 1909.

APPENDIX II

Cunningham, Henry Julian, Lecturer in Ancient History, 1901-4; *b.* 1876; *educ.* Marlborough, Balliol Coll. Oxford; B.A. Oxf. 1898, M.A. 1901; Lecturer 1904-5, Fellow 1905-18, Tutor 1909-18, and Librarian, Worcester Coll., Oxford; Junior Proctor, 1906-7; *d.* 22nd Nov. 1918.

Cushny, Arthur Robertson, Professor of Materia Medica, 1918-26; *b.* Fochabers, Morayshire, 6th March 1866; *educ.* Aberdeen Univ., Berne, Strassburg; M.A. Aberd. 1886; M.B., C.M. Aberd. 1889; M.D. Aberd. 1892; LL.D. Aberd. 1911; F.R.S. 1907; Assistant to Professor of Pharmacology, Strassburg, 1892-93; Professor of Pharmacology, Univ. of Michigan, Ann Arbor, 1893-1905; Professor of Pharmacology, Univ. Coll., London, 1905-18; *d.* Edinburgh, 25th Feb. 1926.

Darbishire, Arthur Dukinfield, Lecturer in Genetics, 1911-15; *b.* 1879; *educ.* Magdalen Coll. School, Balliol Coll. Oxford; B.A. Oxf. 1901, M.A. 1905; B.Sc. Oxf. 1904; Demonstrator in Zoology, Manchester Univ., 1902-5; Senior Lecturer in Zoology, Roy. Coll. of Science, London, 1905-11; *d.* in Gailes Camp, Ayrshire, 26th Dec. 1915.

Darroch, Alexander, Professor of Education, 1903-24; *b.* Greenock, 20th Jan. 1862; *educ.* E.C. Training Coll. Glasgow, Edin. Univ.; M.A. Edin. 1898; Assist. Lecturer in Education, Univ. Coll. of N. Wales, Bangor, 1900-1; Lecturer in Psychology and Education in E.C. Training Coll., Edin., 1901-3; Assistant to Professor of Education, Edin. Univ., 1901-3; Chairman of the Edinburgh Committee for the Training of Teachers, 1909-24; first Chairman of the National Committee for the Training of Teachers in Scotland; Chairman of the Edin. Education Committee, 1920; *d.* in the Island of Jura, *c.* 9th Sept. 1924.

Davidson, Andrew, Lecturer in Diseases of Tropical Climates, 1899-1907; M.D. Brussels 1881; M.R.C.S. Eng. 1862; M.R.C.P. Edin. 1865; F.R.C.P. Edin. 1866; *d.*

Davidson, Hugh Stevenson, Lecturer in Clinical Gynæcology, 1922-29, and in Clinical Midwifery, 1923-32; *b.* Melrose; *educ.* Edin. Instit., Edin. Univ.; O.B.E.; M.B., Ch.B. Edin. 1903; F.R.C.S. Edin. 1906; Gynæcologist, Roy. Infirm., Edin., 1927-32, and Obstetric Physician, Roy. Maternity Hosp.; Gynæcologist, Deaconess Hosp., Edin.; *d.* Edinburgh, 5th Jan. 1932.

Davidson, Leybourne Stanley Patrick, Lecturer in Clinical Medicine, 1928-29, and in Medicine, 1929-30; *b.* 3rd Mar. 1894; *educ.* Cheltenham Coll., Edin. Univ., Trinity Coll. Cambridge; M.B., Ch.B. Edin. 1919; M.D. Edin. 1925; B.A. Camb. 1926; M.R.C.P. Edin. 1921; F.R.C.P. Edin. 1925; Assist. Physician, Roy. Infirm., Edin., 1928-30; Regius Professor of Medicine, Aberdeen Univ., since 1930.

Davie, Robert Chapman, Lecturer in Botany, 1912-19; *b.* Portugal, 1886; *educ.* Glasgow High School, Glasg. Univ.; M.A. 1907; B.Sc. 1909; D.Sc. 1915; Demonstrator 1907-9, Assistant 1909-12, in Botany, Glasg. Univ.; Assistant in Botany, Edin. Univ., 1912; *d.* 4th Feb. 1919.

BIOGRAPHICAL NOTES

DAVIES, Harold Whitridge, Lecturer in Clinical Experimental Methods (Medicine), 1925-27; *educ.* Prince Alfred Coll. Adelaide, Adelaide Univ.; M.B., B.S. Adelaide 1917; Research Assistant with J. S. Haldane at Oxford; Rockefeller Foundation Fellow and Assist. Physician, Hosp. of the Rockefeller Instit., New York; Lecturer in Physiology and Pharmacology, Leeds Univ.; Professor of Physiology, Sydney Univ., since 1930.

DAWSON, James Walker, Lecturer in Practical Pathology, 1918-19; *b.* India, 1870; *educ.* Edin. Instit., Edin. Univ.; M.B., C.M. Edin. 1904; M.D. Edin. 1908; D.Sc. Edin. 1916; F.R.C.P. Edin. 1924; F.R.C.S. Edin. 1926; began his medical training at Edinburgh in 1887; had to abandon his studies owing to ill-health and travelled in America, India and New Zealand, 1891-96; returned to Edinburgh and completed his interrupted studies in 1904; Histologist to the Roy. Coll. of Physicians Laboratory, Edin., 1904-27; *d.* Edinburgh, 26th June 1927.

DICKINS, Bruce, Lecturer 1919-25, Reader 1925-31, in Rhetoric and English Literature; *educ.* Nottingham High School, Magdalene Coll. Cambridge; B.A. Camb. 1913, M.A. 1919; Professor of English Language, Leeds Univ., since 1931.

DICKSON, Alexander, Regius Professor of Botany, 1879-87; *b.* Edinburgh, 21st Feb. 1836; *educ.* privately, Edin. Univ., Würzburg and Berlin; M.D. Edin. 1860; Hon. M.D. Dublin 1868; LL.D. Glasg. 1879; conducted Botany class in Aberdeen Univ., 1862; Professor of Botany at Dublin Univ., 1866, and Roy. Coll. of Science, Dublin, 1868; Professor at Glasgow, 1868-79; *d.* 30th Dec. 1887.

DICKSON, William Elliot Carnegie, Lecturer in Pathological Bacteriology, 1907-14; *b.* Edinburgh, 1878; *educ.* Edin. Acad., Edin. Univ.; B.Sc. 1898; M.B., Ch.B. 1901; M.D. 1905; M.R.C.P. Edin. 1904; F.R.C.P. Edin. 1908; Assistant in Pathology, Edin. Univ., 1904-7; Assist. Pathologist to Roy. Infirm. and to the Roy. Hosp. for Sick Children, Edin., 1906-14; Director of Pathology Dept., Roy. Chest Hosp., London; Cons. Pathologist and Bacteriological Pathologist to West End Hosp. for Nervous Diseases; Hon. Pathologist to Grosvenor Hosp. for Women, London.

DILL, Alfred Vincent, Lecturer in Bacteriology, 1920-21; *educ.* Marlborough, Edin. Univ.; M.B., Ch.B. Edin. 1916; M.D. Edin. 1921; D.P.H. Edin. and Glasg. 1920; House Physician, City Fever Hosp., Edin.; Clinical Tutor in Medicine, Roy. Infirm., Edin.; Assistant in Anatomy, Edin. Univ., 1915-16; now at Stroud, Gloucestershire.

DOBBIN, Leonard, Lecturer in Chemistry, 1894-1921; Lecturer in Agricultural Chemistry, 1904-12; Reader in Chemistry, 1921-24; *b.* Belfast, 1858; *educ.* Roy. Belfast Acad. Instit., Queen's Coll. Belfast 1874-76, Coll. of Science, South Kensington, 1876-78, Univ. of Würzburg 1878-80; Ph.D. Würzburg 1880; Assistant (senior, 1892) in Chemistry, Edin. Univ., 1880-94.

APPENDIX II

Dobie, John, Professor of Hebrew, 1892-94; *b.* Musselburgh, 10th Jan. 1859; *educ.* Edin. Univ.; M.A. Edin. 1878; B.D. Edin. 1882; licensed by Presbytery of Chirnside; Assist. Minister, Park Church, Glasgow; did Oriental Research at Paris and Leipzig; Indian Chaplain at Secunderabad, 1888; Wilson Lecturer in Comparative Philology of Semitic Languages, Bombay Univ., 1892; killed in railway accident at Newtonmore Station, 2nd Aug. 1894.

Douglas, Charles Mackinnon, Lecturer in Moral Philosophy, 1892-98; *b.* Edinburgh, 2nd Oct. 1865; *educ.* Oliphant's School Edin., Edin. Acad., Edin. Univ., Freiburg Univ.; C.B. 1918; M.A. Edin. 1889; D.Sc. Edin. 1892; M.P. for N.W. Division of Lanarkshire, 1899-1906; *d.* Lesmahagow, 3rd Feb. 1924.

Dowden, John Wheeler, Senior Lecturer in Clinical Surgery, 1916-24; *b.* Dublin, 1866; *educ.* Merchiston Castle School, Edin. Univ.; M.B., C.M. 1890; F.R.C.S. Edin. 1894 (Pres. 1931); Lecturer in Surgery, School of Medicine of the Roy. Colleges, Edin., 1902-14; Assist. Surgeon, Roy. Hosp. for Sick Children, Edin., 1898-1901; Assist. Surgeon, Surgeon 1912-24, and Cons. Surgeon, Roy. Infirm., Edin.; Surgeon to Chalmers Hosp., Edin., 1924-28; Chairman of Governors, Merchiston Castle School.

Dryerre, Henry, Lecturer in Physiology, 1923-30; *b.* Blairgowrie, Perthshire, 1881; *educ.* Blairgowrie Public School, Stirling High School, School of Medicine, Royal Colleges, Edinburgh, Edin. Univ.; M.R.C.S. Eng., L.R.C.P. Lond. 1919; Ph.D. Edin. 1923; Interim Lecturer in Physiology, School of Medicine, Roy. Colleges, Edin., 1917-18; Professor of Physiology, Roy. (Dick) Veterinary Coll., Edin.; Physiological Biochemist, Animal Diseases Research Association.

Dunbar, Robert Taylor, Lecturer in Natural Philosophy, 1920-24; *b.* Broughty Ferry, Angus, 8th Feb. 1889; *educ.* Grove Acad. Broughty Ferry, Harris Acad. Dundee, Edin. Univ.; M.A., B.Sc. 1915; Ph.D. 1924; Assistant in Physics, Edin. Univ., 1919-20; Senior Lecturer and Director of the Physics Research Laboratory, Univ. Coll., Cardiff, 1924-30; Professor of Physics, Univ. Coll., Cardiff, since 1930.

Dunlop, George Harry Melville, Lecturer in Clinical Instruction on Diseases of Children, 1906-14; *b.* Leith, 1859; *educ.* Scott's School and Collegiate School Edinburgh, Edin. Univ.; M.B., C.M. 1880; M.D. 1884; M.R.C.P. Edin. 1885; F.R.C.P. Edin. 1887; Senior Physician, Roy. Hosp. for Sick Children, Edin., 1898-1913; Physician, Blind Asylum, Edin.; Physician, Roy. Public Dispensary, Edin.; *d.* Étaples, France, 3rd July 1916.

Dunn, John Petrie, Lecturer in Music, 1920-31; *b.* Edinburgh, 1878; *educ.* George Watson's Coll. Edin., Edin. Univ., Stuttgart Conservatoire; Mus.B. Edin. 1920; Mus.D. Edin. 1928; Vice-Principal, Municipal Conservatoire, Kiel; *d.* following motor accident, Edinburgh, 4th Feb. 1931.

BIOGRAPHICAL NOTES

Dunnill, S., Lecturer in Chemistry, 1921-22; A.R.C.S.

Dyson, Sir Frank Watson, Regius Professor of Astronomy, 1905-10; *b.* Ashby, 8th Jan. 1868; *educ.* Bradford Grammar School, Trinity Coll. Cambridge; K.B.E. 1926; Kt. 1915; B.A. Camb. 1889, M.A. 1893; LL.D. Edin. 1911; Hon. D.Sc. Oxf. 1926; Sc.D. Camb. 1929; Hon. D.Sc. Durham 1929; F.R.S. 1901; Fellow of Trinity Coll., Camb., 1891; Chief Assistant, Roy. Observatory, Greenwich, 1894-1905; Secretary, Roy. Astronomical Soc., 1899-1905; Astronomer Royal for Scotland, 1905-10; Astronomer Royal, 1910-1933.

Eggeling, Hans Julius, Professor of Sanskrit, 1875-1914; *b.* Hecklingen, Germany, 12th July 1842; *educ.* Bernburg Gymnasium, Univs. of Breslau and Berlin; Ph.D.; LL.D. Glasg. 1914; came to England in 1867 to work on Sanskrit MSS. in the libraries of the India Office and Roy. Asiatic Soc.; Assistant to Professor F. Max Müller, Oxford, 1867-69; Secretary and Librarian of Roy. Asiatic Soc., 1869-75; Professor of Sanskrit at Univ. Coll., London, 1872-75; Curator of Edin. Univ. Library, 1900-13; resigned from Edin. Chair, 18th Aug. 1914; *d.* Witten, Germany, 13th Mar. 1918.

Ewart, James Cossar, Professor of Natural History, 1882-1927; *b.* Penicuik, Midlothian, 26th Nov. 1851; *educ.* Penicuik, Edin. Univ.; M.B., C.M. Edin. 1874; M.D. Edin. 1878; LL.D. Edin. 1928; F.R.S. 1893; Demonstrator in Anatomy, Edin. Univ., 1874; Conservator, Univ. Coll. Museum, London, 1875-78; Professor of Natural History, Aberdeen Univ., 1878-82; Member of Fishery Board for Scotland, 1882; Swiney Lecturer in Geology, British Museum, 1907.

Ewing, John, Lecturer in Colonial and Indian History, 1919-27; *educ.* Roy. High School Edinburgh, Edin. Univ.; M.A. Edin. 1907; Assistant in History, Edin. Univ., 1911-19; Professor of History, Rhodes Univ. Coll., Grahamstown, South Africa, since 1927.

Falconer, John Downie, Lecturer in Petrology, 1901-4; *b.* Midlothian, 1st Nov. 1876; *educ.* Univs. of Glasg. and Edin.; M.A. Glasg. 1897; B.Sc. Edin. 1901; D.Sc. Edin. 1906; F.G.S.; F.R.G.S.; Lecturer in Geology, Heriot-Watt Coll., Edin., 1901-4; Principal of the Mineral Survey of Northern Nigeria, 1904-9; Swiney Lecturer in Geology, British Museum, 1914-21; Temporary Assistant District Officer, Northern Nigeria, 1916-18; Lecturer in Geology, Glasg. Univ., 1911-21; Director of Geological Survey, Nigeria, 1918-27; Geologist to the Republic of Uruguay since 1928.

Farquharson, John Malcolm, Lecturer in Diseases of the Larynx, Ear and Nose, 1917-21; *b.* Tillicoultry, 12th Mar. 1864; *educ.* Dollar Acad., Edin. Univ., London and Moorfields Hospitals, Vienna and Berlin; M.B., C.M. Edin. 1887; F.R.C.P. Edin. 1903; House Surgeon, Glasg. Infirm.; Physician, Livingstone Memorial Instit.; Assist. Surgeon 1904, Surgeon 1906-21, now Cons. Surgeon, Ear and Throat Dept., Roy. Infirm., Edinburgh.

APPENDIX II

Fenelon, Kevin Gerard, Lecturer in Economics, 1922-31; *b.* Barnes, London, 6th Dec. 1898; *educ.* Hillside School Farnborough, Merchiston Castle Preparatory School and Merchiston Castle School, Edin. Univ.; M.A. (Ord.) 1920; M.A. (Hons.) 1921; Ph.D. 1926; Director of the Dept. of Industrial Administration, Coll. of Technology, Manchester Univ., since 1931.

Ferguson, James Haig, Lecturer in Clinical Gynæcology, 1913-27, and in Clinical Midwifery, 1923-27; *b.* Edinburgh, 18th Dec. 1862; *educ.* Edin. Collegiate School, Edin. Univ., Medical School, Roy. Colleges, Edin.; M.B., C.M. Edin. 1884; M.D. Edin. 1890; LL.D. Edin. 1928; M.R.C.S. Eng. 1884; F.R.C.P. Edin. 1889; F.R.C.S. Edin. 1902 (Pres. 1929-31); Gynæcologist to Leith Hosp., and Cons. Gynæcologist since 1910; Gynæcologist 1921-27, and Cons. Gynæcologist, Roy. Infirm., Edin.; Obstetric Physician, Roy. Maternity Hosp., Edin., 1915-27; Chairman, Central Midwives Board for Scotland.

Ferrar, William Leonard, Lecturer in Mathematics, 1924-25; *b.* Bristol, 21st Oct. 1893; *educ.* Queen Elizabeth's Hosp., Bristol Grammar School, Queen's Coll. Oxford; M.A. Oxf. 1920; Assistant in Pure Mathematics 1920-22, Lecturer 1922-24, Univ. Coll. of N. Wales, Bangor; Fellow and Lecturer in Mathematics, Hertford Coll., Oxford, since 1925.

Findlay, George William Marshall, Lecturer in Pathology, 1921-1923; *b.* Brailes, Warwickshire, 1893; *educ.* Dean Close School Cheltenham, Edin. Univ.; O.B.E. 1919; M.B., Ch.B. Edin. 1915; M.D. Edin. 1920; D.Sc. Edin. 1922; Lister Research Fellow; Carnegie Research Fellow; Freeland Barbour Fellow; Assistant and Alice Memorial Fellow, Imperial Cancer Research Fund; Assist. Pathologist, Roy. Infirm., Edin.; on staff of Wellcome Bureau of Scientific Research, London.

Fisher, Robert Howie, Lecturer in Apologetics, 1913-16; *b.* Ayrshire, 27th Apr. 1861; *educ.* Sanday, Orkney, George Watson's Coll. Edinburgh, Edin. Univ.; M.A. 1880; B.D. 1884; D.D. 1905; Assist. Minister, St Bernard's Church, Edin., 1884; Minister of Skelmorlie, 1885, of Jedburgh, 1890, of West Parish of St Nicholas, Aberdeen, 1896, of Morningside, Edin., 1900, of St Cuthbert's Parish, Edin., 1914-25; Chaplain-in-Ordinary to the King, 1913; Baird Lecturer, 1922.

FitzHerbert, John Aloysius, Lecturer in Greek, 1922-28; *b.* Tasmania; *educ.* St John's Coll. Sydney, Sydney Univ., Trinity Coll. Cambridge; B.A. Sydney 1913; B.A. Camb. 1920, M.A. 1923; in Australia, 1920-22; Hughes Professor of Classics and Comparative Philology, Adelaide Univ., since 1928.

Fleming, Robert Alexander, Senior Lecturer in Clinical Medicine, 1915-27; *b.* Dundee, 1862; *educ.* Larchfield Acad., Craigmount School, Edin.

Univ., Vienna and Berlin; M.A. Edin. 1884; M.B., C.M. Edin. 1888; M.D. Edin. 1896; LL.D. Edin. 1928; F.R.C.P. Edin. 1892 (Pres. 1927-29); Assistant in Practice of Physic, 1890-94, Clinical Medical Tutor, 1892-97, Edin. Univ.; Physician, now Cons. Physician, Roy. Infirm., Edin.; Lecturer in Practice of Medicine, School of Medicine, Roy. Colleges, Edin.; Physician, Roy. Incurable Hosp., Edin.; Medical Adviser, Prison Dept. for Scotland.

Flett, Sir John Smith, Lecturer in Petrology, 1894-1901; *b.* Kirkwall, Orkney, 1869; *educ.* Kirkwall Burgh School, George Watson's Coll. Edinburgh, Edin. Univ.; K.B.E. 1925; O.B.E. 1918; M.A. Edin. 1892; B.Sc. Edin. 1892; M.B., C.M. Edin. 1894; D.Sc. Edin. 1900; LL.D. Edin. 1912; F.R.S. 1913; F.G.S.; joined H.M. Geological Survey, 1900; investigated, for Roy. Soc., volcanic eruptions at the Soufrière, West Indies, 1901; Petrographer to H.M. Geological Survey, 1902; Assistant to Director, Geol. Survey, in charge of Geol. Survey of Scotland, 1911-20; Director, Geol. Survey of Great Britain, and Museum of Practical Geology since 1920.

Flint, Robert, Professor of Divinity, 1876-1903; *b.* Greenburn, Sibbaldbie, Dumfriesshire, 14th Mar. 1834; *educ.* Evan Water and Moffat Schools, Glasgow Univ.; D.D. (Edin. 1876, Princeton 1896, Glasg. 1901, Aberd. 1906); LL.D. (Glasg. 1876, Yale 1901, Edin. 1904); F.B.A. 1901; licensed by Presbytery of Glasgow, 1858; Assistant to Dr Norman Macleod, Barony, Glasgow; Minister of East Church, Aberdeen, 1859, of Kilconquhar, 1862-64; Professor of Moral Philosophy and Political Economy, St Andrews Univ., 1864-76; Baird Lecturer, 1876-77; Stone Lecturer, Princeton, U.S.A., 1887-88; resigned Chair at Edinburgh, July 1903; appointed Gifford Lecturer at Edinburgh for 1907, but did not lecture owing to ill-health; *d.* Edinburgh, 25th Nov. 1910.

Ford, Lester R., Lecturer in Mathematics, 1914-17; *b.* State of Missouri, U.S.A., 1886; *educ.* Missouri State Normal School (Pd.B.), Missouri State Univ. (A.B. 1911, A.M. 1912), Harvard Univ. (M.A. 1913).

Fordyce, Christian James, Lecturer in Latin, 1926-27; *b.* Fraserburgh, 25th Sept. 1901; *educ.* Glasgow Univ., Balliol Coll. Oxford; M.A. Glasg. 1920; B.A. Oxf. 1924, M.A. 1927; Lecturer in Classics, Reading Univ., 1920-25; Lecturer in Greek, St Andrews Univ., 1925-26; Fellow and Classical Tutor, Jesus Coll., Oxford, since 1927.

Fordyce, William, Lecturer in Clinical Gynæcology, 1913-29, and in Clinical Midwifery, 1923-29; *b.* Liverpool, 1865; *educ.* Anstruther Public School, Clifton Bank School St Andrews, St And. and Edin. Univs.; M.A. St And. 1884; M.B., C.M. Edin. 1888; M.D. Edin. 1893; F.R.C.P. Edin. 1898; Assist. Gynæcologist 1906, Gynæcologist 1921-29, Roy. Infirm., Edin.; Obstetric Physician, Roy. Maternity Hosp., Edin., 1919-29.

Fowler, James Stewart, Lecturer in Clinical Instruction on Diseases of Children, 1913-25; *b.* Pittenweem, 22nd Oct. 1870; *educ.* Edinburgh Acad., Univs. of Edin. and Vienna; M.B., C.M. Edin. 1892; M.D. Edin. 1899; M.R.C.P. Edin. 1895; F.R.C.P. Edin. 1897; House Physician, Roy. Infirm., Edin., to (Sir) James O. Affleck (*q.v.*), and House Surgeon; Physician, Roy. Hosp. for Sick Children, 1906-25; Physician to New Town Dispensary; Assist. Physician, Leith Hosp.; *d.* Elie, 24th Aug. 1925.

Fraser, Alexander Campbell, Professor of Logic, 1856-91; *b.* 3rd Sept. 1819; *educ.* Univs. of Glasg. and Edin.; LL.D. (Glasg. 1871, Edin. 1891, Dublin 1902, Aberd. 1906); Hon. D.C.L. Oxf. 1883; F.B.A. 1903; Junior Minister of Free Church, Cramond, 1844; Professor of Logic and Metaphysics, Free Church Theological Coll., Edin., 1846-56; Dean of the Faculty of Arts, Edin. Univ., 1859-91; Gifford Lecturer at Edin., 1894-96; Member of Edin. Univ. Court, 1877-91; *d.* Edinburgh, 2nd Dec. 1914.

Fraser, Sir Thomas Richard, Professor of Materia Medica, 1877-1918; *b.* Calcutta, 5th Feb. 1841; *educ.* public schools in Scotland, Edin. Univ.; Kt. 1902; M.D. Edin. 1862; LL.D. (Aberd. 1894, Glasg. 1901, Edin. 1919); Hon. Sc.D. Camb. 1907; Hon. M.D. Dublin; F.R.C.P. Edin. 1869 (Pres. 1900-2); F.R.S. 1877; Assistant to Sir Robert Christison, Edin., 1861-70; Lecturer on materia medica in extra-academical school, Edin., 1870; Physician 1878-1918, Roy. Infirm., Edin.; President of Indian Plague Commission, 1898-1901; President of Association of Physicians of Great Britain and Ireland, 1908-9; Dean of the Faculty of Medicine, Edin. Univ., 1881-1900; Hon. Physician to King in Scotland, 1904; Member of Edin. Univ. Court, 1903-13; *d.* Edinburgh, 4th Jan. 1920.

Fream, William, Lecturer in Agricultural Entomology, 1891-1906; LL.D.; F.G.S.; F.L.S.; *d. c.* 1906.

Gardham, Henry Cooper, Lecturer in Geometrical and Graphical Drawing, 1919-20; *b.* Wath-on-Dearne, Yorkshire, 1890; *educ.* Manchester public schools, Roy. High School Edinburgh, Edin. Univ.; B.Sc. 1910; A.M.I.C.E.; Director of Technical Education in Natal, South Africa, and Principal of the Technical Coll., Port Elizabeth, Cape Province.

Geikie, James, Murchison Professor of Geology, 1882-1914; *b.* Edinburgh, 23rd Aug. 1839; younger brother of Sir Archibald Geikie, Professor of Geology, Edin. Univ., 1871-82; *educ.* Roy. High School Edin., Edin. Univ.; LL.D. St And. 1877; D.C.L. Durh. 1889; F.R.S. 1875; F.G.S.; entered H.M. Geological Survey, 1861; District Surveyor, 1869; first Dean of the Faculty of Science, Edin. Univ., 1893-1913; one of the founders, and Pres. (1884-1904), of the Roy. Scottish Geographical Soc.; Munro Lecturer in Archæology, Edin. Univ., 1913; *d.* Edinburgh, 1st Mar. 1915.

Gibb, Andrew Dewar, Lecturer in English Law, 1929-32; M.A. Glasg. 1910; LL.B. Glasg. 1913; Advocate, Scots Bar, 1914, and Barrister-at-Law; Lecturer in the Law of Scotland, Cambridge Univ., since 1932.

BIOGRAPHICAL NOTES

Gloag, William Murray, Lecturer in Evidence and Procedure, 1901-5, in Landlord and Tenant, 1904-5; *b.* 1865; *educ.* Edinburgh Acad., Balliol Coll. Oxford; B.A. Oxf. 1888; LL.D. Edin. 1915; Advocate, Scots Bar, 1889; K.C. 1909; Assistant in Scots Law, Edin. Univ., 1899-1905; Professor of Law, Glasgow Univ., since 1905; Assessor, Dean of Guild Court, Glasgow, since 1926.

Goodhart, Harry Chester, Professor of Humanity, 1891-95; *b.* Wimbledon, 1858; *educ.* Eton, Trinity Coll. Cambridge; B.A. 1881; Fellow and Tutor of Trinity Coll.; Classical Lecturer in Cambridge Univ., 1883; *d.* Edinburgh, 21st April 1895.

Gordon, William, Lecturer in Forest Engineering, 1914-32, and in Strength of Materials, 1919-32; *educ.* George Heriot's School Edin., Lockie's Acad. of Engineering Leith, Edin. Univ.; B.Sc. 1911; Ph.D. 1925; M.I.Mech.E.; served his apprenticeship with Messrs James Milne & Sons, Ltd., general engineers; Chief Lecturer in Mechanical Engineering, Leith Technical Coll., for over thirty years; conducted research with Dr Gulliver (*q.v.*), 1911-13; *d.* Edinburgh, 22nd May 1932.

Gordon, William Thomas, Lecturer in Palæontology, 1910-14; *b.* Glasgow, 27th Jan. 1884; *educ.* George Heriot's School Edinburgh, Edin. Univ., Emmanuel Coll. Cambridge; M.A., B.Sc. Edin. 1906; B.A. Camb. 1910, M.A. 1921; D.Sc. Edin. 1911; F.G.S.; Carnegie Research Fellow in Geology, 1906; Falconer Fellow in Geology and Palæontology, 1908; Lecturer in Geology, King's Coll., Univ. of London, 1914, Reader, 1919; University Professor of Geology, London Univ., at King's Coll., since 1920.

Goudy, Henry, Professor of Civil Law, 1889-93; *b.* Ireland, 16th Sept. 1848; *educ.* private schools, Univs. of Glasg., Edin. and Königsberg; M.A. Edin. 1870; LL.B. Edin. 1871; D.C.L. Oxf. 1894; LL.D. Edin. 1894; Fellow of All Souls, Oxford; Advocate, Scots Bar, 1872; Regius Professor of Civil Law, Oxford, 1893-1919; *d.* Bath, 3rd Mar. 1921.

Grant, Sir Ludovic James, 11th Baronet, Regius Professor of Public Law, 1890-1922; *b.* 4th Sept. 1862; son of Sir Alexander Grant, 10th Bart., Principal of Edin. Univ., 1868-84; *educ.* Fettes Coll., Balliol Coll. Oxford; B.A. Oxf.; LL.D. Glasg. 1904 and Edin. 1923; Advocate, Scots Bar, 1887; Dean of the Faculty of Law, 1894-1910; Secretary of Senatus, 1897-1918; Secretary, Univ. of Edin., 1918-19; Trustee and Commissioner of the Board of Manufacturers, Scotland, since 1901.

Greenfield, William Smith, Professor of Pathology, 1881-1912; *b.* Salisbury, 1846; *educ.* Univ. Coll. London; M.D. Lond. 1874; LL.D. Edin. 1913; M.R.C.S. Eng. 1872; F.R.C.P. Lond. 1879 and Edin. 1881; Fellow of Univ. Coll., Lond., 1876; Medical Registrar to St Thomas's Hosp., Lond., 1872-74; Demonstrator in Morbid Anatomy and Pathology, St Thomas's Hosp., Lond., 1874; Professor of Pathology, Brown Instit., London Univ., 1878; *d.* Juniper Green, Midlothian, 12th Aug. 1919.

APPENDIX II

Gregory Smith, George, Lecturer in English Literature and Language, 1892-1905; *b.* 20th June 1865; *educ.* Edin. Univ., Balliol Coll. Oxford; M.A. Edin. 1884; B.A. Oxf. 1888, M.A. 1894; LL.D. Edin. 1914; Assistant in English, Edin. Univ., 1889-92; Professor of English Literature and Librarian, Queen's Coll., Belfast, 1905-9; Professor of English Literature and University Librarian, Queen's Univ., Belfast, 1909-30; *d.* London, 3rd Mar. 1932.

Grieve, Alexander James, Lecturer in Divinity, 1919-22; *b.* Pembroke Dock, 18th Mar. 1874; *educ.* Univ. Coll. Aberystwyth, Mansfield Coll. Oxford, Berlin Univ.; B.A. Lond. 1894, 1899; B.D. Lond. 1904, 1912; M.A. Oxf. 1904; D.D. Lond. 1914; Registrar, Univ. of Madras, 1900-2; Professor of English, Central Coll., Bangalore, 1902-4; Minister of Congregational Church, Romsey, 1905-9, of St Anne's-on-the-Sea, 1910-11, of Salem, Bradford, 1916-17; Professor of New Testament Studies, Yorkshire United Independent Coll., Bradford, 1909-17; Principal and Professor of Systematic Theology, Scottish Congregational Coll., 1917-21; Lecturer in Church History, Manchester Univ., since 1922, and Dean of the Faculty of Theology since 1931; Principal of Lancashire Independent Coll. since 1922.

Grillo, Ernesto, Lecturer in Italian, 1919-20; *b.* Italy, Dec. 1877; *educ.* Italy, Switzerland, England and Germany; M.A. Urbino 1903; D.Litt. Roy. Instit. of Superior Studies, Florence, 1909; LL.D. and D.C.L. Perugia 1910; Hon. M.A. Glasg. 1924; Director of Anglo-American Instit., Florence, 1908-9; sometime Professor of English and German in the Univ. of Urbino; Head of Italian Dept. at the Athenæum Commercial Coll., Glasgow, since 1911; Director of Italian Studies since 1910, and first Stevenson Professor of Italian Language and Literature, Glasg. Univ., since 1925.

Guild, James Bennett, Lecturer in Political Economy, 1913-20; *b.* Arbroath, 1890; *educ.* Abbey Public School Arbroath, Arbroath High School, Edin. Univ.; M.B.E.; M.A. Edin. 1911; F.R.S.S.; F.R. Econ. Soc.; Interim Lecturer in Economic History, Edin. Univ., 1912-13; Lecturer in History, Heriot-Watt Coll., Edin., 1913; joined Statistical Branch of Ministry of Food and became head during the War; Statistical Officer, National Farmers' Union, 1921-23; General Secretary, Farmers' Union, 1923-32; *d.* Muswell Hill, 5th April 1932.

Gulland, George Lovell, Professor of Medicine, 1915-28; *b.* Edinburgh, 1862; *educ.* Roy. High School Edin., Univs. of Edin. and Halle; C.M.G. 1917; M.A. Edin. 1881; B.Sc. Edin. 1883; M.B., C.M. Edin. 1886; M.D. Edin. 1890; LL.D. Edin. 1928; F.R.C.P. Edin. 1890 (Pres. 1923-25); Resident Physician, Roy. Infirm. and Roy. Hosp. for Sick Children, Edin.; Private Assistant to Sir T. Grainger Stewart (*q.v.*); Senior Lecturer in Clinical Medicine, 1913-15; Physician to Roy. Victoria Hosp., Edin., 1896; Physician, Roy. Infirm., Edin., 1911-28.

R.H.S.

BIOGRAPHICAL NOTES

Gulliver, Gilbert Henry, Lecturer in Experimental Engineering, 1906-14; B.Sc.; D.Sc.; A.M.I.M.E.; Assistant in Engineering, Edin. Univ., 1902-6; Head of Messrs Kirkaldy's Testing Works, London, since 1914.

Gunn, G. O., Lecturer in Actuarial Science, 1920-26; F.F.A.

Gwilt, R. Llewellyn, Lecturer in Actuarial Science, 1925-29; F.F.A.; F.I.A.

Halm, Jacob, Lecturer in Astronomy, 1903-7; Ph.D.

Hardie, Robert Purves, Lecturer in Logic and Metaphysics, 1892-1920, and Reader in Ancient Philosophy, 1920-32; *b.* Edinburgh, 1864; *educ.* Circus Place School Edin., Edin. Univ., Merton Coll. Oxford; M.A. Edin. 1884; B.A. Oxf. 1888, M.A. 1894; Assistant in Logic and Metaphysics, Edin. Univ., 1889-92.

Hardie, William Ross, Professor of Humanity, 1895-1916; *b.* Edinburgh, 1862; *educ.* Edin. Univ., Balliol Coll. Oxford; M.A. Edin. 1880; B.A. Oxf. 1884, M.A. 1887; LL.D. St And. 1913; Fellow and Tutor of Balliol Coll., 1884-95, Junior Proctor, 1893-94; *d.* 3rd May 1916.

Hartley, James Norman Jackson, Lecturer in Clinical Surgery, 1922-27, and in Surgical Pathology, 1924-27; *b.* Keighley, 1889; *educ.* Edin. Univ., Guy's Hosp. London; O.B.E.; M.B., Ch.B. Edin. 1913; F.R.C.S. Eng.; F.R.C.S. Edin. 1915; House Physician, Gynæcological Dept., and House Surgeon, Roy. Infirm., Edin.; Lecturer on surgery in extra-academical school, Edin.; Assist. Surgeon, Roy. Infirm., Edin. 1922-26; Surgeon, Cumberland Infirm., Carlisle, since 1927.

Harvey, John, Lecturer in Procedure and Evidence, 1905-9; *b.* Glasgow, 1865; *educ.* Glasg. Acad., Edin. Acad., Balliol Coll. Oxford, Glasg. Univ., Edin. Univ.; B.A. Oxf.; LL.B.; Advocate, Scots Bar, 1892; *d.* Davos Platz, Switzerland, 28th Oct. 1909.

Harvey, Leslie Arthur, Lecturer in Cytology, 1927-30; *b.* Dulwich, London, 23rd Dec. 1903; *educ.* Bellenden Road L.C.C. School, Bancroft's School, Woodford Green, Essex, Roy. Coll. of Science, Lond. Univ.; B.Sc. 1923; M.Sc. 1925; A.R.C.S. 1923; D.I.C. 1924; F.R.M.S. 1924; F.Z.S. 1924-31; Beit Scientific Research Fellow, Roy. Coll. of Science, 1924-25; Assistant in Zoology, Edin. Univ., 1925-27; Lecturer and Head of the Dept. of Zoology, Univ. Coll. of the South-West of England, Exeter, since 1930.

Hepburn, David, Lecturer in Regional Anatomy, 1894-1903; *b.* Milnathort, Kinross-shire, 1859; *educ.* Brand's School Milnathort, Edin. Univ.; C.M.G. 1917; M.B., C.M. Edin. 1881; M.D. Edin. 1891; V.D.; Hon. Surgeon-Colonel, R.A.M.C.(T.F.); M.R.C.S. Eng.; Resident Physician and Surgeon, Roy. Infirm., Edin., 1881-82; Demonstrator in Anatomy, Edin. Univ., 1882; Professor of Anatomy, Univ. Coll., Cardiff, 1903-28; *d.* Cardiff, 9th Mar. 1931.

APPENDIX II

Herring, Percy Theodore, Lecturer in Histology, 1902-8; *b.* Yorkshire, 1872; *educ.* Christ's Coll. Christchurch, New Zealand, Otago Univ., Edin. Univ., Paris; M.B., C.M. Edin. 1896; M.D. Edin. 1899; M.R.C.P. Edin. 1899; F.R.C.P. Edin. 1903; Resident Physician, Roy. Infirm., 1896; House Physician, Roy. Maternity Hosp., 1896-99; Assistant in Physiology, Edin. Univ., 1899-1908; Chandos Professor of Physiology (and Dean of the Faculty of Science since 1921), St Andrews Univ., since 1908.

Hilton, Irene Alexandra Frances, Lecturer in Zoology, 1927-31; *b.* Liverpool, 24th June 1902; *educ.* Oulton School Liverpool, Liverpool Univ.; B.Sc. 1923; M.Sc. 1928; F.L.S. 1933; Assist. Lecturer in Biology, Univ. Coll., Swansea, 1923-27; Tutor in Natural Science, Somerville Coll., Oxford, since 1931.

Hislop, Gordon, Lecturer in Rhetoric and English Literature, 1920-29; *b.* Edinburgh, 1889; *educ.* Trinity Acad. 1895-98, Leith Acad. 1898-1905, Edin. Univ. 1905-9, New Coll. Oxford; M.A. Edin. 1909; Lecturer in English Literature, Birmingham Univ. and Tutor to the Workers' Educational Association for two years; returned from the War to Birmingham before coming to Edinburgh in 1920; *d.* Edinburgh, 8th Apr. 1929.

Hobson, Alfred Dennis, Lecturer in Cytology and Experimental Zoology, 1926-32; *b.* 1901; *educ.* Christ's Coll. Cambridge; B.A. 1922, M.A. 1926; Professor of Zoology, Armstrong Coll., Newcastle, and Director of the Dove Marine Laboratory, Cullercoats, since 1932.

Hodsdon, Sir James William Beeman, Lecturer 1908-13, Senior Lecturer 1913-22, in Clinical Surgery; *b.* Bermuda, 15th May 1858; *educ.* Sherborne School, Queen's Coll. Belfast, Univ. and School of Medicine Edinburgh, London, Vienna and Paris; K.B.E. 1920; C.B.E. 1919; M.D., M.S. Queen's Coll. Belfast 1881; L.R.C.P. Edin. 1880; M.R.C.P. Edin. 1883; L.R.C.S. Edin. 1880; F.R.C.S. Edin. 1883 (Pres. 1914-17); Lecturer on surgery in the extra-academical school, 1889; Assist. Surgeon 1886, Surgeon and Cons. Surgeon, Roy. Infirm., Edin.; *d.* 28th May 1928.

Hogben, Lancelot Thomas, Lecturer in Zoology, 1922-23, and in Experimental Physiology, 1923-25; *b.* Southsea, 9th Dec. 1895; *educ.* Trinity Coll. Cambridge; B.A. Camb. 1916, M.A. 1920; B.Sc. Lond. 1914; D.Sc. Lond. 1921; Lecturer in Zoology, Imperial Coll. of Science, 1919-22; Assistant Professor of Zoology, McGill Univ., Montreal, 1925-27; Professor of Zoology, Univ. of Cape Town, 1927-30; Professor of Social Biology, Univ. of London, at London School of Economics, since 1930.

Hood, Helen Reid Thomson, Lecturer in Public Health, 1923-26; *b.* Hamilton, Lanarkshire, 25th Jan. 1898; *educ.* Craigneish Coll. Inverness, Edin. Univ.; M.B., Ch.B. 1921; D.P.H. 1922; Assistant in Public Health, Edin. Univ., 1922-23; Clinical Assistant, Dermatological Dept., Roy. Infirm., Edin., 1927; in general practice, Glasgow, 1928-30; Resident Medical Officer, Rockside Hydropathic, Matlock, 1930.

BIOGRAPHICAL NOTES

Howden, Charles Robert Andrew, Lecturer in Landlord and Tenant, 1906-18, and International Private Law, 1909-18; *b.* Edinburgh, 18th Jan. 1862; *educ.* Edin. Acad., Edin. Univ.; M.A. 1883; F.S.A. Scot.; Advocate, Scots Bar, 1886; Sheriff-Substitute of Inverness, Elgin and Nairn at Elgin, since 1917.

Howie, Margaret Dickie (Frau Dr Senft), Lecturer in German, 1923-24; *b.* Midlothian, 1891; *educ.* Kirkcaldy High School, Edin. Univ.; M.A. 1913; Ph.D.

Hutton, G. C., Lecturer in Actuarial Science, 1923-26; M.A.; F.I.A.; Actuary, Scottish Amicable Life Assurance Society, Edinburgh.

Ince, Edward Lindsay, Lecturer in Mathematics, 1931-32; *b.* Amblecote, 30th Nov. 1891; *educ.* Perth Acad., Edin. Univ., Trinity Coll. Cambridge, Paris; M.A., B.Sc. Edin. 1913; B.A. Camb. 1917, M.A. 1922; D.Sc. Edin. 1918; F.R.A.S.; Lecturer, Liverpool Univ., 1920-26; Professor of Pure Mathematics, Egyptian Univ., 1926-31; Lecturer in Mathematics, Imperial Coll. of Science, London, since 1932.

James, Alexander, Lecturer in Infective Diseases, 1908-32; *b.* Edinburgh, 1850; *educ.* Edin. Instit., Univs. of Edin. and Leipzig; M.B., C.M. Edin. 1872; M.D. Edin. 1876; F.R.C.P. Edin. 1877; Lecturer on physiology, 1878, and on medicine, 1889, in the extra-academical school, Edin.; Assist. Physician 1882, Physician 1892, Cons. Physician 1907, Roy. Infirm., Edin.; *d.* Haddington, 7th Apr. 1932.

Jamieson, Francis Robert, Lecturer in Latin, 1892-96; *b.* Sandness, Shetland, 1863; *educ.* Sandness, Shetland, Edin. Univ.; M.A. Edin. 1885; LL.D. Edin. 1924; Assistant in Latin, Edin. Univ., 1886-92; H.M. Inspector of Schools, 1896, at Aberdeen, Dumfries and Galloway, and Glasgow successively; H.M. Chief Inspector in charge of Southern Division; *d.* Edinburgh, 7th Mar. 1927.

Jamieson, William Allan, Lecturer in Clinical Instruction on Diseases of the Skin, 1899-1906; *b.* Dreghorn, 1839; *educ.* Irvine Acad., Glasgow Univ., Edin. Univ.; M.B., C.M. Edin. 1865; M.R.C.P. Edin. 1876; F.R.C.P. Edin. 1877 (Pres. 1908-10); in general practice, Preston 1865-67, Berwick-on-Tweed 1867-76, Edin. 1876; Lecturer on diseases of the skin in extra-academical school, Edin., 1878; Physician, Skin Dept., Roy. Infirm., Edin., 1884-1906; Visiting and Cons. Physician, City Hosp. for Infectious Diseases, Edin., 1886-91; *d.* June 1916.

Jenkin, Henry Charles Fleeming, Regius Professor of Engineering, 1868-85; *b.* near Dungeness, Kent, 25th Mar. 1833; *educ.* Jedburgh, Edin. Acad., Frankfort-on-the-Main, Paris, Genoa, Marseilles; M.A. Genoa; LL.D. Glasg. 1883; A.M.I.C.E. 1859; F.R.S. 1865; Engineer-in-Chief of Reuter's, the French Atlantic and the German Union Telegraph Companies; returned from Continent 1851, and became apprenticed as a Mechanical Engineer at Manchester; Professor of Engineering, Univ. Coll., Univ. of Lond., 1865-68; *d.* Edinburgh, 12th June 1885.

JOHNSTON, Robert McKenzie, Lecturer in Diseases of the Larynx, Ear and Nose, 1903-6; *b.* Edinburgh, 3rd Mar. 1856; *educ.* Edin. Acad., Clifton Coll., Edin. Univ.; M.B., C.M. Edin. 1881; M.D. Edin. 1883; L.R.C.S. Edin. 1881; F.R.C.S. Edin. 1884 (Pres. 1917-19); in general practice till 1890; Assist. Surgeon 1890-1903, Surgeon 1903-6, Cons. Surgeon 1906-30, Ear and Throat Dept., Roy. Infirm., Edin.; Member of the Court 1903-27, Curator of Patronage 1916-28, Edin. Univ.; *d.* Edinburgh, 1st June 1930.

JOHNSTON, Thomas Baillie, Lecturer in Anatomy, 1911-14; *b.* July 1883; *educ.* George Watson's Coll. Edinburgh, Edin. Univ.; M.B., Ch.B. 1906; Lecturer in Anatomy, Univ. Coll., London, 1914-19; Professor of Anatomy (and Dean), Guy's Hosp. Medical School, Univ. of London, since 1919.

JOHNSTONE, Henry Melville, Lecturer in Military Subjects, 1904-16; *b.* India, 1857; *educ.* Edin. Acad., Roy. Military Acad. Woolwich; Lieut. Roy. Engineers, 1877; Capt. 1889; served in Bermuda, Hong-Kong, Cyprus and Egypt; retired from active service, 1895; *d.*

JOLLY, William Tasker Adam, Lecturer in Experimental Physiology, 1908-12; *b.* Edinburgh; *educ.* George Watson's Coll. Edin., Edin. Univ.; M.B., Ch.B. 1906; D.Sc. Edin. 1911; LL.D. Edin. 1926; Assistant in Physiology, Edin. Univ., 1904-12; Carnegie Fellow and Research Student at Leyden Univ., 1908; Professor of Physiology (and Dean of the Faculty of Medicine), Univ. of Cape Town, since 1911.

KAY, Sydney Alexander, Lecturer in Chemistry, 1914-33; *b.* Dundee, 1874; *educ.* Dundee High School, Univ. Coll. Dundee, Stockholm and Leipzig; B.Sc. St And. 1896; D.Sc. St And. 1902; F. Chem. Soc. Lond. 1905; Assistant in Chemistry, St And. Univ., 1899-1909, Edin. Univ. 1909-14; *d.* Fairmilehead, Edinburgh, 26th May 1933.

KENNEDY, Harry Angus Alexander, Lecturer in Divinity, 1919-29; *b.* Dornoch, Sutherlandshire, 1866; *educ.* Edin. Acad., Univs. of Edin., Halle and Berlin, New Coll. Edin.; M.A. Edin. 1889; D.Sc. Edin. 1893; D.D. Edin. 1910; D.D. Queen's Univ., Canada; Minister of United Free Church, Callander, 1893-1905; Professor of New Testament Literature, Knox Coll., Toronto, Canada, 1905-9; Professor of New Testament Language, Literature and Theology, New Coll., Edin., 1909-25; Cunningham Lecturer, United Free Church, 1902-4.

KENNEDY, Neil John Downie, Hon. Lord Kennedy, Lecturer in International Private Law, 1899-1901; *b.* Rosehall, Sutherlandshire, Apr. 1855; *educ.* High School Inverness, Aberd. and Edin. Univs., New Coll. Edin.; M.A. Aberd. 1876; LL.D. Edin. 1903; Advocate, Scots Bar, 1877; K.C. 1906; Professor of Civil and Scots Law, Aberd. Univ., 1901-7; Sheriff of Renfrew and Bute, 1907-12; Chairman of Scottish Land Court, with judicial title of Lord Kennedy, 1912-18; *d.* Edinburgh, 12th Feb. 1918.

BIOGRAPHICAL NOTES

KENNEDY-FRASER, David, Lecturer in Education, 1919-23; *b.* Edinburgh, 10th Feb. 1888; *educ.* George Watson's Coll. Edin., Univs. of Edin., Leipzig, Hamburg and Cornell, U.S.A.; B.Sc. Edin. 1908; M.A. Edin. 1909; Carnegie Scholar and Fellow, 1910-13; Assist. Professor of Education, Cornell Univ., 1914-16; Lecturer in Education, Edin. Training Coll., 1919-23; Lecturer in charge of training of teachers of mentally defective children in Scotland, and Psychologist to Glasgow Education Authority, since 1923.

KER, Claude Buchanan, Lecturer in Infective Diseases, 1904-25; *b.* Cheltenham, 1867; *educ.* Malvern Coll., Edin. Univ.; M.B., C.M. Edin. 1890; M.D. Edin. 1896; M.R.C.P. Edin. 1898; F.R.C.P. Edin. 1901; House Surgeon, Roy. Infirm. and Roy. Maternity Hosp., Edin., 1891; Assist. Medical Officer, Edin. Fever Hosp.; Medical Superintendent, Edin. Fever Hosp., 1896; *d.* Edinburgh, 4th Mar. 1925.

KERR, Douglas James Acworth, Lecturer in Forensic Medicine, 1925-26; *b.* Bradford, 21st Aug. 1894; M.B., Ch.B. Edin. 1920; M.D. Edin. 1927; D.P.H. Edin. and Glasg. 1922; M.R.C.P. Edin. 1924; F.R.C.P. Edin. 1927; Lecturer on forensic medicine in extra-academical school, Edin.; Police Surgeon, Edin., 1927; Assist. Pathologist, Roy. Infirm., Edin.; Assist. Medical Officer, Fife and Kinross District Asylum.

KERR, Robert Browne, Lecturer in Greek, 1920-22, and Lecturer in Education, 1925-27; *b.* Moyness, Auldearn, Nairnshire, 22nd Jan. 1892; *educ.* Auldearn Public School, Spier's School, Beith, Ayrshire, Edin. Univ.; M.A. 1915; B.Ed. 1923; Principal Classical Master, Bearsden Acad., Glasgow, 1923-25; H.M. Inspector of Schools in Scotland since 1927.

KERR, Walter Hume, Lecturer in Engineering Drawing and Design, 1895-1928; *b.* Duns, Berwickshire, 25th June 1861; *educ.* Wellfield Acad. Duns, Edin. Univ. 1877-82, 1891-93, Oxford Univ. 1882-84; M.A. Edin. 1882; B.Sc. Edin. 1893; in New Zealand, 1884-87; apprentice engineer, 1887-91; Assistant in Engineering, Edin. Univ., 1893-95; Sub-Director, Army Education, Étaples, France, and Education Officer, Army of the Rhine, 1918-19.

KIRKPATRICK, John, Professor of History, 1881-1909; *b.* 1835; M.A. Camb.; Dr. Jur. Heidelberg; LL.B. Edin. 1870; LL.D. Glasg. 1890 and Edin. 1910; Advocate, Scots Bar, 1868; Secretary of Senatus and Dean of the Faculty of Law, 1886-97; *d.* Nice, 12th Jan. 1926.

KNOTT, Cargill Gilston, Lecturer 1892-1920, and Reader 1920-22, in Applied Mathematics; *b.* Penicuik, 1856; *educ.* Arbroath High School, Edin. Univ.; B.Sc. Edin. 1876; D.Sc.; LL.D. St And. 1916; F.R.S.; Assistant in Natural Philosophy, Edin. Univ., 1879-83; Professor of Physics, Imperial Univ. of Japan, 1883-91; conducted magnetic survey of Japan, 1887-89; *d.* Edinburgh, 1922.

APPENDIX II

Lackie, James Lamond, Lecturer in Clinical Midwifery, 1923-24; *b.* Montrose, 1868; *educ.* Montrose Acad., Aberd. and Edin. Univs.; M.B., C.M. Edin. 1889; M.D. Edin. 1894; F.R.C.P. Edin. 1896; on staff of Edin. Maternity Hosp., Leith Hosp., and Edin. Hosp. for Diseases of Women; *d.* Edinburgh, 4th Jan. 1924.

Laird, Thomas Patrick, Professor of Accounting, 1919-27; *b.* 1860; *educ.* Sharp's Instit. Perth, Perth Acad.; C.A. 1886; Secretary of Society of Accountants, Edinburgh, 1916-20; Chairman of British Assets Trusts, Ltd.; Senior Partner of Moncreiff & Horsburgh, Edin.; Lecturer in Accounting and Business Method, Edin. Univ., 1919; Member of Edin. Univ. Court, 1922-27; *d.* Edinburgh, 11th June 1927.

Lambie, Charles George, Lecturer in Materia Medica, 1919-23, and in Clinical Medicine, 1922-29; *b.* Trinidad, British West Indies, 24th July 1891; *educ.* Stanley House, Bridge of Allan, Edin. Univ.; M.C. 1918; M.B., Ch.B. Edin. 1914; M.D. Edin. 1927; M.R.C.P. Edin. 1921; F.R.C.P. Edin. 1924; Resident Physician, Roy. Infirm., Edin., 1914-15; Beit Memorial Fellow, 1923-26; Lister Fellow, 1928; Bosch Professor of Medicine, Univ. of Sydney, since 1929.

Laurie, Simon Somerville, Professor of Education, 1876-1903; *b.* Edinburgh, 13th Nov. 1829; *educ.* High School Edin., Edin. Univ.; M.A. Edin. 1849; LL.D. (St And. 1887, Edin. 1903, Aberd. 1906); Hon. F.E.I.S.; Secretary to Education Committee of the Church of Scotland; Secretary to the Endowed Schools (Scotland) Commission, 1872-75; Gifford Lecturer, Edin. Univ., 1905-6; Member of Edin. Univ. Court, 1898-1903; *d.* Edinburgh, 2nd Mar. 1909.

Lennie, Alice Brown, Lecturer in Geography, 1919-29; *b.* Edinburgh, 1875; *educ.* Edin. Ladies' Coll., Edin. Univ.; M.A. Edin. 1898; B.Sc. Edin. 1902; Assistant in Geography, Edin. Univ., 1912-19; previously private Assistant to George Goudie Chisholm.

Leslie, Robert, Lecturer in Political Economy, 1909-13; *b.* Buckie, Fife, 1885; *educ.* George Watson's Coll. Edin., Edin. Univ.; M.A. Edin. 1907; Assistant Professor of Political Economy, Calcutta Univ., 1913-14; Professor of Political Economy, Univ. of Cape Town, since 1914.

Lewin, R. F. H., Lecturer in Forest Engineering, 1930-32.

Lewis, Walter James, Lecturer 1910-22, Reader 1922-31, in Evidence and Procedure; *b.* Hemel Hempstead, Hertfordshire, 15th Nov. 1857; *educ.* Oliphant's School, Roy. High School and George Watson's Coll., Edinburgh, Edin. Univ.; B.L. 1879; S.S.C. 1887; admitted Law Agent 1881; in legal practice 1888-1909; partner of Lewis & Somerville, W.S., since 1909; Examiner, Law Agents in Scotland, since 1919; Auditor of the Sheriff Court, Edin., since 1922.

BIOGRAPHICAL NOTES

LIM, Robert Kho-Seng, Lecturer in Histology, 1919-23; *b.* Singapore, 1896; *educ.* George Watson's Coll. Edinburgh, Edin. Univ.; M.B., Ch.B. 1919; Ph.D. 1921; D.Sc. 1924; Professor of Physiology, Peking Union Medical Coll., Peking, China.

LITTLEJOHN, Sir Henry Duncan, Regius Professor of Forensic Medicine, 1897-1906; *b.* Edinburgh, 1828; *educ.* Perth Acad., High School Edin., Edin. Univ., Paris; Kt. 1895; M.D. Edin. 1847; LL.D. Edin. 1893; L.R.C.S. Edin. 1847; F.R.C.S. Edin. 1854 (Pres. 1875-77); Lecturer in Forensic Medicine, Surgeons' Hall, 1855; Medical Officer of Health, Edin., 1862-1908; Pres., Roy. Instit. of Public Health, 1893; *d.* Bendreoch, Arrochar, 30th Sept. 1914.

RHS

LITTLEJOHN, Henry Harvey, Regius Professor of Forensic Medicine, 1906-27; *b.* Edinburgh, Oct. 1862; *educ.* Edin. Acad., Brunswick, Germany, Edin. Univ., Vienna, Berlin, Paris; M.A. Edin. 1882; M.B., C.M. Edin. 1886; B.Sc. (Public Health) Edin. 1888; F.R.C.S. Edin. 1890; assisted his father, Sir Henry Duncan Littlejohn, in teaching and practice of medical jurisprudence; Medical Officer of Health, Sheffield, 1891-97; Lecturer in Medical Jurisprudence, Surgeons' Hall, Edin., 1898; Lecturer to Edin. School of Medicine for Women; Dean of the Faculty of Medicine, Edin. Univ., 1908-19; President of the Section of Forensic Medicine, International Medical Congress, 1913; Member of Edin. Univ. Court, 1913-20; *d.* Edinburgh, 16th Aug. 1927.

LODGE, Sir Richard, Professor of History, 1899-1925; *b.* Penkhull, Staffordshire, 20th June 1855; *educ.* Christ's Hosp., Balliol Coll. Oxford; Kt. 1917; B.A. Oxf. 1878, M.A. 1881; LL.D. Glasg. 1905 and Edin. 1926; Hon. Litt.D. Manchester 1912; Fellow and Lecturer of Brasenose Coll., Oxford, 1878, Tutor 1883, Hon. Fellow 1911; Professor of History, Glasgow Univ., 1894-99; Dean of the Faculty of Arts, Edin. Univ., 1911-24; Member of Edin. Univ. Court, 1911-24; Pres. of the Roy. Historical Soc. since 1928.

LONGSTAFF, James Patrick, Lecturer in Chemistry, 1914-16; *b.* Edinburgh, 23rd July 1860; *educ.* Roy. High School, Circus Place School, Edin., Edin. Univ.; B.Sc. Edin. 1901; D.Sc. Edin. 1909; Assistant in Chemistry, Edin. Univ., 1896-1901, 1904-16; Assistant in Chemistry, Heriot-Watt Coll., Edin., 1901-4; General Secretary, Soc. of Chemical Industry, 1916-29.

RHS

LORIMER, James, Regius Professor of Public Law, 1862-90; *b.* Aberdalgie, Perthshire, 4th Nov. 1818; *educ.* Perth High School, Univs. of Edin., Berlin and Bonn, Acad. of Geneva; M.A. Edin. 1856; LL.D. Glasg. 1882; Dr Jur. Bonn; Advocate, Scots Bar, 1845; Principal Lyon Clerk, 1848; *d.* Edinburgh, 13th Feb. 1890.

Luke, Thomas Davey, Lecturer in Anæsthetics, 1904-1909; M.B., B.S., B.O. 1894, M.D. 1908, Roy. Univ. of Ireland; F.R.C.S. Edin. 1902; Managing Director, Ochil Hills Sanatorium, Kinross; Staff-Surgeon, R.N.A. Hosp., Peebles; Resident Physician, Smedley's Hydropathic, Matlock, and Hydropathic, Grange-over-Sands; Medical Superintendent, Peebles Hydropathic; *d.* Peebles, 1921.

McBride, Peter, Lecturer in Diseases of Larynx, Ear and Nose, 1897-1903; *b.* Hamburg, 1854; *educ.* Edin. Collegiate School, Clifton Coll., Edin. Univ., Vienna; M.B., C.M. Edin. 1876; M.D. Edin. 1881; L.R.C.P. Edin. 1876; F.R.C.P. Edin. 1880; Lecturer on diseases of the ear in the extra-academical school, Edin., 1882; Surgeon, Ear, Nose and Throat Dept., Roy. Infirm., Edin., 1883-1903; Surgeon to the Edin. Ear Dispensary; retired from practice, 1910.

McCallum, Peter, Lecturer in Pathology, 1920-21; *b.* Glasgow, 1885; *educ.* East Christchurch Public School, Christ's Coll. Grammar School and Canterbury Univ. Coll., Christchurch, New Zealand, Edin. Univ.; M.A. N.Z.; M.Sc. N.Z.; M.B., Ch.B. Edin. 1914; D.P.H. Edin. and Glasg. 1923; Professor of Pathology, Univ. of Melbourne, since 1925.

McCartney, James Elvins, Lecturer in Bacteriology, 1920-25; *b.* Warwick, 1891; *educ.* Westgate School, Warwick, 1894-1902, Warwick School 1903-10, Edin. Univ.; M.B., Ch.B. Edin. 1915; M.D. Edin. 1922; D.Sc. Edin. 1924; Fellow, Rockefeller Instit., New York, 1922-23; Director of Research in Pathological Sciences, London County Council, since 1925.

McClelland, William Wither, Lecturer in Education, 1923-25; *b.* Newton-Stewart, 10th June 1889; *educ.* Ewart High School, Leith Acad., Edin. Univ.; M.A. Edin. 1913; B.Sc. Edin. 1913; B.Ed. Edin. 1918; Executive Officer to Wigtownshire Education Authority, 1919; Lecturer in Education, Aberd. Univ., 1921; Principal Lecturer in Education, Edin. Training Centre, 1923; Visiting Professor of Education, Columbia Univ., 1930-31; Professor of Education, St And. Univ., and Director of Studies, St Andrews, and Dundee Training Coll., since 1925.

McCrea, William Hunter, Lecturer in Mathematics, 1929-32; *b.* Dublin, 13th Dec. 1904; *educ.* Chesterfield Grammar School 1916-23, Trinity Coll. Cambridge 1923-28, Göttingen Univ. 1928-29; B.A. Camb. 1926, M.A. 1931; Ph.D. Camb. 1929; B.Sc. Lond. 1924, Part II. 1925; F.R.A.S. 1929; Lecturer in Astronomy, Edinburgh Workers' Educational Assoc., 1930-31; Reader in Mathematics, Imperial Coll. of Science, London Univ., since 1932.

MacDougall, Robert Stewart, Steven Lecturer 1906-20, Reader 1920-29, in Agricultural and Forest Zoology; *b.* Edinburgh, 1862; *educ.* George Heriot's School Edin., Edin. Univ., Munich Univ.; M.A. Edin. 1889; B.Sc. Edin. 1892; D.Sc. Edin. 1898; LL.D. Edin. 1932; Professor of Biology, Roy. (Dick) Veterinary Coll., Edin.; Acting Technical Adviser in Zoology, Board of Agriculture and Fisheries, 1904-13.

BIOGRAPHICAL NOTES

McEwen, Bruce, Lecturer in Apologetics, 1907-13; *b.* Stonehaven, 1876; *educ.* Fettes Coll., Edin. Univ.; M.A. 1897; B.D. 1900; D.Phil. 1906; licensed by Presbytery of Edin., 1900; ordained as Assistant Minister and successor, Gladsmuir, 1903; Minister of Old Machar's, Aberdeen, 2nd charge 1913-16, 1st charge 1919-23; Gunning Lecturer, Edin. Univ., 1913; *d.* Aberdeen, 8th June 1923.

MacGregor, James Gordon, Professor of Natural Philosophy, 1901-13; *b.* Halifax, Nova Scotia, 1852; *educ.* Free Church Acad. Halifax, Dalhousie Coll. Halifax 1867-71, Univs. of Edin. 1871-74, and Leipzig 1874-76; B.A. Dalhousie 1871; M.A. Dalhousie 1874; M.A. Edin. 1874; B.Sc. Lond. 1874; D.Sc. Lond. 1876; LL.D. Glasg. 1901; F.R.S. 1900; Lecturer in Physics, Dalhousie Coll., 1876-77; Chief Physics Master, Clifton Coll., Bristol, 1877-79; Munro Professor of Physics, Dalhousie Coll., 1879-1901; *d.* 21st May 1913.

Mackay, George, Lecturer in Diseases of the Eye, 1905-13; *b.* Palaveram, India, 1862; *educ.* Clifton Coll., Inverness Coll., Edin. Univ., Vienna, Leipzig, Paris and London; M.B., C.M. Edin. 1883; M.D. Edin. 1888; M.R.C.S. Eng. 1883; F.R.C.S. Edin. 1886 (Pres. 1919-21); Ophthalmic Surgeon, Roy. Infirm., Edin., 1895-1913; Lecturer on ophthalmology, extra-academical school, Edin., 1896; Ophthalmic Medical Referee under the Workmen's Compensation Act; Surgeon and later Cons. Surgeon, Roy. Infirm., Deaconess Hosp., Roy. Blind Asylum and the Deaf and Dumb Institution, Edinburgh.

Mackenzie, Ronald Douglas Hunter, Lecturer in Pathology, 1925-29; *b.* Edinburgh, 1894; *educ.* Edin. Acad., Edin. Univ.; M.B., Ch.B. Edin. 1919; F.R.C.P. Edin. 1928; Dipl. Bact. Lond. School of Hygiene and Tropical Med., 1929; now in London.

Mackinnon, Donald, Professor of Celtic, 1882-1914; *b.* Colonsay, 18th Apr. 1839; *educ.* locally, Church of Scotland Training Coll. Edinburgh, Edin. Univ.; M.A. Edin. 1870; school teacher, 1860-63; Clerk to Church of Scotland's Education Scheme, 1869; Clerk to Endowed Schools and Hospitals Commission, 1872; Clerk and Treasurer to Edinburgh School Board, 1873-82; Member of Crofters Roy. Commission, 1883; *d.* Balnahard, in Colonsay, 25th Dec. 1914.

Mackinnon, James Alexander Rudolf, Lecturer in Jurisprudence, 1927-32; *b.* Edinburgh, 1887; *educ.* George Watson's Coll. Edinburgh, Madras Coll. St Andrews, St And. Univ., Edin. Univ.; M.A. Edin. 1911; LL.B. Edin. 1914; Advocate, Scots Bar, 1915; Sheriff-Substitute at Forfar since 1932.

Mackinnon, James, Regius Professor of Ecclesiastical History, 1908-30; *b.* Turriff, Aberdeenshire, 1860; *educ.* Univs. of Edin., Bonn and Heidelberg; M.A., Ph.D. Heidelberg 1890; D.D. St And. 1912; D.Th. Halle 1930; LL.D. Edin. 1931; Lecturer in History, Queen Margaret Coll., Univ. of Glasgow, 1892; Lecturer in History, St Andrews Univ., 1896-1908.

APPENDIX II

McLachlan, Donald Gordon Stewart, Lecturer in Bacteriology, 1926-31; *b.* Star, Markinch, Fife, 1897; *educ.* Star Public School 1903-9, Buckhaven Higher Grade School 1909-10, Warrender Park School Edinburgh, 1910-11, George Heriot's School Edin. 1911-16, Edin. Univ.; M.B., Ch.B. Edin. 1924.

Maclagan, Sir Andrew Douglas, Regius Professor of Forensic Medicine, 1862-97; *b.* Ayr, 17th Apr. 1812; *educ.* High School Edin., Edin. Univ., Berlin, London and Paris; Kt. 1886; M.D. Edin. 1833; LL.D. Glasg. 1891 and Edin. 1897; F.R.C.S. Edin. 1833 (Pres. 1859-61); F.R.C.P. Edin. 1864 (Pres. 1884); Lecturer on materia medica, extra-academical school of medicine, Edin.; *d.* Edinburgh, 5th Apr. 1900.

Maclennan, Roderick Diarmid, Lecturer in Philosophy, 1927-33; *b.* Laggan, Inverness-shire; *educ.* New Zealand, Kingussie and Oban High Schools, Edin. Univ.; M.A. Edin. 1924; Assistant in Philosophy, Edin. Univ., 1924-27; first Warden of Cowan House; Lecturer to Edin. Workers' Educational Association; Professor of Philosophy, McGill Univ., Montreal, 1933.

Macpherson, Norman, Professor of Scots Law, 1865-88; *b.* Aberdeen, 13th June 1825; *educ.* Aberd. Grammar School, Aberd. Univ., King's Coll. London, Jesus Coll. and Trinity Coll. Cambridge, Edin. Univ.; M.A. Aberd. 1842; LL.D. Aberd. 1865 and Edin. 1888; assisted his father, Professor of Greek at Aberd., 1847-48; Advocate, Scots Bar, 1851; Secretary to Law Courts Commission, 1868; Chairman of Solway Fisheries Commission, 1877; Sheriff of Dumfries and Galloway, 1880-90; *d.* Edinburgh, 2nd Aug. 1914.

Mair, Alexander William, Professor of Greek, 1903-28; *b.* Keith, 9th June 1875; *educ.* Keith Grammar School, Aberdeen Univ. 1889-93, Gonville and Caius Coll. Cambridge 1893-98; M.A. Aberd. 1893; B.A. Camb. 1898, M.A. 1901; Litt.D. Aberd. 1911; Fellow of Caius Coll. Camb., 1899-1905; Lecturer in Greek, Aberd. Univ., 1898-99; Lecturer in Greek, Edin. Univ., 1899-1903; *d.* Edinburgh, 13th Nov. 1928.

Malcolm, John, Lecturer in Physiological Chemistry, 1902-5; *b.* Halkirk, Caithness, 1873; *educ.* Crossroads School Dunnet, Edin. Univ.; M.B., Ch.B. 1897; M.D. 1899; Assistant in Physiology, Edin. Univ., 1899-1902; Professor of Physiology, Otago Univ., Dunedin, New Zealand, since 1905.

Marshall, Daniel Grove, Lecturer in Tropical Medicine, 1908-23; *b.* Shrewsbury, 1860; *educ.* Brightwell's Acad. Shrewsbury, Edin. Univ.; M.B., C.M. Edin. 1885; House Surgeon, Roy. Infirm., Edin., 1886; joined Indian Medical Service, 1888; served in Burma 1891-92, N.W. Frontier of India 1897-98, in China 1900; Lecturer and later Professor of Medicine,

Medical Coll., Lahore; retired from I.M.S. with rank of Major; Lieut.-Col. 1919; Lecturer on tropical medicine, extra-academical school, Edin., 1905-19; *d.* Edinburgh, 16th Dec. 1923.

MARSHALL, Francis Hugh Adam, Lecturer in Physiology of Reproduction, 1905-8; *b.* High Wycombe, 11th July 1878; *educ.* St Mark's School Windsor, Univ. Coll. London, Christ's Coll. Cambridge; B.A. Camb. 1899, M.A. 1905; D.Sc. Edin. 1904; Sc.D. Camb. 1912; F.R.S. 1920; came to Edinburgh, 1900; Research Student; Assistant in Zoology, 1903-5; Carnegie Fellow, 1904; Fellow of Christ's Coll., Camb., 1909, Tutor, 1912-23; Reader in Agricultural Physiology, Cambridge Univ., since 1908.

MARSHALL, Hugh, Lecturer in Mineralogy and Crystallography, 1894-1908, and Lecturer in Chemistry, 1902-8; *b.* Edinburgh, 1868; *educ.* Moray House Normal School Edin., Edin. Univ., Munich, Ghent; B.Sc. Edin. 1886; D.Sc. Edin. 1890; Assistant in Chemistry, Edin. Univ., 1887-1908; Professor of Chemistry, Univ. Coll., Dundee, 1908; *d.* 1913.

MASSON, David Mather, Regius Professor of Rhetoric and English Literature, 1865-95; *b.* Aberdeen, 2nd Dec. 1822; *educ.* Aberd. Grammar School 1831-35, Marischal Coll. Aberd. 1835-39, Divinity Hall, Edin. Univ., 1839-42; M.A. Aberd. 1839; LL.D. (Aberd. 1864, Edin. 1896, St And. 1905); Hon. Litt.D. Dublin 1892; Hon. R.S.A. 1896; Hon. degree of Univ. of Moscow; Editor of *The Banner* 1842-44; on staff of W. & R. Chambers, 1844-47; moved to London 1847; Professor of English Literature, Univ. Coll., Lond., 1853; Editor of *Macmillan's Magazine*, 1859-67; Historiographer Royal for Scotland, 1893; *d.* 6th Oct. 1907.

MATTHEWS, James Robert, Lecturer in Botany, 1920-29; *b.* Duncrub, Dunning, Perthshire, 8th Mar. 1889; *educ.* Dunning Public School, Perth Acad., Edin. Univ., Edin. Provincial Training Coll. for Teachers; M.A. 1911; F.L.S. 1919; Teacher, North Berwick School, 1912-13; Lecturer in Botany, Birbeck Coll., London Univ., 1913-16, 1919-20; Protozoologist to Western Command at Liverpool School of Tropical Medicine, 1916-19; Professor of Botany, Reading Univ., since 1929.

MEAKINS, Jonathan Campbell, Christison Professor of Therapeutics, 1919-24; *b.* Hamilton, Canada, 16th May 1882; *educ.* Hamilton Coll., McGill Univ.; M.D., C.M.; LL.D. Edin. 1927; F.R.C.P. Edin.; Hon. F.R.C.S. Edin. 1930; F.R.C.P.S. Canada (and first President); Resident Physician, Roy. Victoria Hosp., Montreal, 1904-6; Assistant in Medicine, Johns Hopkins Hosp., Baltimore, 1906-7; Resident Pathologist, Presbyterian Hosp., New York, 1907-10; Assist. Physician, Roy. Victoria Hosp., Montreal; Lecturer in Medicine and Pathology, McGill Univ., Montreal; Director of Experimental Medicine, McGill Univ.; Professor of Medicine and Director of the Department of Medicine, McGill Univ.; Physician-in-chief, Roy. Victoria Hosp., Montreal, since 1924.

MEIKLE, Henry William, Lecturer in Scottish History, 1909-19 ; *b.* Edinburgh, 1880 ; *educ.* Daniel Stewart's Coll. Edin., Edin. Univ. ; M.A. Edin. 1904 ; D.Litt. Edin. 1912 ; Lecteur d'Anglais, Univ. of Lyons, 1904-5 ; Master in George Watson's Coll., Edin., 1905-8 ; Carnegie Scholar in History, 1908-9 ; Assistant in English 1908-11, and in History 1911-15, Edin. Univ. ; Administrative Officer, Ministry of Munitions and Ministry of Labour, 1917-22 ; Secretary and Librarian of the Instit. of Historical Research, London Univ., 1923-27 ; Keeper of MSS., 1927-31, and Chief Librarian, National Library of Scotland, since 1931.

MEIN, C. B., Lecturer in Actuarial Science, 1926-29 ; B.A. ; F.F.A. ; Scottish Equitable Life Assurance Society, Edinburgh.

MEKIE, David Clark Thomson, Lecturer in Geography (Economic Ethnography), 1926-28 ; *b.* Edinburgh, 17th Oct. 1873 ; *educ.* Daniel Stewart's Coll. Edin., Edin. Univ., Roy. Coll. of Science London ; M.A. Edin. 1894 ; Ph.D. Edin. 1925 ; F.R.S.G.S. ; in Education service, Edin. ; Headmaster, Darroch Intermediate School, Edin., since 1932.

MILES, Alexander, Senior Lecturer in Clinical Surgery, 1913-25 ; *b.* Leith, 1865 ; *educ.* George Watson's Coll. Edin., Edin. Univ. ; M.B., C.M. Edin. 1888 ; M.D. Edin. 1891 ; LL.D. Edin. 1925 ; F.R.C.S. Edin. 1890 (Pres. 1927-29) ; Lecturer on surgery, extra-academical school, Edin., 1901-10 ; Surgeon 1910-24, and Cons. Surgeon, Roy. Infirm., Edin., and Leith Hosp. ; Member of Edin. Univ. Court since 1927.

MILL, James, Lecturer in Latin, 1896-1927 ; *b.* Arbroath, 1862 ; *educ.* Arbroath High School, Daniel Stewart's Coll. Edin., Edin. Univ., Trinity Coll. Oxford ; M.A. Edin. 1885 ; B.A. Oxf. 1889, M.A. 1894 ; Assistant to Principal Peterson, Dundee Univ. Coll., 1884-85 ; Classical Master, Dunfermline High School, 1889-90 ; Rector, Waid Acad., Anstruther, 1890-96.

MILLAR, John Hepburn, Professor of Constitutional History, 1909-25 ; *b.* 1864 ; son of Lord Craighill, Senator of the Coll. of Justice, Scotland ; *educ.* Edin. Acad., Balliol Coll. Oxford, Edin. Univ. ; B.A. Oxf. 1887 ; LL.B. Edin. 1889 ; LL.D. Glasg. 1919 and Edin. 1926 ; Advocate, Scots Bar, 1889 ; Lecturer in Private International Law, Edin. Univ., 1902-9 ; Lecturer in Scottish Literature, Glasg. Univ., 1911-12 ; *d.* Edinburgh, 13th Feb. 1929.

MILLER, James, Lecturer in Pathology, 1916-19, and in Morbid Anatomy, 1919-20 ; *b.* Edinburgh, 1875 ; *educ.* Edin. Acad., Univs. of Edin. and Freiburg ; B.Sc. Edin. 1896 ; M.B., Ch.B. Edin. 1899 ; M.D. Edin. 1903 ; D.Sc. Birmingham 1904 ; F.R.C.P. Edin. 1910 ; Resident Physician, Roy. Infirm., Edin., 1899-1900 ; Lecturer in Pathology and Bacteriology, Birmingham Univ., 1902-9 ; Visiting Pathologist to Birmingham General Hosp., 1906-9 ; Professor of Pathology, Queen's Univ., Kingston, Canada ; Bacteriologist to Ontario Board of Health.

MILROY, Thomas Hugh, Lecturer in Physiological Chemistry, 1899-1902; *b.* Kirkcowan, Wigtownshire, 1870; *educ.* George Watson's Coll. Edin.; Univs. of Edin., Berlin and Marburg; M.B., C.M. Edin. 1891; B.Sc. Edin. 1892; M.D. Edin. 1896; LL.D. Edin. 1927; Assistant in Physiology, Edin. Univ., 1897-1902; Professor of Physiology, Queen's Univ., Belfast, since 1902.

MITCHELL, William McKutcheon, Lecturer in Political Economy, 1920-21; *b.* Edinburgh, 1893; *educ.* George Heriot's School Edin., Edin. Univ.; M.A. Edin. 1915; LL.B. Edin. 1920; *d.* 1921.

MOORE, James Middleton, Professor of French, 1931-32; *b.* Lauder, Berwickshire, 13th Oct. 1871; *educ.* Edin. Univ.; M.A. Edin. 1894; Class Master, Campbeltown Grammar School, 1895-99; Headmaster, Darroch Burgh School, 1899-1907; Language Master, Boroughmuir School, Edin., 1907-9; Senior French Master, Roy. High School, Edin., 1909-15; Rector, Madras Coll., St Andrews, 1915-20; Lecturer in French, Edin. Univ., 1920-31; *d.* Grenoble, 21st July 1932.

MORISON, John Miller Woodburn, Lecturer in Radiology, 1925-30; *educ.* Glasg. Univ.; M.B., C.M. Glasg. 1896; M.D. Glasg. 1924; M.R.C.P. Edin. 1925; F.R.C.P. Edin. 1929; D.M.R.E. Camb. 1924; Radiologist, Roy. Infirm., Edin., 1925-30; Director, Radiological Dept., Cancer Hospital, Fulham; Professor of Radiology, London Univ., since 1930.

MOUNSEY, John Little, Professor of Conveyancing, 1900-22; *b.* Lockerbie, 30th Oct. 1852; *educ.* Corrie Parish School, Annan Acad., Edin. Univ.; Writer to the Signet, 1883; LL.D. Edin. 1923; Partner in Messrs John Clerk Brodie & Sons, W.S.; *d.* Edinburgh, 26th June 1933.

MOUNTFORD, James Frederick, Lecturer in Latin, 1919-24; *b.* 15th Sept. 1897; *educ.* Birmingham Univ., Oriel Coll. Oxford; M.A. Birmingham 1917; D.Litt. Birmingham 1921; M.A. Oxf. 1924; Fereday Fellow of St John's Coll., Oxford; Lecturer in Classics, Armstrong Coll., Newcastle, 1918; Schiff Lecturer, Cornell Univ., 1924; Professor of Classics, Cornell Univ., 1924-27; Professor of Latin, Univ. Coll. of Wales, Aberystwyth, since 1928.

MUIR, Robert, Lecturer in Pathological Bacteriology, 1894-98; *b.* Balfron, Stirlingshire, 5th July 1864; *educ.* Hawick High School, Teviot Grove Acad., Edin. Univ.; M.A. Edin. 1884; M.B., C.M. Edin. 1888; M.D. Edin. 1890; Hon. Sc.D. Dublin 1912; LL.D. Edin. 1925; D.C.L. Durham 1931; F.R.C.P. Edin. 1895; F.R.F.P.S. Glasg. 1901; F.R.S. 1911; Senior Assistant in Pathology, Edin. Univ., and Pathologist to Roy. Infirm., Edin., 1892; Professor of Pathology, St Andrews Univ., 1898-99; Professor of Pathology, Glasgow Univ., since 1899.

APPENDIX II

Muirhead, James, Professor of Civil Law, 1862-89; *b.* 1831; LL.D. Glasg. 1885; spent two years in a merchant's office in Leith and several years in the office of the *Edinburgh Advertiser;* enrolled as a student of the Inner Temple, London, 1853; admitted to English and Scots Bars, 1857; Advocate-Depute, 1874; Sheriff of Chancery; Sheriff of Stirling, Dumbarton and Clackmannan, 1886; *d.* Edinburgh, 8th Nov. 1889.

Munro, James, Lecturer in Colonial and Indian History, 1912-19; *b.* Edinburgh, 1882; *educ.* Daniel Stewart's Coll. Edin., Edin. Univ.; M.A. Edin. 1905; Assistant in History, Edin. Univ., 1906-10; Beit Lecturer in Colonial History, Oxford, 1910-12; *d.* Hendon, 15th July 1924.

Murdoch, Hector Burn. *See* Burn-Murdoch, H.

Murdoch, Thomas Monck Burn. *See* Burn-Murdoch, T. M.

Myles, William Harris, Lecturer in Realistic Economics, 1919-20; *b.* East Barnes, Dunbar, 5th Apr. 1891; *educ.* Dunbar H.G. School, Edin. Univ.; M.A.(Ord.) Edin. 1911; M.A.(Hons.) Edin. 1914; F.S.S.; Assistant in Political Economy, Edin. Univ., 1911-15; Chief Instructor (Commercial) Army General and Commercial Coll., Cologne, 1919; Professor of Economics, Univ. of the Punjab, Lahore, India, 1920-30; Senior Marketing Investigator, Ministry of Agriculture and Fisheries, London, since 1930.

Nicholson, Harry Oliphant, Lecturer in Clinical Midwifery, 1923-24; *b.* Edinburgh, 13th Mar. 1870; *educ.* privately, Gordon's Coll. Aberdeen, Aberd. Univ., Berlin Univ.; M.B., C.M. Aberd. 1891; M.D. Aberd. 1901; M.R.C.P. Edin. 1901; F.R.C.P. Edin. 1904; House Physician and Surgeon, Roy. Hosp. for Sick Children, Edin.; Clinical Assistant, Roy. Infirm., Edin., 1901; Obstetric Physician, New Town Dispensary, Edin., 1903; Assist. Obstetric Physician, Roy. Maternity Hosp., Edin., 1904-23.

Nicholson, Joseph Shield, Professor of Political Economy, 1880-1925; *b.* Wrawby, Lincolnshire, 9th Nov. 1850; *educ.* Preparatory School, Banbury, Congregational School, Lewisham, Kent, King's Coll. London 1865, Edin. Univ. 1872, Trinity Coll. Cambridge 1873, Heidelberg; B.A. Lond. 1870; B.A. Camb. 1877, M.A. 1886; M.A. Lond. 1877; Sc.D. Camb. 1887; LL.D. St And. 1911 and Edin. 1926; F.B.A. 1903; private tutor, Cambridge, 1876-80; *d.* Edinburgh, 12th May 1927.

Nicol, David Bruce, Lecturer in Divinity, 1924-27; *b.* Edinburgh, 22nd Feb. 1886; *educ.* George Watson's Coll. Edin., Aberdeen Grammar School, Aberd. Univ.; M.A. Aberd. 1905; B.D. Aberd. 1908; licensed by Presbytery of Aberd., 1908; Assist. Minister, Scots Church, Buenos Aires and St Cuthbert's, Edin.; ordained 1911; Minister, Skelmorlie, 1911-20, St Margaret's Church, Edin., 1920-25, St Mark's, Dundee, 1925-29, Govan, 1929-30; Chaplain to the Forces, 1916-19; *d.* 23rd Mar. 1930.

BIOGRAPHICAL NOTES

Niecks, Frederick Maternus, Reid Professor of Music, 1891-1914; *b.* Düsseldorf, 3rd Feb. 1845; *educ.* privately, Univ. of Leipzig; Mus.D. Dublin 1898; LL.D. Edin. 1915; violinist and teacher of music at Düsseldorf till 1868, when he came to Scotland and settled in Dumfries; organist of St Mary's Presbyterian Church, Dumfries, and teacher of music there; became a naturalised British subject in 1880; first Dean of the Faculty of Music, Edin. Univ., 1893-1914; *d.* Edinburgh, 24th June 1924.

Oakeley, Sir Herbert Stanley, Reid Professor of Music, 1865-91; *b.* Ealing, 22nd July 1830; second son of Sir H. Oakeley, 3rd Baronet; *educ.* Rugby, Christ Church Oxford; Kt. 1876; B.A. Oxf. 1853, M.A. 1856; Mus. D. (Camb. 1871, Lambeth 1871, Oxf. 1879, Dublin 1887, St And. 1878, Adelaide 1895, Edin. 1899); D.C.L. Trinity Coll. Toronto 1876; LL.D. (Aberd. 1881, Edin. 1891, Glasg. 1901); Director of Music at St Paul's Episcopal Church, Edinburgh; Composer of Music to the Queen in Scotland, 1881; *d.* Eastbourne, 26th Oct. 1903.

Oppenheim, Alexander, Lecturer in Mathematics, 1930-31; *educ.* Balliol Coll. Oxford; B.A. 1925; Tutor and Lecturer in Mathematics, Exeter Coll., Oxford; Professor of Mathematics, Raffle's Coll., Singapore.

Orr, John, Lecturer in Materia Medica (to women), 1916-18; *b.* Edinburgh, 1870; *educ.* George Watson's Coll. Edin., Edin. Univ.; M.B., C.M. 1891; M.D. 1896; M.R.C.S. Eng., L.R.C.P. Lond. 1891; M.R.C.P. Edin. 1894; F.R.C.P. Edin. 1896; Physician, Western Dispensary, Edin.; Lecturer on materia medica in the extra-academical school, Edin.; Dean of School of Medicine of Roy. Colleges, Edin., 1924; Resident Physician, Roy. Infirm., Edin. 1891-92; Resident Surgeon, Roy. Maternity Hosp., Edin.; Resident Medical Officer, Chalmers Hosp., Edinburgh.

Paterson, James Veitch, Lecturer in Diseases of the Eye, 1917-27; *b.* Dumfriesshire, 1866; *educ.* Edin. Acad., Edin. Univ., Vienna; M.A. Edin. 1888; M.B., C.M. Edin. 1893; F.R.C.S. Edin. 1897; Surgeon 1913-27; now Cons. Ophthalmic Surgeon, Roy. Infirm., Edinburgh.

Patrick, John, Regius Professor of Biblical Criticism, 1898-1915; *b.* Lochwinnoch, 15th Sept. 1850; *educ.* Lochwinnoch School, Univs. of Glasg., Edin. and Heidelberg; M.A. Glasg. 1875; B.D. Edin. 1877; D.D. Edin. 1895; LL.D. Edin. 1919; licensed by Presbytery of Paisley, 1877; Assistant at High Church, Kilmarnock, 1877-79, Assistant and Successor, 1879; Minister of Monkton and Prestwick, 1880, of Greenside, Edin., 1887; Dean of the Faculty of Divinity, Edin. Univ., 1899-1912; Croall Lecturer, 1899-1900; *d.* Edinburgh, 17th Jan. 1933.

Pattison, Andrew Seth Pringle. *See* Pringle-Pattison, A. S.

APPENDIX II

Patton, Walter Scott, Lecturer in Zoology, 1920-27; *b.* 7th Oct. 1876; *educ.* Stoke's School, Mussoorie, India, Univs. of Edin. and Marburg; M.B., Ch.B. Edin. 1901; joined Indian Medical Service, 1902; Bacteriologist, I.M.S., 1908-21; Assistant Director and Director, King Instit. of Preventive Medicine, Madras, 1908-14; Entomologist, Mesopotamia Expeditionary Force, 1917; Director, Pasteur Instit., Southern India, 1919-21; retired from I.M.S. in 1921 with rank of Major; Dutton Memorial Professor of Entomology, Liverpool Univ. and Liverpool School of Tropical Medicine, since 1927.

Pealling, Robert John, Lecturer in Plant Physiology, 1919-20; *b.* Dalbeattie, 17th May 1882; *educ.* George Heriot's School Edinburgh, Edin. Univ.; M.A. Edin. 1905; B.Sc. Edin. 1912; Science Master, Sinclairtown School, Kirkcaldy, 1905-6, Fyvie H.G. School 1908-11, Fort William High School 1912, Galashiels Acad. 1912-14, Edin. Ladies' Coll. 1915-16, Inverness Roy. Acad. since 1920; Organiser, Inverness Continuation Classes, since 1924.

Peddie, William, Lecturer in Natural Philosophy, 1892-1907; *b.* Papa Westray, Orkney, 1861; *educ.* Orkney, George Watson's Coll. Edinburgh, Edin. Univ.; B.Sc. 1887; D.Sc. 1888; Neil Arnott Demonstrator in Natural Philosophy 1881, and Assistant 1882-1907, Edin. Univ.; Harris Professor of Physics, Univ. Coll., Dundee, since 1907.

Pickard-Cambridge, Arthur Wallace, Professor of Greek, 1929-30; *b.* 20th Jan. 1873; *educ.* Weymouth Coll., Balliol Coll. Oxford; B.A. Oxf. 1895, M.A. 1898; D.Litt. Oxf. 1929; Fellow of Oriel Coll., 1895-97; Fellow of Balliol Coll., 1897-1929; Univ. Lecturer in Greek and Latin Literature, Oxford, 1926-28; Hon. Fellow of Balliol Coll. and St Hilda's Coll., Oxford; Vice-Chancellor of Sheffield Univ. since 1930.

Playfair, John Menzies, Lecturer in Clinical Instruction on Diseases of Children, 1889-1900; *b.* Perthshire, 14th Sept. 1849; *educ.* Edin. Univ., Paris, Vienna; M.B., C.M. Edin. 1872; M.D. Edin. 1892; L.R.C.S. Edin. 1872; F.R.C.P. Edin. 1876 (Pres. 1904-6); Hon. F.R.C.S. Edin. 1905; Medical Officer, New Town Dispensary, Edin.; Physician 1884-1900, and Cons. Physician, Roy. Hosp. for Sick Children, Edinburgh.

Ponder, Eric Haldane, Lecturer in Physiology, 1921-27; *b.* Darjeeling, India, 23rd May 1898; *educ.* George Watson's Coll. Edinburgh, Edin. Univ.; M.B., Ch.B. 1919; D.Sc. 1925; M.D. 1926; F.R.M.S. 1927; Carnegie Teaching Fellow and Crighton Research Fellow, 1923-26; Professor of General Physiology, New York Univ., since 1927.

Pringle, Harold, Lecturer in Histology, 1908-19; *b.* Clones, Co. Monaghan, Ireland, 1876; *educ.* Trinity Coll. Dublin; B.A. 1899; M.B., Ch.B. 1899; M.D. 1902; F.R.C.S.I. 1902; F.R.C.P.I. 1921; Fellow of the Roy. Acad. of Medicine of Ireland; Fellow of the Roy. Acad. of Ireland; Assistant in Physiology, Trinity Coll., Dublin, 1904-8; Professor of Physiology, Trinity Coll., Dublin, since 1919.

BIOGRAPHICAL NOTES

PRINGLE-PATTISON, Andrew Seth, Professor of Logic, 1891-1919; [original name was Andrew Seth; assumed name of Pringle-Pattison on succeeding to The Haining estate, 1898]; *b.* Edinburgh, 1856; *educ.* Roy. High School Edin., Edin. Univ.; M.A. Edin. 1878; LL.D. St And. 1892 and Edin. 1920; Hon. D.C.L. Durham 1902; F.B.A. 1904; Assistant to Professor Campbell Fraser, 1880-83; Balfour Lecturer in Philosophy, 1883-91; first Professor of Logic and Philosophy, Univ. Coll., Cardiff, 1883-87; Professor of Logic, Rhetoric and Metaphysics, St And. Univ., 1887-91; Member of Edin. Univ. Court, 1903-11; Gifford Lecturer, Aberd. 1911-13, Edin. 1921-23; Hibbert Lecturer, 1921; *d.* at The Haining, Selkirk, 1st Sept. 1931.

RHS

PROTHERO, Sir George Walter, Professor of History, 1894-99; *b.* Wiltshire, 14th Oct. 1848; *educ.* Eton, King's Coll. Cambridge, Univ. of Bonn; K.B.E. 1920; M.A. Camb. 1872; Litt.D. Camb. 1894; LL.D. Edin. 1899; Litt. D. Harvard 1910; F.B.A. 1903; Fellow (and Hon. Fellow) of King's Coll., Camb.; Assistant Master at Eton; Lecturer under Univ. Extension Scheme at Nottingham, Leicester, etc.; Univ. Lecturer in History and Tutor of King's Coll., Camb., 1876-94; Editor, *Quarterly Review,* 1899; Pres., Roy. Historical Soc., 1901-5; Member of Roy. Commission for Ecclesiastical Discipline, 1904-6; Director of Historical Section, Foreign Office, 1918-19; Member of British Peace Delegation, 1919; *d.* London, 10th July 1922.

PURSER, George Leslie, Lecturer in Zoology, 1920-26; *b.* Moseley, Birmingham, 23rd Dec. 1891; *educ.* King Edward VIth High School Birmingham, Trinity Coll. Cambridge; B.A. 1914, M.A. 1918; F.Z.S.; Assistant in Zoology 1915-18, in Botany 1916-18, in Anatomy 1917-19, Glasgow Univ.; Assistant in Natural History, Edin. Univ., 1919-20; Lecturer in Embryology, Aberdeen Univ., since 1926.

RAINY, Harry, Lecturer in Physical Methods in the Treatment of Diseases, 1912-20, and Senior Lecturer in Clinical Medicine, 1918-23; *b.* Glasgow, 1864; *educ.* Edin. Acad., Edin. Univ., Vienna and London; M.A. Edin. 1885; M.B., C.M. Edin. 1891; M.D. Edin. 1899; Hon. M.D. Upsala; M.R.C.P. Edin. 1895; F.R.C.P. Edin. 1896; Assistant to Professor Chrystal (*q.v.*) for a year; Resident Medical Officer, Chalmers Hosp., Edin.; Tutor in Clinical Medicine, Edin. Univ., 1894-1900; Physician, Roy. Infirm., Edin., 1915-23; Medical Electrician, Roy. Hosp. for Sick Children, Edin., 1906; Physician, Longmore Hosp., Edin.; *d.* Edinburgh, 4th Jan. 1923.

RANKINE, Sir John, Professor of Scots Law, 1888-1922; *b.* Sorn, Ayrshire, 18th Feb. 1846; *educ.* Sorn, Ayrshire, Edin. Acad., Univs. of Edin. and Heidelberg; Kt. 1921; M.A. Edin. 1865; LL.D. Glasg. 1892; Advocate, Scots Bar, 1869; Advocate-Depute, 1885; Q.C., 1897; resigned Chair at Edin., 1922; Member of Edin. Univ. Court, 1901-22; *d.* Threepwood, Roxburghshire, 8th Aug. 1922.

APPENDIX II

Rees, James Frederick, Lecturer 1913-24, and Reader 1924-25, in Economic History; *b.* Milford Haven, Pembrokeshire, 13th Dec. 1883; *educ.* Univ. Coll. Cardiff, Lincoln Coll. Oxford; B.A. Wales 1904; B.A. Oxf. 1908, M.A. 1912; Tutor in History, Normal Coll., Bangor, 1908; Assistant Lecturer in History, Univ. Coll., Bangor, 1908-12; Lecturer in Economic History, Queen's Univ., Belfast, 1912-13; Professor of Commerce, Birmingham Univ., 1925-29; Principal of Univ. Coll. of South Wales and Monmouthshire, Cardiff, since 1929.

Rettie, Theodore, Lecturer in Pathology, 1921-33; *b.* Edinburgh, 1871; *educ.* Clifton Bank School St Andrews, George Watson's Coll. Edin., Edin. Univ.; B.Sc. Edin. 1891; D.Sc. Edin. 1907.

Reynolds, Francis Esmond, Lecturer in Practical Pathology, 1922-24, in Neuropathology, 1924-32; *b.* Ilkley, Yorkshire, 19th Aug. 1882; *educ.* King Edward VIth High School Birmingham, Edin. Univ.; M.B., Ch.B. Edin. 1908; M.D. Edin. 1930; L.M., Coombe Hosp., Dublin 1908; M.R.C.P. Edin. 1930; D.T.M. & H., R.C.P. Lond. and R.C.S. Eng. 1920; D.T.M. & H. Camb. 1920; Pathologist, Devonshire Hosp., Buxton, 1911; Assistant in Pathology, Edin. Univ., 1912-13, 1921-22; Bacteriologist, North Manchurian Plague Commission, 1913-14; Professor of Pathology, Egyptian Government School of Medicine, Cairo, 1920-21; Pathologist to the City of Glasgow and Hon. Lecturer in Pathology, Glasg. Univ., since 1932.

Ritchie, James, Professor of Bacteriology, 1913-23; *b.* Duns, 1864; *educ.* Roy. High School Edinburgh, Edin. Univ., New Coll. Oxford; M.A. Edin. 1884; M.B., C.M. Edin. 1888; B.Sc. Edin. 1889; M.D. Edin. 1895; B.Sc. Oxf. 1901; M.A. Oxf. 1907; F.R.C.P. Edin. 1910; House Surgeon, Roy. Infirm., Edin., 1889; Lecturer, Reader and Professor (1902) of Pathology successively at Oxford, 1890-1907; Fellow of New Coll., Oxford, 1902-7; Hon. Physician 1897-1906, and Pathologist 1900-7, Radcliffe Infirm., Oxford; Superintendent, Roy. Coll. of Physicians Laboratory, Edin., 1907-20; Member of Edin. Univ. Court, 1920-23; *d.* Edinburgh, 28th Jan. 1923.

Ritchie, Robert Lindsay Graeme, Lecturer in French, 1909-19; *b.* Glasgow, 16th Nov. 1880; *educ.* Aberd. Grammar School, Aberd. Univ., Strassburg Univ. 1903, École des Hautes Études Paris 1904-8; M.A. Aberd. 1904; D.Litt. Aberd. 1922; Docteur de l'Univ. de Paris; Carnegie Research Scholar 1904-6, and Fellow 1908-9; Professor of French Language and Literature, Birmingham Univ., since 1919.

Robertson, Douglas Moray Cooper Lamb Argyll, Lecturer in Diseases of the Eye, 1883-1896; *b.* Edinburgh, 1837; *educ.* Edin. Instit., Neuwied, Germany, Univs. of Edin. and St And.; M.D. St And. 1857; F.R.C.S. Edin. 1862 (Pres. 1885-87); LL.D. Edin. 1896; House Surgeon, Roy. Infirm., Edin., 1857; Assistant to Professor John Hughes Bennett;

Assist. Ophthalmic Surgeon 1867, Surgeon 1882-96, Cons. Surgeon 1896, Roy. Infirm., Edin.; Pres., Ophthalmological Soc. of Great Britain, 1893-95; Surgeon Oculist to H.M. in Scotland; retired from practice, 1904; *d.* Gondal, India, 3rd Jan. 1909.

ROBERTSON, Edward, Lecturer in Arabic, 1913-21; *b.* Cameron, Fife, 10th Oct. 1879; *educ.* Cameron School, Madras Coll. St Andrews, Univs. of Leipzig, Berlin and Heidelberg; M.A. St And. 1902; B.D. St And. 1904; D.Litt. St And. 1913; D.D. St And. 1929; Assistant in Hebrew, St And. Univ., 1905-6; Carnegie Research Scholar, 1909-10; Gunning Lecturer, Edin. Univ., 1929-32; Professor of Semitic Languages and Literature since 1921, Dean of the Faculty of Theology since 1922, and Vice-Principal, 1926-28, Univ. of N. Wales, Bangor.

ROBERTSON, George Matthew, Professor of Psychiatry, 1920-32; *b.* India, 1864; *educ.* Madras Coll. St Andrews, Edin. Univ.; M.B., C.M. Edin. 1885; M.D. Edin. 1913; LL.D. St And. 1931; M.R.C.P. Edin. 1891; F.R.C.P. Edin. 1893 (Pres. 1925-27); Hon. F.R.C.S. Edin. 1927; Physician Consultant in Psychiatry, Roy. Infirm., Edin., 1923-29; Assistant, Roy. Edin. Asylum till 1892; Physician Superintendent, Perth District Asylum, Murthly, 1892, Stirling District Asylum, Larbert, 1899-1908, Roy. Edin. Asylum, 1908-32; Lecturer on mental diseases, extra-academical school, Edin.; Lecturer in Mental Diseases, Edin. Univ., 1910-20; *d.* Edinburgh, 26th March 1932.

ROBERTSON, William, Lecturer in Sanitary Administration, 1925-30; *b.* Beyrout, Palestine, 8th Sept. 1865; *educ.* George Watson's Coll. Edinburgh, Glasgow High School, Glasg. Univ.; M.B., C.M. 1887; M.D. 1891; D.P.H. Edin. and Glasg. 1893; M.R.C.P. Edin. 1921; F.R.C.P. Edin. 1923; Resident Surgeon and Physician, Glasg. Western Infirm.; Medical Officer of Health, Perth; general practice, Perth, for ten years; M.O.H., Paisley 1901, Leith 1902; Lecturer on public health, extra-academical school, Edin.; M.O.H. Edin. 1921-30 (retired).

ROBERTSON, William Alexander, Lecturer in Actuarial Science, 1922-23; *b.* Edinburgh, 8th Dec. 1877; *educ.* George Watson's Coll. Edin.; F.F.A. 1900; F.C.I.I. 1912; Actuary, Century Insurance Company, Limited, 1908, and Assist. General Manager and Actuary since 1920.

ROBINSON, Arthur, Professor of Anatomy, 1909-31; *b.* Manchester, 8th Apr. 1862; *educ.* Edin. Univ.; M.B., C.M. Edin. 1883; M.D. Edin. 1890; F.R.C.S. Eng. and Edin. 1912; Hon. R.S.A.; Fellow of King's Coll., London, 1913; Demonstrator in Anatomy, Edin. Univ., 1883; Demonstrator in Anatomy, Owens Coll., Manchester; Lecturer in Victoria Univ. of Manchester; Lecturer in Anatomy, Middlesex Hosp., London; Hunterian Professor, Roy. Coll. of Surgeons, 1903; Professor of Anatomy, Birmingham Univ., 1906-9.

APPENDIX II

ROBINSON, George, Lecturer in Mathematics, 1921-25; M.A.; B.Sc.

ROBINSON, Harold Roper, Lecturer 1923-24, and Reader 1924-26, in Natural Philosophy; *b.* 26th Nov. 1889; B.Sc. Manchester 1911, M.Sc. 1912, D.Sc. 1917; Ph.D. Trinity Coll. Cambridge 1924; F.R.S. 1929; Lecturer and Assist. Director of Physical Laboratories, Manchester Univ.; Mosely Research Student of the Roy. Soc.; Professor of Physics, Univ. Coll., Cardiff, 1926-30; Professor of Physics, East London Coll., London Univ., since 1930.

ROBSON, Andrew, Lecturer in Engineering Drawing and Structural Design, 1920-21; *b.* Hawick, 26th Apr. 1888; *educ.* Teviot Grove Acad. Hawick 1900-4, Edin. Univ. 1909-12; B.Sc. Edin. 1912; B.Com. Lond. 1926; A.M.I.Mech.E. 1914; engineer apprentice, Hawick, 1905-9; draughtsman with Dorman Long & Co., Ltd., Middlesbrough, 1912-13; Assist. Engineering Master, West Hartlepool Technical Coll., 1913-14, Allan Glen School, Glasgow, 1914-15; draughtsman 1915-16, Works' Manager of Optical Dept. 1916-20, with Barr & Stroud, Ltd., Glasgow; head of Engineering Dept. 1921-22, Principal 1922-33, West Hartlepool Technical Coll.; Principal, Handsworth Technical Coll., Birmingham, 1933.

ROMANES, George John, Lecturer in Philosophy of Natural History, 1886-91; *b.* Kingston, Canada West, 20th May 1848; *educ.* Gonville and Caius Coll. Cambridge, Univ. Coll. London; B.A. Camb. 1870; LL.D. Aberd. 1882; *d.* Oxford, 23rd May 1894.

ROSS, John David McBeath, Lecturer in Chemistry, 1919-26; *b.* Edinburgh, 3rd Nov. 1889; *educ.* George Heriot's School Edin., Edin. Univ.; B.Sc. 1912; M.A. 1913; D.Sc. 1926; F.C.S. 1919; F.S.C.I. 1919; Imperial Coll. of Science and Technology, London, for Trench Warfare Dept. and Chemical Warfare Dept. of Ministry of Munitions, 1915-18, and Demonstrator in Chemistry, 1918-19; Lecturer in Physical Chemistry, Univ. Coll., Dundee, since 1926.

RUSSELL, William, Moncrieff Arnott Professor of Clinical Medicine, 1913-19; *b.* Isle of Man, 1852; *educ.* Wick Acad., Thurso Acad., F.C. Instit. Castle Douglas, Edin. Univ.; M.B., C.M. Edin. 1876; M.D. Edin. 1884; LL.D. Edin. 1920; F.R.C.P. Edin. 1887 (Pres. 1916-18); House Physician and Pathologist, General Hosp., Wolverhampton; Pathologist, Roy. Infirm., Edin., and Lecturer on pathology, extra-academical school, Edin.; Senior Lecturer in Clinical Medicine, Edin. Univ., 1913; Physician, Roy. Infirm., Edin., 1907-19.

RUTHERFORD, Andrew, Lecturer in Clinical Medicine, 1925-29; *b.* 1890; M.B., Ch.B. Edin. 1912; B.Sc. Edin. 1915; Assistant in Pathology, Edin. Univ.; Assist. Physician, Roy. Infirm., Edin., 1924-30; *d.* Edinburgh, 4th July 1930.

BIOGRAPHICAL NOTES

RUTHERFORD, William, Professor of Physiology, 1874-99; *b.* Ancrum Craig, Roxburghshire, 20th Apr. 1839; *educ.* Jedburgh Grammar School, Edin. Univ.; M.D. Edin. 1863; Assistant Demonstrator in Anatomy, Surgeons' Hall, 1864; travelled on Continent, 1864-5; Assistant to John Hughes Bennett, Edin. Univ., 1865; Professor of Physiology, King's Coll., London, 1869-74; Fullerian Professor of Physiology, Roy. Instit. of London, 1871; one of the founders of the Edin. Univ. Musical Soc., 1866; *d.* 21st Feb. 1899.

RYRIE, Benjamin James, Lecturer in Pathology, 1920-21; *b.* Fraserburgh, 1888; *educ.* Townhead School Montrose, Montrose Acad., Edin. Univ.; M.B., Ch.B. 1916; Assistant in Anatomy, Edin. Univ., 1915-16; Professor of Pathology, Univ. of Cape Town, since 1925.

SAINTSBURY, George Edward Bateman, Regius Professor of Rhetoric and English Literature, 1895-1915; *b.* Southampton, 23rd Oct. 1845; *educ.* King's Coll. School London, Merton Coll. Oxford; B.A. Oxf. 1868, M.A. 1873; LL.D. Aberd. 1898 and Edin. 1919; Hon. D.Litt. Durham 1906 and Oxf. 1912; F.B.A. 1911; Fellow, King's Coll., Lond., 1892; Hon. Fellow, Merton Coll., 1909; Assistant Master, Manchester Grammar School, 1868; Senior Classical Master, Elizabeth Coll., Guernsey, 1868-74; Headmaster, Elgin Educational Instit., 1874-76; journalist in London, 1876-95; in retirement at Bath, 1915-33; *d.* Bath, 28th Jan. 1933.

SAROLEA, Charles, Professor of French, 1918-31; *b.* Tongres, Belgium, 25th Oct. 1870; *educ.* Roy. Athénee, Hasselt, Liège Univ. (and Paris, Palermo, Naples, 1892-3); O.O.L. 1918; K.O.L. 1902; Ph.D. Liège 1892; D.Litt. Liège 1892; Hon. D.Ph. Brussels 1904; LL.D. Montreal 1915; D. Juris Cleveland 1915; first Consul for Scotland, Free Congo State, 1903; Belgian Consul at Edinburgh, 1901; Lecturer in French, Edin. Univ., 1894-1918.

SCHAFER, Sir Edward Albert Sharpey, Professor of Physiology, 1899-1933; *b.* London, 2nd June 1850; Kt. 1913; LL.D. (Aberd. 1897, McGill 1908, St And. 1911); Sc.D. (Dublin 1905, Camb. 1914, Melbourne 1914, Oxf. 1926); Hon. M.D. Berne 1910 and Groningen 1914; D.Sci. Méd. Louvain 1930; Hon. D.Sc. Nat. Univ. of Ireland 1933; Hon. F.R.C.P. Edin. 1931; F.R.S. 1878; Assistant Professor of Physiology, Univ. Coll., Lond., 1874-83; Jodrell Professor of Physiology, Lond. Univ., 1883-99.

SCHLAPP, Otto, Professor of German, 1926-29; *b.* Erfurt, 15th May 1859; *educ.* Erfurt, Jena, Edinburgh 1880-81, Berlin, Leipzig and Strassburg Univs.; Dr Philos. Strassburg; LL.D. Edin. 1930; Teacher of German in George Watson's Coll. and Edin. Ladies' Coll., 1887-94; Lecturer in German, Edin. Univ., 1894-1920, Reader 1920-26.

APPENDIX II

SCOT-SKIRVING, Archibald Adam, Senior Lecturer in Clinical Surgery, 1918-28; *b.* East Lothian, 29th June 1868; *educ.* Edin. Acad., Cheltenham Coll., Edin. Univ., Paris, Berlin; C.M.G. 1900; M.B., C.M. Edin. 1893; M.R.C.S. Eng., L.R.C.P. Lond. 1895; F.R.C.S. Edin. 1897; House Surgeon to Professor Chiene, 1893; Senior Surgeon, Leith Hosp., till 1916; Assist. Surgeon 1910-16, Surgeon 1916-28, Cons. Surgeon 1928-30, Roy. Infirm., Edin.; *d.* Edinburgh, 14th June 1930.

SELLAR, William Young, Professor of Humanity, 1863-90; *b.* Morvich, Sutherlandshire, 22nd Feb. 1825; *educ.* Edin. Acad., Glasgow Univ., Balliol Coll. Oxford; B.A. Oxf. 1847, M.A. 1850; LL.D. St And. 1863; Fellow of Oriel Coll., Oxford, 1848; Lecturer in Durham Univ.; Assistant to Professor Ramsay, Glasg. Univ., 1851-53; Assistant in Greek, St And. Univ., 1853-59; Professor of Greek, Glasg. Univ., 1859-63; *d.* Dalry, Kirkcudbrightshire, 12th Oct. 1890.

SETH, Andrew. *See* PRINGLE-PATTISON, Andrew Seth.

SETH, James, Professor of Moral Philosophy, 1898-1924; *b.* Edinburgh, 1860; younger brother of Andrew Seth Pringle-Pattison (*q.v.*); *educ.* George Watson's Coll. Edin., Edin. Univ., Free Church Coll. Edin., Leipzig, Jena and Berlin; M.A. Edin. 1881; LL.D. Dalhousie 1919; licensed by Free Church Presbytery of Edin.; Assistant to Professor Campbell Fraser, 1883-85; Professor of Philosophy, Dalhousie Coll., Halifax, Nova Scotia, 1886-92; Professor of Philosophy, Brown Univ., U.S.A., 1892-96; Sage Professor of Moral Philosophy, Cornell Univ., U.S.A., 1896-98; *d.* Edinburgh, 24th July 1924.

SHENNAN, Theodore, Lecturer in Morbid Anatomy, 1913-14; *b.* Bathgate, West Lothian; *educ.* Roy. High School Edinburgh, Edin. Univ.; M.B., C.M. Edin. 1890; M.D. Edin. 1895; F.R.C.S. Edin. 1898; Pathologist, Leith Hosp. 1896, Hosp. for Sick Children 1900, and Roy. Infirm., Edin., 1902; Lecturer in Pathology and Bacteriology, Surgeons' Hall, Edin., 1899-1913; Professor of Pathology, Aberdeen Univ., since 1914.

RHS

SHOESMITH, John Baldwin, Lecturer in Chemistry, 1921-31; *b.* 1896; *educ.* Manchester Univ.; B.Sc. Manchester 1919, M.Sc. 1920; D.Sc. Edin. 1925; *d.* Edinburgh, 18th Nov. 1931.

SILLAR, William Cameron, Lecturer in Experimental Pharmacology, 1894-1924; *b.* London; *educ.* Blackheath School, Edin. Univ., London and Strassburg; M.B., C.M. Edin. 1887; B.Sc. Edin. 1889; M.D. Edin. 1906; Assistant in Pharmacology, Edin. Univ., 1890-94.

SIMPSON, Sir Alexander Russell, Professor of Midwifery, 1870-1905; *b.* Bathgate, 30th Apr. 1835; *educ.* Bathgate Acad., Edin. Univ., Montpellier, Halle, Berlin, Vienna and Würzburg; Kt. 1906; M.D. Edin. 1856; Hon. D.Sc. Manchester 1902; LL.D.; F.R.C.P. Edin. 1865 (Pres. 1891-93); apprenticed to Professor John Goodsir; Assistant for seven years to his uncle, Sir James Young Simpson, Bart.; in private practice in Glasgow for five years; Dean of the Faculty of Medicine, Edin. Univ., 1900-4; killed by a motor car, Edinburgh, 5th Apr. 1916.

Simpson, Sutherland, Lecturer in Experimental Physiology, 1902-8; *b.* Flotta, Orkney, 3rd Feb. 1863; *educ.* Flotta Parish School, Heriot-Watt Coll. Edinburgh 1882-85, Edin. Univ.; B.Sc. Edin. 1894; M.B., Ch.B. 1899; M.D. 1901; D.Sc. 1903; Assistant in Physiology, Edin. Univ., 1899-1908; Professor of Physiology and Head of the Dept. of Physiology and Biochemistry, Cornell Univ., Ithaca, U.S.A., 1908-26; *d.* 1926.

Sinclair, Arthur Henry Havens, Lecturer in Diseases of the Eye, 1920-32; *b.* Kenmore, Perthshire, Feb. 1868; *educ.* Acharn School, Perthshire, privately Edinburgh, Edin. Univ., London, Utrecht; M.B., C.M. Edin. 1893; M.D. Edin. 1899; F.R.C.S. Edin. 1900; Ophthalmic Surgeon, Roy. Infirm., Edin., 1920-32; Cons. Ophthalmic Surgeon, Edin. Eye, Ear and Throat Infirm. and Leith Hosp.; Hon. Surgeon Oculist to H.M. in Scotland, 1928; Pres., Ophthalmological Soc. of the United Kingdom, 1932.

Skirving, Archibald Adam Scot. *See* Scot-Skirving, Archibald Adam.

Slight, David, Lecturer in Psychology, 1924-25; *b.* Falkirk, 1899; *educ.* Victoria School Falkirk 1903-11, Falkirk High School 1911-16, Edin. Univ. 1916-22; M.B., Ch.B. 1922; D.P.M. R.C.P.S.Eng. 1924; F.R.C.P.S. Canada; Assist. Physician, Edin. Roy. Asylum; Maudsley Hosp., Denmark Hill; Lecturer and Rockefeller Fellow, 1927-8, and Assist. Professor of Psychiatry, McGill Univ., Montreal, since 1928.

Smeal, Glenny, Lecturer in Mathematics, 1919-21; B.Sc.; Assistant in Mathematics, Edin. Univ., 1914-16, 1918-19.

Smith, Allan Edward Holmes, Lecturer in Plant Physiology, 1911-14; *b.* Edinburgh, 20th March 1881; *educ.* Edin. Instit., Edin. Univ.; B.Sc. Edin. 1907; Demonstrator in Botany, Edin. Univ., 1906-7; conducted Flax Research, Belgium, 1907-8; Economic Botanist, India, 1908-11, and Acting Deputy Director of Agriculture, Bombay, 1910-11; Lecturer in Agricultural Botany and Plant Pathology, Union Dept. of Agriculture, South Africa, 1914-19; Senior Lecturer in Agricultural Botany and Mycology, Manchester Univ., and Advisory Plant Pathologist, Ministry of Agriculture and Fisheries, since 1919.

Smith, George Gregory. *See* Gregory Smith, George.

Smith, James Lorrain, Professor of Pathology, 1912-31; *b.* Half Morton, Dumfriesshire, 21st Aug. 1862; *educ.* George Watson's Coll. Edinburgh, Univs. of Edin., Oxford, Cambridge 1892, Strassburg and Copenhagen; M.A. Edin. 1884; M.B., C.M. Edin. 1889; M.D. Edin. 1893; LL.D. Belfast 1922; D.Sc. Manchester 1930; F.R.S. 1909; Demonstrator in Pathology, Camb. Univ.; Hon. Pathologist, Roy. Infirm., Edin., 1913; Lecturer 1895, and Professor 1901, Queen's Coll., Belfast; Professor of Pathology, Manchester Univ., 1904; Member of the Roy. Commission on Irish University Education, 1901; Dean of the Faculty of Medicine, Edin. Univ., 1919-31; *d.* Edinburgh, 18th Apr. 1931.

APPENDIX II

Smith, William G., Lecturer in Plant Physiology, 1894-98.

Smith, William George, Lecturer in Psychology, 1906-18; *b.* Half Morton, Dumfriesshire, 1866; younger brother of J. Lorrain Smith (*q.v.*); *educ.* George Watson's Coll. Edinburgh, Edin. Univ., Leipzig Univ.; M.A. Edin. 1889; Ph.D. Leipzig 1894; Assistant in Moral Philosophy, Edin. Univ., 1889-91; Harvard Psychological Laboratory, 1895; Professor, Smith's Coll., Northampton, Mass.; Lecturer in Psychophysics, King's Coll., London; Assist. Lecturer in Physiology, Liverpool Univ.; *d.* Edinburgh, 22nd Nov. 1918.

Smyth, Charles Piazzi, Regius Professor of Astronomy, 1846-89; *b.* Naples, 3rd Jan. 1819; LL.D. Edin. 1890; Assistant at Cape Roy. Observatory, 1835; Astronomer Royal for Scotland, 1845-89; resigned his Fellowship of the Roy. Soc., 1874; *d.* Clova, Ripon, Yorkshire, 21st Feb. 1900.

Somerville, Sir William, Lecturer in Forestry, 1889-91; *b.* Lanarkshire, 1860; *educ.* Roy. High School Edinburgh, Univs. of Edin. and Munich; K.B.E. 1926; B.Sc. Edin. 1888; D.Œcon. Munich 1889; Hon. D.Sc. Durh. 1897; Hon. M.A. Durh. 1898; M.A. Camb. 1899; D.Sc. Oxf. 1911; LL.D. Edin. 1922; M.A. Oxf. 1924; F.L.S.; Professor of Agriculture and Forestry, Durham Coll. of Science, 1891-99; Professorial Fellow of King's Coll., and Professor of Agriculture, Cambridge Univ., 1899-1901; Sibthorpian Professor of Rural Economy, Oxford, 1906-1925; Assist. Secretary of the Board of Agriculture and Fisheries, 1902-6; Hon. Fellow of St John's Coll., Oxford, 1926-32; *d.* Boar's Hill, Oxford, 17th Feb. 1932.

Sprague, Alfred Ernest, Lecturer in Actuarial Science, 1919-21; *b.* Blackheath, Kent, 15th Aug. 1868; son of Thomas Bond Sprague, M.A., LL.D.; *educ.* Edin. Collegiate School, 1875-83, Edin. Univ. 1883-87, Trinity Coll. Cambridge 1887-90; B.Sc. Edin. 1888; B.A. Camb. 1890, M.A.; D.Sc. Edin. 1905; F.F.A. 1892; F.I.A. 1893; Assistant Secretary 1901-11, Secretary and Actuary 1911-27, Edin. Life Assurance Company, Limited (now Edin. Assurance Company Limited); retired from business 1927.

Steen, Stourton William Peile, Lecturer in Mathematics, 1925-26; *educ.* Christ's Coll. Cambridge; B.A. 1921, M.A. 1925; Fellow of Christ's Coll., Camb., 1923; Univ. Lecturer in Mathematics, Cambridge.

Stephenson, John, Lecturer in Zoology, 1920-29; *b.* Padiham, Lancashire, 1871; *educ.* Burnley Grammar School, Univs. of Manchester and London; C.I.E. 1919; B.Sc. Lond. 1890; M.B., Ch.B. Manchester 1893; M.B. Lond. 1894; D.Sc. Lond. 1909; F.R.C.S. Eng. 1905; F.R.S. 1930; House Physician, Manchester Roy. Infirm., 1893-94; House Physician, Roy. Hosp. for Diseases of the Chest, London, 1894; joined Indian Medical Service, 1895; Professor of Biology, Government Coll., Lahore, 1906, Professor of Zoology 1912, Principal 1912; Vice-Chancellor, Punjab University, 1918; retired from I.M.S. in 1920 with rank of Lieut.-Colonel; *d.* London, 2nd Feb. 1933.

BIOGRAPHICAL NOTES

Steuart, Ethel Mary, Lecturer in Latin, 1921-26; *b.* Mumbles, Glamorgan.; *educ.* North London Collegiate School, Univ. Coll. London, Girton Coll. Cambridge, Berlin Univ.; B.A. Lond. 1908; M.A. Lond. 1914; Dipl. in Pedagogy, Lond. Univ., 1914; D.Litt. Edin. 1923; Fellow of Girton Coll.; did research work in Paris and at the British School of Archæology, Rome; Assist. Lecturer in Latin, Univ. Coll., Cardiff; Headmistress, High School for Girls, Bootle, Liverpool, since 1926.

Stevenson, George Hope, Lecturer in Ancient History, 1905-7; *educ.* Glasgow Univ., Balliol Coll. Oxford; M.A. Glasg. 1900; B.A. Oxf. 1904, M.A. 1907; Fellow of Univ. Coll., Oxford, 1906, re-elected 1913; Praelector in Ancient History and Secretary, Univ. Coll., Oxford; Univ. Lecturer in Ancient History and Curator of Taylor Instit., Oxford.

Stewart, Charles Hunter, Bruce and John Usher Professor of Public Health, 1898-1924; *b.* Edinburgh, 29th Sept. 1854; *educ.* Edin. Univ., Munich, Amsterdam and Paris; B.Sc. Edin. 1882; M.B., C.M. Edin. 1884; D.Sc. Edin. 1894; Assistant to Professor Sir Douglas Maclagan (*q.v.*), 1884-97; first occupant of the Bruce and John Usher Chair of Public Health, 1898; Director of the John Usher Instit. of Public Health, Edin. Univ., 1902; *d.* Edinburgh, 30th June 1924.

Stewart, J. F., Lecturer in Forestry, 1927-30.

Stewart, Sir Thomas Grainger, Professor of Medicine, 1876-1900; *b.* Edinburgh, 23rd Sept. 1837; *educ.* High School Edin., Universities and Hospitals of Edin., Berlin, Prague and Vienna; Kt. 1894; M.D. Edin. 1858; M.D. Roy. Univ. Ireland 1887; Hon. M.D. Dublin 1892; LL.D. Aberd. 1897; F.R.C.P. Edin. 1861 (Pres. 1889-91); Hon. F.R.C.P. Ireland 1887; Hon. F.C.P. Philadelphia 1892; Lecturer on materia medica and dietetics 1861, on pathology 1862, on clinical medicine 1869, on practice of physic 1873, in extra-academical school, Edin.; Pathologist 1862, Physician 1869-1900, Roy. Infirm., Edin.; Physician, Sick Children's Hosp., Edin., 1862; Physician-in-Ordinary to the Queen in Scotland, 1882; *d.* Edinburgh, 3rd Feb. 1900.

Stiles, Sir Harold Jalland, Regius Professor of Clinical Surgery, 1919-25; *b.* Spalding, Lincolnshire, 21st March 1863; *educ.* Totteridge Park 1872-79, Univs. of Edin., Freiburg and Berne; K.B.E.; M.B., C.M. Edin. 1885; Hon. D.Sc. Leeds 1922; LL.D. St. And. 1922 and Edin. 1925; F.R.C.S. Edin. 1889 (Pres. 1923-25); Hon. F.R.C.S. Ireland; Hon. F.A.C.S.; Assistant in Anatomy, 1887-89 and Assistant in Surgery, 1889-1900, Edin. Univ.; Lecturer in Applied Anatomy, Edin. Univ., 1903-19; Assist. Surgeon, Surgeon 1919-25, now Cons. Surgeon, Roy. Infirm., Edin.; Surgeon 1898-1919, and Cons. Surgeon, Roy. Hosp. for Sick Children, Edin.; Surgeon 1904, now Cons. Surgeon, Chalmers Hosp., Edin.; Member, Edin. Univ. Court, 1923-25; Surgeon to H.M. in Scotland.

APPENDIX II

Stump, Claude Witherington, Lecturer in Anatomy, 1923-24; *b.* Malvern, South Australia, 1891; *educ.* Unley School, Kyre Coll., Edin. Univ.; M.B., Ch.B. Edin. 1917; M.D. Edin. 1923; D.Sc. Edin. 1924; Professor of Anatomy, Roy. Medical Coll., Univ. of Bangkok, Siam, 1924-27; Professor of Embryology and Histology, Univ. of Sydney, since 1927.

Sym, William George, Lecturer in Diseases of the Eye, 1912-20; *b.* Edinburgh, 1864; *educ.* Craigmount House School Edin. 1878-80, Edin. Univ.; M.B., C.M. 1886; M.D. 1889; L.R.C.S. Edin. 1888; F.R.C.S. Edin. 1889; Assist. Ophthalmic Surgeon 1891, Surgeon 1905, Cons. Surgeon 1920, Roy. Infirm., Edin.; Lecturer on diseases of the eye in the extra-academical school, Edin., 1905; Ophthalmic Surgeon, Eye, Ear and Throat Infirm., Edin.; Cons. Ophthalmic Surgeon, Leith Hosp. and Roy. Maternity Hosp., Edinburgh.

Tait, John, Lecturer in Experimental Physiology, 1911-19; *b.* Orkney, 1878; *educ.* Edin. Univ., Göttingen, Berlin; B.Sc. Edin. 1901; M.B., Ch.B. Edin. 1903; M.D. Edin. 1906; D.Sc. Edin. 1907; Drake Professor of Physiology, McGill Univ., Montreal, since 1919.

Tait, Peter Guthrie, Professor of Natural Philosophy, 1860-1901; *b.* Dalkeith, 28th Apr. 1831; *educ.* Dalkeith Grammar School, Edin. Acad. 1841-47, Edin. Univ. 1847, Peterhouse Cambridge 1848; B.A. Camb. 1852; Hon. Sc.D. Univ. of Ireland, 1875; LL.D. Glasg. 1901; Fellow of Peterhouse 1852, Hon. Fellow 1885; Professor of Mathematics, Queen's Coll., Belfast, 1854; resigned Chair at Edin., 1901; *d.* Edinburgh, 4th July 1901.

Taylor, John Orr, Lecturer in Military History, 1921-25, and in Industrial Law, 1928-32; M.A. Glasg. 1908; LL.B. Glasg. 1911; Advocate, Scots Bar, 1914; *d.* Elie, 9th Sept. 1932.

Taylor, Malcolm Campbell, Regius Professor of Ecclesiastical History, 1876-1908; *b.* Dalinlongard, Argyllshire, 1832; *educ.* Parish School of Bowmore, Univs. of Glasgow, St Andrews, Heidelberg and Tübingen; D.D. Glasg. 1866; LL.D. Edin. 1909; Licentiate of the Church of Scotland, 1860; ordained to Parish of New Kirk (Greyfriars), Dumfries, 1862, Montrose 1865, Crathie and Braemar 1867, Morningside, Edinburgh, 1873; Extra Chaplain to the Queen in Scotland, 1873; Extra Chaplain-in-Ordinary to the King in Scotland, 1901-22; Dean of the Faculty of Divinity, Edin. Univ., 1884-99; Secretary to Edin. Univ. Court 1892-1916, Member 1889-93; *d.* Edinburgh, 10th Mar. 1922.

Taylor, William White, Lecturer in Chemistry, 1902-15, and in Biochemistry, 1915-30; *b.* Alnwick, 1869; *educ.* Darlington Grammar School 1882-87, Edin. Univ.; M.A. Edin. 1893; B.Sc. Edin. 1896; D.Sc. Edin. 1901; Assistant in Chemistry, Edin. Univ., 1893-1902.

TEMPLETON, James, Lecturer in Plant Physiology, 1920-21; *b.* Annan, 1891; *educ.* Annan Public School, Broughton H.G. School Edinburgh, Broughton Junior Student Centre Edin., Edin. Univ.; B.Sc. 1914; D.Sc. 1927; Assistant in Botany, Edin. Univ.; Senior Botanist, Ministry of Agriculture, Cotton Research Board, Cairo.

THOMSON, Alexander Douglas, Lecturer in Greek, 1892-99; *b.* Kinross-shire, 9th Nov. 1864; *educ.* Roy. High School Edin., Edin. Univ.; M.A. Edin. 1888; D.Litt. Edin. 1897; Assistant in Greek, St And. Univ., 1888-89; Interim Assistant in Greek, Edin. Univ., 1889; Classical and English Master, Kelvinside Acad., Glasgow, 1888-91; Rector of Stranraer Acad., 1891; Assistant in Greek, Edin. Univ., 1891; H.M. Inspector of Schools (Scotland), 1899, Chief Inspector, 1922-29; retired, 1929.

THOMSON, Henry Alexis, Professor of Surgery, 1909-23; *b.* Edinburgh, 1863; *educ.* Roy. High School Edin., La Villette Vaud, Realschule Hanover, Edin. Univ., St Thomas's Hosp. London; C.M.G. 1916; M.B., C.M. Edin. 1885; B.Sc. (Public Health) Edin. 1888; M.D. Edin. 1889; M.R.C.S. Eng. 1885; F.R.C.S. Eng. 1920; F.R.C.S. Edin. 1888; Assist. Surgeon 1892-1909, Surgeon 1909-23, Roy. Infirm., Edin.; Surgeon to Deaconess Hosp., Edin., 1894-1909; *d.* Algeciras, 5th Mar. 1924.

THOMSON, John, Lecturer in Clinical Instruction on Diseases of Children, 1913-17; *b.* Edinburgh, 23rd Nov. 1856; *educ.* Edin. Acad., Univs. of Edin., Vienna and Berlin; M.B., C.M. Edin. 1881; M.D. Edin. 1891; LL.D. Edin. 1922; F.R.C.P. Edin. 1888; Hon. F.R.C.P. Lond. 1926; Hon. Member American Pediatric Soc.; Physician 1889-1917, Cons. Physician 1917-26, Roy. Edin. Hosp. for Sick Children; Cons. Physician, Roy. Scottish National Instit., Larbert; *d.* Edinburgh, 2nd July 1926.

THOMSON, Robert Black, Lecturer in Anatomy, 1909-11; *b.* Thornhill, Dumfriesshire, 1880; *educ.* Wallace Hall Acad., Edin. Univ.; M.B., Ch.B. Edin. 1905; M.D.; Assistant in Anatomy, Edin. Univ., 1906-9; Professor of Anatomy, Cape Town University.

THORNTON, Cecil Taylor, Lecturer in Practical Theology, 1927-31; *b.* Edinburgh, 26th Mar. 1886; *educ.* Merchiston Castle School, Oxford Univ., Edin. Univ.; B.A. Oxf. 1911; B.D. Edin. 1910; licensed by Presbytery of Edinburgh, 1910; Assistant Minister, St Marks, Dundee; ordained, 1913; Minister of St Columba's, Blackhall, Edin., 1913, of St Margaret's Parish Church, Edin., since 1926.

TILLIE, Joseph, Lecturer in Experimental Pharmacology, 1894-96; *b.* Edinburgh, 1859; *educ.* Daniel Stewart's Hosp. Edin., Edin. Univ., Leipzig; M.B., C.M. Edin. 1886; M.D. Edin. 1889; Assistant in Materia Medica, 1888-96, and Tutor, Clinical Medicine, 1891-96, Edin. Univ.; Physician, Western Dispensary, 1893; Resident Surgeon, Roy. Maternity Hosp., Edin.; Resident Physician, Roy. Infirm., Edin.; *d.* Springfontein, Orange Free State, 28th Nov. 1898.

APPENDIX II

TILLYARD, Henry Julius Wetenhall, Lecturer in Greek, 1908-17, and in Russian, 1917-19; *b.* Cambridge, 18th Nov. 1881; *educ.* Tonbridge School, Gonville and Caius Coll. Cambridge; B.A. Camb. 1904, M.A. 1910; D.Litt. Edin. 1918; Member of the British School at Athens, 1904-12; Professor of Latin, Univ. Coll., Johannesburg, 1919-21; Professor of Russian, Birmingham Univ., 1921-26; Professor of Greek, Univ. Coll., Cardiff, since 1926.

TODD, James Eadie, Lecturer in Economic History, 1910-12; *b.* Duns, Berwickshire, 1885; *educ.* George Watson's Coll. Edinburgh, Edin. Univ., Balliol Coll. Oxford; M.A. Edin. 1907; M.A. Oxf. 1914; F.R.H.S.; Lecturer in History, McGill Univ., Montreal, 1912-13; Professor of History and Economics, Dalhousie Univ., Nova Scotia, 1913-16; Professor of Modern History, Queen's Univ., Belfast, since 1919.

TURNER, Arthur Logan, Lecturer in Diseases of the Larynx, Ear and Nose, 1906-24; *b.* 6th May 1865; *educ.* Fettes Coll., Edin. Univ.; M.B., C.M. Edin. 1889; M.D. Edin. 1894; LL.D. Edin. 1926; F.R.C.S. Edin. 1891 (Pres. 1925-27); Hon. F.R.C.P. Edin. 1927; Assist. Surgeon 1903, Surgeon 1906-21, Surgeon-Consultant 1921-24, and Cons. Surgeon since 1924 to the Ear and Throat Dept., Roy. Infirm., Edinburgh.

TURNER, Sir William, Professor of Anatomy, 1867-1903; Principal of the University, 1903-16; *b.* Lancaster, 7th Jan. 1832; *educ.* private schools, St Bartholomew Hosp., London Univ., 1850-54; K.C.B. 1901; Kt. 1886; M.B. Lond. 1857; M.R.C.S. Eng. 1853; F.R.C.S. Edin. (Pres. 1882-83); D.C.L. (Durham 1889, Oxf. 1890, Toronto and McGill 1897); LL.D. (Glasg. 1884, St And. 1902, Aberd. 1906); Sc.D. Dublin 1892 and Camb. 1909; F.R.S. 1877; invited to Edinburgh by John Goodsir to be Senior Demonstrator, 1854; Univ. Demonstrator in Anatomy, 1861; Dean of the Faculty of Medicine, Edin. Univ., 1878-81; represented Univs. of Edin. and Aberd. 1873-83, and Edin. 1886-1905, on General Medical Council; Pres., General Medical Council, 1898-1904; Lecturer on Anatomy and Physiology to Roy. Coll. of Surgeons, Eng., 1875-76; Professor of Anatomy, Roy. Scottish Acad.; Member of Edin. Univ. Court, 1889-1916; Curator of Patronage, 1906; given Freedom of Edin., 1908; *d.* Edinburgh, 15th Feb. 1916.

TWEEDIE, Charles, Lecturer in Mathematics, 1892-1922; *b.* Swinton, Duns, 1868; *educ.* Swinton School 1873-83, George Watson's Coll. Edin. 1883-85, Edin. Univ.; M.A. 1890; B.Sc. 1890; *d.* Edinburgh, 14th Sept. 1925.

TYTLER, James Stuart Fraser, Professor of Conveyancing, 1866-91; *b.* Woodhouselee, 1820; grandson of Lord Woodhouselee, Senator of the Coll. of Justice; *educ.* Edin. Acad., Edin. Univ.; Writer to the Signet, 1849; LL.D. Glasg. 1874; *d.* Edinburgh, 26th Nov. 1891.

BIOGRAPHICAL NOTES

UNDERHILL, Charles Edward, Lecturer in Clinical Instruction on Diseases of Children, 1887-90; *b.* 8th Mar. 1845; *educ.* Shrewsbury, Gonville and Caius Coll. Cambridge, Edinburgh School of Medicine; B.A. Camb. 1867; M.B. Camb. 1870; F.R.C.S. Edin. 1872; M.R.C.S. Eng. 1872; F.R.C.P. Edin. 1876 (Pres. 1906-8); Lecturer on midwifery 1876, and on diseases of children 1886, extra-academical school of medicine, Edin.; Obstetric Physician, Roy. Maternity Hosp., Edin.; Hon. Physician and Cons. Physician, Roy. Hosp. for Sick Children, Edin.; *d.* Juniper Green, Midlothian, 24th Apr. 1908.

UNWIN, George, Lecturer in Economic History, 1908-10; *b.* Stockport, 7th May 1870; *educ.* Univ. Coll. Cardiff 1890-93, Lincoln Coll. Oxford 1893-97, Berlin Univ. 1897-98; B.A. Oxf. 1897; Research Scholar at London School of Economics, 1898-99; Private Secretary to Lord Courtney of Penwith, 1899-1907; Lecturer at London Univ., 1905-7; Professor of Economic History, Manchester Univ., 1910-25; *d.* Manchester, 30th Jan. 1925.

URQUHART, John, Lecturer in Mathematics, 1911-14; *b.* Poolewe, Ross-shire, 1883; *educ.* Poolewe School, Gairloch School, Aberdeen Grammar School, Aberd. Univ., Jesus Coll. Cambridge; M.A. Aberd. 1906; B.A. Camb. 1909; Assistant in Mathematics, Edin. Univ., 1909; *d.* 1914.

VINOGRADOFF, Igor, Lecturer in European History, 1926-31; son of Sir Paul Vinogradoff; *educ.* New Coll. Oxford; B.A. 1924.

WALKER, Sir James, Professor of Chemistry, 1908-28; *b.* Dundee, 6th Apr. 1863; *educ.* Dundee High School, Univs. of Edin. 1882, Munich 1887 and Leipzig 1888; Kt. 1921; B.Sc. Edin. 1885; D.Sc. Edin. 1886; Ph.D. Leipzig 1889; LL.D. St And. 1909 and Edin. 1929; F.R.S. 1900; Demonstrator in Chemistry, 1886-87, and Assistant to Professor of Chemistry, Edin. Univ., 1889-92; Professor of Chemistry, Univ. Coll., Dundee, 1894-1908; Pres., Chemical Soc., 1921-23.

WALKER, Sir Norman Purvis, Lecturer in Diseases of the Skin, 1906-24; *b.* Dysart, Fife, 2nd Aug. 1862; *educ.* Edin. Acad., Univs. of Edin., Vienna, Prague; Kt. 1923; M.B., C.M. Edin. 1884; M.D. Edin. 1888; LL.D. St And. 1920 and Edin. 1926; F.R.C.P. Edin. 1892 (Pres. 1929-31); Resident Physician 1885, Assist. Physician 1892, and Physician 1906-25, to the Dept. for Diseases of the Skin, Roy. Infirm., Edin.; in general practice, Cumberland, 1885-90; Pres., General Medical Council, 1931.

WALLACE, Sir David, Lecturer 1910-13, and Senior Lecturer 1913-23, in Clinical Surgery; *b.* July 1862; *educ.* Dollar Acad., Edin. Univ.; K.B.E. 1920; C.B.E. 1918; C.M.G. 1900; D.L. City of Edin.; M.B., C.M. 1884; LL.D. Edin. 1930; F.R.C.S. Edin. 1887 (Pres. 1921-23); War service, South Africa 1900-2; Surgeon 1908-23, now Cons. Surgeon, Roy. Infirm., Edin.; Surgeon, Roy. Hosp. for Incurables, Edinburgh.

APPENDIX II

WALLACE, Robert, Professor of Agriculture, 1885-1922; *b.* 24th June 1853; *educ.* Edin. Univ.; M.A.; LL.D. Edin. 1923; F.R.S.G.S.; Professor of Agriculture, Roy. Agricultural Coll., Cirencester, 1882-85; made agricultural investigations in Italy and India 1887, Australia and New Zealand 1889, U.S.A. 1879, 1890, 1893, 1898, 1907-10, Egypt 1891, Greece 1891-92, South Africa (for Government of the Cape) 1895, Canada and Mexico 1907, Rhodesia (for the Chartered Company) 1908, Tonkin, F.M.S., Java, Japan and Canada 1910, 1923; adviser to Victoria Government at Inter-colonial Cattle-tick Conference, Sydney, 1896; Hon. Secretary, Roy. Empire Soc.; Garton Lecturer in Colonial and Indian Agriculture, 1900-22.

WATERSTON, David, Lecturer in Anatomy, 1903-9; M.A. Edin. 1892; M.B., C.M. Edin. 1895; M.D. Edin. 1900; F.R.C.S. Edin. 1898; Demonstrator in Anatomy, Edin. Univ.; Professor of Anatomy and Dean of the Faculty of Science (Medical), King's Coll., London, 1909-14; Bute Professor of Anatomy, St And. Univ., since 1914.

WATSON, Benjamin Philp, Professor of Midwifery, 1922-26; *b.* Anstruther, 1880; *educ.* Waid Acad. Anstruther, Univs. of Aberd. and Edin.; M.B., Ch.B. Edin. 1902; M.D. Edin. 1905; F.R.C.S. Edin. 1905; F.A.C.S.; Tutor in Gynæcology, Edin. Univ., 1905-10; Lecturer in School of Medicine of the Roy. Colleges, Edin., 1910-12; Professor of Obstetrics and Gynæcology, Toronto Univ., 1912-22; Gynæcologist, Roy. Infirm., Edin., 1922-26; Obstetric Physician, Roy. Maternity Hosp., Edin., 1922-26; Professor of Obstetrics, Columbia Univ., New York, since 1926.

WATSON, James Anderson Scott, Professor of Agriculture, 1922-25; *b.* Forfar, 16th Nov. 1889; *educ.* Harris Acad. Dundee, Edin. Univ., Roy. Agricultural Coll. Berlin, Iowa State Coll. of Agriculture, U.S.A.; M.A. Edin.; B.Sc. Edin. 1908; M.A. Oxf. 1925; Fellow of St John's Coll., Oxf., 1925; Assistant in Agriculture 1910, Lecturer 1911-22, Edin. Univ.; Sibthorpian Professor of Rural Economy, Oxford Univ., since 1925.

WATSON, William Heriot, Lecturer in Natural Philosophy, 1924-28; *b.* Edinburgh, 1900; *educ.* Craiglockhart School, Broughton School, Broughton H.G. School, Broughton Junior Student Centre, Edin., Edin. Univ.; M.A. Edin. 1921; Ph.D. Camb. 1931; Carnegie Research Fellow, Cavendish Laboratory, Cambridge, 1928; Assist. Professor of Physics, McGill Univ., Montreal, since 1931.

WATT, Sir George, Lecturer in Indian Forest Trees, 1920-25; *b.* Old Meldrum, Aberdeenshire, 24th Apr. 1851; *educ.* Aberdeen Grammar School, Aberd. Univ., Glasg. Univ.; Kt. 1903; C.I.E. 1886; M.B., C.M. Glasg. 1873; LL.D. Aberd. 1904 and Glasg. 1907; F.L.S.; Professor of Botany, Calcutta

Univ., 1873-84; Scientific and Medical Officer, Burma-Manipur Boundary Commission, 1882; Scientific Assist. Secretary, Supreme Government Secretariat, 1884; Reporter on Economic Products, Government of India, 1887-1903; in charge of Industrial Museum, Calcutta, 1894-1903; on duty in London, 1904-8; retired from Indian service, 1906.

Webster, Adam Blyth, Lecturer in Rhetoric and English Language, 1905-20; *b.* Girvan, Ayrshire, 1882; *educ.* Boys' High School, Canterbury, New Zealand, Edin. Univ.; M.A. Edin. 1905; LL.D. California 1930; Lecturer in English, Edin. Provincial Training Coll. for Teachers, 1909-16; Visiting Professor, California Univ., 1926, 1929, 1930; Berry Professor of English Literature, St Andrews Univ., since 1920.

Wedderburn, Joseph Henry Maclagan, Lecturer in Mathematics, 1905-10; *b.* Forfar, 1882; *educ.* Forfar Acad., George Watson's Coll. Edinburgh, Edin. Univ.; M.A. 1903; D.Sc. 1908; F.R.S. 1933; Assistant in Natural Philosophy, Edin. Univ., 1902-4; Preceptor in Mathematics 1910-11, Assist. Professor and Preceptor 1911-21, Associate Professor 1921-28, Professor since 1928, Princeton Univ., New Jersey, U.S.A.

Welsh, David Arthur, Lecturer in Pathological Bacteriology, 1898-1901; *b.* Montrose, 1866; *educ.* Colliston Parish School, Arbroath High School, Edin. Univ; M.A. Edin. 1887; B.Sc. Edin. 1890; M.B., C.M. Edin. 1893; M.D. Edin. 1897; F.R.C.P. Edin. 1911; Assistant in Pathology, Edin. Univ., 1895-1901; Resident Physician and Pathologist, Roy. Infirm., Edin.; Pathologist, Roy. Hosp. for Sick Children, Edin.; Professor of Pathology (and Dean of the Faculty of Medicine, 1927-29), Sydney Univ., Australia, since 1902.

Wemyss, Herbert Lindesay Watson, Lecturer in Clinical Medicine, 1921-29; *b.* Broughty Ferry, 1885; *educ.* Seafield House, Broughty Ferry, 1896-99, Marlborough Coll. 1899-1903, Edin. Univ.; M.B., Ch.B. Edin. 1908; M.D. Edin. 1910; M.R.C.P. Edin. 1911; F.R.C.P. Edin. 1914; Tutor to Professor William Russell, 1913; Assistant Physician, Leith Hosp. and Deaconess Hosp.; Assistant Physician, Roy. Infirm., Edin., 1921-33; *d.* Edinburgh, 3rd Feb. 1933.

White, Adam Cairns, Lecturer in Materia Medica, 1924-29; *b.* Edinburgh, 1901; *educ.* Preston Street and Regent Road Schools Edin., Roy. High. School Edin., Edin. Univ.; M.B., Ch.B. Edin. 1923; Ph.D. Edin. 1925; Assist. Pharmacologist, Wellcome Physiological Research Laboratory, Beckenham, Kent.

RHS

White, Margaret Pirie (Mrs R. T. Dunbar), Lecturer in Natural Philosophy, 1920-21; *b.* Edinburgh, 30th May 1892; *educ.* George Watson's Ladies' Coll. Edin., Edin. Univ.; M.A. 1915; B.Sc. 1916; Ph.D. 1921; Assistant in Natural Philosophy, Edin. Univ., 1916-20; *m.* 1921.

APPENDIX II

WHITTAKER, John Macnaghten, Lecturer in Mathematics, 1927-30; *educ.* Edin. Univ., Trinity Coll. Cambridge; M.A. Edin. 1924; B.A. Camb. 1927, M.A. 1931; D.Sc. Edin. 1929; Fellow, 1929, and Lecturer in Mathematics, Pembroke Coll., Cambridge; Professor in Pure Mathematics, Liverpool Univ., 1933.

WILLIAMS, Alexander Mitchell, Lecturer in Chemistry, 1918-20; M.A. Edin. 1910; D.Sc. Edin. 1918; *d.*

WILLIAMS, Carrington Bonsor, Steven Lecturer in Agricultural Zoology, 1929-31, and Lecturer in Forest Zoology, 1929-31; *b.* Liverpool, 7th Oct. 1889; *educ.* Birkenhead School, Clare Coll. Cambridge; B.A. Camb. 1911, M.A. 1916; Sc.D. Camb. 1931; Entomologist at John Innes Horticultural Instit., Surrey, 1911-16; Sugar Cane Entomologist, Dept. of Agriculture, Trinidad, British West Indies, 1916-21; Sub-Director and Director, Entomological Service, Ministry of Agriculture, Egypt, 1921-27; Entomologist to East African Agricultural Research Station, Amani, Tanganyika, 1927-29; Guest Professor of Entomology, Univ. of Minnesota, U.S.A., 1932; Chief Entomologist, Rothamsted Experimental Station, since 1931.

WILSON, John, Professor of Agriculture, 1854-85; *b.* London, Nov. 1812; *educ.* privately, Univ. Coll. London, Paris; LL.D. Edin. 1886; in charge of the Admiralty coals' investigation under Sir Henry de la Beche, 1845-46; Principal of the Roy. Agricultural Coll., Cirencester, 1846-50; Secretary to the Senatus, Edin. Univ., 1868-85; *d.* Tunbridge Wells, 27th Mar. 1888.

WOOD, John Philp, Professor of Conveyancing, 1892-1900; *b.* 1847; *educ.* Edin. Acad., Edin. Univ.; Writer to the Signet, 1871; LL.D. Edin. 1900; Partner in Messrs Melville and Lindsay, W.S.; *d.* Edinburgh, 14th Jan. 1906.

WOOD, Philip Francis, Lecturer 1904-28, Reader 1928-32, in Administrative Law; *b.* 1858; *educ.* Edin. Univ., Balliol Coll. Oxford; C.B. 1921; M.A. Edin. 1876; LL.B. Edin. 1884; B.A. Oxf. 1881, M.A. 1885; B.C.L. Oxf. 1884; Advocate, Scots Bar, 1884; Barrister, Inner Temple, 1884; K.C. 1912; Junior Counsel to the Secretary for Scotland under the Private Legislation Procedure (Scotland) Act, 1900, and Senior Counsel since 1908.

WRIGHT, Hedley Duncan, Lecturer in Pathology, 1920-21; *b.* Ulverstone, Tasmania, 3rd Mar. 1891; *educ.* Queen's Coll., Hobart, Tasmania, Edin. Univ.; B.A. Tasmania 1910; M.B., Ch.B. Edin. 1916; M.D. Edin. 1925; D.Sc. Edin. 1927; M.R.C.P. Edin. 1921; Assist. Superintendent, Research Laboratory, Roy. Coll. of Physicians, Edin., 1921-22; Lecturer and Reader (1928) at Univ. Coll. Hosp., London Univ., 1923-30; Professor of Bacteriology, Univ. of Sydney, since 1930.

BIOGRAPHICAL NOTES

WYLLIE, John, Professor of Medicine, 1900-15; *b.* Ratho, Midlothian, 1844; *educ.* school at Bolton, East Lothian, Edin. Instit., Edin. Univ., Paris; M.D. Edin. 1865; LL.D. Edin. 1897; F.R.C.P. Edin. 1870; Resident Physician, Roy. Infirm., Edin., 1865-66; House Physician, General Hosp., Birmingham, 1866-68; in general practice, Selkirk, 1868; Lecturer on pathology 1871-78, on medicine 1878-97, and on clinical medicine 1882-97, in extra-academical school, Edin.; Pathologist, Roy. Infirm., 1875-77; Assist. Physician, Fever Wards, 1876-82, Physician 1882-97 and 1900-15, Cons. Physician 1897-1900 and 1915-16, Roy. Infirm., Edin.; Cons. Physician, City Fever Hosp., Edin., 1896-1900; *d.* Edinburgh, 25th Jan. 1916.

YOUNG, James Buchanan, Lecturer in Public Health, 1921-28; *b.* Edinburgh, 1866; *educ.* Grange Acad. Edin., Edin. Univ. 1881-90; M.B., C.M. 1890; B.Sc. 1892; D.Sc. 1893; Assistant in Forensic Medicine and Public Health, 1894-99, in Public Health, 1899-1921, Edin. Univ.; *d.* Edinburgh, 17th Mar. 1928.

APPENDIX III

CHANCELLORS, PRINCIPALS AND VICE-CHANCELLORS, RECTORS, REPRESENTATIVES IN PARLIAMENT, MEMBERS OF THE UNIVERSITY COURT AND THE CURATORS OF PATRONAGE, 1883-1933

CHANCELLORS

1868 Right Hon. John Inglis, Lord Glencorse
1891 Right Hon. Arthur James Balfour (the Earl of Balfour)
1930 Sir James Matthew Barrie, Bt.

PRINCIPALS AND VICE-CHANCELLORS

1868 Sir Alexander Grant, Bt.
1885 Sir William Muir
1903 Sir William Turner
1916 Sir James Alfred Ewing
1929 Sir Thomas Henry Holland

RECTORS

1883 Right Hon. Sir Stafford H. Northcote, Bt. (the Earl of Iddesleigh)
1887 Most Hon. the Marquess of Lothian
1890 Right Hon. George Joachim Goschen (Viscount Goschen)
1893 Right Hon. James Patrick Bannerman Robertson (the Lord Robertson of Forteviot)
1896 Right Hon. the Lord Balfour of Burleigh
1899 Most Hon. the Marquess of Dufferin and Ava
1902 Right Hon. Sir Robert Bannatyne Finlay (Viscount Finlay of Nairn)
1905 Right Hon. Richard Burdon Haldane (Viscount Haldane of Cloan)
1908 Right Hon. George Wyndham
1911 Right Hon. the Earl of Minto
1914 Field-Marshal Right Hon. the Earl Kitchener of Khartoum
1917 Admiral Right Hon. the Earl Beatty
1920 Right Hon. David Lloyd George
1923 Right Hon. Stanley Baldwin
1926 Right Hon. Sir John Gilmour
1929 Right Hon. Winston Leonard Spencer Churchill
1932 General Sir Ian Standish Monteith Hamilton

REPRESENTATIVES IN PARLIAMENT

St Andrews and Edinburgh (one member)

1885-86 Right Hon. John Hay Athole Macdonald (Lord Kingsburgh)
1888 Moir Tod Stormonth Darling (Lord Stormonth Darling)
1890-92 Right Hon. Sir Charles J. Pearson (Lord Pearson)
1896 Sir William Overend Priestley
1900-6 Sir John Batty Tuke
1910 Right Hon. Sir Robert Bannatyne Finlay
1916 Sir Christopher Nicholson Johnston (Lord Sands)
1917 Sir William Watson Cheyne, Bt.

The Four Scottish Universities (three members)

1918-22 Sir William Watson Cheyne, Bt.
1918 Dugald McCaig Cowan
1918-27 Right Hon. Sir Henry Craik
1922-31 Sir George Andreas Berry
1927 John Buchan
1931 Archibald Noel Skelton

MEMBERS OF UNIVERSITY COURT

UNIVERSITY COURT

The Principal of the University is a member of the Court and, in the absence of the Rector, presides at the meetings of the Court.

Chancellor's Assessors

1881 Archibald Campbell Swinton, Advocate
1887 Thomas Graham Murray, W.S.
1891 Æneas James George Mackay, Advocate
1901 Hon. Lord Stormonth Darling
1907 Hon. Lord Dundas
1922 Hon. Lord Blackburn

Rector's Assessors

1880 Right Hon. Lord Young
1883 Thomas Graham Murray, W.S.
1887 Hon. Lord Stormonth Darling
1900 Hon. Lord Dundas
1907 James Walker, C.A.
1922 Hon. Lord Constable
1928 Right Hon. Lord Salvesen
1933 Alexander Stevenson Blair, W.S.

The Lord Provosts of Edinburgh

1882-85 Sir George Harrison
1885-88 Sir Thomas Clark, Bt.
1888-91 Sir John Boyd
1891-94 Sir James Alexander Russell
1894-97 Sir Andrew McDonald
1897-1900 Sir Mitchell Mitchell-Thomson, Bt.
1900-3 Sir James Steel, Bt.
1903-6 Sir Robert Cranston
1906-9 Sir James Puckering Gibson, Bt.
1909-12 Sir William Slater Brown
1912-16 Sir Robert Kirk Inches
1916-19 Sir John Lorne MacLeod
1919-21 John William Chesser
1921-23 Sir Thomas Hutchison, Bt.
1923-26 Sir William Lowrie Sleigh
1926-29 Sir Alexander Stevenson
1929-32 Sir Thomas Barnby Whitson
1932 William Johnston Thomson

Town Council Assessors

1882 Thomas Clark
1886 James Colston
1897 Andrew Mitchell
1901 William Lang Todd
1905 Robert Menzies
1909 Alfred Alexander Arbuthnot Murray
1913 John McGill Rusk
1921 Francis John Robertson
1925 Thomas Barnby Whitson
1929 Joseph David Philips Smith

General Council Assessors

1883-87 Daniel Rutherford Haldane, M.D.
1887-1903 Sir Patrick Heron Watson, F.R.C.S. Edin.
1889-93 Right Hon. John Hay Athole Macdonald
1889-95 John Duncan, M.D.
1889-93 Thomas McKie, advocate
1893-1901 John Hope Finlay, W.S.
1893-1901 Alexander Taylor Innes, Advocate
1895-1911 Joseph Bell, F.R.C.S. Edin.
1901-3 Francis Grant Ogilvie, B.Sc.
1901-9 John Campbell Lorimer, Advocate
1903-17 David Fowler Lowe, M.A.
1903-27 Robert McKenzie Johnston F.R.C.S. Edin.
1909-21 David Donaldson Buchan, S.S.C.
1911-23 Sir George Andreas Berry, M.B.
1917 John Brown Clark, M.A.
1921-32 James Roberton Christie, Advocate
1923 Sir Norman Purvis Walker, M.D.
1927 Alexander Miles, F.R.C.S. Edin.
1932 Alexander Morgan, D.Sc.

APPENDIX III

Senatus Assessors

1877-91 Professor Alexander Campbell Fraser
1889-93 Professor Malcolm Campbell Taylor
1889-1903 Professor Sir William Turner
1889-1908 Professor Alexander Crum Brown
1891-1901 Professor Samuel Henry Butcher
1892-97 Professor Henry Calderwood
1898-1903 Professor Simon Somerville Laurie
1901-22 Professor Sir John Rankine
1903-13 Professor Sir Thomas Richard Fraser
1903-11 Professor Andrew Seth Pringle-Pattison
1908- Professor Sir Thomas Hudson Beare
1911-24 Professor Sir Richard Lodge
1913-20 Professor Henry Harvey Littlejohn
1920-23 Professor James Ritchie
1922-27 Professor Thomas Patrick Laird
1923-25 Professor Sir Harold Jalland Stiles
1924-32 Professor Norman Kemp Smith
1925-32 Professor Sir Robert W. Philip
1927-30 Professor Edmund Taylor Whittaker
1930 Rev. Professor William Alexander Curtis
1932 Professor Thomas Jones Mackie
1932 Professor Frederick Wolff Ogilvie

CURATORS OF PATRONAGE

Representatives of the Town Council

1881 James Colston
1882 Sir Thomas Jamieson Boyd, Lord Provost
John Boyd
Duncan MacLaren
1884 George Harrison, Lord Provost
1885 John Clapperton
1886 Thomas Clark, Lord Provost
1886 James Cowan
1889 James McIntosh
1891 James Alexander Russell, Lord Provost
1892 George Auldjo Jamieson
1895 Andrew McDonald, Lord Provost
1898 Sir Mitchell Mitchell-Thomson, Bt., Lord Provost
1898 Alexander Forbes MacKay
1900 Robert Cranston
1901 James Steel, Lord Provost
1903 William Slater Brown
1904 Richard Clark
1906 William Fraser Dobie
1906 James Puckering Gibson, Lord Provost
1907 John Murray
1909 John Harrison
1912 William Allan Carter
1913 John Lorne MacLeod
1913 Robert Kirk Inches, Lord Provost
1918 John William Chesser
1918 William Wallace Dunlop
1918 George Malcolm Stuart
1919 David Wright Deas
1921 Thomas Hutchison, Lord Provost
1923 William Lowrie Sleigh, Lord Provost
1924 Edward Graham Guest
1924 Alexander Stevenson
1925 James Hastie
1926 Joseph David Philips Smith
1927 George Freeland Barbour Simpson
1928 Andrew Young
1929 Thomas Barnby Whitson, Lord Provost
1929 William James Harvey
1932 Thomas Adams
1932 Peter Given
1932 William Johnston Thomson, Lord Provost

CURATORS OF PATRONAGE

Representatives of the University

1881 Hon. Lord Kinnear
1883 Principal Sir Alexander Grant, Bt.
1884 Right Hon. the Lord Balfour of Burleigh
1884 Thomas Graham Murray, W.S.
1887 Principal Sir William Muir
1890 Right Hon. John Hay Athole Macdonald
1891 Sir Patrick Heron Watson
1896 Right Hon. James Patrick Bannerman Robertson
1900 Hon. Lord Stormonth Darling
1902 Hon. Lord Dundas
1906 Principal Sir William Turner
1909 Joseph Bell, F.R.C.S. Edin.
1911 David Fowler Lowe, M.A., LL.D.
1916 Robert McKenzie Johnston, M.D.
1916 Principal Sir James Alfred Ewing
1922 Hon. Lord Blackburn
1922 Sir George Andreas Berry, M.B.
1928 Sir Norman Purvis Walker, M.D.
1929 John Brown Clark, M.A., LL.D.
1929 Principal Sir Thomas Henry Holland

APPENDIX IV

DONORS AND BENEFACTIONS

1884-1933

Donor	Purpose	Year	Amount
Abercromby, John, Lord	Chair of Prehistoric Archæology	(1925)	£17,000
Anderson, Lady, Beechmount, Edinburgh	General Purposes	(1926)	5,163
Anonymous	Lectureship on Orthopædics	(1919)	16,600
Anonymous	Furnishing of New Masson Hall	(1931)	5,000
Anonymous	Chair of Forestry	(1890)	1,000
Anonymous per Professor Sir James Walker	General Purposes	(1924-29)	2,500
Arnott, James Moncrieff, M.D. of Chapel, Fife, and his daughter	Endowment of Chair of Therapeutics	(1907)	22,300
Association for Better Endowment of the University	Endowment	(1890 and later)	12,787
Barbour, A. H. Freeland, M.D., Edinburgh	Fellowship in Midwifery	(1888 and 1928)	3,848
Baxter Fund	Augmentation of Various Stipends	(1889)	17,961
Beaverbrook, Maxwell, Lord	Medical Purposes	(1929)	1,000
Beit, Sir Otto John, Bt., LL.D.	Tutorship in Midwifery	(1930)	6,000
Bell, Rev. Andrew, D.D., of Egmore	Additional Endowment of Chair of Education	(1889)	4,500
Berwick, Miss J. L., Edinburgh	Research in Medicine and Science. House No. 14 Heriot Row and Endowment Fund of	(1923)	1,000
Black, Charles Bertram	Scholarships in Greek	(1906)	4,000
British Association for the Advancement of Science	Travelling, etc., Expenses of Science Students	(1921)	1,364
Brown, Professor G. Baldwin, Edinburgh	Scholarships in Fine Art	(1932)	8,200
Brown, Misses Janet, Isabella, and Anne, Edinburgh	Bursaries in Divinity	(1899)	1,000
Brown, Professor P. Hume, Edinburgh	Prize in Scottish History	(1919)	1,500
Brown, Richard, Edinburgh	Research Scholarship	(1929)	2,000
Bruce, Charles, Banker, Edinburgh	Lectureship in Banking	(1909)	5,000
Bruce, John, M.B.	Bursary in Medicine	(1911)	1,193
Bruce, Alexander Low, Edinburgh, and members of his family	Bruce and John Usher Chair of Public Health	(1897)	5,663
Bruce, Peebles & Co. Ltd., Edinburgh	General Purposes	(1926-1930)	2,500
Bucher, Signor Théophile, Edinburgh	Scholarships in Music	(1893)	3,913
Cameron, Mrs A. M.	Lewis Cameron Fund, Faculty of Medicine	(1930)	80,000
City of Edinburgh (Common Good)	General Purposes	(1925)	2,000

Donor	Purpose	Year	Amount
Clark, Edward, Trustees of late, Printer, Edinburgh	Chair of Child Life and Health and Equipment of Geography Department	(1931)	£17,320
Clark, Mrs James, Ravelston, Edinburgh	General Purposes	(1925)	2,000
Clark, Miss Stewart, Edinburgh	General Purposes	(1925)	1,000
Cobb, Miss Matilda J., Broughty Ferry	Scholarship in Divinity . . .	(1889)	1,000
Cochrane, Richmond I., Edinburgh	Reid Orchestra Endowment . .	(1931)	2,000
Combe Trust (founded by George Combe, M.D., Edinburgh)	Psychology	(1906 to 1933)	14,368
Commerce, Chamber of, Edinburgh; Leith Chamber of Commerce, The Merchant Company of Edinburgh, The Leith Shipowners' Society, The Society of Accountants and The Institute of Bankers, Edinburgh	Chairs of Accounting and of Organisation of Industry and Commerce	(1918)	30,490
Cowan, Sir John, LL.D., Edinburgh	General Purposes	(1925-29)	1,500
Cowan, Thomas, LL.D., Leith	For Building and Endowment of Hall of Residence and residential Scholarships for Students £75,000, and Endowment of Surgery Department £5000	(1924-29)	80,000
Crabbie, George, of Blairhoyle	General Purposes	(1924)	1,000
Crawford, William . . .	General Purposes	(1925)	2,000
Crichton, Major Robert Orr, M.D., of Lynn	Bursaries and Scholarships in Medicine	(1890)	28,555
Currie, Sir Donald, of Garth, G.C.M.G.	Lectureship Endowment Fund .	(1909)	21,444
Davidson, Sir Leybourne, of Huntly	Research Fellowship in Bacteriology	(1928)	5,000
Davidson, Lady, of Huntly .	Apparatus for Bacteriological Research	(1926)	1,000
Dick, Miss Mary, Edinburgh .	Chair of Comparative Anatomy .	(1910)	12,126
Dickson, William, Edinburgh .	Travelling Fund for Students .	(1888)	2,665
Distillers Co., Ltd. . . .	General Purposes	(1925)	1,000
Divinity Chair Augmentation Fund, Trustees of	Chair of Divinity	(1920)	1,196
Donaldson, Miss H. C., of Aucharnie	Bursaries in Arts	(1906)	4,385
Doyle, Sir Arthur Conan . .	Prizes in Medicine	(1902)	1,000
Dundas, Heirs of the late Hon. Lord	Study of Latin	(1922)	1,000
Dunlop, Dr A. Vans, H.E.I.C.S.	Further Scholarships . . .	(1885 to 1933)	21,132
Dunn, Sir William, London, Trustees of the late	Towards Reconstruction of Medical Buildings	(1928)	20,000
Elliott, Samuel, New York .	Scholarships and Prizes in Arts .	(1917)	1,443
Edinburgh School of Social Study, Trustees of	Endowment, etc., on transfer to University	(1928)	1,734
Findlay, Sir John R., Bt., of Aberlour	General Purposes £6500, and for Geology £1000	(1924-29)	7,500
Forbes, Daniel Mackintosh, M.A., East India Merchant	General Purposes	(1916)	106,816

APPENDIX IV

Forteviot, John Alexander, Lord	Endowment of Animal Breeding Research Department	(1928)	£2,000
Fraser, Mrs Isabella W. . .	Travelling Scholarship in Music .	(1930)	3,000
Fulton, John	General Purposes	(1888)	3,000
Garton, R. and J., Newton-le-Willows, Lancashire	Lectureship on Colonial and Indian Agriculture	(1920)	4,786
Gibson, Alexander, Advocate, Edinburgh	Library Purposes	(1887)	2,000
Gifford, Adam (The Honourable Lord Gifford)	Lectureship in Natural Theology	(1887)	22,500
Goodsir, Robert A., M.D. .	Additional Sum for Goodsir Memorial Fellowship	(1895)	2,200
Grant, Sir Alexander, Bt., of Logie	For General Purposes £50,000, and for New Geology Department £50,000	(1924-29)	100,000
Gunning, His Excellency Robert H., M.D., LL.D.	Gunning (Victoria Jubilee) Prizes and Lectureship	(1900)	11,720
Haldane, Viscount, of Cloan .	Library, etc.	(1928)	1,000
Harvie, J. Clason, of Brownlee, Lanarkshire	Chairs of French and German .	(1911 and 1925)	7,766
Hastie, Miss Margaret, Edinburgh	Scholarship in Law . . .	(1926)	1,500
Highland and Agricultural Society of Scotland	Endowment of Animal Breeding Research Department	(1928)	1,000
Highland and Agricultural Society and Scottish Arboricultural Society	Lectureship in Forestry . .	(1893)	1,485
Hood, James A., LL.D., of Midfield	Chair of Mining	(1922)	15,000
Howden, Miss Catherine Spence	Research Scholarship . . .	(1925)	5,000
Hay, Dr Alfred, D.Sc., London	Physical Laboratory . . .	(1933)	1,000
International Education Board	Erection and Equipment of Building for Animal Genetics and Zoology and Endowments for Expenses and for Chair	(1927)	104,000
Irvine, Robert, F.C.S., Edinburgh	Chair of Bacteriology and Equipment	(1902)	31,021
Jackson, Sir John, O.B.E., London	Physical Research . . .	(1907)	4,000
Jardine, Charles, of Thorlieshope	Further Bursaries in Arts . .	(1896)	8,473
Jeffrey, Miss Jane, Portobello .	Bursary in Divinity . . .	(1888)	4,500
Kay, Walter S., M.D., Harrogate	Research Scholarships in Psychiatry	(1931)	4,557
Kidd, Miss Mary Laing, Aigburth, Liverpool	James Fairbairn Scholarship in Arts	(1887)	1,000
Kirkpatrick, Miss Jane and Professor John	History Library	(1910)	1,184
Lang, General William . .	Bursaries	(1917)	2,790
Leverhulme, William Hesketh, Viscount	General Purposes	(1920)	1,000
Lockerby, Thomas, of Addiscombe, Surrey	Bursary in Divinity . . .	(1891)	1,000
Macaulay, Thomas B., LL.D., of Montreal	Animal Breeding Research . .	(1929-33)	15,930
McCosh, John, M.D. . .	Bursary in Medicine . . .	(1897)	5,115

Macdonald, William, Publisher, Edinburgh	Bursaries in Arts	(1923)	£3,310
McEwan, Rt. Hon. Wm., LL.D.	The McEwan Hall and for its Endowment a sum of	(1897)	6,450
McGuffie, Rev. George, Bridge of Earn	Bursaries in Arts, Divinity and Medicine	(1915)	2,000
Mackay, Sheriff Æneas J. G., LL.D.	Augment Salary of Assistant to Professor of History	(1900)	2,244
Mackie, Dr James, Greenock .	Bursaries in Medicine and Divinity	(1887)	1,855
McKie, Thomas, Advocate .	Research in Medicine, Surgery and Science; Study of English and of Modern Languages	(1924)	54,678
Maclaurin, Daniel, London .	Bursaries in Arts	(1889)	2,000
Maitland, Mrs Alexander, Edinburgh	Reid Orchestra Endowment . .	(1931)	8,044
Mann, Peter Campbell, of Seaham Harbour	Bursaries in Arts	(1886)	2,000
Milne, Miss Isabella . . .	Falconer Memorial Fellowship .	(1921)	1,500
Moray, Edmund Archibald, the Earl of	To promote Research . . .	(1895)	20,000
Maule, Rev. Thomas, Glasgow .	Bursaries in Arts	(1893)	2,907
Mouat, Frederick J., M.D., London	Scholarship in Medicine . .	(1897)	1,831
Munro, Robert, M.D., LL.D., of Largs	Lectureship in Anthropology .	(1909)	5,164
Nasmyth, Thomas G., M.D., Edinburgh	General Purposes	(1924)	1,000
Newton, Robert Pillans, of Castlandhill and Drumcross	Bursary in Natural Philosophy and Mathematics	(1887)	2,250
Nichol, Mrs Elizabeth, Edinburgh	Assistantship in Physical Laboratory	(1895)	2,000
Ormerod, Miss Eleanor, LL.D.	General Purposes	(1901)	5,000
Pullar, Laurence, of Dunbarney, LL.D.	Department of Zoology . . .	(1923)	20,000
Rawdon, W. F., M.D., York .	Building Fund	(1896)	1,000
Ritchie, James, formerly of Edinburgh	Scholarships in Arts . . .	(1895)	3,100
Ritchie, James, Upper Norwood, London	Physical and Chemical Research .	(1925)	7,000
Robertson, J. L., C.B., LL.D., Inverness	Endowment of Lewis Bursary .	(1924)	1,000
Rockefeller Foundation . .	Reconstruction of Medical Buildings; Erection and Equipment of Clinical Laboratory; Endowments of Chair of Surgery and for Expenses	(1925-29)	93,832
Romanes, Miss Isabella D., Edinburgh	Romanes Lectureship in Chemistry	(1932)	2,000
Royal Edinburgh Hospital for Mental and Nervous Disorders, Managers of	Chair of Psychiatry . . .	(1918)	10,000
Royal Victoria Hospital Tuberculosis Trust, Edinburgh, Trustees of	Chair of Tuberculosis . . .	(1916)	18,392
Ryder, Col. F. J., C.M.G. .	Study of Mental Illness . .	(1922)	5,332
Salvesen, F. G., Edinburgh .	General Purposes	(1924)	1,000
Sanderson, James, Galashiels .	Engineering and Chemistry . .	(1928)	50,000
Scott, George, London . .	Scholarship in Arts . . .	(1895)	1,066

Donor	Purpose	Year	Amount
Skirving, David, London	Scholarship in Arts	(1913)	£1,072
Small, Miss Jemima L., Edinburgh	Library	(1924)	5,000
Stark, John, M.D., Auchtermuchty	Scholarship in Medicine	(1884)	1,400
Steven, Misses Elizabeth and Grace, of Bellahouston	Lectureship in Agriculture	(1889)	3,000
Sutherland, Miss Marion, Edinburgh	General Purposes	(1917)	3,520
Tait, W. A., D.Sc., Edinburgh, and other Donors	Tait Chair of Mathematical Physics	(1922)	10,324
Thomson, T. S., Edinburgh	Surgery Department	(1925)	1,000
Tweedie, General William, of Lettrick	Research	(1925)	4,081
Trevelyan, Mrs Elizabeth	Scholarship in Engineering	(1892)	1,000
Usher, Sir John, Bt., of Norton and Wells	The Building of the John Usher Institute, and for part Endowment of Chair of Public Health, a sum of	(1902)	8,000
Usher, Sir Robert, Bt., of Norton and Wells	General Purposes	(1921)	10,000
Wardlaw, Miss Margaret, Edinburgh	Indigent and Deserving Students	(1911)	2,504
Watson, Mrs Chalmers, M.D., Edinburgh, and Others	Medical Education of Women	(1917)	2,150
Westminster Hospital Medical Society	Houldsworth Scholarship in Medicine	(1896)	1,709
Woolavington, James, Lord	Chair of Animal Genetics	(1926)	10,000
Younger, Mrs, of Harmeny, Balerno	Scholarship in Music	(1932)	1,500
Younger, Wm. & Co., Ltd., Edinburgh	Towards Endowment of Chair of Public Health and for General Purposes	(1897 and 1924)	2,000
			£1,401,408
Aggregate amount of gifts under £1000 received during the period from Donors not mentioned above			32,853
			£1,434,261

APPENDIX V

DISTRIBUTION OF GRADUATES OF THE UNIVERSITY OF EDINBURGH IN THE BRITISH ISLES AND OVERSEAS.

A. THE BRITISH ISLES—16,204.

SCOTLAND (with Orkney and Shetland)—		
Edinburgh and Midlothian	5,405	
Rest of Scotland	5,377	
	——	10,782
ENGLAND (with the Channel Islands)—		
London and Middlesex	1,473	
Rest of England	3,570	
	——	5,043
WALES		213
IRELAND		166
		16,204

B. OVERSEAS—3,297.

AFRICA—			
South Africa—			
Cape Town and Province	365		
Transvaal	211		
Orange Free State	69		
Natal	66		
Rhodesia	41		
General	17		
	——	769	
West Africa		86	
North Africa—			
Egypt	75		
The Sudan	4		
	—	79	
East Africa		69	
		——	1,003

APPENDIX V

America (North)—			
United States of America—			
New York State	68		
California	23		
Pennsylvania	16		
New Jersey	12		
Illinois	11		
Massachusetts	10		
Maryland	4		
Other States	72		
		216	
Canada and Newfoundland—			
Canada	166		
Newfoundland	8		
		174	
			390
America (Central) and **British West Indies**			139
America (South)			62
Asia—			
India and Ceylon		751	
China		134	
Straits Settlements		89	
Turkey, Persia, Palestine and Iraq		25	
Indian Ocean Islands		24	
Japan		9	
Philippine Islands		2	
			1,034
Australia and Tasmania			333
Europe—			
Eastern Europe		25	
France		20	
Scandinavia		11	
Italy		11	
Switzerland		8	
Spain and Portugal		5	
Germany		6	
Gibraltar		4	
Malta		3	
Cyprus		3	
			96
New Zealand			240
			3,297

INDEX

INDEX

INDEX

INDEX

INDEX

INDEX

INDEX

INDEX

INDEX

INDEX

INDEX

INDEX

INDEX

INDEX

INDEX

INDEX

INDEX

INDEX

INDEX

INDEX

INDEX

INDEX